Interactive Learning for Innovation

Interactive Learning for Innovation

A Key Driver within Clusters and Innovation Systems

Edited by

Bjørn T. Asheim
Professor of Economic Geography, Lund University, Sweden

and

Mario Davide Parrilli
*Associate Professor of Economics, University of Deusto,
Senior Research Fellow, Orkestra,
Bilbao and San Sebastian, Spain*

Editorial Matter and Selection © Bjørn T. Asheim and Mario Davide Parrilli 2012
Preface © Bengt-Åke Lundvall 2012
Foreword © José Luis Curbelo 2012
Individual Chapters © Contributors 2012

All rights reserved. No reproduction, copy or transmission of this publication may be made without written permission.

No portion of this publication may be reproduced, copied or transmitted save with written permission or in accordance with the provisions of the Copyright, Designs and Patents Act 1988, or under the terms of any licence permitting limited copying issued by the Copyright Licensing Agency, Saffron House, 6–10 Kirby Street, London EC1N 8TS.

Any person who does any unauthorized act in relation to this publication may be liable to criminal prosecution and civil claims for damages.

The authors have asserted their rights to be identified as the authors of this work in accordance with the Copyright, Designs and Patents Act 1988.

First published 2012 by
PALGRAVE MACMILLAN

Palgrave Macmillan in the UK is an imprint of Macmillan Publishers Limited, registered in England, company number 785998, of Houndmills, Basingstoke, Hampshire RG21 6XS.

Palgrave Macmillan in the US is a division of St Martin's Press LLC, 175 Fifth Avenue, New York, NY 10010.

Palgrave Macmillan is the global academic imprint of the above companies and has companies and representatives throughout the world.

Palgrave® and Macmillan® are registered trademarks in the United States, the United Kingdom, Europe and other countries.

ISBN: 978–0–230–29876–7

This book is printed on paper suitable for recycling and made from fully managed and sustained forest sources. Logging, pulping and manufacturing processes are expected to conform to the environmental regulations of the country of origin.

A catalogue record for this book is available from the British Library.

A catalog record for this book is available from the Library of Congress.

10 9 8 7 6 5 4 3 2 1
21 20 19 18 17 16 15 14 13 12

Printed and bound in Great Britain by
CPI Antony Rowe, Chippenham and Eastbourne

Contents

List of Tables	vii
List of Figures	ix
Preface Bengt-Åke Lundvall	xi
Foreword José Luis Curbelo	xiv
List of Contributors	xvi

Introduction: Learning and Interaction – Drivers for Innovation in Current Competitive Markets 1
Bjørn T. Asheim and Mario Davide Parrilli

Part I Theoretical Insights from the Literature on STI and DUI Innovation, Learning Organizations and the 'Related Varieties' Approach

1. Innovation and Competence Building in the Learning Economy: Implications for Innovation Policy 33
   Bengt-Åke Lundvall and Edward Lorenz

2. Labor Market Institutions, Skills, and Innovation Style: A Critique of the 'Varieties of Capitalism' Perspective 72
   Edward Lorenz

3. Organization and Innovation: The Topic of Creative Cities 90
   Björn Johnson

4. Knowledge Economy Spillovers, Proximity, and Specialization 100
   Philip Cooke

Part II Clusters, Firms and Innovation Systems

5. Combined and Complex Mode of Innovation in Regional Cluster Development: Analysis of the Light-Weight Material Cluster in Raufoss, Norway 115
   Arne Isaksen and James Karlsen

6 Facilitating Cluster Evolution in Peripheral Regions:
The Role of Clusterpreneurs 137
Jesper Lindgaard Christensen and Dagmara Stoerring

7 Social Capital, Knowledge, and Competitiveness: The
Cases of the Basque Paper and Electronics/ICT Clusters 161
*Jesus María Valdaliso, Aitziber Elola,
Maria José Aranguren, and Santiago López*

8 Firm Heterogeneity and Trajectories of Learning:
Applications and Relevant Policy Implications 181
Miren Larrea, Maria José Aranguren, and Mario Davide Parrilli

9 Innovation Capabilities and Learning:
Virtuous and Vicious Circles 206
Joost Heijs

10 Typologies of Innovation Based on Statistical
Analysis for European and Spanish Regions 234
Mikel Navarro and Juan José Gibaja

11 Academia and Public Policy: Towards the
Co-generation of Knowledge and Learning Processes 275
Maria José Aranguren, Miren Larrea, and James R. Wilson

Index 291

Tables

1.1	Frequency of the four clusters by firm size, sector, group ownership, and production type	47
1.2	Logistic regression of learning clusters on product/service innovation	48
1.3	Changes in task content for employees, 1993–1995, for firms that had made organizational changes, compared with firms that had not made organizational changes	50
1.4	National differences in organizational models	53
1.5	Index of trust in 14 European countries based upon the European Social Survey	61
1.6	National differences in organizational models	62
1.7	Work organization across classes: EU-27 and Norway	63
1.8	Differences between countries in forms of work organization	66
2.1	Cluster analysis of types of workers	81
2.2	National differences in types of learners: EU-27	82
5.1	Characteristics of the STI and the DUI modes of innovation	119
5.2	Characteristics of different modes of innovation	121
5.3	Sample of firms in the Raufoss cluster	124
7.1	Lifecycle of the Basque paper cluster and electronics/ICT clusters	168
8.1	Types of learners in Ezagutza Gunea	195
9.1	Motives for cooperation with research centers	210
9.2	Short description of the surveys and the main variables	211
9.3	Impact of R&D project in relation to several modes of learning	213
9.4a	Principal results of the exploratory analyses of generic impact	215
9.4b	Principal results of the exploratory analyses of generic impact	216
9.5	Explanatory factors for learning capability: a logistic regression model	218
9.6	Impact of public support projects on form of learning	222

9.7	Direction or orientation of knowledge transfer (learning) between firm and research center	223
9.8	A logistic regression model to reflect the profile of the firms or R&D centers with a lower or higher learning effect	226
10.1	Review of RIS conceptual typologies	237
10.2	Synoptic review of works on statistical typologies of innovation for the EU regions	240
10.3	Review of typologies of innovation for the Spanish regions	248
10.4	Variables used to obtain the innovation typologies of EU-25 and Spanish regions	252
10.5	Groups of EU-25 regions obtained through the cluster analysis	258
10.6	Relation coefficients between groups	268

Figures

0.1	The innovation gap and the interdependences among the factors	11
1.1	Discretionary learning and tertiary education	54
1.2	Discretionary learning and employee vocational training	55
1.3	Trust in people and economic inequality	60
2.1	Labor market mobility by initial vocational training	76
2.2	Percentage of new-to-firm innovators by percentage of creative workers	83
2.3	Percentage of new-to-market innovators by percentage of creative workers	84
2.4	Labor market mobility by percentage of creative workers	85
2.5	Flexible security by percentage of creative workers	86
4.1	EU S&T specialization, 2005	102
4.2	EU regional S&T over GDP variations	103
4.3	Technology convergence in cleantech	109
5.1	Simplified overview of the regional innovation network at Raufoss	129
7.1	Social capital, knowledge, and competitive advantage of clusters	164
8.1	Taxonomy of learners (firms)	186
10.1	Aspects considered to build an RIS typology	254
10.2	Results of the principal components analysis for the EU-25 regions	256
10.3	Location of the EU-25 regions in terms of the first two principal components: regional typology according to the cluster analysis	260
10.4	Results of the principal components analysis for the Spanish regions, using Eurostat data	261
10.5	Dendrogram of Spanish regions, using Eurostat data	262
10.6	Location of Spanish regions in terms of the first two principal components, using Eurostat data	262
10.7	Results of the principal components analysis for the Spanish regions, using data from Eurostat and Spanish sources	264
10.8	Dendrogram of Spanish regions, using data from Eurostat and Spanish sources	265

10.9	Location of Spanish regions in terms of the first two principal components of the factorial analysis, using data from Eurostat and Spanish sources	266
10.10	Geographical location of Spanish regions and their cluster groups	267
10.11	Comparison between the regions' location in terms of the two principal components in the two-factor analyses, using only Eurostat data and using data from Eurostat and Spanish sources	268
11.1	The Basque Institute of Competitiveness model of operation	280

Preface

Today, all regions of the world are involved in global competition – both in the sense that economic activities and economic agents have become more mobile at the global level and in the sense that local economic activities compete with activities worldwide. This book helps us to understand the character of this competition.

Nations and regions use different strategies to engage in global competition. One option is a low-cost strategy, which seems to be the philosophy behind the European Competitiveness Pact and the prescription for strengthening the competitiveness of countries such as Greece, Portugal, and Spain. With this strategy, nations compete by offering lower tax rates for business, lower wages, and a less generous state welfare system. Regions may make themselves more attractive by offering loose regulations and subsidized access to land and other natural resources.

An alternative strategy is for nations and regions to invest in knowledge infrastructure and human resources and to offer high-quality public services to support development and to attract resources. This was the idea behind the Lisbon Strategy, developed in 2000. This book explains why the second strategy is the only sustainable one and why the focus should be on promoting the knowledge base of a region.

How can it be that firms located at high-cost sites are more competitive than firms located at low-cost sites? If the firms were producing the same products and used the same production process, those located at low-cost sites would, of course, increase their market share. The major reason why this does not happen is that 'knowledge' about products and processes does *not* move freely in geographical space. Most of the chapters in this book focus on the processes whereby localized knowledge is produced and reproduced in the interactions among local as well as external agents.

Why does knowledge not flow freely in geographical space? If one takes the view that knowledge equals information, the answer is not obvious. Technology makes it possible to transmit information worldwide swiftly and with low costs. Taking knowledge as equivalent to natural science, we would also expect knowledge to be highly mobile. But, as shown in this book, successful innovation requires more than science-based knowledge. Learning by doing, using, and interacting

(DUI learning) is a prerequisite for successful innovation and it results in tacit knowledge that is embodied in people and embedded in organizations that are rooted in specific localities.

One reason why important elements of knowledge remain localized is thus that knowledge resides in individuals in the form of 'tacit knowledge'. Individuals know how to do things without being able to explain why, and they cannot transfer their full set of competences to others. One way to overcome this 'stickiness' of knowledge is therefore to increase the mobility of individuals. And it is clear that regions are increasingly competing to attract people with scarce talents and skills. But, as demonstrated in this book, moving people is not enough.

Knowledge is not only embodied in individuals; it is also embedded in organizations. This leads us to assume that attracting firms to a region may involve a more significant transfer of knowledge than just attracting individuals. There is a substantial literature on the impact on economic development of spillover effects from the inflow of foreign direct investments. These studies demonstrate that the impact is dependent upon the 'absorptive capacity' of the local innovation system.

This capacity is itself constituted by knowledge that is embedded in relationships between individuals and organizations. This collective knowledge includes shared specialized codes of communication as well as shared norms and common understandings of how to do business. It often reflects the product specialization of a region and is built in close connection to specific industries and industrial clusters.

A specialized knowledge base and close-knit clusters within a region may constitute a competitive advantage, and sometimes the advantage will last for a long time. Conversely, long periods of success may result in practices at the regional level that are rigid and do not respond to changes in markets, technologies, and business practices. The success of Silicon Valley (originally specialized in the production of fruit) and the relative stagnation of Rust Belt areas with a long industrial history, such as Detroit, can be viewed in this light.

Building regional competitive advantage therefore requires a twofold strategy. To promote learning and adaptability it is rational to encourage close interaction and a common understanding among regional agents. But the regional system also needs mechanisms that help it to move away from its own routines when it reaches maturity and is threatened by stagnation. This is why a certain degree of openness, diversity, and even internal contradiction is required for retaining a sustainable regional advantage.

In terms of the organization of regional policy, this may imply either a strong concentration of power in a regional authority that combines integration with autonomy in relation to the business community or a more diffuse distribution of power whereby several authorities with different aims and practices are in competition when it comes to stimulating regional development.

All these issues are discussed from different perspectives in this book. The lessons for public policy are not simple. The promotion of innovation and economic development at the regional level in a globalized context necessarily involves elements of experimentation and trial and error. Attracting top-level scientists and experts needs to be combined with investing broadly in human skills and with the delegation of responsibility to employees.

Mario Davide Parrilli and his co-editor Bjørn T. Asheim should be congratulated on this book. It combines contributions by international scholars on the general issues with contributions on the reality in the Basque region from scholars connected to the research unit Orkestra, which was established only in 2006. On the basis of this collaboration I would say that Orkestra has the potential to become an important international research center for understanding innovation in its regional and global contexts.

Bengt-Åke Lundvall
Aalborg May 11, 2011

Foreword

The second *Competitiveness Report of the Basque Country*, which was compiled and published by the Basque Institute of Competitiveness in 2009, exposed a phenomenon that is characteristic of many national and regional economies, the *competitive paradox*. In the Basque Country this paradox involves the counter-intuitive fact that the comparatively high levels of economic performance and welfare (measured in terms of exports, growth rate, and per capita income) are not explained by the relatively low levels of applied knowledge inputs used within the regional production system (measured in terms of investment in human capital formation, expenditure on R&D, number of patents, and so on).

Comparative economic analysis shows that this paradox is not a local exception. It is a situation that can be found in several countries, though in each case the 'contradiction' exhibits its own specificities. As a result, direct linear relationships such as 'an amount x of knowledge inputs leads to an identical amount x of economic output' represent an extraordinary situation. Non-linear ties ('inputs x lead to output y, which could be either lower or higher than x') are more common than generally supposed.

This book collects together a set of seminal contributions that study in depth the process of business and territorial innovation, including its impact on competitiveness and welfare. These critical thoughts analyze the 'black box' of innovation that connects inputs and outputs in the hypothetical linear relation. In this sense, the chapters of this book unpack the broad concept of innovation by clarifying the processes through which societies, and more specifically firms, transform (public and private) financial resources into, on the one hand, knowledge and, on the other, goods and services that are demanded and valued by the market.

The authors are unanimous in recognizing the need to broaden our understanding of innovation processes beyond the standard input–output relationship that links investment/expenditure with competitive products. They take into account a social relation in which innovation and economic output are determined to a large extent by the *capacity to learn* of each specific society. This capacity highlights the need for broader and more practice-oriented learning processes involving learning-by-doing, learning-by-using, and learning-by-interacting. The formalization of this learning path is currently called the *DUI mode of innovation* (from 'doing', 'using,' and 'interacting').

Contributing to this debate and to the literature on innovation, the chapters of this book emphasize the capacity of experience/practice-based economies to develop both incremental and radical innovations owing to the strength of collective learning processes that act not only to help improve the working of social and economic systems, institutions, and firms but also to catalyze new interactions and actions that on a one-off basis produce entirely novel effects in the organization of production activities and generate a substantial impact on economic performance.

One of the critical outcomes of such reflection is the gradual deepening of knowledge about how innovation processes materialize, become more complex, and acquire richness, which may be exploited in the spheres of business management and economic policy. For managers and policy-makers, the enhancement of business or territorial competitiveness is not restricted to the management of inputs – which in its simplest form is equivalent to increasing the budget devoted to R&D activities and to developing strategic product lines and institutions (universities, technology centers, and so on). In contrast to this more traditional approach, the DUI mode of innovation demands deeper understanding, acquisition, and transformation of the forms in which knowledge is generated and conveyed to firms and to society as a whole. In this effort, local and regional territories acquire importance insofar as innovation and development processes are social processes articulated in a plurality of public and private institutions within specific geographical boundaries.

The 'microeconomics' and 'mesoeconomics' of these innovation and development processes need to be analyzed in the long term because such processes have to be sustained over time in order to secure the reproduction of appropriate resources for this and future generations. This analysis is also essential for optimizing both the effectiveness and the efficiency of invested resources (result-oriented exploitation of inputs).

The Basque Institute of Competitiveness, in collaboration with leading experts in the field, aims to participate in and promote the analysis of – and the related academic and policy debate on – the complex macro, meso, and micro factors that affect the competitiveness of territorial (regional or local) economies such as those of the Basque Country or the Scandinavian countries discussed in this book, which might be representative of other territorial economies worldwide.

José Luis Curbelo
Director, Basque Institute of Competitiveness

Contributors

Maria José Aranguren, Head of the Territory, Innovation, and Clusters Unit, Basque Institute of Competitiveness (Orkestra), and Associate Professor of Economics, University of Deusto, San Sebastian.

Bjørn T. Asheim, Full Professor of Economic Geography, Department of Social and Economic Geography, and Co-Founder and Deputy Director of CIRCLE, University of Lund.

Jesper-Lindgaard Christensen, Associate Professor of Economics, Department of Business Studies, University of Aalborg.

Philip Cooke, Full Professor and Director of the Centre for Advanced Studies, University of Wales, Cardiff.

Aitziber Elola, Research Fellow in the Strategy Unit, Basque Institute of Competitiveness (Orkestra-Institut), San Sebastian.

Juan José Gibaja, Associate Professor of Quantitative Methods, Faculty of Economics and Business Administration, University of Deusto, San Sebastian.

Joost Heijs, Associate Professor of Economics and Director of the Centre for Financial and Industrial Analysis, Complutense University, Madrid.

Arne Isaksen, Full Professor of Regional Innovation and Governance, Institute of Employment and Innovation, University of Agder.

Björn Johnson, Senior Associate Professor, Innovation and Knowledge and Economic Dynamics (IKE) Group, Department of Business Studies, University of Aalborg.

James Karlsen, Senior Research Fellow, University of Agder and Agder Research, and Senior Research Fellow Basque Institute of Competitiveness (Orkestra).

Miren Larrea, Senior Research Fellow, Territory, Innovation, and Clusters Unit, Basque Institute of Competitiveness (Orkestra), San Sebastian.

Santiago López, Associate Professor, Department of Economics and Economic History, University of Salamanca.

Edward Lorenz, Full Professor of Economics, GREDEG-CNRS and University of Sophia-Antipolis, Nice.

Bengt-Åke Lundvall, Full Professor, Department of Business Studies, University of Aalborg, and Professor, Science-Po, Paris; founder and coordinator of the international network GLOBELICS; co-founder of the academic conference DRUIDS.

Mikel Navarro, Full Professor of Economics, University of Deusto, and Senior Research Fellow, Basque Institute of Competitiveness (Orkestra), San Sebastian.

Mario Davide Parrilli, Associate Professor of Economics and Director of the PhD program in Economics and Business, University of Deusto, San Sebastian, and Senior Research Fellow, Basque Institute of Competitiveness (Orkestra), San Sebastian.

Dagmara Stoerring, Officer at the European Parliament, Brussels.

Jesus María Valdaliso, Full Professor of Economic History, University of the Basque Country, Bilbao.

James R. Wilson, Senior Research Fellow, Territory, Innovation, and Clusters Unit, Basque Institute of Competitiveness (Orkestra), and Lecturer in Economics, University of Deusto, San Sebastian.

Introduction: Learning and Interaction – Drivers for Innovation in Current Competitive Markets

Bjørn T. Asheim and Mario Davide Parrilli

Europe's competitive landscape after the global economic and financial crisis

The challenge for Europe after the global economic and financial crisis is substantially different from the scenarios envisaged by the 2000 Lisbon Strategy. Then, optimistic perspectives of Europe catching up with the United States and becoming the most competitive region during a ten-year period were opened up, and the means of achieving this vision were to spend at least 3% of GDP on R&D, as stated in the Barcelona Declaration of 2002, following what Lundvall and Lorenz (2006) call the STI mode of innovation (Science, Technology, Innovation). Globalization having been identified as the basis of an understanding of the dynamics of contemporary capitalism, there was strong agreement that innovation was the key factor in promoting competitiveness in a globalizing knowledge economy (Porter, 1987; Lundvall, 2007). It is about twenty years since eminent academics acknowledged the role of innovation as the main driver of competitiveness, opening up the global market to new firms and developing countries capable of producing at very low cost (Drucker, 1985; Freeman, 1987; Porter, 1987; Dosi et al., 1988; Pyke and Sengenberger; 1992; Lundvall, 1992; Nelson, 1993; Asheim, 1994; Cooke, 2004). The solution points to leaving the low-road type of competition to enter markets for more sophisticated, specialized or niche products that can be produced by selected firms and/or systems/clusters of firms. For these reasons, these market segments are less price competitive and potentially highly remunerative.

Competition based on innovation implies choosing the high-road strategy, which is the only sustainable alternative for developed, high-cost regional and national economies. For a long time such a strategy was thought to be identical with promoting high-tech, R&D-intensive industries in accordance with the linear view of innovation. Up to the 1990s, scholars in economics and business studies identified expenditure on private and public R&D as the activity that most directly helped to create new products and processes and that represented the fundamental basis on which to promote the innovation capacity of firms and territories (Griliches, 1979; Cohen and Levinthal, 1989; Audretsch and Feldman, 1996). Together with R&D, human capital was recognized as the complementary key determinant; in fact, a high level of capability – evidenced, for instance, by a significant number of doctors and engineers in a company – increased its absorptive capacity and, as a consequence, helped to improve the impact of R&D activities, that is its capacity to innovate (Cohen and Levinthal, 1989; Romer, 1994).

On the basis of these hypotheses and grounded on research results supported by varying degrees of empirical evidence, countries and public agencies, together with private firms, started to invest capital in R&D activities that generated new products, processes and organizational forms that would help them to differentiate themselves from other firms and production systems and gain a competitive edge to increase market share or, more simply, avoid low-cost competition from emerging economies such as BRIMC countries, including Thailand, Malaysia, Vietnam, Chile and South Africa (OECD, 1992; EU, 1994).

However, it has since increasingly been recognized that a broader and more comprehensive view of innovation has to be applied to retain and develop competitiveness in the heterogeneity of Europe's regions. This implies that regional advantage has to be constructed on the basis of the uniqueness of the capabilities of firms and regions rather than solely on the basis of R&D efforts (Barney, 1991; Malmberg and Maskell, 1999; Eisenhardt and Martin, 2000; Cooke, 2004; Asheim et al., 2006). This reflects recent research pointing to the complexity of modern products and their innovation processes (Lam, 2002), which requires a differentiated knowledge base perspective (synthetic, analytical and symbolic) to be fully understood (Asheim and Gertler, 2005; Asheim et al., 2007). Such a broad-based innovation policy is in line with the definition of innovation as interactive learning, combining an STI and a DUI (doing, using, interacting) mode of innovation (Lorenz and Lundvall, 2006).

DG Research launched the idea of 'constructing regional advantage' in 2006 as the new way of taking on and combating the new challenges and problems of globalization confronting European regions (Asheim et al., 2006), and presented perspectives of how innovation policies and strategies can resolve the tension between competition and cohesion (Asheim et al., 2006). Constructing regional advantage means turning comparative advantage into competitive advantage through an explicit policy push promoting a Chamberlinian monopolistic competition based on product differentiation promoting unique products, an assumption which was fundamental also to Porter's cluster approach. While building on the lessons from the dynamic principle of the theory of competitive advantage as well as the innovation system approach that competitive advantage can be influenced by innovation policies and supporting regulatory and institutional frameworks, the constructed advantage approach recognizes the important interplay between industrial and institutional dynamics at the same time as calling for greater attention to multi-level governance. What is especially highlighted is the role of a proactive public–private partnership and impact of the public sector and public policy support by acknowledging to a greater extent the importance of institutional complementarities in knowledge economies. This approach represents an improved understanding of key regional development challenges as well as a better anticipation and response to the problems by addressing system failures of lack of connectivity in regional innovation systems.

Two main ideas lie behind and inform this approach: first, the observation that the strong push of R&D and science-driven innovation, following the Lisbon and Barcelona declarations, can fully resolve neither the competitiveness challenges nor the cohesion challenges in regional development. Secondly, inspired by the work for DG Research on 'Constructing Regional Advantage' (Asheim et al., 2006), we argue that in order to resolve the competitiveness–cohesion tension regions need to proactively construct regional advantage by improving the connectivity in regional innovation systems. In the globalizing knowledge economy, imitation and adaptation is no longer a sufficient strategy for creating unique competitive advantages.

There are at least two main problems with a too strong focus on R&D and science-driven innovation. Such a policy tends to give a one-sided priority to emerging, science-based industries building on an analytical knowledge base at the cost of more traditional, engineering-based industries building on a synthetic knowledge base as well as of rapid growing cultural industries building on a symbolic knowledge base. While new and emerging science-based industries are very important in the continuous strengthening of the competitiveness of regions and nations, we should still keep in mind that when it comes to economic impact and employment non-R&D/science-based economic activities clearly dominate. In addition, the success rate of science-driven innovations in terms of returns is quite low, which is one of the arguments for pursuing user-driven innovations. Moreover, an R&D and science-driven innovation policy favors larger cities and regions, which have the capabilities and capacities to carry out the knowledge exploration and exploitation required for innovation. Human capital, universities and research organizations tend to concentrate in the centre, leaving more peripheral and less advanced regions (the 'ordinary' regions) without sufficient innovation policy support. Furthermore, jobs will primarily be created for the well educated and highly skilled part of the workforce (the creative class).

Thus, EU policy discourses traditionally pay much attention to the quantitative aspects of knowledge creation, particularly with respect to investments in R&D. However, countries with high investments in R&D do not always perform better economically than those that invest less. One way to gain insight into the conditions in which knowledge leads to economic and social development is to study how the relationship between creation of knowledge and its social and economic effects is conditioned by differences in economic, institutional, political and social factors. International comparative studies on how governance and institutions, as well as broader social and cultural factors, influence innovation, diffusion and economic growth in other countries will provide valuable insights into factors that need to be taken into account to achieve the objectives of national policies, that is into the conditions under which knowledge creation leads to economic and social development (see, for example, Abramovitz, 1986; Cohen and Levinthal, 1990; Fagerberg et al., 2007).

The traditional approach to innovation and its limitations

Looking at the countries that have handled the global economic and financial crisis best reveals some striking patterns. First, countries organized around a coordinated market economy, such as the Nordic countries, Germany and the Netherlands, are doing much better than countries with a liberal market economy (the UK, Ireland and the United States). The only exception is economies with a large resource-based economy, such as Australia and Canada, due to the strong demand, especially from China, that has made these economies highly resilient to the crisis. Second, countries with a micro foundation of learning work organizations (Norway, Denmark, Sweden and the Netherlands) – often underpinning synthetic, knowledge-based industries – are clearly outperforming countries dominated by Taylorist and more artisanal forms of work organization (typically Southern European countries as well as Ireland, that is the Taylorist form).

Thus, it can be questioned if countries and regions that invest a high proportion of their GDP in R&D and human capital are those that exhibit the highest development and innovation capacity (UNU-MERIT, 2008), as it is currently evident that large (public) investments in R&D may be not sufficiently efficient and effective (Arundel et al., 2007; Jensen et al., 2007; Bitard et al., 2008; Parrilli et al., 2010). From the academy, a broad call has been opened on the false expectation that direct investment in R&D and human capital generate innovation automatically according to the linear model. In fact, after many years of investment in infrastructures and policies, policy-makers and public agency managers and officers have verified that such investments are not enough to guarantee substantial or efficient results. This may be due to regional, national or sector idiosyncrasies that influence the type of innovation that is generated in each territory in a way that generates significant variations. In some cases the flow of codified and analytical knowledge might be more important (e.g. in territories based on high-tech industries such as aeronautics, biotechnology and nano-materials), whereas in other cases tacit and synthetic knowledge bases are more relevant (e.g. in territories based on traditional industries of medium to low technology content or on industries based on symbolic and/or artistic knowledge) (see Asheim and Coenen, 2006). For these reasons, academics and policy-makers have been working to identify fundamental factors to promote an efficient and effective process of innovation among firms and territories.

To establish a proper framework for formulating as well as evaluating a fine-tuned regional innovation policy, a distributed knowledge base perspective should be introduced together with the idea that different modes of innovation co-exist in regional economies. We make the distinction between analytical (science-based), synthetic (engineering-based) and symbolic (arts-based) knowledge bases (Asheim, 2007; Asheim et al., 2007). The two main reasons for using this typology are first that knowledge creation and innovation can take place in all kind of industries but take place in different ways, need different kinds of knowledge and skilled people and require different kinds of innovation support. Second, no type of knowledge should a priori be given priority with regard to being 'superior' in terms of providing economic growth and jobs (as is done using a linear view of innovation giving priority to high-tech industries). Here Porter's position of partly recommending that a region should continue to build on industries in which it has traditionally been strong, as well as his view on basing competitive advantage on the uniqueness of products and services (which could be founded on analytical, synthetic or symbolic knowledge), should be the starting point when formulating policies for promoting regional competitiveness and innovativeness. This view accords well with the research of Lorenz and Lundvall (2006), identifying at least two main modes of innovation: DUI (doing, using and interacting) and STI (science, technology and innovation). The STI mode of innovation is mostly associated with the analytical knowledge base but is also applied engineering research (synthetic but also to a certain extent symbolic knowledge) carried out at technical universities. The DUI mode of innovation is based on synthetic and symbolic knowledge; it is experience-based with a much larger tacit component than is found in analytical, research-based knowledge, and it is mainly carried out in companies dominated by highly skilled workers from technical universities and polytechnics. If the DUI mode of innovation has learning forms of work organization as its micro foundation, which is the case in the Nordic countries as well as in the Netherlands, and is characterized by a high degree of work autonomy (which requires highly skilled workers and a flat organizational structure), which provides a significant learning dynamic, the potential for being highly innovative is clearly present.

The innovative potential that a learning work organization can display is theoretically based on the argument that learning not only is reproductive or adaptive (resulting in imitation) but also can be developmental and creative. Ellström (1997) uses these categories to make a distinction between developmental learning as the 'logic' of knowledge exploration on the one hand, and reproductive or adaptive learning which represents the 'logic' of knowledge exploitation on the other. New research on the relationship between forms of work organization and economic performance in EU confirms that learning also can be developmental and creative due to the high degree of work autonomy and learning dynamics found in learning form work organization (Chapter 2 in this book) (Lorenz and Valeyre, 2006; Michie and Sheehan, 2003). The studies show that in addition to providing better and more qualified jobs, the learning work organization promotes superior conditions for learning and innovation and even a greater propensity for patenting. This implies that a DUI mode of innovation which has learning work organizations as its micro foundation should not only be expected to produce incremental innovations but also have the potential for creating radical innovations due to the presence of developmental learning, as argued by Lorenz in Chapter 2 in this book.

Research has shown that combining the two modes of innovation (STI and DUI), and consequently different knowledge bases, increases the economic performance of firms; in other words that firms which have relied almost exclusively on one of the modes would benefit from integrating the other mode. Research confirms this by showing that firms that source knowledge on a broad base rather than one-sidedly focusing on collaboration with either R&D institutes or non-R&D-based sources of innovation are more innovative. To achieve such a combination of modes of innovation the cognitive distance between actors in the regional innovation systems (RIS) has to be reduced and the absorptive capacity of firms and at system level has to be increased. In the case of many less developed regions in Europe the most important challenge would be to link non-R&D-based firms with R&D institutes and universities. This requires well functioning technological transfer organizations and other forms of brokers, as well as mobility schemes whereby the hiring of university-trained candidates in non-R&D based firms is partly subsidized by the public sector, to increase their absorptive capacity (this is especially important for SMEs). Such policy measures represent important parts of improving the connectivity in the RIS.

The potential benefits of combining the two modes of innovation make it necessary to reflect upon which types of R&D efforts it would be most beneficial to support as part of a regional innovation policy. In this context it is important to remember the point already made that the STI mode is not limited to an analytical knowledge base but must also include synthetic and symbolic knowledge bases, and that the DUI mode is not limited to industries based on synthetic or symbolic knowledge, since predominantly analytical knowledge-based industries (e.g. pharmaceutical and biotech industries) make use of synthetic knowledge in specific phases of their innovation processes (Laursen and Salter, 2004; Herstad et al., 2008; Moodysson et al., 2008). In the case of synthetic knowledge and STI the argument that the STI mode of innovation also includes the synthetic knowledge base can be illustrated by reference to applied research undertaken at (technical) universities, which clearly must be part of the STI mode but operates mainly on the basis of synthetic (engineering) knowledge. An important distinction in this case is made between application development and technology development. Application development means solving concrete problems in connection with building specific equipment for customers. This draws on internal engineering competence as well as requiring interaction with suppliers and customers, and is, thus, an example of the DUI mode of innovation. Technology development means development of more general platform technologies, which represents the basic technological competence for carrying out application development. While application development is carried out only in-house or in user–producer relationships, technological development takes place in cooperation with (technical) universities as applied research projects, and thus represents the STI mode of innovation.

Clearly this points towards R&D which could directly be used to upgrade more traditional and non-R&D-based industry. However, such R&D should not only be focusing on the existing technological trajectory but also have an eye on how to transcend the dominating trajectory to avoid path dependency leading to negative, lock-in situations. However, it would be even more interesting to apply a related variety perspective on how to combine R&D-intensive and less intensive sectors (Frenken et al., 2007). Generic technologies such as ICT, biotechnology and nanotechnology stand out as being of special importance in achieving a related variety-based combination of the modes of innovation. Examples of this, using biotechnology as the generic technology, would be within green biotechnology, where the production of functional food requires collaboration between R&D-intensive biotech firms in science parks and traditional dairy firms, or in white biotechnology, where biotech input is used to upgrade and diversify products and processes in traditional metal and chemical industries.

When it comes to supporting emerging firms based on newly created knowledge from universities and R&D institutes through innovation policy, it is of strategic importance that the knowledge created is unique and of international excellence, and that a critical mass of research exists. In addition a successful policy requires competent technology transfer offices and organizations, science parks with incubators having well established links to the relevant university departments, research centers and R&D institutes as well as a regional entrepreneurial culture. Experience has shown that if R&D resources are too evenly spread, their positive impact disappears. While Finland was highly successful in its Centers of Expertise (CoE) policy in ICT, which was concentrated in a few places with research capacity of world class and NOKIA as the major private actor, applying the same CoE strategy to biotechnology was a failure because the public R&D funding was distributed among far too many CoEs. This has led Finland to reformulate its CoE policy and to revert to a much more centralized approach.

It is also important to keep in mind that not all relevant knowledge can be provided within a region, and that a related variety strategy can also be obtained by linking regional industry with universities and R&D institutes outside the region and even internationally in a distributed knowledge network. Experiences in Sweden show that only a few regions – those that have high-quality research universities, international competitive industries and a pro-active regional government – can support international competitive industries. This is even more valid for less developed regions and should be remembered when deciding on how innovation policy and support should be designed.

The black box of innovation and the learning processes

On the basis of the discussion presented so far , a number of scholars and their schools focused on identifying the different 'national and regional paradoxes' that point at the lack of correspondence between knowledge inputs introduced in the system, the innovation output and the related economic result. For example, in the case of the 'Swedish paradox' it has been argued that significant financial and human capital has traditionally been invested in R&D without producing correspondingly high GDP growth rates (Bitard et al., 2008). This interpretation of the 'Swedish paradox' has, however, been contested in a forthcoming article in *Research Policy*, where the conclusion is that there is no a paradox at all. The authors argue that if such a system failure existed, the paradox would manifest itself in slow growing sectors which could not transform R&D into growth. However, what they found was that the paradox occurs only in fast-growing manufacturing and service sectors. This can be explained by the diminishing marginal return on R&D investment in high-tech sectors, which are dependent on R&D for their international competitiveness (Ejermo et al., 2011).

In the 'Basque paradox', on the other hand, despite the quite limited resources invested in R&D and the even lower innovation output (e.g. patents and high-tech spin-off companies), the economic performance of the region is such that it has the highest per capita income in Spain (Navarro, 2009). A similar case of a high level of productivity and GDP combined with low R&D input in the economy is presented by Norway and was described as the Norwegian 'puzzle' by the OECD (OECD, 2008). What is it then that determines differentiated ratios between knowledge inputs, innovation output and economic results?

What justifies different models of innovation promotion such as can be found in the Swedish and Finnish cases, which are based on significant investments in R&D in the context of the STI mode of innovation, and the Norwegian and Danish cases, which are based on more intensive flows of tacit knowledge, in other words on innovation based on accumulated experience, learning-by-doing, and interaction with other agents in a DUI mode of innovation? This is the basis of important new studies in which the need is set to overcome the analysis of R&D alone to incorporate a series of new indicators that take into account new aspects related to tacit and interactive knowledge. These aspects have been and are relevant for the success obtained in the last few decades by the above-mentioned Scandinavian economies – principally Norway and Denmark – and by other systems based on small and medium-sized enterprises such as the industrial districts regional economies of Italy, Spain and the clustered economies of other EU regions and beyond, such as China and Brazil (Sforzi, 1992; Cassiolato and Lastres, 2001; Bellandi and Di Tommaso, 2005; Boix and Galletto, 2008). An example of these novel efforts to elaborate a more appropriate and comprehensive methodology to fully analyze innovation processes is represented by the European Innovation Surveys realized over the past ten years on the basis of the 'Oslo Manual' endorsed by the OECD (1997/2006).

For these reasons, many schools of thought as well as many academics, program managers, consultants, entrepreneurs and policy-makers recognize that a soft element exists in the processes of innovation that has not been taken sufficiently into account up to now ('soft' in contrast to the traditional 'hard' investment in R&D and infrastructures). Some researchers have focused on these 'soft' aspects that promote innovation, sometimes even independently from investments in R&D and human capital. Various academics have highlighted the important role of 'learning' (Archibugi and Lundvall, 2001; Lundvall and Nielsen, 2007; Arundel et al., 2007; Jensen et al., 2007; Stoneman, 2007; Parrilli and Sacchetti, 2008; Parrilli et al., 2010) and of the related 'absorptive capacity', taken as the capacity to absorb and to adapt external knowledge to the local entrepreneurial context and thus transform it into higher productivity and innovation (Cohen and Levinthal, 1989; Zahra and George, 2002; Langlois, 2003; Lazaric et al., 2008). One explanation of Norway's strong performance with respect to productivity and high GDP is precisely its high level of absorptive capacity due to one of the highest levels of participation in tertiary education in Europe. This – among other factors – has resulted in a high level of adoption of new technologies, efficient knowledge diffusion and frequent cooperation in innovation (Fagerberg et al., 2009). According to Fagerberg et al. such characteristics of a national innovation system are 'typically not captured by conventional indicators of innovation input or output' (Fagerberg et al., 2009). More and more international experts have started focusing on this direct basis of innovation, in other words on the learning process as a means to metabolize codified knowledge flows that are generated in knowledge organizations and infrastructures (e.g. universities, research and excellence centers, technology centers) and that in a more or less fluid way reach the production system (Jensen et al., 2007; Laranja, 2009; Parrilli et al., 2010; Parrilli and Elola, 2011).

Figure 0.1 synthetically shows that the learning processes improve the relationships between the system of production (manufacturing firms and private services) and the system of infrastructures of innovation (with a strong public nature) by reducing the gap between them, and so strengthen the system efficiency in developing new processes

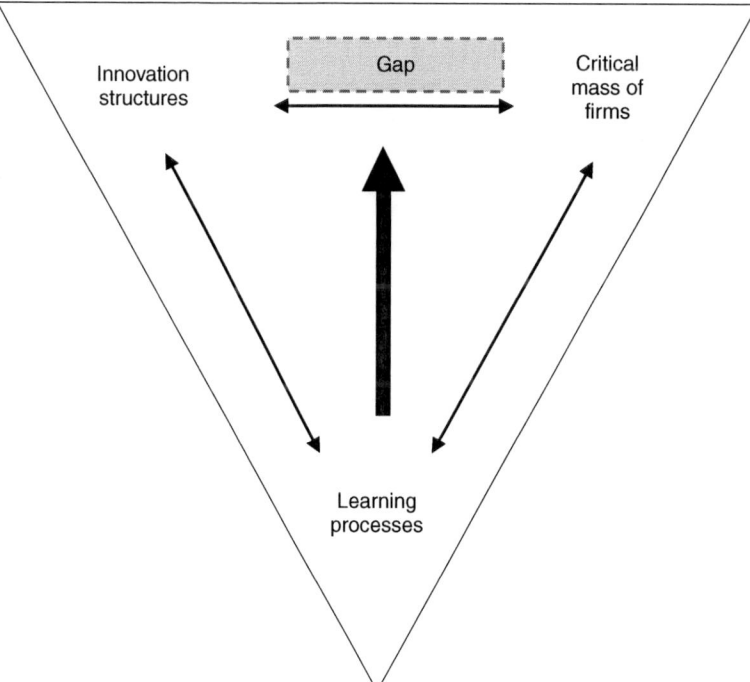

Figure 0.1 The innovation gap and the interdependences among the factors
Source: Parrilli et al. (2010).

and products. As can be seen in Figure 0.1, we highlight the mutual dependence of these three variables in the promotion of innovatio in the system of production and, in particular, show the importance of the 'learning' driver as a factor capable of reducing the distance between the institutions of the system of innovation (e.g. universities, technology and excellence centers, science and technology parks, training centers) and the firms agglomerated in clusters, districts and local production systems in general. With no learning processes at work the two 'hard' components – institutions/infrastructures and firms – remain far from one another and do not communicate on key production issues and on the required knowledge inputs. As a result, the potential benefits of investing in such institutions/infrastructures are minimized, as are those of the practical activity of these organizations for the firms (e.g. projects of technology centers to support innovation in specific industries) measured in terms of innovations and economic results. In contrast, learning processes based on interaction and experience promote this relationship, which helps to increase the flows of useful knowledge among these agents, and helps the firms and their territories to build up competitive advantages that are critical in the new economy of innovation.

Learning processes constitute a strategic element of the innovation process because they help the active subjects (e.g. entrepreneurs, managers, workers, etc.) to metabolize external knowledge and to convert it into useful inputs for the creation of product and process innovations, and for the strategic design of the organization and its innovation plans and management. Complementarily, learning processes make entrepreneurs, managers and workers active subjects capable of transforming these inputs in new products, processes and organizational routines and mechanisms; in other words, they create what Zahra and George (2002) call the capacity to transform potential absorptive capacities into realized absorptive capacities (see also Langlois, 2003; and Lazaric et al., 2008). From a market perspective, learning processes are the foundation of the capacity to 'perceive and identify the new market opportunities, incorporate these in the organization through mechanisms and solutions that are useful to activate it, and at the same time, find new and better paths to connect knowledge, resources and factors in innovative combinations' (Teece, 2007: p. 1346).

The learning subject is fundamental for the promotion of innovation in all local, regional and country production systems where significant gaps are found between the volume of knowledge inputs to the system (measured, for example, as investment in education and as expenditure in R&D), the expected output of innovation (measured, for example, in terms of patents, licenses and/or sales or exports of new products) and economic output (measured through GDP, growth rate and GDP per capita). In this sense, in the past few years many relevant research groups have started focusing on the existence of a 'black box' of the innovation process in each territorial system, a black box that represents local idiosyncrasies in the conversion of knowledge inputs into innovation output and economic performance (NESTA, 2006/2007; Jensen et al., 2007; Bitard et al., 2008; Ejermo et al., 2011; Parrilli and Elola, 2011). In some cases it seems that the innovation system is not efficient in transforming the inputs into output; in other cases it seems that the territorial systems (national and regional innovation systems) have a great capacity to convert these into material innovations and economic growth. In the case of the Basque country, for example, one can observe a sort of hourglass, since on the one hand there is a first bottleneck: significant knowledge inputs generate a small innovation output (e.g. patents); this bottleneck turns upside down in the second half of the hourglass as small innovation outputs are transformed, rather surprisingly, into relevant economic results. The weakness of the innovation output is counterbalanced by a very strong economic growth and performance over the last two decades (Navarro, 2009). Of course, past success does not guarantee future performance, as the (global) economy will have changed and the exploitation of natural resources or low manufacturing costs, which might have explained that performance, are no longer an option in Western economies.

Besides the possible idiosyncrasies related to each case, the aforementioned paradoxes could be explained by the weakness or limitation of the selected indicators in measuring 'all' the inputs and outputs of the innovation process, as is shown in the Norwegian case. In effect, the academic debate and the related innovation policy debate center upon this topic, with many academic and consultancy organizations focused on identifying new indicators that allow a more complete view of the innovation process in the various production systems (OECD, 2006; NESTA, 2006/2007; among others). Most of these works single out the importance of interactive flows of knowledge based on practical/tacit experience in promoting both incremental and radical innovations (Lorenz and Lundvall, 2006; Jensen et al., 2007; see also Lorenz in this book (Chapter 2)). One example of this is the distinction that is made in synthetic, engineering-based industries involved in technologically advanced 'batch' production (e.g. equipment to the oil and gas industry) between *technological* development and *application* development.

In a study of the Norwegian oil and gas industry it is shown that even though around 30% of all firms in (a wider defined) oil and gas industry spent at least 4% of sales income on R&D (though with wide variations between the various industry sub-sectors) 'most past innovations were driven by the close cooperation between operators and suppliers in the development of the large fields' (Sasson and Blomgren, 2011). This type of innovation as a result of practical challenges related to either field development or improved recovery is a typical example of what we have called application development. Thus, none of these major innovations, which 'relied on well-developed engineering competence and highly competent labor, depended on large-scale, intra-firm R&D programs. Indeed, many such innovations [...] may not even be classified as innovations by CIS-type surveys that mainly focus on technological (product and process) innovations' (Fagerberg et al., 2009a: p. 11). This implies that 'learning-by-doing and engineering based activities such as the design of large process plants in oil refining or basic metals are not captured by the Frascati manual definitions of R&D and may not be captured by the design category in the CIS innovation expenditures question' (Fagerberg et al., 2009b: p. 141). This measurement problem together with the importance of learning work organizations as the micro foundation of the DUI mode of innovation may well explain why the Norwegian 'puzzle' is not a 'puzzle' after all.

New studies have increasingly focused on the role of the 'learning organization', which in this context refers to new forms of organizing work within a firm, such as self-determined and auto-organized work targets and work pace, continuous on-the-job training, and multi-function and multidisciplinary team work (Arundel et al., 2007; Lorenz and Valeyre, 2006), which also help to explain the innovation capacity of the firms and their productive systems. Other research highlights the different types of innovation, including innovations in services and in commercialization activities that are realized with different objectives from pure manufacturing (e.g. less emphasis on product and process and more on client assistance; see, for instance, Stoneman, 2007; and NESTA, 2006/2007). All these areas of innovation generation are based less on the traditional science and technology approach to innovation (the STI mode of innovation) and more on interactive and tacit forms of knowledge exchange. These learning forms and innovation modes seem to offer a more interesting and useful interpretation of the Danish, Norwegian and Basque paradoxes or puzzles among others as they might represent their specific 'engines of innovation'.

Interactive drivers, radical innovation and a novel policy approach

This discussion has a further impact on innovation today. Contributions in this book highlight the key influence of DUI drivers and of learning organizations on the kinds and the value of innovation that may develop. Up to now, scholars and DUI supporters have believed that these drivers act on production by promoting small, imperceptible changes that assume the form of incremental innovations (Lundvall, 1992; Johnson and Lundvall, 1994) such as when workers and managers work together and identify minimal modifications in the factory layout or in the sequence of operations that are needed to improve the efficiency of the production process, or when client and producer discuss and identify tiny process variations or slight product differentiations. Simultaneously and complementarily, scholars who classify the 'varieties of capitalism' (Hall and Soskice, 2001) view liberal market economies 'with a comparative advantage in radical innovation because labor markets with few restrictions on firing and educational systems favor investments in industry-specific skills, thus making it easier for companies to rapidly reconfigure their knowledge bases in order to develop new product lines' (Lorenz in this book). This is said to be true especially in cases where radical innovations destroy former competences, as when new technologies replace former technologies or materials (e.g. synthetic materials replacing cotton in the textile industry).

In spite of this strong tradition, current work by scholars helps us to propose a new way forward in innovation studies. The interactive way to innovation does not result into incremental innovation only; rather, it is very likely to have a meaningful impact on radical innovations too. From this perspective, Lorenz argues that 'labour market mobility is more likely to contribute to the development and accumulation of the largely tacit industry-specific technical and organizational skills needed for many, if not most, radical innovations when it is embedded in a system of "flexible security" characterized by high levels of unemployment protection combined with active labour market policies'. This opportunity depends on the capacity of the 'flexible security' system to 'encourage individuals to commit themselves to what would otherwise be considered unacceptably risky career paths'. Lorenz uses data from EU-25 countries based on the 5th Community Innovation Survey (CIS) to support his hypothesis and to outline the success of those economies – especially Nordic countries and Germany.

It is the seminal hypothesis proposed by Lorenz in this book that sets the basis for a revolutionary thinking in the debate on innovation that has an impact also on policy-making. In fact, the evidence provided by Lorenz shows that countries that invest most in 'flexible security' and competence-building within firms and/or as part of labour market policies are also the ones that promote interactive learning and DUI innovation. Thus a circle is established which modifies the parameters that are traditionally applied to the promotion of innovation in firms and systems. In their initial chapter, Lundvall and Lorenz argue that if such a hypothesis is true – as some evidence suggests – then a special approach to education needs to be adopted, an approach that focuses on amplifying the kinds of competences and skills that are required of workers who are expected to be innovative and creative and of organizations that wish to promote participation, creativity and innovation among workers. Competences and skills will have to be measured not only in terms of individual codified knowledge capabilities, but also in terms of the tacit and relational skills and competences that will be required for different education models, courses and practices. The education system should thus improve not only students' ability with math and English or their degree of specialization in a specific subject, but also their ability to create and maintain contacts, dialogue and cooperation with others, who will later become suppliers, clients, workers and managers. Innovation is mostly developed through these interactive networks and exchanges, which need specific investments in the education system first, and in the firms themselves later on (in continuous training and learning programs, for example). This is why Lundvall and Lorenz emphasize the importance of focusing education schemes and programs not only on PISA test capabilities but also on 'collective entrepreneurship' models, which are also likely to have a significant impact on economic development. This approach will then be reflected in the social security system that backs up the production system. As we have said, the promotion of flexible security norms and practices related to employment favor the commitment of workers to maintain, improve and devote their competences to radical and incremental innovation activities and outputs within their firms and systems.

Within this framework and approach, such a new education model and such a new employment system are possible if the society has a strong social capital, meaning in this case 'the willingness and capability of citizens to make commitments to each other, collaborate with each other and trust each other in processes of exchange and interactive learning [...] where new insights into technologies and good organizational practices are diffused rapidly both within organizations and across organizational borders' (Lundvall and Lorenz, Chapter 1). As a general conclusion, STI efforts are important, but 'if they stand alone they cannot be expected to constitute a strong innovation system. It is necessary to take a broader and more systemic approach to competence building' (Ibid.), an approach that includes the DUI driver, which helps firms to become 'learning organizations' and so accumulate the advantages of both codified and tacit knowledge flows, science and technology drivers with practice and interaction-based drivers, resulting in both radical and incremental innovations.

Layout of the book

This book includes the variety of contributions presented in the workshop on 'Innovation and Learning', which are presented in two parts. The first part presents and discusses some of the main advances in economic theory of innovation processes; within it particular attention is devoted to the dynamics of innovation based on learning-by-doing, learning-by-using and learning-by-interacting (DUI) as a key component in the innovation process that has often been neglected by neoclassical/new growth theories centered on science and technology (STI) drivers. The second part consists of a discussion on the application of STI and DUI drivers to specific contexts, which in some cases represent whole regional innovation systems (such as Spanish regions and the Basque Country) and in other cases represent local production systems or even firms. The cases of local production systems and firms (in Norway, Denmark and Spain) presented here help clarify ideas on how the processes of innovation in individual firms and in significant groups of firms (e.g. the clusters) do prosper.

Overall, these contributions shed light on the importance of adopting a broader approach to innovation than the classical science- and technology-based approach. In turn, they help to answer the need of less high-tech-based economies, such as those of Southern Europe, to boost innovation and economic growth. This approach helps to identify and build up the competitive advantage of these countries. In this second part, some of the chapters also discuss the role of DUI type innovation policies in particular as a means to promote efficient and effective relations between the local or regional production system and the regional innovation system consisting of infrastructures and organizations that generate and disseminate specialized knowledge to the firms in the territory.

Part I: Theoretical insights from the literature on STI and DUI innovation, learning organizations and the 'related varieties' approach

In this first part, Bengt-Åke Lundvall and Edward Lorenz discuss the importance of the 'learning economy' that is superseding the traditional 'knowledge economy', promoted for years as the innovation model of the twentieth century (Abramowitz and David, 1996). For this new approach, it is relevant to distinguish between codified and tacit knowledge and, , between two different forms of innovation: one based mainly upon formal education activities related to investment in infrastructures and organizations centred on science and technology activities (STI), the other more based on experience, observation, knowledge exchange and the sharing of good practices based on learning by doing, using and interacting (DUI). Grounded on empirical bases (Jensen et al., 2007), the discussion concludes by acknowledging the importance of activating both processes of innovation in a complementary form as a means to create firms and territories that are capable of becoming leaders in innovation. Simultaneously, Lundvall and Lorenz stress the relevance of applied education models (such as creating specialized courses for engineers similar to MBAs for managers). In this way, the education system could promote the formation of complementary skills and capabilities that have been implemented successfully and 'naturally' in some Nordic countries thanks to a specific social capital formed in these areas over time that stimulates collective, interactive and practical learning processes, which go well beyond individual and formal methods.

In Chapter 2, Edward Lorenz focuses on different styles of innovation within the 'learning organization' and on the contribution of the labor force to innovation. Lorenz discusses the theory of the 'varieties of capitalism' that shows how 'coordinated market economies' tend to produce incremental innovations, whereas 'liberal market economies' produce more radical innovations. Contrarily to this interpretation, Lorenz argues that the capacity to generate radical innovations depends more on the 'flexible security' guaranteed by the production system in connecting high levels of mobility in the labour market with generous unemployment benefits and active policies for the labour market. This is one of the hot topics of the learning organization literature, which also proposes organizational forms that promote autonomy and creativity among workers, and greater emphasis on continuing on-the-job training and education as a means to generate new capabilities across the whole personnel and to make it participate creatively in the innovation process of the firm. Overall, Lorenz claims that the capacity to generate radical innovations does not depend on the liberal market economy approach, but rather on a perspective that values the accumulation of collective, tacit and institutional knowledge that is fundamental to the encouragement of both radical and incremental innovation processes.

Another relevant contribution is Bjorn Johnson's chapter on creative cities. This work applies the approaches of STI and DUI innovation to the context of urban agglomerations. In particular, Johnson puts emphasis on the importance of a variety of structural elements of the population (age, culture, preferences, skills, and so on), together with density of communication means and physical proximity among economic agents. These three types of factor promote interactions that increase knowledge and skills in the productive activities of a territory. At the same time, Johnson argues for the importance of a social and moral order and an inclusive governance model adequate for the promotion of interactions and the achievement of optimal variety, controlled for the size of the towns/cities, that permits the control of 'centrifugal forces' and can transform these urban concentrations into creative cities. In this sense, the 'triple helix' approach can be limited, whereas a wider approach ('quadruple helix') could be set up to take into account the position and the interests of a wider and representative public (consumers).

Phil Cooke's contribution further enriches this conceptual discussion by means of focusing on the value of geographical proximity and its potential for the generation of knowledge spillovers. Cooke stresses that geographical proximity, so much valued in the 1990s through clustering processes and cluster policy, should be upgraded on the basis of the creation of new industrial poles that cannot strictly center on the local area but have to broaden their borders in order to absorb knowledge spillovers produced by related industries in the wider (regional or national) territory. This argument is quite solid in high-technology sectors, although it could benefit the traditional industrial sectors too. Moreover, it creates a foundation to support the readjustment of public programs and development strategies centered on sub-sectors that are related to the current production and knowledge strengths (the 'related varieties' discussed in Cooke, 2006; and Asheim et al., 2011) with a view to promoting the competitive advantage of countries and regions in the near future.

Part II: Clusters, firms and innovation systems

Part II of this book includes a series of contributions related to clusters of firms, individual firms and innovation systems in selected Scandinavian countries as well as in southern Europe, mainly in Spain. This part helps to connect the theoretical discussion on innovation with the innovation and performance capacity of local production systems and their firms. It focuses on applied experiences of innovation activities from the perspective of the firms (such as how they elaborate new products, processes and organizational modalities, and how they improve their creative capacity) as well as from the perspective of public organizations. With regard to the regional innovation system, comparative analyses are realized together with efficiency and effectiveness assessments whose objective is the strengthening of the regional innovation system, which is based on the support of dynamic interactions among the agents of the RIS itself. A set of concluding remarks is deduced for the definition of innovation policies.

In their chapter, Arne Isaksen and James Karlsen analyze the modes of innovation that are adopted in the context of the cluster of light materials in Raufoss, Norway. In particular, they contend that the innovation mode applied in this context is a mix of STI and DUI factors, which in this case is called 'complex and combined innovation' (CCI) as this approach shows the meaning of knowledge flows and interactive learning in networks of innovation that transcend the local level. This capacity is based upon high absorptive capacity and the dynamic capacities of the local production agents. For this reason, the authors stress the importance of utilizing the concept of 'related varieties' in cases such as Raufoss as this cluster seems to be quite disconnected from other local clusters in spite of needing cross-fertilization of knowledge and competences with other clusters and production sectors. In part this can be obtained by means of good relationships with international partners or clusters that can help them acquire knowledge and thus prosper economically. Yet, a higher interrelation of Raufoss with other clusters in the country may generate knowledge spillovers that strengthen its overall competitiveness.

In Chapter 6, Jesper Lindgaard Christensen and Dagmara Stoerring discuss the creation of high-tech clusters in regions that are traditionally oriented towards low-tech production. The authors focus on the biomedical cluster in the North of Jutland, Denmark. They identify the role of the 'clusterpreneur' – a key actor in the process of emergence of clusters – having an entrepreneurial stimulus with a territorial basis that can arise from the private sector or from universities, public policy, or even service firms – in order to develop a cluster. Although difficult, the creation of competitive clusters in marginal regions can benefit from a series of elements that are present in successful cases such as this biomedical cluster. These elements include the diffusion of knowledge with a scientific and technological basis rooted in the work of technical consultants who support local SMEs, the support of collective and joint learning processes (STI+DUI), support services for high-tech small firms and policies oriented toward the specific needs of a selected region, not to mention other key aspects such as the critical mass of firms and the social capital that mobilizes local capabilities as a means to achieve appropriate economies of scale and scope.

Jesus Valdaliso, Aitziber Elola, Maria Jose Aranguren and Santiago López utilize the diamond of competitiveness elaborated by Porter as a frame to introduce social capital and knowledge as drivers in the evolution of the clusters of pulp and paper, and electronics and ICT systems in the Basque Country. The authors argue that social capital – which implies an intense flow of tacit and interactive knowledge – contributes to the competitiveness of the territory by creating sticky factor conditions, in other words by favoring the creation of client–producer networks, encouraging an entrepreneurial technology regime, and stimulating higher levels of diversification, which are fundamental for innovation. These conclusions have value for public policies that can focus on generating higher social capital as a basis for increasing territorial competitiveness.

In Chapter 8, Maria Jose Aranguren, Miren Larrea and Mario Davide Parrilli analyze the heterogeneity of small firms in relation to their approach/mode of innovation, and the related policy implications. The authors focus on a local production network that involves producers of furniture, machine tools and metallic products and identify firms that exhibit different types of approach to innovation ('artisanal', 'structured', 'non-systematic', 'advanced-though-looking-inward' and 'advanced-along-the-value-chain'). Only the last two modes involve – to different extents – both DUI and STI modes of innovation that in one case alone stretch beyond the firm (including external agents such as suppliers and clients). This study permits the identification of a typology of innovation behaviors as a potential trajectory to innovation implementation in small and medium-sized firms. As a consequence, public support programs with instruments that respond to these different types of behavior and attitude can be set up, thus helping to attain a more sustained economic impact.

In Chapter 9, Joost Heijs focuses on technology policy and, in particular on how expenditure on R&D influences learning processes in firms, measured by improvements in the training of personnel, absorption of knowledge and improvement in management models and practices. The result is positive as the investment in R&D and the related technology transfer supports the process of learning within enterprises and helps them to become more competitive. For this reason, Heijs confirms that 'the technology policy has achieved one of its main objectives, by generating synergies and a process of collective learning among the different agents of the innovation system'. However, an in-depth analysis shows differences in the learning process between innovative and less innovative firms: the first achieve stronger learning processes that depend on their technology capacity in a sort of virtuous circle, whereas the second type of firm presents a more limited learning process that depends on their lower technology capacity (vicious circle). This negative circle can be overcome only through a reduction in technology gaps; this objective requires a great effort, both public and private, in the design of instruments, including financial instruments, technical support and training.

Mikel Navarro and Juan José Gibaja implement an inductive, empirical analysis based on the theory of the knowledge production function, which is complemented with two further approaches: the agglomeration economies and the contribution of 'social filters' (Rodríguez-Pose's version of social capital). Through this combined approach (see also Navarro et al., 2009), the authors analyze and compare the different Spanish regions through a typology that permits them to group these communities not only in terms of production homogeneity and innovation potential, but also for their potential development trajectories based on their traditional economic structure and competence bases; in this way, this analysis delivers useful instruments to innovation policy as a means to improve its overall efficiency.

In the final chapter, Mari Jose Aranguren, Miren Larrea and James R. Wilson explore the relationship between universities and policy-makers with the aim of overcoming the dilemma of whether universities should convert to technical consultancies or retain their independent function in terms of academic thinking and the analysis of public policy. The authors argue for the importance of working out financial mechanisms and arrangements that promote the functioning of research institutes and universities insofar as these can guarantee an effective interaction between scientists and policy-makers. In addition, they claim the importance of introducing formal schemes that include academic training in applied research methods (such as action research) for development agents and policy-makers.

A synthetic view

This book presents a discussion of the processes of innovation and learning in the globalized economy and the role that regional innovation systems play in it, together with clusters of firms and firms themselves. It is a discussion that becomes crucial in the current globalized economy, in which several countries find themselves under pressure and need to find competitive advantages as a means to grow their economies.

The value of acquiring an open approach to innovation is stressed; in particular, the relevance of explicit and tacit knowledge flows is emphasized. The former tend to be grounded in science and technology (STI), whereas the latter rely more on interaction and learning-by-doing and -by-using (DUI). In spite of acknowledging the importance of both types of driver, this volume signals the relevance of DUI drivers as the 'engine of innovation' for many local, regional and even national economies, which have traditionally invested fewer resources in classical technology policy based on R&D expenditure and have been able to benefit from more interactive and tacit mechanisms of knowledge creation and innovation performance. In this respect, this work highlights the opportunities for local and national policy-makers to build innovation policy frameworks that recognize the DUI approach (and drivers) while pursuing it within the boundaries of a useful complementarity with the more classical STI approach. Such policy represents what is called a broad-based innovation policy, which is now implemented in Finland and is increasingly being diffused to other European countries as well as international organizations such as the OECD and EU as part of their policy recommendations.

Interestingly and originally, some of the contributions that enrich this book emphasize the capacity of learning organizations and local production systems to produce radical innovations (and not only incremental innovations) on the basis of a more 'coordinated market economy' (as opposed to the 'liberal market economy' propelled by the literature on the 'varieties of capitalism') that, in addition to a higher recognition of the importance of taking a more complete approach to innovation (that adds the DUI drivers to the classical STI factors), acknowledges the relevance of setting up a 'creative knowledge environment' which values the variety of creative knowledge and social inputs insofar as it establishes the bases for a more supportive 'flexibly secure' social and economic system. Appropriate policies are to be developed so as to respond to this more complex approach to innovation and development in the context of local and regional territories.

Such an approach should also offer higher options for innovation and development across firms, especially the thousands of small and medium-sized enterprises operating in local and regional territories worldwide. In fact, local production systems are often based on SMEs, which usually have less capital to invest in R&D as a means to realize new-to-market innovations; this option is obviously more feasible for groups of small firms on a territorial basis (clusters), sectoral basis (associations of firms) or even value-chain basis, as larger resources can be pulled together to facilitate economies of scale and scope.

In the selected cases, successful and useful examples of collective learning and innovation are presented, sometimes supported through effective innovation policies and public programs. In other cases, the different features of various groups of firms are visible; this observation is useful as a means to define public policies and innovation programs. These elements help to clarify the new landscape of competitiveness and innovation in globalized markets, the new challenges faced by firms and their production and innovation systems, and the challenges that also public innovation agencies and their regional, national and even international governments (EU) face and have to address if they want to open a more prosperous and sustainable future for their socioeconomic agents.

This is particularly important in the current scenario of globalization and also of the global economic crisis, which is putting particular pressure and uncertainty on the capacity of the Western economies to respond to the new challenges set by the entry of a large number of emerging economies in their traditional markets. The broader approach to innovation (STI+DUI) and to the relevant types of knowledge (analytical, synthetic and symbolic) is more likely to help a large set of non-leading economies to identify their true potential for growth in particular sectors as a means to create their own national and regional competitive advantage, which represents their way to join globalized markets in a unique and competitive way.

These lines of reasoning point to critical issues at the level of both the firm and the public research system subsectors of a RIS, and consequently to the system as a whole. Such a broad-based innovation policy needs both narrowly and broadly defined innovation systems to be implemented, in other words its knowledge diffusion infrastructure must be able to combine actor groups that individually are placed at different points on the DUI–STI continuum into processes of experimental recombination and co-evolution. These actors represent different but potentially related internal knowledge development processes, and different but potentially complementary extra-regional networks.

In this perspective learning regions should be looked upon as a strategy for formulation of long-term public–private partnership-based development strategies initiating learning-based processes of innovation and change (Asheim, forthcoming). Of crucial importance in this context is the capacity of people, organizations, networks and regions to learn (Lundvall, 2007). The concept of a learning region can, thus, be used to describe a region characterized by innovative activity based on localized, interactive learning, and co-operation promoted by organizational innovations in order to exploit learning-based competitiveness (Amin and Thrift, 1994).

The attractiveness of the concept of learning regions to planners and politicians is to be found in the fact that it promises not only economic growth and job generation but also social cohesion. As such, learning regions may be seen as an answer to the challenges of the global economy at the regional level, especially for regions with weak territorial competence bases. Learning regions , underline the strategic role played by social capital facilitating collective action for mutual benefit (Woolcock, 1998). Thus, it is not accidental that this approach to learning regions has been used since the 1990s by the Regional Innovation Strategies pilot scheme of the EU Commission as part of new policy developments in Europe to promote less developed regional economies within the EU through innovation (Bellini and Landabaso, 2007). In this sense, deep reflections on the policy approach to promoting innovation across these economies are necessary to help them build up such capacities in the near future.

References

Abramowitz, M. (1986), 'Catching up, forging ahead, and falling behind', *Journal of Economic History*, 46(2), 385–406.

Abramowitz, M. and David, P. (1996), 'Technological change and the rise of intangible investments: The US economy's growth path in the XX Century', in D. Foray and B.-Å. Lundvall (eds), *Employment and Growth in the Knowledge-based Economy*, Paris, OECD.

Amin, A. and Thrift, N. (1994), *Globalisation, Institutions and Regional Development in Europe*, Oxford, Oxford University Press.

Archibugi, D. and Lundvall, B.-Å. (2001), *The Globalizing Learning Economy*, Oxford University Press.
Arundel, A., Lorenz, E., Lundvall, B.-Å. and Valeyre, A. (2007), 'Europe's economies learn: a comparison of work organization and innovation modes for the EU-15', *Industrial and Corporate Change*, 16(6), 1175–1210.
Asheim, B.T. (1994), 'Industrial districts, inter-firm cooperation and endogenous technological development: the experience of developed countries', in *UNCTAD, Technological Dynamism in Industrial Districts*, Geneva & New York, pp. 91–142.
Asheim, B.T. (2007), 'Differentiated knowledge bases and varieties of regional innovation systems', *Innovation – The European Journal of Social Science Research*, 20(3), 223–241.
Asheim, B.T. (2011), 'The changing role of learning regions in the globalising knowledge economy: A theoretical re-examination', Special issue of *Regional Studies*, forthcoming.
Asheim, B.T. and Coenen, L. (2006), 'Contextualising regional innovation systems in a globalising learning economy: on knowledge bases and institutional frameworks', *Journal of Technology Transfer*, 31, 163–173.
Asheim, B.T. and Gertler, M. (2005), 'The geography of innovation: regional innovation systems', in J. Fegerberg, D. Mowery and R. Nelson (eds), *The Oxford Handbook of Innovation*, Oxford University Press, pp. 291–317.
Asheim, B.T., Cooke, P. and Martin, R. (2006), *Clusters and Regional Development: Critical Reflections and Explorations*, Routledge, London.
Asheim, B.T., Coenen, L., Moodysson, J. and Vang, J. (2007), 'Constructing knowledge-based regional advantage', *International Journal of Entrepreneurship and Innovation Management*, 7(2–5), 140–155.
Asheim, B.T., Boschma, R. and Cooke, P. (2011), 'Constructing regional advantage', *Regional Studies*, 45 (7), 893–904
Audretsch D.B. and Feldman M. (1996), R&D spillovers and the geography of innovation and production, *American Economic Review*, Vol.86(3), pp.630–640.
Barney, J. (1991), 'Firm resources and sustained competitive advantage', *Journal of Management*, 17(1), 99–120.
Bellandi, M. and Di Tommaso, M. (2005), 'The case of specialized towns in Guangdong, China', *European Planning Studies*, 13(5), 707–729.
Bellini, N. and Landabaso, M. (2007), 'Learning about innovation in Europe's regional policy', in R. Rutten and F. Boekema (eds), *The Learning Region: Foundations, State of the Art, Future*, Elgar, Cheltenham.
Bitard, P., Edquist, C., Hommen, L. and Rickne, A. (2008), *The Paradox of High R&D Input and Low Innovation Output: Sweden*, Circle Working Papers no. 14. CIRCLE, Lund University.
Boix, R. and Galletto, V. (2008), 'Innovation and industrial districts: a first approach to the measurement and determinants of the I-district effect', *Regional Studies*, 43, 1117–1133.
Cassiolato, J. and Lastres, H. (2001), 'Arranjos y sistemas produtivos locais na industrial brasileira', *Revista de Economia Contemporanea*, 5, Special Issue, 103–135.
Cohen, W.M. and Levinthal, D.A. (1989), 'Innovation and learning: the two faces of R&D', *Economic Journal*, 99(397), 569–596.

Cohen, W.M. and Levinthal, D.A. (1990), 'Absorptive capacity: a new perspective on learning and innovation', *Administrative Science Quarterly*, 35(1), 128–152.
Cooke, P. (2006), 'Reflections on the research and conclusions for policy', in P. Cooke, C. De Laurentis, F. Todtling and M. Trippl (eds), *Regional Knowledge Economies*, Elgar, Cheltenham.
Cooke, P. (2004), 'Regional innovation systems: an evolutionary approach', in Cooke, P., Heidenreich, M. and Braczyck, H-J. (eds), *Regional Innovation Systems: Governance in the Globalized World*, Routledge, London.
Dosi, G., Freeman, C., Nelson, R., Silverberg, G. and Soete, L.L. (1988), *Technical Change and Economic Theory*, Pinter, London; Columbia University Press, New York.
Drucker, M. (1985), *Innovation and Entrepreneurship: Principles and Practice*, Harper and Row, New York.
Eisenhardt, K. and Martin, J. (2000), 'Dynamic capabilities: what are they?', *Strategic Management Journal*, 21, 1105–1121.
Ejermo, O., Kander, A. and Svensson Henning, M. (2011) 'The R&D-growth paradox arises and fast-growing sectors', *Research Policy*, forthcoming.
Ellström, P.E. (1997), 'The many meanings of occupational competence and qualification', *Journal of European Industrial Training*, 21(6–7), 266–273.
EU (1994), *The European Report on Science and Technology Indicators 1994*, Report 15897, European Commission, Luxembourg.
Fagerberg, J. (2007), 'The dynamics of technology, growth and trade: a Schumpeterian perspective', in H. Hanusch and A. Pyka (eds), *Elgar Companion to New-Schumpeterian Economics*, Elgar, Cheltenham.
Fagerberg, J., Mowery, D. and Verspagen, B. (2009a), 'The evolution of Norway's national innovation system', *Science and Public Policy*, 431–444.
Fagerberg, J., Mowery, D. and Verspagen, B. (2009b), *Innovation, Path Dependency and Policy. The Norwegian Case*, Oxford, Oxford University Press.
Freeman, C. (1987), *Technology Policy and Economic Performance: Lessons from Japan*, Pinter, London.
Griliches Z. (1979), Siblings models and data in economics: beginnings of a survey, *Journal of Political Economy*, Vol. 87(5), 37–64.
Hall, P. and Soskice, D. (2001), *Varieties of Capitalism: the Institutional Foundations of Comparative Advantage*, Oxford, Oxford University Press.
Herstad, S., Bloch, C., Ebersberger, B. and van de Velde, E. (2008), 'Open innovation and globalization: theory, evidence and implications', *Projektbericht des ERA-NETS Vision*, Helsinki.
Jensen, M., Johnson, B., Lorenz, E. and Lundvall, B.-Å. (2007), 'Forms of knowledge and modes of innovation', *Research Policy*, 36, 680–693.
Lam, A. (2002), 'Los modelos societales alternativos de aprendizaje e innovación en la economía del conocimiento', *Revista de Ciencias Sociales*, 171, 51–61.
Langlois, R. (2003), 'The vanishing hand: the changing dynamics of industrial capitalism', *Industrial and Corporate Change*, 12(2), 351–385.
Laranja, M. (2009), 'The development of technology infrastructure in Portugal and the need to pull innovation using proactive intermediation policies', *Technovation*, 29(1), 23–34.
Laursen, K. and Salter, A. (2004), 'Searching low and high: what types of firm use universities as a source of innovation?', *Research Policy*, 33(8), 1210–1215.

Lazaric, N., Longhi, C. and Thomas, C. (2008), 'Gatekeepers of knowledge versus platforms of knowledge: from potential to realized absorptive capacity', *Regional Studies*, 42(6), 837–852.

Lorenz, E. and Lundvall, B.-Å. (2006), *How Europe's Economies Learn: Coordinating Competing Models*, Oxford, Oxford University Press.

Lorenz, E. and Valeyre, F. (2006), 'Organizational forms and innovative performance: a comparison of the EU-15', in E. Lorenz and B.-Å. Lundvall, *How Europe's Economies Learn: Coordinating Competing Models*, Oxford, Oxford University Press.

Lundvall, B.-Å. (1992), *National Systems of Innovation: Towards a Theory of Innovation and Interactive Learning*, Pinter, London.

Lundvall, B.-Å. and Johnson, B. (1994), 'The learning economy', *Journal of Industry Studies*, 1(2), 23–42.

Lundvall, B.-Å. and Nielsen, P. (2007), 'Knowledge management and information performance', *International Journal of Manpower*, 28(3/4), 207–223.

Lundvall, B.-Å. (2007), 'National innovation systems: analytical concept and development tools', *Industry and Innovation*, 14(1), 95–119.

Malmberg, A. and Maskell, P. (1999), 'The Competitiveness of firms and regions: "ubiquitification" and the importance of localized learning', *European Urban and Regional Studies*, 6(1), 9–25.

Michie, J. and Sheehan, M. (2003), 'Labour market deregulation, flexibility and innovation', *Cambridge Journal of Economics*, 27(1), 123–143.

Moodysson, J., Coenen, L. and Asheim, B. (2008), 'Explaining spatial patterns of innovation: analytical and synthetic modes of knowledge creation in the Medicon Valley life science cluster', *Environment and Planning A.*, 40 (5), 1040–1056.

Navarro, M. (2009), *El sistema de innovación de la CAPV a partir de las estadísticas de I+D*, Orkestra Institute, San Sebastian.

Nelson, R. (1993). *National Innovation Systems: a Comparative Analysis*, Oxford University Press.

NESTA (2006/2007), *Hidden Innovation*, University of Manchester, Manchester.

OECD (1992), *Technology and Economy: The Key Relationship*, Paris.

OECD (1997/2006), Oslo Manual: Guidelines for collecting and interpretating innovation data, OECD-EUROSTAT, Paris, various editions.

OECD (2008), OECD reviews of innovation policy: Norway, Organization for Economic Cooperation and Development, Paris.

Parrilli, M.D. and Sacchetti, S. (2008), 'Linking learning with governance in clusters and networks: key issues for analysis and policy', *Entrepreneurship and Regional Development*, 20(4), 387–408.

Parrilli, M.D., Aranguren, M.J. and Larrea, M. (2010), 'The role of interactive learning to close the "innovation gap" in SME-based economies', *European Planning Studies*, 18(3), 351–368.

Parrilli M.D. and Elola A. (2011), 'The strength of science and technology drivers for SME innovation', *Small Business Economics*, (15 March 2011), pp. 1–11, doi:10.1007/s11187–011-9319–6.

Porter, M. (1987), *The Competitive Advantage of Nations*, Prentice Hall, New York.

Pyke, F. and Sengenberger, W. (1992) 'Introduction', in F. Pyke and W. Sengenberger (eds), *Industrial Districts and Inter-firm Cooperation*, ILO, Geneva.

Romer, P. (1994), 'The origins of endogenous growth', *Journals of Economic Perspectives*, 8(1), 3–22.

Sasson, A. and Blomgren, A. (2011), 'Knowledge-based oil and gas industry', Research Report 3/2011, BI Norwegian Business School.

Sforzi, F. (1992), 'The quantitative importance of Marshallian industrial districts in the Italian economy', in F. Pyke and W. Sengenberger (eds), *Industrial Districts and Local Economic Regeneration*, ILO, Geneva.

Stoneman, P. (2007), 'Soft innovation: change in product aesthetics to aesthetic products', Working Paper, Mimeo, Warwick Business School.

Teece, D. (2007), 'Explicating dynamic capabilities: the nature and microfoundations of (sustainable) enterprise performance', *Strategic Management Journal*, 28(13), 1319–1350.

UNU-MERIT (2008), *European Innovation Scoreboards*, PRO-INNO EUROPE, Mastricht.

Woolcock, M. (1998), 'Social capital and economic development', *Theory and Society*, 27(2), 151–208.

Zahra, S. and George, G. (2002), 'Absorptive capacity: a review, reconceptualization and extension', *Academy of Management Review*, 27, 195–203.

Part I

Theoretical Insights from the Literature on STI and DUI Innovation, Learning Organizations and the 'Related Varieties' Approach

1
Innovation and Competence Building in the Learning Economy: Implications for Innovation Policy

Bengt-Åke Lundvall and Edward Lorenz

1.1 Introduction

The idea that knowledge matters for the economy is far from new. Adam Smith (1776) refers to the division of labor among specialized 'men of speculation' as an important source of innovation. Friedrich List (1841) argues that the most important form of capital is 'mental capital'. Karl Marx (1868) pointed to science as an important productive force. In the twentieth century the British scholar Bernal (1936) proposed that raising investments in R&D from 0.2 to 2% in Great Britain would stimulate the economy and bring a new kind of economic growth, and a similar message was formulated in *The Endless Frontier* by Vannevar Bush (1945), which laid the foundation of post-war science policy in the United States.

In the late 1950s Kenneth Arrow (1962b) and Richard Nelson (1959) gave economic arguments for why governments should support or even organize the production of scientific knowledge. In the following decades, the OECD played a major role in the analysis of science as a productive factor (OECD 1963, 1971). Most of this work was based upon a linear model in which it was assumed that advances in science would more or less automatically be transformed into new technology and market success. In OECD (1992) new insights from innovation research changed this perspective. It was realized that innovation came out of an interaction among several actors and that feedback from markets was critical for innovation. The concept of an innovation system was taken aboard.

In the mid-1990s the OECD initiated a new discourse on knowledge and economic development and started to refer to the knowledge-based economy, the learning economy and the learning society (Foray and Lundvall 1996; OECD 1996, 2000). The concept of 'the new economy' took hold widely in OECD (2001). With inspiration from Alan Greenspan, President of the US Federal Reserve, many OECD economists began, for the first time, to see science and technology as a factor that should be taken into account when analyzing macro-economic dynamics.

In this chapter we will not dwell upon the details of this history. Rather we will present a synthesis of what has come out of these research efforts and relate them to some of the main characteristics of the Nordic countries. We will make the following points:

1. The distinction between knowledge about the world, easy to codify, and know-how, embodied in people or embedded in organizations, is crucial for theory and policy.
2. The corresponding distinction between science- and experience-based learning helps us to understand why the link from the science base to innovation performance is weak.
3. The skill-biased technical changes characterizing the current era reflect 'the learning economy', in which the rate of change in technologies and organization has accelerated.
4. In the learning economy there is a need to rethink the role of education, and in particular of universities, and give more attention to personal skills and the interaction between knowledge and practice.
5. Nordic countries perform well in both the long and the medium term on the basis of a kind of social capital and trust that supports organizational and interactive learning.

Rather than moving directly to public policy issues, this chapter first gives attention to conceptual issues and to new empirical results relevant to the design of public policy. After each section we will discuss principles and implications for public policy without aiming at detailed recommendations – these need to be worked out in the concrete context of the specific national system and in a dialogue with major social partners.

1.2 The economics of knowledge

Today there is a quite widespread assumption that knowledge is important for the economy. But the effort to understand what knowledge is and how it is translated into economic performance is not correspondingly great. There is a bias in much of the economics literature as well as in policy practice in favour of knowledge as information and this has serious negative consequences both for analysis and policy.

1.2.1 Is knowledge a public good?

Sidney Winter concluded his seminal paper on knowledge management strategy by pointing out that there is "a paucity of language" and "a serious dearth of appropriate terminology and conceptual schemes" (Winter, 1987). Since then, the number of relevant publications has grown (see for instance Foray, 2000; OECD, 2000; Amin and Cohendet, 2004) but still there is little agreement on what distinctions between different kinds of knowledge are most useful for understanding the interaction between knowledge and economic development.

Knowledge and information appear in economic models in two different contexts. The most fundamental assumption of standard microeconomics is that the economic system is based on *rational choices made by individual agents*. Thus, *how much and what kind of information* agents have about the world and their *ability to process the information* are crucial issues.

The other major perspective is one in which knowledge is regarded as an *asset*. Here, knowledge may appear as both input (competence) and output (innovation) in the production process. Under certain circumstances, it can be privately owned and/or bought and sold in the market as a commodity. The economics of knowledge is to a high degree about specifying the conditions for knowledge to appear as 'a normal commodity', that is, as something similar to a producible and reproducible tangible product.[1]

In what follows, attention is on knowledge in this latter sense. When analyzing knowledge as an *asset*, its properties in terms of transferability across time, space, and people is central. This fundamental issue is at the core of two quite different strands of economic policy debate. One is about the public/private dimension of knowledge and the role of governments in knowledge production; the other is about the formation of industrial districts and the local character of knowledge.

Is knowledge a private or a public good? In economic theory, the characteristics that give a good the attribute of 'public' are that benefits can be enjoyed by many users concurrently as well as sequentially without being diminished (non-rivalry) and that it is costly for the provider to exclude unauthorized users (non-excludability).

One reason for the interest in this issue is that it is crucial for defining the role of government in knowledge production. If knowledge is a public good that can be accessed by anyone, there is no economic incentive for rational private agents to invest in its production. More generally, if it is less costly to imitate than to produce new knowledge, the social rate of return would be higher than the private rate of return and, again, resource allocation would be inefficient since private agents would invest too little. Nelson's (1959) and Arrow's (1962b) classical contributions demonstrated that, in such situations, there is a basis for government policy either to subsidize or to take charge directly of the production of knowledge. The public funding of schools and universities, as well as of generic technologies, has been motivated by this kind of reasoning, which also brings to the fore the need for the legal protection of knowledge, for instance by patent systems.

This fundamental problem remains at the core of the economics of knowledge production, and recent developments have led to a reinforcement of intellectual property rights (Granstrand, 2005). At the same time, another strand of thought, with roots in the history of economic thought, has become more strongly represented in the debate in the last decades, especially among regional economists. Marshall (1923) was preoccupied by the phenomenon of the *industrial district*: why is it that certain specialized industries locate themselves in certain regions in England and why do they remain competitive for long periods?

He argued that "knowledge is in the air". But his principal explanation was that knowledge was localized in the region because it was rooted in the local labor force and in local institutions and organizations. This perspective, with its focus on localized knowledge, has resurfaced strongly among industrial and regional economists over recent decades – one reason was the Silicon Valley phenomenon and the growing interest in promoting knowledge-based regional industrial clusters.[2]

These two perspectives, while seemingly opposed in their contrasting emphasis on, respectively, the need to protect and the difficulty of sharing knowledge, raise fundamental questions: Is the consent of the producer needed or can knowledge be copied against the will of the producer? How difficult is it to transfer knowledge and what are the transfer mechanisms? Is it possible to change the form of knowledge (through codification) so that it becomes easier (or more difficult) to mediate? How important is the broader socio-cultural context for the transferability of knowledge? The distinctions between different kinds of knowledge proposed below aim at throwing light upon these issues.

1.2.2 A terminology of knowledge

In earlier work we have proposed that it is useful to divide knowledge into four categories (Lundvall and Johnson, 1994).

- Know-what
- Know-why
- Know-how
- Know-who.

Know-what refers to knowledge about 'facts'. How many people live in New York, what are the ingredients of pancakes are, and when the battle of Waterloo took place are examples of this kind of knowledge. Here, knowledge is close to what is normally called information – it can be broken down into bits and communicated as data.

Know-why refers to knowledge about principles and laws of motion in nature, in the human mind and in society. This kind of knowledge is extremely important for technological development in certain science-based areas, such as the chemical and electric/electronic industries. Access to this kind of knowledge will often make advances in technology more rapid and reduce the frequency of errors in procedures involving trial and error.

Know-how refers to skills – that is, the ability to do something. It may be related to the skills of artisans and production workers. But it plays a key role in all important economic activities. The businessman judging the market prospects for a new product or the personnel manager selecting and training staff use their know-how. One of the most interesting and profound analyses of the role and formation of know-how is actually about scientists' need for skill formation and personal knowledge (Polanyi, 1958/1978).

Know-who involves information about who knows what and who is expert in dealing with specific tasks. But it also involves the social ability and social capital that makes it possible to cooperate and communicate with people and experts. Know-who becomes increasingly important with the general trend towards a more composite knowledge base. New products typically combine many technologies, rooted in several different scientific disciplines, and this makes access to many different sources of knowledge essential (Pavitt, 1998). No single person or organization can host all the kinds of expertise needed to pursue innovation processes.

1.2.3 How public or private are the four kinds of knowledge?

Databases bring together know-what in a more or less user-friendly form. The effectiveness of search machines is highly relevant in this context (Shapiro and Varian, 1999). Yet even today, the most effective medium for obtaining pertinent facts may be through the know-who channel, that is, contacting an expert in the field to obtain directions on where to look for a specific piece of information.

Scientific work aims at producing know-why, and some of this work is placed in the public domain. Academics have strong incentives to publish and make their results accessible (although new regulations introducing intellectual property rights to university administrations may undermine the public character of science). The Internet offers new possibilities for speedy electronic publishing. Open and public access is, of course, a misnomer, in that it often takes enormous investments in learning before scientific information has any meaning for a user. Again know-who, directed towards academia, can help the non-specialist to obtain a translation into something comprehensible.

Know-how is characterized by limited public access and mediation is complex. The basic problem is that it is impossible to separate the competence to act from the person or organization that acts. The outstanding expert – cook, violinist, manager – may write a book explaining how to do things, but what is done by the amateur on the basis of that explanation is, of course, less perfect than what the expert would do. Attempts to use information technology to develop expert systems show that it is difficult and costly to transform expert skills into information that can be used by others. It has also been demonstrated that the transformation always involves changes in the content of the expert knowledge (Hatchuel and Weil, 1995).

Know-who refers to a combination of information and social relationships. Telephone books that list professions as well as databases that list producers of certain goods and services are in the public domain and can, in principle, be accessed by anyone. In the economic sphere, however, it is extremely important to get access to highly specialized competencies and to find the most reliable experts; hence the importance of good personal skills and relationships with key people one can trust. These social and personal relationships are by definition not public. They cannot be transferred and, more specifically, they cannot be bought or sold on the market. As pointed out by Arrow (1971), "you cannot buy trust and, if you could, it would have no value whatsoever".

The social context may support, to a greater or lesser degree, the formation of know-who knowledge while the cultural context determines the form it takes. This is an important aspect of the concept of social capital (Woolcock, 1998). In this chapter we will go as far as arguing that the unique levels of trust in the Nordic countries may be seen as the most important and generic explanation of their (paradoxically) strong economic performance (see Section 1.6).

1.2.4 Knowledge is both public and private

It is clear from what has been said that very little knowledge is 'perfectly public'. Even information of know-what type may be impossible to access for those not connected to the right telecommunications or social networks. Scientific and other types of complex knowledge may be accessible in principle, but for effective access the user must have invested in building absorptive capacity.

On the other hand, little economically useful knowledge is completely private, at least not in the long run. Tricks of the trade are shared within the profession. Know-how can be taught and learnt in interaction between the master and the apprentice. Even when the possessor of private knowledge does not want to share it with others, there are ways to obtain it, such as engaging in reverse engineering. If necessary, private agents will engage in intelligence activities aimed at getting access to competitors' secrets.

Different parts of economic theory handle this mixed situation differently. Underlying much of the neoclassical theory of production and growth is the simplifying assumption that there is a global bank of blueprints of which anybody can get a copy to use in starting production. Knowledge is here assumed to be public and to correspond to information. The resource-based theory of the firm takes the opposite view and assumes that the unique competence of the firm determines the directions in which it expands its activities (Penrose, 1958).

In real life there is not one common knowledge base, nor is knowledge completely private and individualized. The most appropriate understanding may be to refer to a multitude of *knowledge pools*, to which access is limited by law, organizational borders, physical distance or professional background. It implies that in order to get access to relevant pools, individuals have to engage simultaneously in copying well known routines from others, exploiting internal capabilities, and building new competencies. Below we will refer to these activities as individual and organizational learning. This is what makes management a difficult art, quite different from firms' effortless information access modelled in neoclassical economics text-books.

1.2.5 On the tacitness and codification of knowledge

There has been a lively debate among economists about the role of tacitness and codification with relation to knowledge (Cowan et al., 2000; Johnson et al., 2001). The reason for the interest is, of course, that tacitness relates to the transferability and the public character of knowledge. Codified knowledge is potentially shared knowledge, while non-codified knowledge remains individual – at least, until it can be learnt in direct interaction with the possessor. An important issue in this context is how much effort should be made to codify knowledge.

Sectors where the knowledge base is dominated by non-codified but codifiable knowledge are those in which progress towards more efficient practices is difficult. Economists have used education as a typical example of a production process characterized by tacit techniques (Murname and Nelson, 1984). OECD (2000) presents a unique attempt to compare the production, diffusion, and use of knowledge across some important economic and societal sectors – information technology and management science as well as health and education.

In the bases of important attributes of knowledge (public/private; codified/tacit) it can be suggested that there may be marked differences among various sectors with regard to their knowledge base. Some science-based sectors depend upon codified knowledge while others operate and compete mainly on the basis of unstructured and experience-based implicit knowledge. But there are no pure cases and one of the points made in Section 1.4 is that firms with a weak foundation in codified/scientific knowledge may have the most to gain from engaging in science-based learning; conversely, firms specialized in the use of scientific knowledge may have the most to gain from engaging in organizational learning and focusing on customer needs in order to promote the formation of tacit knowledge.

1.2.6 Policy implications

At this general level only limited conclusions can be drawn for public policy. One obvious conclusion is that knowledge politics needs to have two aims. One is about the protection of strategic knowledge and the other is about promoting the absorption and diffusion of knowledge. To strike the right balance between the two dimensions is far from a trivial task. While knowledge owners may be very outspoken in favour of greater protection, the general interest of public access may have less powerful spokespersons.

Another conclusion, strongly supported by the analysis in OECD (2000) is that the mix of private and public, as well as tacit and codified, knowledge differs across different sectors in the economy. This implies that whatever general policy measures are implemented will turn out to be selective policy since they affect different sectors differently (e.g. sectors producing codified knowledge versus sectors using codified knowledge). If governments become hostages to the private interest of knowledge producers, there may be negative consequences for the diffusion and wide use of knowledge.

1.3 Toward the learning economy

Many indicators show that there has been a shift in economic development in the direction of a more important role for knowledge production and learning in both the long and the medium term. Moses Abramowitz and Paul David (1996) have demonstrated that this century has been characterized by increasing knowledge intensity in the production system. The OECD's structural analysis of industrial development in the post-war period points in the same direction. It has been shown that the sectors that use knowledge inputs such as R&D and skilled labor most intensively are the ones that grow most rapidly. At the same time, the skill profile is on an upward trend in almost all sectors. In most OECD countries, in terms of employment and value added, the most rapidly growing sector is knowledge-intensive business services (OECD, 1999).

These observations have led more and more analysts to characterize the new economy as 'knowledge-based', and there is in fact a shift in the demand for labor towards more skilled workers. Perhaps the most pertinent finding of the OECD Jobs Study, covering the period 1985–1995 (OECD, 1994), was that in *all* member countries the position of highly skilled workers became stronger while that of unskilled workers was weakened in terms of pay and employment.

Below we will argue that this shift in demand can be explained most adequately with reference to 'the learning economy'. While the 'skill-based technical progress' approach leaves it open why there has been a shift in the demand for knowledge, the learning-economy perspective may contribute to an explanation of the phenomenon. To explain this change we need to ask the question why and under what circumstances highly educated people contribute more to the economy than those with little education. We will refer to Nelson and Phelps (1966) and to Schultz (1975) in order to provide some of the answers.

Nelson and Phelps (1966) present a simple growth model in which people with higher education contribute to economic growth through two mechanisms. First, they are able to conduct regular activities more efficiently than the average worker. Second – and here is the new insight brought by this article – *they are more competent when it comes to exploiting new technical opportunities*. The conclusion from the analysis is that the marginal productivity of the highly educated will reflect the rate of technical change (exogenously given in the model). *In other words the rate of return on investment in higher education will be positively correlated with the rate of technical progress*. In a stationary economy we would expect the rate of return to be low while we would expect it to be high in an economy characterized by rapid technical change. *A general conclusion is that the role of higher education needs to be assessed in the wider context of the national innovation system and that higher education policy needs to be coordinated with a wider set of innovation policies.*

Schultz (1975) follows a similar line of thought but takes the reasoning some steps further. His title ('The Value of the Ability to Deal with Disequilibria') and his reasoning are intriguing, not least since it comes from an economist belonging to the Chicago tradition of economics, which is based upon general equilibrium analysis. Schultz argues on the basis of empirical observations that education makes individuals better prepared to deal with disequilibria. When the individual is exposed to change in terms of new technological opportunities, he/she will be more or less competent in finding a solution and it is assumed that one major impact of education is to enhance this competence, which Schultz refers to as 'entrepreneurial'.

In a series of PhD dissertations for the Department of Business Studies, Aalborg University, different aspects of the role of higher education in processes of innovation have been analyzed (Vinding, 2004; Nielsen, 2007). Taking into account a number of factors that may affect the propensity to innovate, we find a positive effect in having employees with a graduate degree. This effect is especially strong in small and medium-sized firms operating in low- and medium-technology sectors (see Vinding, 2004). The role of graduates in small firm innovation has been analyzed more in depth in Nielsen (2007). The analysis is focused upon 200 small Danish firms originally without academic personnel. The analysis demonstrates that – taking into account a series of relevant control variables – the first-time hiring of a graduate with an engineering background has a significant positive impact on the propensity to introduce a new product (Nielsen, 2007).

This points to an interpretation of the increase in the demand for skilled labor: those who have a higher education and thereby can be expected to be better prepared to cope in an economy characterized by rapid change. Higher rates of innovation and the permanent opening-up of new disequilibria lie behind what has been called skill-biased technical progress. The implications for the content and organization of education will be discussed in Section 1.5.

1.3.1 The learning economy

As argued in the last section, the observed skill bias in OECD (1994) supports the hypothesis that since the middle of the 1980s there has been an acceleration in the rate of economic and technical change, imposing a strong transformational pressure, not least on small, open, high-income economies (Lundvall, 1992; Drucker, 1993; Lundvall and Johnson, 1994; Archibugi and Lundvall, 2001). Behind the acceleration of change lie shorter product life-cycles and intensified international trade as well as politically driven deregulation. At the level of the firm, an intensification of competition is registered. At the level of the individual it is experienced as a need permanently to renew skills and competencies in order to remain 'employable'.

Change and learning are two sides of the same coin. The speed-up of change confronts people and organizations with new problems, and tackling the new problems requires new skills (OECD, 2000). The process is characterized by cumulative circular causation (cf. Myrdal, 1968). The selection by employers of more learning-oriented employees and the market selection in favour of change-oriented firms accelerate further innovation and change. There is nothing to indicate that the process will be slowed down in the near future. Rather, the further deregulation of markets for services, the growth of exports from China and India, and the radical change in relative prices of energy and raw materials are all giving new momentum to the process.

1.3.2 Policy implications

In a small, open economy within global learning dynamics, the key to economic success is to transform the economy so that exposed activities are either upgraded or replaced by more competency-intensive activities. It is a major task to design institutions that regulate education and labor markets so that they promote processes of learning and the formation and diffusion of learning organizations in the private and public sector. As will be demonstrated in the next section it is not sufficient to promote R&D efforts and the training of scientists and engineers. We will argue that the broad participation of workers in processes of change has been fundamental for the relative success of the Nordic countries.

This indicates a fundamental internal contradiction in the learning economy that may require public intervention in the process. If left to itself, it leads to increasing inequality that erodes its foundation in social cohesion and trust. This reflects a Matthews syndrome when it comes the distribution of knowledge. The highly skilled have privileged access to formal training at enterprise level (Lundvall, 2001) and they get jobs offering more learning opportunities (Tomlinson, 1999). Acceleration in the rate of change may result in a growing gap between highly skilled and unskilled workers in terms of employment opportunities and income. This has important implications for public policy related to the creation of competencies, especially among the low-skilled segments of the workforce.

1.4 Modes of innovation and innovation performance

1.4.1 Introduction

In Section 1.2 we made a distinction between codified and tacit knowledge. In this section we will introduce two modes of learning related to this distinction. We present recent data and analysis showing that firms that combine R&D efforts (STI learning) with organizational learning and interaction with customers (DUI learning) are the most innovative (Jensen et al., 2007). The idea that it is useful to make a distinction between these two modes of innovation is far from new. In the introduction to the *Wealth of Nations* Adam Smith presents a case story about a worker who, on the basis of his experience, finds a way to make a machine more efficient, and in the following paragraphs he points to "men of speculation" who specialize in finding new production methods (Smith, 1776, pp. 8–9).

Inspired by Adam Smith and by the more recent distinction between tacit and codified knowledge, we define two modes of innovation (Jensen et al., 2007). On the one hand there are innovation strategies that emphasize promoting R&D and creating access to explicit codified knowledge (Science, Technology, and Innovation: the STI mode). On the other hand there are innovation strategies based on learning by doing, using, and interacting (Doing, Using, and Interacting: the DUI mode). We show that firms using mixed strategies that combine a strong version of the STI mode with a strong version of the DUI mode excel in product innovation.

The *STI mode of innovation* refers to the way firms use and develop a body of science-like understanding in the context of their innovative activities. Over the twentieth century, and still today, a major source of the development of this knowledge about artefacts and techniques has been the R&D laboratory of the large industrial firm (Mowery and Oxley, 1995; Chandler, 1977). The STI mode of learning, even when it starts from a local practical problem, will make use of 'global' knowledge all the way through and, ideally, it will end up with 'potentially global knowledge' – that is, knowledge that could be used widely if it were not protected by intellectual property rights.

The *DUI mode of innovation* refers to learning on the job as employees face ongoing changes that confront them with new problems and learning in an interaction with external customers. Finding solutions to problems enhances the skills and know-how of the employees and extends their repertoires. The DUI mode of learning refers to knowledge that is tacit and often highly localized. While this kind of learning may occur as an unintended by-product of the firm's design, production, and marketing activities, the point we want to make here is that the DUI mode can be intentionally fostered by building structures and relationships that enhance and utilize learning by doing, using, and interacting. In particular, we assume that interaction with users and organizational practices such as project teams, problem-solving groups, and job and task rotation, which promote learning and knowledge exchange, contribute to innovation performance.

1.4.2 Illustrating empirically how DUI and STI learning promote innovation

In what follows we will show that the probability of successful product innovation increases when the firm has organized itself in such a way that it promotes DUI learning. We will also show that firms that establish a stronger science base will be more innovative than the rest. But the most significant and important result is that firms using mixed strategies, which combine organizational forms promoting learning with R&D efforts and cooperation with researchers at knowledge institutions, are much more innovative than the rest. *It is the firm that combines a strong version of the STI mode with a strong version of the DUI mode that excels in product innovation.*

Two of three measures we use to capture STI mode learning are standard measures used to benchmark science and technology development in innovation policy studies: expenditures on R&D; and the employment of personnel with third-level degrees in science or technology. The third measure – cooperation with researchers attached to universities or research institutes – is, though of recognized importance, less commonly used in policy studies due to the lack of survey data. For

DUI-mode learning we use organizational characteristics assumed to characterize the learning organization (such as integration of functions and interdisciplinary workgroups), including also an indicator of interaction with users.

1.4.3 The four clusters

In order to find out how the different aspects of establishing a learning organization tend to be combined with the capacity to handle scientific and codified knowledge, we have pursued a cluster analysis across firms using latent class analysis. The first cluster is a static or low-learning cluster and encompasses about 40% of the firms. The second cluster, which we refer to as the STI cluster, encompasses about 10% of the firms. Firms belonging to the STI cluster have activities that indicate a strong capacity to absorb and use codified knowledge. The third cluster, which we refer to as the DUI cluster, brings together about one third of the firms in a group that is characterized by an over-average development of organizational characteristics typical of the learning organization but without activities that indicate a strong capacity to absorb and use codified knowledge. The fourth cluster includes firms using mixed strategies that combine the DUI and STI modes. It includes one fifth of the firms and these firms tend to combine the characteristics indicating a strong capacity for informal, experience-based learning with activities that indicate a strong capacity to absorb and use codified knowledge.

Table 1.1 shows the frequency distribution of the different clusters by firm size, industry, group ownership, and production. It is clear that the different clusters are distributed unevenly across industry, size, and ownership. In terms of sector, it is not surprising to find that construction, trade, and other services are underrepresented in the STI and DUI/STI clusters given the relatively low levels of R&D expenditure that characterize these sectors.

One interesting observation is that *the match between high-tech manufacturing sectors and STI learning is far from perfect*. Almost 50% of the high-tech firms do not appear to be strong in STI learning while more than 35% of the low-tech manufacturing firms do have a strong STI learning mode. This confirms that the traditional definition of high versus low technology sectors is highly problematic, especially if the size of the high-tech sector is used as an indicator of innovation performance.

In order to examine the effect of the learning modes on a firm's innovative performance we use logistic regression analysis as reported in

Table 1.1 Frequency of the four clusters by firm size, sector, group ownership, and production type (% horizontal)

Variables	Low learning cluster	STI cluster	DUI cluster	DUI/STI cluster	N
Fewer than 50 employees	0.5605	0.0855	0.2566	0.0973	*339*
50–99 employees	0.3314	0.1775	0.3018	0.1893	*169*
100 or more employees	0.2457	0.1257	0.2686	0.3600	*175*
Manufacturing, high tech	0.2231	0.2645	0.2314	0.2810	*121*
Manufacturing, low tech	0.3522	0.1321	0.2893	0.2264	*159*
Construction	0.6139	0.0495	0.2574	0.0792	*101*
Trade	0.5780	0.0462	0.3064	0.0694	*173*
Business services	0.2727	0.0909	0.2576	0.3788	*66*
Other services	0.6512	0.0465	0.2791	0.0233	*43*
Danish group	0.4073	0.1371	0.2460	0.2097	*248*
Foreign group	0.2903	0.1694	0.2903	0.2500	*124*
Single firm	0.4890	0.0789	0.2776	0.1546	*317*
Standard product	0.3574	0.1687	0.2851	0.1888	*249*
Customized product	0.4518	0.0871	0.2635	0.1976	*425*
All firms	0.4249	0.1171	0.2673	0.1908	*692*

Source: Jensen et al. (2007).

Table 1.2. The dependent variable for this exercise is whether or not the firm has introduced to the market a new product or service (P/S innovation) over the last three years. The independent variables in the Model 1 specification are binary variables indicating whether or not the firm belongs to a particular cluster. In the Model 2 specification we include control variables to account for the effects of industry, firm size, ownership structure, and whether the firm produces customized or standard products.

Overall, the results of the logistic analysis show that adopting DUI mode enhancing practices and policies tends to increase firm innovative performance. Further, they support the view that firms adopting mixed strategies combining the two modes tend to perform better than those relying predominantly on one mode or the other.

Our cluster analysis indicates that many firms that are involved in STI learning have established organizational elements related to the DUI

Table 1.2 Logistic regression of learning clusters on product/service innovation

Variables	Model 1 (without controls) Odds ratio estimate	Coefficient estimate	Model 2 (with controls) Odds ratio estimate	Coefficient estimate
STI Cluster	3.529	1.2611**	2.355	0.8564**
DUI Cluster	2.487	0.9109**	2.218	0.7967**
DUI/STI Cluster	7.843	2.0596**	5.064	1.6222**
Business services			1.433	0.3599
Construction			0.491	−0.7120*
Manufacturing (high tech)			1.805	0.5905*
Manufacturing (low tech)			1.250	0.2229
Other services			0.747	−0.2923
100 and more employees			1.757	0.5635*
50–99 employees			0.862	−0.1481
Danish group			0.859	−0.1524
Single firm			0.521	−0.6526*
Customized product			1.378	0.3203
Pseudo R^2	0.1247	0.1247	0.1775	0.1775
N	692	692	692	692

** = significant at the .01 level; * = significant at the .05 level.

mode. They operate in sectors where there is supply-driven – and sometimes radical – change in products and processes. To cope with these changes the need for learning by doing, using, and interacting will be strongly felt. Likewise, for firms in traditional sectors it is no longer sufficient to base competitiveness on know-how and DUI learning. Firms that connect more systematically to sources of codified knowledge may be able to find new solutions and develop new products that make them more competitive. Moreover, the cluster analysis shows that what really improves innovation performance is using mixed strategies that combine strong versions of the two modes.

1.4.4 Policy implications

Our results strongly suggest a need for the realignment of policy objectives and priorities, given the tendency to develop innovation policy with a one-sided focus on promoting the science base of high-technology firms. Actually both a strategy that promotes organizational learning in STI firms and one that promotes STI learning in DUI firms may have greater effect on innovation than promoting R&D in firms that are already experienced in pursuing it. Too little attention is being given to policies that serve to strengthen linkages to sources of codified knowledge for firms operating in traditional manufacturing sectors and services more generally. The fact that the first-time hiring of a graduate has a significant positive impact on the propensity to innovate (Nielsen, 2007) indicates that there are cultural barriers to implementing elements of the STI mode in such sectors – barriers that could be overcome through temporary marginal employment subsidies addressed specifically to small and medium-sized firms in traditional sectors.

Thinking in terms of the two modes and their evolution in the learning economy may also have implications for wider aspects of public policy and institution building. In the following section we will argue that the education of graduates and their hiring in industry is the best way to transmit both codified and tacit knowledge and upgrade both DUI and STI learning in the business sector. Organizing innovation policy and distributing responsibility between ministries of education, science, industry, and economic affairs, for instance, needs to balance the two modes in innovation policy. If the main responsibility is given to a ministry of science, the STI bias in innovation policy will be reinforced.

1.5 Education in the learning economy

Education systems and schools are often seen as sites where knowledge about the world is transmitted from the teacher to the student. But education also forms personalities and individual social skills. The idea of education as a process of filling empty bottles, the form of which is determined elsewhere, is as widely held as it is inadequate (Guile, 2003). In the learning economy this dimension of education becomes especially important. This is true for all categories of worker, from the top management to the man/woman on the floor. One crucial issue is to what degree a specific education system creates social barriers between the two categories and between professions (Lundvall et al., 2008).

In this section we start with a closer look at how management in Danish firms referred to changes in the content of work in the 1990s. In a context of accelerating change it is of particular interest to focus on changes in the competencies demanded within firms that had engaged in organizational change (Gjerding, 1997). We will move on to new data on how people learn on the job in different parts of Europe and see how learning on the job is related to national educational efforts. Finally we will discuss in more detail the role of universities in the national innovation system and especially the implications for the design of higher education programs.

1.5.1 Skill requirements and organizational change – challenges for education

Table 1.3 reveals substantial differences in the pattern of answers between the firms that have introduced new forms of organization and those that have not (percentage of firms with numbers in parenthesis).

The importance of general skills – reflected in growing demands for independence in the work situation, cooperation with management and colleagues, and cooperation with external partners (especially customers) – has grown remarkably in firms that have pursued organizational change and much less so in firms that have not changed their organization.

All firms, and especially those that engage in organizational change, require that employees be able to communicate and collaborate internally

Table 1.3 Changes in task content for employees, 1993–1995, for firms that had made organizational changes (outside the parentheses) compared with those of firms that had not made organizational changes (in parentheses).

	More (%)	Less (%)	Unchanged (%)	No answer (%)
a. Independence of work	72.6 (37.1)	4.2 (2.7)	21.2 (56.3)	2.0 (3.8)
b. Professional qualifications	56.4 (36.3)	7.5 (5.3)	33.3 (53.8)	2.8 (4.4)
c. Degree of specialization	33.9 (26.2)	20.8 (7.8)	39.3 (58.4)	6.0 (7.5)
d. Routine character of tasks	5.6 (8.2)	41.8 (15.5)	45.0 (67.1)	7.7 (9.1)
e. Customer contact	51.6 (29.3)	5.1 (3.1)	37.2 (59.9)	6.1 (7.6)
f. Contact with suppliers	34.9 (18.0)	7.1 (4.3)	46.4 (62.0)	11.6 (15.6)
g. Contact with other firms	24.7 (14.0)	5.5 (4.3)	56.8 (68.9)	13.0 (13.7)
h. Cooperation with colleagues	59.1 (27.1)	5.8 (4.5)	31.8 (63.3)	3.2 (5.0)
i. Cooperation with management	64.9 (28.6)	5.9 (4.2)	26.1 (62.2)	3.1 (4.9)

Note: Management representatives in 4000 Danish private firms, excluding agriculture, were asked: "Did the firm introduce a non-trivial change in the organization in the period 1993–1995?". The response rate was close to 50%. For more detailed information see Lundvall (2002a).

Source: Voxted, 1999, DISKO Survey, N=952 (981)

and externally. In Section 1.5.4 we argue that this is of major relevance to the design of higher education programs. It should be noted that the higher the education level of the employee, the more demanding and time-consuming is on-the-job learning (Tomlinson, 1999). To see the graduate as ready-made in terms of competencies and reserve on-the-job training for low-skilled workers is thus a mistake.

Above we referred to Nelson and Phelps (1966) and Schultz (1975), who argue in different ways that education becomes more important in contexts of rapid and radical change. Here we can add that promoting entrepreneurship and initiative at the secondary level of technical training becomes increasingly important. When management can rely on these categories of worker to engage in change it frees valuable time for the more demanding tasks to those with a higher education.[3]

1.5.2 How Europe's economies learn

Lorenz and Valeyre (2006) developed an original and informative EU-wide mapping of how employees in the private sector work and learn. Later it was shown that it has wider implications for innovation and growth. In Arundel et al. (2007) international comparisons show that there is a positive correlation between the national share of employees engaged in advanced forms of learning in the workplace and the percentage of private sector enterprises engaged in more radical forms of innovation.

Cluster analysis is used to identify four systems of work organization:

- Discretionary learning (DL)
- Lean
- Taylorist
- Traditional.

Two of these, the discretionary learning and lean forms, are characterized by high levels of learning and problem solving in work. The principal differences between the discretionary learning and the lean clusters are the higher levels of discretion or autonomy in work and of task complexity enjoyed by employees in the former.

Discretionary learning thus refers to work settings where a lot of responsibility is allocated to the employee, who is expected to solve problems on his or her own. Employees operating in these modes are constantly confronted with 'disequilibria' and, as they cope with these, they learn and become more competent. But in this process they also discover that some of their earlier insights and skills have become obsolete.

Lean production also involves problem solving and learning but here the problems are more narrowly defined and the set of possible solutions less wide and diverse. The work is highly constrained and this points to a more structured or bureaucratic style of organizational learning, which corresponds quite closely to the characteristics of the Japanese-inspired 'lean production' model.

The other two clusters are characterized by relatively low levels of learning and problem solving. The taylorist form leaves very little autonomy to the employee in decision making. In the traditional cluster there is more autonomy but learning and task complexity are the lowest among the four types of work organization. This cluster includes employees working in small firms providing services and transport where methods are for the most part informal and non-codified.

Table 1.4 shows that people working in different national systems of innovation and competence work and learn differently. Discretionary learning is most widely diffused in the Netherlands, the Nordic countries, and (to a lesser extent) Austria and Germany. The lean model is most in evidence in the UK, Ireland, and Spain. Taylorist and traditional forms are more in evidence in Portugal, Spain, Greece, and Italy.[4] Within the Nordic group, Denmark is extreme in terms of its high share of discretionary learning and low share of taylorist workplaces. The share of discretionary learning is higher in Germany than it is in the UK and France.

Table 1.4 indicates unequal access to learning between different parts of Europe. The three Nordic countries, together with the Netherlands, have few taylorist organizations left in the economy while a majority of employees operate in jobs that are demanding in terms of both skills and autonomy.[5]

In the next subsection, which draws upon recent work by Lorenz (2007), we take a closer look at how national learning modes relate to national patterns of education. Here we will find that on-the-job training and vocational training are fundamental prerequisites for developing discretionary learning – much more so than the training of science graduates.

1.5.3 Education and training for learning organizations

Since discretionary learning depends on the capacity of employees to undertake complex problem-solving tasks, it can be expected that nations with a high frequency of these forms will have made substantial investments in education and training. In what follows we

Table 1.4 National differences in organizational models (% of employees by organizational class)

	Discretionary learning	Lean production learning	Taylorist organization	Simple organization
North				
Netherlands	64.0	17.2	5.3	13.5
Denmark	60.0	21.9	6.8	11.3
Sweden	52.6	18.5	7.1	21.7
Finland	47.8	27.6	12.5	12.1
Centre				
Austria	47.5	21.5	13.1	18.0
Germany	44.3	19.6	14.3	21.9
Luxembourg	42.8	25.4	11.9	20.0
Belgium	38.9	25.1	13.9	22.1
France	38.0	33.3	11.1	17.7
West				
United Kingdom	34.8	40.6	10.9	13.7
Ireland	24.0	37.8	20.7	17.6
South				
Italy	30.0	23.6	20.9	25.4
Portugal	26.1	28.1	23.0	22.8
Spain	20.1	38.8	18.5	22.5
Greece	18.7	25.6	28.0	27.7
EU-15	39.1	28.2	13.6	19.1

Source: Adapted from Lorenz and Valeyre (2006).

compare tertiary education in universities and other institutions of higher education with the continuing vocational training offered by enterprises.

Tertiary education develops both problem-solving skills and formal and transferable technical and scientific skills. While most of the qualifications acquired through third-level education are relatively general and hence transferable on the labor market, the qualifications an employee acquires through continuing vocational training are more firm-specific. Some of this training will be designed to renew employees' technical skills and knowledge in order to respond to the firm's requirements in terms of ongoing product and process innovation.

Figure 1.1 shows the correlations between the frequency of the discretionary learning forms and two of the four measures of human resources for innovation used in Trendchart's innovation benchmarking exercise: the proportion of the population with third-level education and the number of science and engineering graduates since 1993 as a percentage of the population aged 20–29 years in 2000.

The results show a modest positive correlation (R-squared =.26) between the discretionary learning forms and the percentage of the population with third-level education, and no discernible correlation between the discretionary learning forms and the number of new science and engineering graduates.

Figure 1.2 shows that there are fairly strong positive correlations (R-squared =.75 and .52 respectively) between the frequency of the discretionary learning forms and two measures of firms' investments in continuing vocational training: the percentage of all firms offering such training and the participants in continuing vocational education as a percentage of employees in all enterprises. The results suggest that these forms of firm-specific training are key complementary resources in the development of a firm's capacity for knowledge exploration and innovation. The diagram also points to a strong north/south divide within Europe. The Nordic countries are characterized by relatively high levels of vocational training and use of the discretionary learning forms. This may be seen as one of the common characteristics that contribute to their relative success in the learning economy.

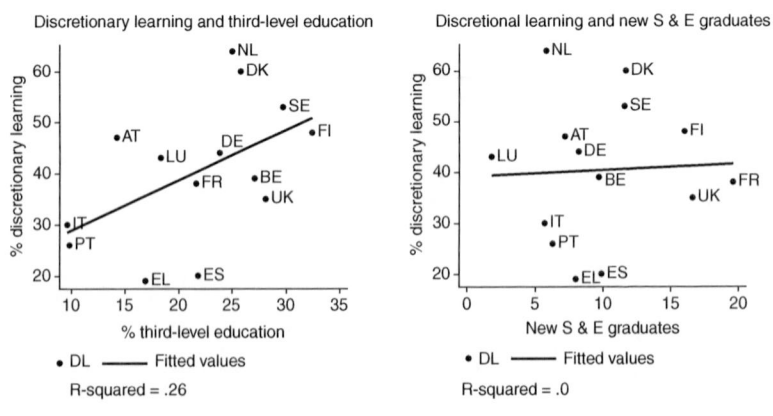

Figure 1.1 Discretionary learning and tertiary education

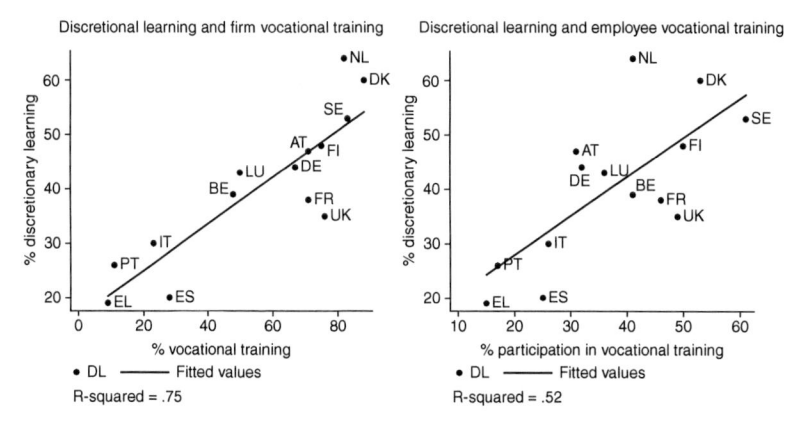

Figure 1.2 Discretionary learning and employee vocational training

These results indicate that national educational systems in which the emphasis is on the formal training of scientists and engineers at the expense of the broader forms of vocational training may be vulnerable in the context of the learning economy. The more drastic the status difference and the distinction between theory and practice in education programs, the more difficult it will be to install participatory learning in the private sector. The strong element of vocational training in the Nordic countries contributes to engaging workers more actively in processes of change.

1.5.4 The role of universities in the innovation system

When it comes to linking universities to economic development, the emphasis is currently on how universities may serve industry through direct flows of information from ongoing research. To illustrate, in a recent book with the title *How Universities Promote Economic Growth* edited by World Bank Economists Yusuf and Nabeshima (2007) the only dimension covered is the formation of university–industry links related to research. We believe that this narrow agenda, in which the role of higher education is neglected, reflects a biased interpretation of the sources of innovation (as STI-driven) as well as an underestimation of the importance of transmitting the tacit knowledge embodied in people (Lundvall, 2002, 2007).

In some of the Nordic countries the prevailing 'university models' are the world-leading US universities in the Boston and the San Francisco area, and to a lesser extent the universities of Cambridge or Oxford.

While this search for academic excellence may seem commendable it is not unproblematic to combine it with intentions to serve domestic industry. It is not realistic to expect front-line research to be absorbed by domestic firms, and for advanced research there is a need to collaborate with global rather than domestic firms.

The advanced commercial users of the most ambitious science and technology breakthroughs are thus more often located abroad rather than in the domestic economy. The greatest transmission of advanced knowledge relevant to domestic firms takes place as graduates move into industry. *Universities' most important contribution to innovation in the domestic economy remains their production of graduates with a good problem-solving ability.* This view is widely shared among innovation scholars (see for instance the report by Salter et al., 2000).

The strong emphasis policy makers and university administrators put on a separate 'third mission', as compared with the much lesser attention they give to reforming 'ordinary education', is highly problematic since it results in a neglect of the substantial gains that could be achieved by modernizing the education system. Especially in the fields of engineering and management such educational reforms would have as one central element to deepen and widen the network relationships between university and industry.[6]

Seen from this perspective there may be a need to consider how well teaching programs prepare students for the transfer and practical use of scientific knowledge. Innovation is a process requiring close interaction between individuals and organization. Therefore, while skills in mathematics and language are fundamental, they need to be combined with the social skills that make it possible to cooperate vertically in hierarchies as well as horizontally with experts with a different educational background.

This implies that the teaching at universities needs to be adjusted in order to prepare the students for communication and cooperation with other categories of worker and expert. The way students study and learn at university affects their social skills and so does the broader cultural context of the university. Traditional learning forms such as mass lectures do not prepare students to use the theory and methods in a real-life context and neither does it replicate the kind of learning that is required in a future professional life. In professional life most learning takes place through problem solving, often in a context of collaboration with others with a different background. *Problem-based learning and combining theoretical work with periods of practical work is an obvious response to these problems.*

This also implies that there is a need for a concept and indicators of quality with several dimensions. PISA-tests in mathematics, physics, and language capabilities need to be combined with tests of interactive capabilities. A high level of the first type of capability is of limited value for innovation if the level of the second type is low. A principal task for higher education is to contribute to *collective entrepreneurship* – that is, to general skills supporting interaction with others resulting in innovation.[7]

1.5.5 Policy implications

The transition to a learning economy has important *implications for education*. The most obvious is that the education system needs to give attention to *enhancing the learning capacity* of students. This does not conflict with teaching basic skills and complex bodies of theory. But it implies that the way teachers teach and the way students learn becomes crucial since the methods used affect the future learning capability of the student. In the previous subsection we developed this argument further in a critical and policy-oriented discussion of the role of the university in the innovation system.

A second major implication is that education institutions need to be ready to support *continuous and life-long learning*. Especially in fast-moving fields of knowledge there is a need to give regular and frequent opportunities to experts to renew their professional knowledge. The current boom in MBA and MPA programs may be seen as indicating the growing insight among individuals and management that continuously renewing competencies is of great importance. But so far such programs tend to operate mainly in relation to management functions. Similar programs are needed in areas where effective demand is less strong.

Finally, rapid change in science and technology and the need to move quickly from invention to innovation presents a strong argument for keeping a reasonably *close connection between education and research*, especially in higher education. Teachers who have little knowledge about what is going on in current research or obsolete knowledge are not helpful when it comes to giving students useful insights into dynamic knowledge fields.

1.6 Social capital, trust and the egalitarian Nordic model

According to standard economic analysis, Nordic countries should not perform very well in a global context where knowledge and innovation are key to economic success. One of the few clear conclusions of new growth theory is that the small scale of a system should be a handicap and it is only recently that firms in Denmark, Finland, and Norway have increased their R&D effort. Small scale should be a handicap both because there are economies of scale to be achieved in the production of new knowledge in some of the so-called high-technology fields and also because it is so much less expensive to apply knowledge than it is to create knowledge. In this section we use the conceptual ideas developed above to demystify this paradox.

At the core of our analysis has been the importance of tacit knowledge and experience-based learning. The most interesting forms of learning take place through interaction between people. The master interacts with the apprentice. Within the business organization, interaction among specialized experts and across departments is a prerequisite for successful innovation. When it comes to implementing innovation, a close interaction between workers and managers is crucial for success. Firms that interact with customers, suppliers, and knowledge institutions are more successful in terms of innovation than those that operate in isolation (Rothwell, 1977; Rosenberg, 1982; Lundvall, 1985).

How people interact and with whom will reflect the society in which they live and the education systems that has shaped them. We will argue that in the Nordic countries social capital and trust are fundamental resources that make their national systems strong in terms of incremental innovation, the absorption of knowledge produced elsewhere, and rapid adaptation. First we discuss the role of the welfare state and how it can be seen as contributing to broad participation in processes of change. Second we demonstrate that the level of trust and the level of income equality is highest in the Nordic countries (and the Netherlands). Third we show how a more fundamental and dynamic dimension of equality – access to on-the-job learning – is also strongest in the Nordic countries and the Netherlands. [8]

1.6.1 Welfare states and economic performance

Welfare states may be defined as countries where the public sector is heavily engaged in the provision of basic services such as education and health. Welfare states are also characterized by social security arrangements, with the public sector as the last resource guaranteeing the social standard of citizens when exposed to unemployment, health problems, and old age. Finally, welfare states interfere in income distribution through taxes and subsidies aimed at reducing the degree of income inequality.

According to the analysis of standard neoclassical economic theory ambitious welfare states should not be expected to perform well. Here it is assumed that, in the absence of market failure, perfect competition will result in an efficient allocation of resources. Seen from this point of view most of the public sector activities characterizing the welfare state are alien and unnecessary.

The pro-market bias of standard economics is reflected in policy advice offered by international organizations such as the OECD and the World Bank. Much of the advice on economic policy coming from the European Commission has also, at least until recently, pointed in the same direction – often with lofty references to the need for 'structural reform' in member countries. Big public expenditure, high and progressive tax rates and generous public social schemes have been characterized as hampering growth and, in countries with ambitious welfare policies, more free market and more individual entrepreneurship have been hailed as keys to higher economic growth. This general message has been reinforced through references to the threat from globalization. It has been argued that, ceteris paribus, capital will move out of the ambitious welfare states to national systems with reduced public employment and low taxes.

However, globalization does not affect welfare states uniformly, and the Scandinavian welfare model seems to have prospered in the context of globalization. Since 1990, the Scandinavian countries have outperformed not only Continental European countries on employment, economic growth, and labor productivity but also the neo-liberal models of the UK and the United States. For instance, from 1990 to 2005, average annual growth in labor productivity in the private sector was 2.6% in the Nordic countries, as against 1.3% in the Eurozone as a whole, 2.0% in the US, and 2.1% in the UK. In the World Economic Forum's 2005 ranking of all countries according to international competitiveness, the Scandinavian countries occupied five of the upper nine positions. A key to understand this relative success is social capital and trust.

1.6.2 Social capital and trust as key elements in the Nordic model

In the US-dominated literature social capital has been presented as rooted in civil society and the frequency of participation in civic activities has been used as an indicator of 'social capital'. It has been argued that big government and big public sectors undermine civil society and thereby also social capital. The Scandinavian experience shows that growth in the welfare state does not necessarily reduce participation in civic organizations. Levels of trust are much higher in the Scandinavian countries than in countries with less extensive welfare states. There is an especially strong correlation between general (rather than selective) social welfare programs and generalized trust. Social capital is a somewhat amorphous concept and it has referred both to individual access to social resources and to societal characteristics affecting social interaction. Here we define it as 'the willingness and capability of citizens to make commitments to each other, collaborate with each other, and trust each other in processes of exchange *and* interactive learning'.

In Figure 1.3 the four Nordic countries, together with Netherlands and Canada, stand out in terms of both degree of trust and economic equality.

According to the European Social Survey, trust among agents seems to be consistently higher in the Nordic countries than in most other countries (see Table 1.5) and, combined with the small size of the system, results in a high degree of *interaction* among agents both within and across organizations.

This not only gives rise to low transaction costs but, more importantly, it facilitates processes of interactive learning where new insights into technologies and good organizational practices are diffused rapidly both within organizations and across organizational borders. The most important impact of high degrees of trust is *high learning*

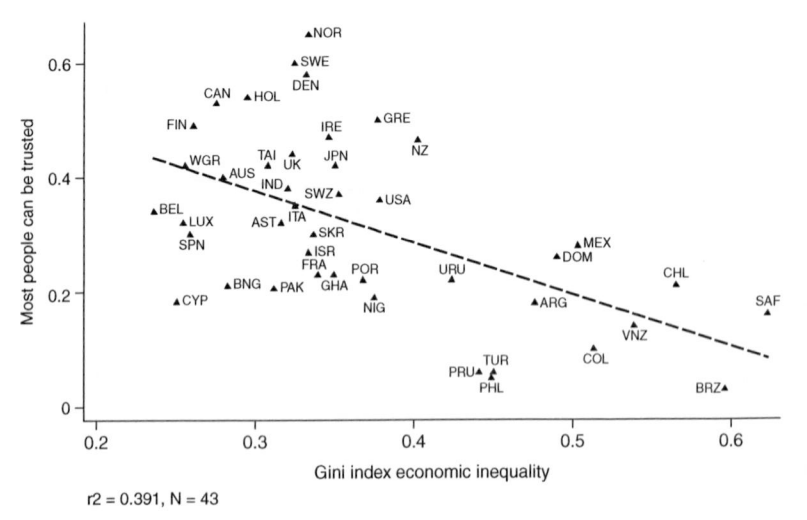

Figure 1.3 Trust in people and economic inequality

Table 1.5 Index of trust in 14 European countries based upon the European Social Survey

	2002	2004	2006
Denmark	7.2	7.0	7.2
Finland	6.7	6.7	6.7
Norway	6.8	6.8	6.9
Sweden	6.4	6.3	6.5
France	5.0	5.1	5.1
UK	5.3	5.3	5.6
Germany	5.2	5.2	5.2
Netherlands	5.9	6.0	6.0
Belgium	5.2	5.2	5.4
Ireland	5.7	6.0	5.6
Austria	5.3	5.5	5.4
Spain	5.0	5.0	5.3
Hungary	4.5	4.3	4.5
Switzerland	5.9	6.1	6.1

Note: In the European Social Survey, respondents are asked the two questions relating to trust ("Do you trust most people?" and "Do you think that most people would take advantage of you if they got the chance?"), to which they must answer on a scale of 1–10. The index above gives the average response.

benefits. Low social distance between managers and workers and willingness to trust partners are key elements behind the relative success of the Nordic countries.

While the innovation systems in the Nordic countries are handicapped in the production of codified knowledge because of negative scale effects, they have been highly successful in terms of learning by doing, learning by using, and learning by interacting.

1.6.3 Degree of inequality in access to organizational learning in Europe

An egalitarian income distribution might not be the most important dimension of social equality; when it is combined with growing gaps in competence between the highly skilled and the low-skilled workers it might result in underemployment of the low-skilled. From a more theoretical welfare point of view, Sen (2000) argues that inequality should be related more to capabilities than to the static distribution of income. The data referred in Table 1.4 on organizational models of learning in different European countries make it possible to find indicators of more adequate measures of inequality. In Table 1.6 we present an indicator for the social distribution of workplace learning opportunities.

Table 1.6 National differences in organizational models (% of employees by organizational class)

	Discretionary learning model	Share of managers with access to discretionary learning	Share of workers with access to discretionary learning	Learning Inequality index*
North				
Netherlands	64.0	81.6	51.1	37.3
Denmark	60.0	85.0	56.2	35.9
Sweden	52.6	76.4	38.2	50.3
Finland	47.8	62.0	38.5	37.9
Austria	47.5	74.1	44.6	39.9
Centre				
Germany	44.3	65.4	36.8	43.8
Luxembourg	42.8	70.3	33.1	52.9
Belgium	38.9	65.7	30.8	53.1
France	38.0	66.5	25.4	61.9
West				
UK	34.8	58.9	20.1	65.9
Ireland	24.0	46.7	16.4	64.9
South				
Italy	30.0	63.7	20.8	67.3
Portugal	26.1	59.0	18.2	69.2
Spain	20.1	52.4	19.1	63.5
Greece	18.7	40.4	17.0	57.9

*The index is constructed by dividing the share of 'workers' engaged in discretionary learning by the share of 'managers' engaged in discretionary learning and subtracting the resulting percentage from 100. If the share of workers and managers was the same, the index would equal 0, and if the share of workers was 0 the index would equal 100.

Source: Lundvall, Rasmussen, and Lorenz (2008).

Table 1.7 Work organization across classes: EU-27 and Norway

		Discretionary learning	Lean production	Taylorist	Traditional or simple	All
Learning		87.7	89.3	38.1	27.1	68.3
Problem-solving activities		96.4	92.7	53.2	47.5	78.9
Complexity		79.1	83.7	34.8	18.1	61.4
Monotony		21.9	61.3	73.9	36.7	44.5
Repetitiveness of tasks		10.2	41.5	40.4	17.7	25.3
Task rotation		41.2	78.8	40.8	27.8	48.5
Teamwork	Members decide on task division	33.8	47.9	13.2	19.0	31.0
	Members do not decide on task division	24.9	40.4	45.6	17.5	31.4
Quality	Self-assessment	81.7	91.5	56.9	25.5	69.9
	Norms	77.7	95.7	91.8	35.3	77.8
Autonomy in methods		88.8	66.4	9.8	45.4	60.6
Autonomy in speed or rate of work		87.7	66.3	20.8	53.6	63.6
Work pace constraints	Automatic	3.8	46.4	59.9	5.9	25.8
	Norm-based	42.2	76.1	73.8	14.6	52.2
	Hierarchical	24.6	65.7	69.7	30.0	44.6
	Horizontal	36.0	85.0	64.2	24.8	52.0
Sample		38.2	25.7	19.0	17.1	100.0

We distinguish between 'workers' and 'managers' and we compare their access to discretionary learning in different national systems.[9]

Table 1.6 shows that employees at the high end of the professional hierarchy have better access to jobs involving discretionary learning. This is true for all the countries listed.

It is also noteworthy, however, that the inequality in access to learning is quite different in different countries. In the Nordic countries and the Netherlands the inequality in the distribution of learning opportunities is moderate while it is very substantial in the less developed South. For instance, the proportion of the management category engaged in discretionary learning in Portugal (59%) is almost as high as in Finland (62%), but the proportion of workers engaged in discretionary learning is much lower in Portugal (18.2% versus 38.2%).

This pattern indicates that the Nordic countries are relatively egalitarian not only in terms of income distribution. Also when it comes to access to learning the distribution is more equal than elsewhere in Europe. The combination of welfare states offering basic security, equal income distribution, and low social distance is reflected in high degrees of trust and broad participation in change. While there are tendencies toward polarization in the current context even in the Nordic countries, the latter still benefit from a kind of social capital that supports dynamic economic efficiency.

So while it might be true that higher education fosters people who are successful as equilibrators and innovators, at least in the Nordic countries, it seems to be when those people interact with broader segments of the workforce in promoting or coping with change that the innovation system as a whole turns out to be most efficient.

1.6.4 Policy implications

Traditionally the focus of innovation policy has been on strengthening R&D effort, strengthening the link between universities and industry, and increasing the numbers and the formal qualifications of engineers and scientists (Lundvall and Borras, 2005). Such efforts are useful and necessary in the current era. But if they stand alone they cannot be expected to constitute a strong innovation system. It is necessary to take a broader and more systemic approach to competence building.

1.7 Summing up and broadening the perspective

This chapter is built around the assumption that innovation and competency-building policy may become more balanced and adequate through a better understanding of the tacit dimension of knowledge and experience-based dimension of learning. We have also argued that the relative success of the small Nordic countries is rooted in social capital and trust, contributing not only to low transaction costs but also to dynamic effects reflecting a highly developed division of labour and high benefits from interactive learning within and across organizational borders.

From this point of view we have criticized strategies that focus almost exclusively on promoting science-based learning in what is regarded as high-technology sectors. We have also raised questions about the current drive to transfer scientific knowledge directly from academic research to the business sector and the tendency toward the commercialization of universities that it involves. By defining the role of graduates in innovation processes we have argued that much greater emphasis should be placed on higher education and that the flow of graduates to industry constitutes the single most important transmission mechanism.

We see the development of policies aiming at supporting DUI learning as a major task, which should involve an interaction between policy makers on the one hand and innovation scholars, management, and employees on the other. There is a need for new indicators, data sets, and case studies. Comparisons between several small national systems (the Nordic countries, the Netherlands, and Ireland, for instance) may be the most relevant strategy.

It is important to note that historical patterns and strengths change over time. In the Nordic countries, a stronger element of science-based learning in more traditional sectors is necessary for the upgrading of activities exposed to global competition. The low proportion of low-skilled jobs in the Nordic countries will become even smaller and there is a need for a 'new new deal' where the focus is upon supporting competency-building among those who are weak in the labor market – namely, workers with low skills and workers with a non-Nordic ethnic background.

So far the focus in the small Nordic countries has been on the capability to innovate and adapt in a rapidly changing environment with focus on absorbing new technology from abroad. The policies involved are oriented mainly toward market repair and support. The new challenge for innovation that relates to sustainability requires more ambitious policies (Smith, 2008).

Environmental threats call for radical trans-disciplinary and multi-technological breakthroughs, which must be realistically anchored in

Table 1.8 Differences between countries in forms of work organization (weighted % of employees by organizational class)

	Classes of work organization			
	Discretionary learning	Lean production	Taylorist	Traditional or simple
Belgium	41.2	25.2	16.8	16.9
Czech Republic	30.2	25.1	22.8	21.9
Denmark	54.1	28.4	7.9	9.6
Germany	43.3	19.8	18.3	18.6
Estonia	40.8	32.7	11.4	15.1
Greece	22.9	28.9	24.5	23.6
Spain	20.6	24.9	26.3	28.2
France	46.7	24.8	17.6	10.9
Ireland	42.3	26.8	10.9	20.1
Italy	38.2	24.4	21.4	16.0
Cyprus	27.9	24.7	21.6	25.8
Latvia	35.2	32.6	17.1	15.1
Lithuania	24.5	30.8	22.0	22.7
Luxembourg	44.2	29.0	13.1	13.7
Hungary	39.6	16.4	23.9	20.1
Malta	47.0	34.3	10.6	8.1
Netherlands	52.8	22.7	11.9	12.6
Austria	48.1	21.4	17.9	12.6
Poland	33.5	31.3	20.0	15.2
Portugal	24.8	30.3	32.1	12.9
Slovenia	34.0	31.0	16.9	18.1
Slovakia	28.9	19.0	34.3	17.8
Finland	44.9	30.9	11.3	12.9
Sweden	67.2	14.9	7.1	10.8
UK	30.3	33.3	16.7	19.7
Bulgaria	20.3	28.1	30.2	21.3
Romania	24.3	32.5	28.2	15.0
Norway	55.6	28.2	6.0	10.2
All	38.2	25.7	19.0	17.1

Continued

Table 1.8 Continued

Regional patterns	Discretionary learning	Lean production	Taylorist	Traditional or simple
Nordic countries				
Sweden	67.2	14.9	7.1	10.8
Norway	55.6	28.2	6.0	10.2
Denmark	54.1	28.4	7.9	9.6
Finland	44.9	30.9	11.3	12.9
Continental countries				
Netherlands	52.8	22.7	11.9	12.6
Austria	48.1	21.4	17.9	12.6
France	46.7	24.8	17.6	10.9
Luxembourg	44.2	29.0	13.1	13.7
Germany	43.3	19.8	18.3	18.6
Belgium	41.2	25.2	16.8	16.9
Anglo-Saxon countries				
Ireland	42.3	26.8	10.9	20.1
UK	30.3	33.3	16.7	19.7
Mediterranean countries				
Malta	47.0	34.3	10.6	8.1
Italy	38.2	24.4	21.4	16.0
Portugal	24.8	30.3	32.1	12.9
Cyprus	27.9	24.7	21.6	25.8
Greece	22.9	28.9	24.5	23.6
Spain	20.6	24.9	26.3	28.2
Former socialist countries				
Estonia	40.8	32.7	11.4	15.1
Latvia	35.2	32.6	17.1	15.1
Lithuania	24.5	30.8	22.0	22.7
Hungary	39.6	16.4	23.9	20.1
Czech Republic	30.2	25.1	22.8	21.9
Poland	33.5	31.3	20.0	15.2
Slovenia	34.0	31.0	16.9	18.1
Slovakia	28.9	19.0	34.3	17.8
Bulgaria	20.3	28.1	30.2	21.3
Romania	24.3	32.5	28.2	15.0
All	38.2	25.7	19.0	17.1

an understanding of the role of institutional barriers as well as social movements and interest groups (Jamison and Østby, 1997). In this context it is useful to think in terms of *building new technological systems*, seen as combinations of interrelated sectors and firms, institutions, and regulations (Carlsson and Stankiewitz, 1991). It is a major challenge for the Nordic countries to find ways through specialized efforts to contribute to the building of such systems. Here there will be a need for more ambitious domestic policies as well as for far-reaching international collaboration.

In the case of environmental innovation, coordinating the following three policies may be crucial for success:

1. Creating markets for green products through procurement policies activating private and public users and establishing standards in an interaction between users and producers.
2. Strengthening the institutes responsible for measuring and evaluating the crucial parameters related to the environment, and building new institutions for training and research.
3. Strengthening the links between environmental policy, innovation policy, and general economic policy.

Notes

1. Knowledge differs from tangible assets in many important respects and market failure is the rule rather than the exception (Arrow, 1971, 1974). In markets for knowledge it is difficult for the buyer to assess its value without knowing the content, but if the content were known the buyer would not pay for it. The seller does not lose access to it when it is sold. It may be expensive to produce but often it is much less expensive to reproduce. Most important is that some forms of knowledge it is not scarce in the same sense as a tangible asset – the more know-how is used the more it grows and develops. This is why it is problematic to apply standard economic models and why the design of an institutional framework that supports the formation and distribution of knowledge is a major task for governments.
2. Markusen (1996) gives an excellent overview of the analytical work on industrial districts, showing why and how some knowledge remains 'sticky' in a 'slippery' space.
3. This point was made by professor emeritus Reinhard Lund with reference to a series of his case studies of innovation processes in Danish firms.
4. Lorenz and Valeyre (2006) use logit regression analysis to control for differences in sector, occupation, and establishment size when estimating the impact of nation on the likelihood of employees being grouped in the various forms of work organization. The results show a statistically significant 'national effect' also when controlling for the structural variables, thus

pointing to considerable latitude in how work is organized for the same occupation or within the same industrial sector.
5. Lorenz has, for the sake of this article, made a similar analysis for 2000 that includes 28 countries, including Norway – see Appendix A. Here Sweden comes out as the country with the biggest share of discretionary learning followed by Denmark and Norway, with remarkably similar patterns of work organization and learning.
6. The reason that such reforms are neglected may reflect that they are both more difficult to realize and less visible for the public. They need to take place at the core of the university function and they will not have the same symbolic effect as when a minister opens yet another science park.
7. In this section on education we have not referred to the 'human capital' literature. The reason is that much of this literature is based upon rates of return on human capital calculated assuming general equilibrium. As argued by Schultz (1975), the rate of return on investment in human capital will more than anything else reflect the 'degree of disequilibrium'. If this is correct, it is not logically satisfactory to make calculations assuming the reign of equilibrium.
8. In Appendix A we present a bold theory about economic development where social capital is linked to the division of labor and the division of labor is linked to interactive learning and innovation.
9. The class of managers includes not only top and middle management but also professionals and technicians (ISCO major groups 1, 2 and 3). The worker category includes clerks, and service and sales workers as well as craft, plant, and machine operators, and unskilled workers (ISCO major groups 4 through 9).

References

Abramowitz, M. and David, P. (1996), 'Technological change and the rise of intangible investments: The US economy's growth path in the twentieth century', in Foray, D. and Lundvall B.-Å. (eds.), *Employment and Growth in the Knowledge Based Economy*, Paris, OECD.

Amin, A. and Cohendet, P. (2004), *Architectures of Knowledge: Firms, Capabilities, and Communities*. Oxford, Oxford University Press.

Arrow, K.J. (1962a), 'The economic implications of learning by doing', *Review of Economic Studies*, Vol. XXIX, No. 80.

Arrow, K.J. (1962b) 'Economic welfare and the allocation of resources for invention', in Nelson, R.R. (ed.) *The Rate and Direction of Inventive Activity: Economic and Social Factors*, Princeton, Princeton University Press.

Arrow, K.J. (1971), 'Political and economic evaluation of social effects and externalities', in Intrilligator, M. (ed.), *Frontiers of Quantitative Economics*, North Holland.

Arrow, K.J. (1974), *The Limits of Organisation*, New York, W.W. Norton and Co.

Bernal J.D. (1939), *The Social Function of Science*, Cambridge, MA, MIT Press.

Bush, V. (1945), *Science: The Endless Frontier*, A Report to the President, Washington.

Carlsson, B. and Stankiewitz, R. (1991), 'On the nature, function and composition of technological systems', *Journal of Evolutionary Economics*, Vol. 1, pp. 93–118.

Cowan, R., P.A. David, D. Foray (2000), 'The explicit economics ok knowledge codification and tacitness', *Industrial and Corporate Change*, Vol. 9, pp. 211–253.

Foray, D. (2000), *The Economics of Knowledge*, Cambridge, MA, The MIT Press.

Foray, D. and B.-Å. Lundvall (1996), 'The knowledge-based economy: from the economics of knowledge to the learning economy' in Foray, D. and B.-Å. Lundvall (eds.), *Employment and Growth in the Knowledge-based Economy*, OECD Documents, Paris, OECD.

Granstrand, O. (2004), 'Innovation and intellectual property rights' in Fagerberg, J., D.C. Mowery, and R.R. Nelson (eds.), *The Oxford Handbook of Innovation*, Oxford, Oxford University Press.

Johnson, B., Lorenz, E. and Lundvall B.-Å. (2002) 'Why all this about codified and tacit knowledge?', *Industrial and Corporate Change*, Vol. 11, No. 2, pp. 245–262.

List, F. (1841): *Das Nationale System der Politischen Ökonomie*, Basel: Kyklos (translated and published under the title: The National System of Political Economy' by Longmans, Green and Co., London).

Lundvall, B.-Å. (1985), *Product Innovation and User-Producer Interaction*, Aalborg, Aalborg University Press.

Lundvall, B.-A. (2002), 'The university in the learning economy', *DRUID Working Paper* no. 6, Aalborg Universitet.

Lundvall, B.-Å. (2006), 'Interactive learning, social capital and economic performance', Foray, D. and Kahin, B. (eds.), *Advancing Knowledge and the Knowledge Economy*, Cambridge MA, Harvard University Press.

Lundvall, B. Å. (2007), Higher Education, Innovation and Economic Development, Paper presented at the World Bank's *Regional Bank Conference on Development Economics*, Beijing, 16–17 January 2007.

Lundvall, B.-Å. and Borras, S. (2005), 'Science, technology, innovation and knowledge policy', in Fagerberg, J., D. Mowery and R.R. Nelson (eds.), *The Oxford Handbook of Innovation*, Norfolk, Oxford University Press.

Lundvall, B.-Å and Johnson, B. (1994), 'The learning economy', *Journal of Industry Studies*, Vol. 1, No. 2, December 1994, pp. 23–42.

Lundvall, B.-Å, Rasmussen, P. and Lorenz, E. (2008), 'Education in the learning economy: a European perspective', *Policy Futures in Education*, Vol. 6, No. 2., 681–700.

Markusen A. (1996), 'Sticky places in slippery space: A typology of industrial districts', Economic Geography, Vol. 72, No. 3, 293–313.

Marshall, A.P. (1923), *Industry and Trade*, London, Macmillan.

Murnane, R.J. and Nelson, R.R. (1984), 'Production and innovation when techniques are tacit', *Journal of Economic Behaviour and Organization*, Vol. 5, pp. 353–373.

Nelson, R.R. (1959), 'The simple economics of basic economic research', *Journal of Political Economy*, Vol. 67, pp. 323–348.

Nelson, R. R. and E. S. Phelps (1966), 'Investment in humans, technological diffusion, and economic growth', *American Economic Review*, Vol. 56, No. 1/2, pp. 69–75.

Nielsen, R.N. (2007), Innovation, human resources, and academic labour: Introduction of highly educated labour in small Danish firms, Unpublished Ph.D. dissertation, *Department of Business Studies*, Aalborg University.
OECD (1963), *Science, Economic Growth and Government Policy*, Paris, OECD.
OECD (1971), *Science, Growth and Society*, Paris, OECD.
OECD (1992), *Technology and the Economy*, Paris, OECD.
OECD (1994), *The OECD Jobs Study – Facts, Analysis, Strategies*, Paris, OECD
OECD (1996), *Transitions to Learning Economies and Societies*, Paris, OECD.
OECD (1999), *OECD Science, Technology and Industry Scoreboard 1999: Benchmarking Knowledge-based Economies*, Paris, OECD.
OECD (2000), *Knowledge Management in the Learning Society*, Paris, OECD.
OECD (2001), *The New Economy: Beyond the Hype*, Paris, OECD.
Pavitt, K. (1998), 'Technologies, products and organisation in the innovating firm: What Adam Smith tells us and Joseph Schumpeter doesn't', paper presented at the *DRUID 1998 Summer conference*, Bornhom, June 9–11.
Penrose, E. (1959/1995), *The Theory of the Growth of the Firm*, Oxford, Oxford University Press.
Rosenberg, N. (1982), *Inside the Black Box: Technology and Economics*, Cambridge, Cambridge University Press.
Rothwell, R. (1977), 'The characteristics of successful innovators and technically progressive firms', *R&D Management*, Vol. 7, No 3, pp. 191–206.
Shapiro, C. and Varian, H.R. (1999), *Information Rules: A Strategic Guide to the Network Economy*, Boston, Harvard Business School Press.
Senge, P. (1990), *The Fifth Discipline: The Art and Practice of Learning*, New York, Doubleday.
Tomlinson, M. (1999), 'The learning economy and embodied knowledge flows in Great Britain', *Journal of Evolutionary Economics*, Vol. 9, No. 4, pp. 431–451.
Polanyi, M. (1958/1978), *Personal Knowledge*, London, Routledge and Kegan Paul.
Polanyi, M. (1966), *The Tacit Dimension*, London, Routledge and Kegan Paul.
Schultz, T. W. (1975), 'The value of the ability to deal with disequilibria', *Journal of Economic Literature*, pp. 827–846.
Sen, A. (1999), *Development as Freedom*, Oxford, Oxford University Press.
Smith, A. (1776/1904), *An Inquiry into the Nature and Causes of the Wealth of Nations* (5th edition), London, Methuen and Co. Ltd.
Vinding, A.L. (2004), 'Human resources, absorptive capacity and innovative performance', in Christensen J.L. and Lundvall, B.-Å. (Eds.), *Product Innovation, Interactive Learning and Economic Performance*, Amsterdam, Elsevier.
Yusuf, S. and Nabeshima, K. (eds.) (2007), *How Universities Promote Economic Growth*, Washington, DC, The World Bank.

2
Labor Market Institutions, Skills, and Innovation Style: A Critique of the 'Varieties of Capitalism' Perspective

Edward Lorenz

2.1 Introduction

Recent work on innovation performance within the national systems of innovation (NSI) framework has sought to go beyond the focus in the seminal contributions on science–industry links and the R&D activities of industrial firms (Nelson, 1993) or on the nature of user–producer relations promoting interactive learning (Lundvall, 1992). The more recent work has sought to widen the NSI perspective by exploring the way labor market institutions and systems of social protection impact on employee learning and innovation outcomes (Lorenz and Lundvall, 2006; Holms et al., 2010). A focus on the institutional determinants of the innovative performance of firms is also a hallmark of research on the varieties of capitalism (VoC) by Hall and Soskice (2001), who were perhaps the first to emphasize the way labor markets and vocational training systems shape differences in innovation style across nations.

In this chapter I begin by presenting a critique of the VoC view that those nations with relatively fluid labor markets and a predominance of general over industry or company-specific skills will be specialized in the more radical forms of innovation. Then, drawing on prior research on the relation between creativity at work and innovative style (Lorenz and Lundvall, 2009), I present evidence to support the view that for the EU-27 the more radical forms of innovation are more developed in nations with systems of 'flexible security' characterized by high levels of labor market mobility combined with generous systems of unemployment insurance and active labor market policies;

2.2 The VoC perspective on labor market institutions and innovation style

The VoC perspective draws a broad distinction between liberal market economies (LME) such as the United States and the UK, and coordinated market economies (CME) such as Germany and Japan. A central idea developed in the VoC approach is that of 'comparative institutional advantage', and Hall and Soskice (2001: 38–40) in particular argue that the institutional arrangements of different national systems will be more or less suited to different styles of innovation, with CMEs excelling in incremental innovation and LMEs excelling in more radical innovation. Drawing inspiration from prior research on the adoption of strategies of 'diversified quality production' by German enterprises (Streeck, 1991, 1992), they argue that incremental innovation thrives in corporate settings where workers are skilled and autonomous enough to contribute to continuous improvements in products and processes and secure enough in their tenures to take the risk of promoting changes that might alter their job situation. These relational requirements for incremental innovations are more likely to be achieved under the institutional arrangements characteristic of CMEs, including industrial relations systems characterized by works councils and consensus decision making, vocational training systems providing an appropriate mix of company- and industry-specific skills, and corporate governance arrangements favoring long-term employment tenures.

LMEs, on the other hand, will have a comparative advantage in radical innovation because labor markets with few restrictions on firing and educational systems which favor the development of general over industry-specific skills will make it easier for companies to rapidly reconfigure their knowledge bases in order to develop new product lines. Further, the hierarchical structure of companies in LMEs, with power concentrated at the top, will make it easier for senior management to implement new business strategies than for management in CME enterprises, who are constrained by the requirements of consensus decision making (Hall and Soskice, 2001: 40–41).

This hypothesis of the VoC approach regarding innovation style has recently been subject to some criticism and debate. Focusing on the biotech industry, Herrmann (2008) and Lange (2009) observe that German companies perform better than the VoC perspective would allow in market segments of the industry, such as therapeutics discovery, that are characterized by radical technological change. The authors do not contest the basic claim of the VoC approach that the institutions of CMEs are unsupportive of radical innovation. Rather, they oppose the idea that corporate strategy and performance are directly determined by the national institutional configuration by arguing that German biotech companies have displayed considerable innovativeness in circumventing the disadvantages of their institutional setting, notably by tapping into international markets for technical expertise and finance.

While the evidence of Herrmann (2008) and Lange (2009) would appear to be at odds with the VoC notion of comparative institutional advantage, the validity of the VoC hypothesis concerning differences in innovation style across nations obviously should not hinge on evidence concerning the performance of a limited number of companies in a single sector of activity. Hall and Soskice (2001: 43–44) support their argument on the basis of patent data comparing patterns of technological specialization between the United States and Germany for the periods 1983–1984 and 1993–1994. More general tests of the VoC hypothesis on the basis of patent data for larger populations of LMEs and CMEs have been undertaken by Taylor (2004) and by Akkermanns et al. (2009). Using the NBER patent database Taylor refutes the basic proposition on the basis of a series of tests using indices of patent specialization[1] across six LMEs (Australia, Canada, Great Britain, Ireland, New Zealand, and the United States) and ten CMEs (Austria, Belgium, Denmark, Finland, Germany, Japan, Netherlands, Norway, Sweden, and Switzerland). For example, he observes that for the period 1983–1984, also examined by Hall and Soskice, the LMEs have higher degrees of patent specialization in three industries that are characterized by Hall and Soskice as incremental (mechanical elements, basic materials, and polymers) while the CMEs have greater specialization in two radical industries (new materials and audiovisual technology). Taylor also observes that the United States stands out as a clear outlier in terms of specialization in sectors that are characterized as radical, and when the United States is removed from the population of LMEs the success of the VoC hypothesis in accounting for international patterns of patent specialization is substantially reduced.

Akkermanns et al. (2009), also using the NBER data set, arrive at similar conclusions using a measure of the radicalness of an innovation based on the number of citations a patent receives. The basic idea in this measure, introduced by Trajtenberg (1990), is that patents that receive more citations than others have a more important impact on subsequent technical development and therefore can be seen as more radical. One finding of Akkermanns et al. (2009) is that LMEs other than the United States and Ireland do not systematically show stronger specialization in radical innovation, and that in four of eight industries examined in more detail, CMEs tend to be more directed towards generating radical innovation.[2]

While the empirical literature cited appears to provide convincing evidence that CMEs can generate radical innovations and can perform well in industries that are characterized as radical, this literature does not question the saliency of Hall and Soskice's portrayal of the CME institutions, nor does it question Hall and Soskice's view regarding the types of institutions that support incremental versus radical innovation. While the dichotomous distinction between LMEs and CMEs has been criticized as inadequate for capturing the distinctive features of nations such as France, where the state has traditionally played a strong role in coordinating economic activity, less critical attention has been paid to the way the VoC literature portrays the differences in institutions and corporate strategies that serve to distinguish the core CME nations from the core LME nations.

Hall and Soskice (2001: 40) argue that the weak initial vocational training systems of LMEs combined with fluid labor markets and short-term tenures make it rational for employees to concentrate of the development of general skills rather than industry or company-specific skills. The notion of institutional complementarities that is implicit here means that across nations one should observe a negative relation between the degree of fluidity of labor markets and the extent to which nations have established strong initial vocational training systems that generate desirable mixes of company and industry-specific skills.. In order to test this hypothesis for the EU-27, we use data from UNESCO to develop a measure of the strength of the initial vocational training system, and data available on Eurostat's electronic database to develop a measure of the degree of labor market mobility. The scatter plot diagram presented in Figure 2.1 below does not support the view that there is a negative relation between the strength of a nation's initial vocational training system and the degree of labor market mobility.[3]

A recent article by Busemeyer (2009), focusing on the links between skill-specificity on the one hand and national training regimes and systems of social protection on the other, argues convincingly that there are important differences between the initial vocational training systems of different core CME nations. One important distinction is between CMEs such as Sweden, Norway, Belgium, and the Netherlands,

[Figure: scatter plot of Labour market mobility vs Initial vocational training for European countries, R-squared = .00]

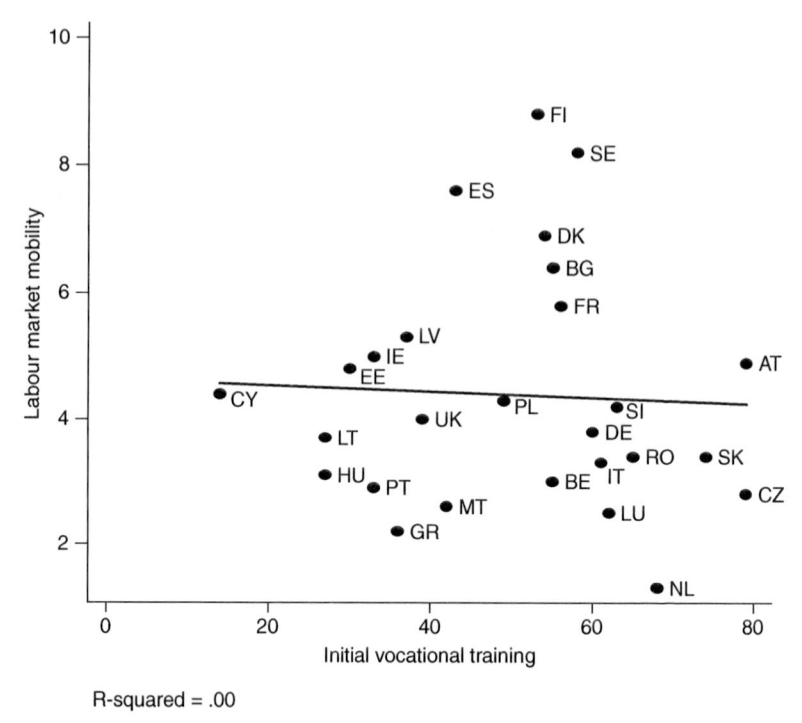

Figure 2.1 Labor market mobility by initial vocational training

which have extended school-based initial vocational training systems and referred to by Busemeyer as "integrationist" skill regimes, and CME's such as Germany, Austria, and Switzerland, which have strong workplace apprenticeship systems that are referred to by Busemeyer as "differentiated" skill regimes. The stronger involvement of employers and firms in setting the curricula and organizing initial training in the differentiated skills systems might be expected to reinforce the company-specific component of training and skills relative to that in integrationist regimes, where skills would tend to be more transferable.

The other important distinction discussed by Busemeyer has to do with the 'conservativeness' of the welfare regime. Germany's is presented as a prototypically conservative welfare regime, with an emphasis on employment protection combined with relatively generous unemployment benefit. This is contrasted with the welfare systems of the Scandinavian nations, which are characterized by lower employment protection and greater emphasis on unemployment protection combined with active labor market policies in the forms of lifelong learning and continuous vocational training in order to promote the mobility of workers from unproductive to productive occupations and sectors.

The upshot of these differences is that one might expect skills to be more transferable and labor mobility to be greater in CMEs such as Sweden, which combine extended school-based systems of initial vocational training with welfare systems emphasizing unemployment protection and active labor market policies rather than employment protection. While Busemeyer does not draw out the implications of these differences for innovation style and performance, one possibility is that the relatively good innovative performance of countries such as Sweden and Finland over the last decade in high-tech sectors such as ICT is connected to the flexibility of their local labor markets, which promote diversity in the enterprise knowledge base.

2.2.1 Labor market fluidity and radical innovation

Before accepting this hypothesis, however, it is important to revisit the argument about the positive relation between fluid labor markets and a capacity for radical innovation. The argument appears to be based on the idea that radically innovative firms will need the freedom to fire their employees in order to rapidly configure their knowledge base. The interest a radically innovative firm has in firing its employees will, however, depend on the extent to which its innovation activities are strongly competency destroying. Competency destroying in this context refers not only to competencies that are specific to a particular firm but also to competencies that are specific to a particular technology or class of product, and consequently all firms specialized in those products or technologies will be affected.

If we define radical innovations in the strong sense as those that destroy existing competencies, the issue of how competency destroying such innovations are is settled. However, if we work with a more general definition of radical innovation as technological discontinuities in the form of new products or processes that are order-of-magnitude improvements in price/performance (Tushman and Anderson, 1986), there will be variations in the extent to which radical innovations are competency destroying with respect to industry-specific technical skills. Historically, certain radical innovations, such as entirely new product lines in the form of automobiles or airlines, or process substitutions such as industrial gems for natural gems, were strongly competency destroying. Others, such as the introduction of the screw propeller, which improved the speed of ocean-going vessels, or the development of electric typewriters, were at least in part competency enhancing.

This distinction within the class of radical innovation does not mean that the value of having fluid labor markets is restricted to instances where radical innovations are strongly competency destroying. Major innovations that are competency enhancing require creative thinking and new ideas, and labor market mobility can be important for generating diversity of knowledge within an organization. However, these considerations do imply a need to qualify the idea in the VoC literature that companies in the United States or other LME nations necessarily succeed at radical innovation through their regular use of massive layoffs in order to entirely reconfigure their skills and knowledge base.

First, this vision of the radically innovative firm as a unitary structure in which powerful senior management imposes new business strategies irrespective of their impact on the jobs and tenures of their existing employees is at odds with work in strategic management focusing on the internal organization of creative and innovative firms. For example, the classic taxonomy of Mintzberg (1979) identifies "adhocracies" as the most suitable organizational design for high performance in new technology sectors characterized by rapid changes in technology and products. Such firms depend on relatively decentralized structures that support the autonomous ability of their skilled technical and managerial staff to coordinate their activities through an informal process that Mintzberg refers to as "mutual adjustment." The ability of employees to coordinate in this manner depends on relation-specific knowledge built up through processes of team and enterprise learning that are largely tacit and hence by definition difficult to reproduce in new corporate settings. Some of these relational requirements for success in sectors characterized by radical changes in technology do not sound all that different from the organizational features that Hall and Soskice (1991: 39) describe as characteristic of incremental innovators in CMEs.

Second, while it is true that the literature on innovation management points to an increasing role for a new type of expert whose career is punctuated by a series of short-term employment contracts working within project team structures across multiple firms, there is little appreciation in the VoC literature that such career paths and forms of mobility are typical in settings where there are regional clusters of firms competing in the same technology areas. As Lam and Lundvall (2006) have observed, this is linked to the fact that labor market mobility is a two-edged sword for the creative firm. Highly creative firms draw their capability from the industry- and technology-specific know-how and problem solving skills that are embodied in individual experts. Formal professional knowledge may play only a limited role and the expert's problem solving capabilities have more to do with experience and tacit knowledge generated through interaction, trial and error, and experimentation. Because these tacit skills cannot be easily codified, the creative firm faces a problem of reproducing what has been learnt into an organizational memory and such firms are highly vulnerable when it comes to individuals leaving the organization.

These problems of accumulating and transferring experience-based tacit knowledge take a different form when firms are organized into localized networks and industry clusters. Mobility across organizational borders within industrial clusters contributes to professional and social relationships, which provide the 'social capital' and 'information signals' needed to ensure the efficient accumulation and transfer of tacit knowledge in an inter-firm career framework (Saxenian, 1996). While it is possible to identify radical innovations that completely break with the know-how and practice specific to a sector or technology, many, if not most, innovations that are order-of-magnitude improvements in price/performance will build on existing industry-specific skills, and firms that are well placed to draw on local pools of experienced scientists and technicians will show a competitive advantage.

I would argue that the localized or industry-specific professional and social networks that facilitate the accumulation and transfer of experts' tacit knowledge are more likely to arise in institutional settings that where high levels of labor market mobility are combined with both well developed systems of unemployment protection and active labor market policies designed to increase the employability of the unemployed. Generous unemployment protection can encourage individuals to commit themselves to what would otherwise be considered unacceptably risky career paths punctuated by transitions between employment and unemployment or part-time employment. Further, unemployment protection combined with active labor market polices can help to ensure that extended periods of unemployment will not lead individuals to accept downgrading or take job offers that do not make use of and build on the experience and knowledge they have gained through previous employment.

For these reasons, it can be argued that labor market mobility is more likely to contribute to the development and accumulation of the largely tacit industry-specific technical and organizational skills needed for many, if not most, radical innovations when it is embedded in a system of 'flexible security' characterized by high levels of unemployment protection combined with active labor market policies.

In order to present empirical evidence that is pertinent to this claim, in what follows I draw on empirical research presented in a recent co-authored paper with Bengt-Åake Lundvall on the relation between innovation and creative work activity (Lorenz and Lundvall, 2009). The paper develops a measure of the degree of creativity at work for private sector employees across the EU-27 and then, drawing on the results of the 5th Community Innovation Survey (CIS) on the innovative activities of firms, demonstrates that there is a positive association between degree of creativity and the more radical forms of product innovation. In what follows I summarize these results and extend the research by examining the relation between our measure of creativity at work and measures of labor market mobility and flexible security.

2.3 Creativity, systems of flexible security, and innovation style

In order to develop a measure of the creativity at work that is suitable for a comparative analysis of the EU-27, we drew on the results of the 4th European Working Condition Survey carried out in 2005 by the European Foundation for the Improvement of Living and Working Conditions. The analysis draws on the results for private sector establishments of the EU-27 employing ten or more salaried people and the total size of the sample is 9240 salaried people.[4] The measure of creativity at work is based on a factor analysis that identifies the underlying associations that exist among six binary variables that capture key features of creative work activity (see Table 2.1). We then used hierarchical clustering in order to group the population of employees into three basic types of worker: creative workers, constrained problem-solvers, and taylorized workers.

The first column in Table 2.1 lists the six variables used in order to classify a worker as creative and the last column shows the percentage of the population characterized by each of the variables. Creative workers are identified as those that engage in learning and complex problem-solving activities drawing on their own ideas. Further, they are identified as people who exercise considerable discretion over their work methods or task order. This corresponds to Florida's (2002) characterization of creative professionals as people who are able to "think on their own" and that take on "increased responsibility to interpret their work and make decisions."

Columns 2 through 4 of Table 2.1 show the composition of the three groups resulting from the hierarchical cluster analysis. The first group,

Table 2.1 Cluster analysis of types of workers

Variable	Creative workers	Constrained problem-solvers	Taylorized workers	Average
Problem solving activities in work	96	87	37	79
Learning new things in work	87	84	16	68
Undertaking complex tasks	80	81	8	62
Using own ideas in work	77	24	19	50
Able to choose or change own work methods	94	21	29	60
Able to choose change the order of own tasks	92	14	25	56
Total share of occupied people	51	24	25	100

(% of occupied persons by type of learner reporting each variable)

Source: 4th Working Conditions Survey, 2005. European Foundation for the Improvement of Living and Working Conditions.

which accounts for 51% of the population, is distinctive for high levels of problem solving, learning, and task complexity. The people grouped in this cluster use their own ideas and exercise considerable autonomy in carrying out their jobs. We refer to them as "creative workers." The second group is characterized by slightly lower levels of problem solving and learning and comparable levels of task complexity. However, there is little use of own ideas and levels of autonomy or discretion in work are low. This cluster groups employees who, while regularly solving technical or other problems at work, do so in highly supervised settings offering little scope for developing original or creative solutions based on their own ideas. We refer to them as "constrained problem solvers." The third group is composed largely of people doing unskilled work. Levels of learning, problem solving, and task complexity are low. There is little use of own ideas and there is limited scope for exercising discretion in how work is carried out. We refer to this group as "taylorized workers."

Table 2.2 shows differences in the frequency of creative work activity across the EU-27 in 2005. The Figures show that creative work is more

Table 2.2 National differences in types of learners: EU-27 (% of occupied persons by country and type of learner)

	Creative workers	Constrained problem solvers	Taylorized workers	Total
Belgium	60	21	19	100
Czech Republic	40	30	30	100
Denmark	70	15	14	100
Germany	52	23	26	100
Estonia	58	22	20	100
Greece	39	33	28	100
Spain	35	30	36	100
France	63	18	19	100
Ireland	58	18	24	100
Italy	37	29	34	100
Cyprus	42	26	32	100
Latvia	53	19	27	100
Lithuania	35	27	38	100
Luxembourg	60	20	20	100
Hungary	44	31	25	100
Malta	70	14	16	100
Netherlands	67	16	16	100
Austria	50	28	23	100
Poland	43	34	23	100
Portugal	46	24	29	100
Slovenia	50	25	25	100
Slovakia	33	32	35	100
Finland	66	21	13	100
Sweden	82	10	8	100
United Kingdom	51	22	27	100
Bulgaria	39	30	31	100
Romania	35	38	27	100
EU-27	51	24	25	100

Source: 4th Working Conditions Survey, 2005. European Foundation for the Improvement of Living and Working Conditions.

prevalent in the Nordic countries, the Netherlands, and Malta than it is in the other EU nations. Levels of creative work activity are at, or somewhat above, the EU average in the Continental nations, the UK, and Ireland. Levels are below the EU average in the four southern nations. Creative work activity is considerably below the average in a number of the new member nations, including Lithuania, Poland, Slovakia, the Czech Republic, Bulgaria, and Romania. It is close to, or above, the average in Estonia and Slovenia.

Figures 2.2 and 2.3 examine the relations between the frequency of creativity and two measures of innovation performance based on the results of the 5th Community Innovation Survey. The first, presented in Figure 2.2, is firms that have introduced new-to-the-firm innovations. This is a broad measure of innovative firms that includes not only firms relying on intensive in-house R&D to develop products or services that are new to the market, but also those that have expended minimal effort to introduce new products developed mainly by other enterprises or organizations. Figure 2.2 nonetheless shows a positive correlation ($R^2 = .18$) between the frequency of creative work activity and this measure of national innovative performance.[5]

The second measure, presented in Figure 2.3, is firms that have introduced products or processes that are not only new to the firm but

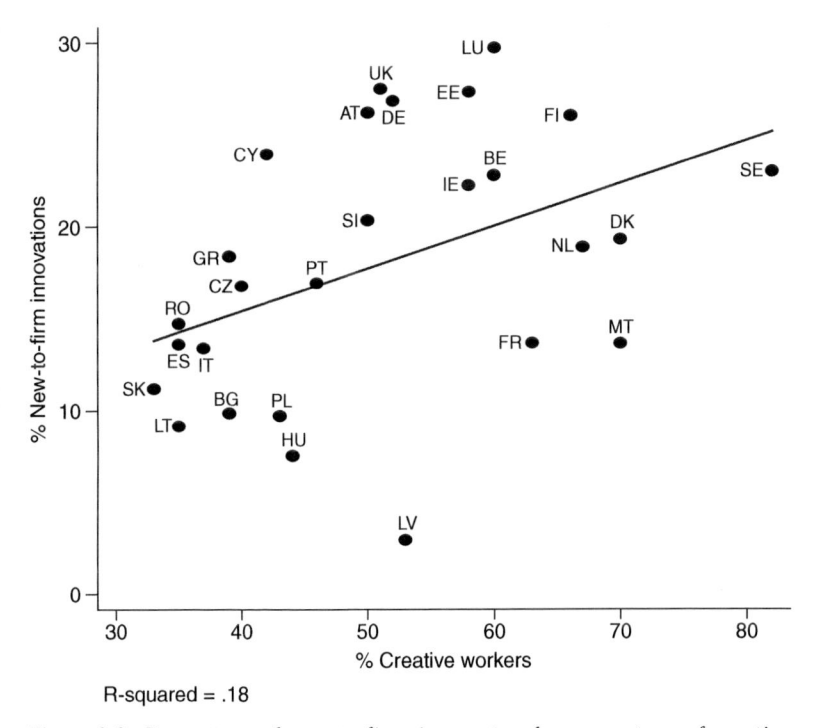

Figure 2.2 Percentage of new-to-firm innovators by percentage of creative workers

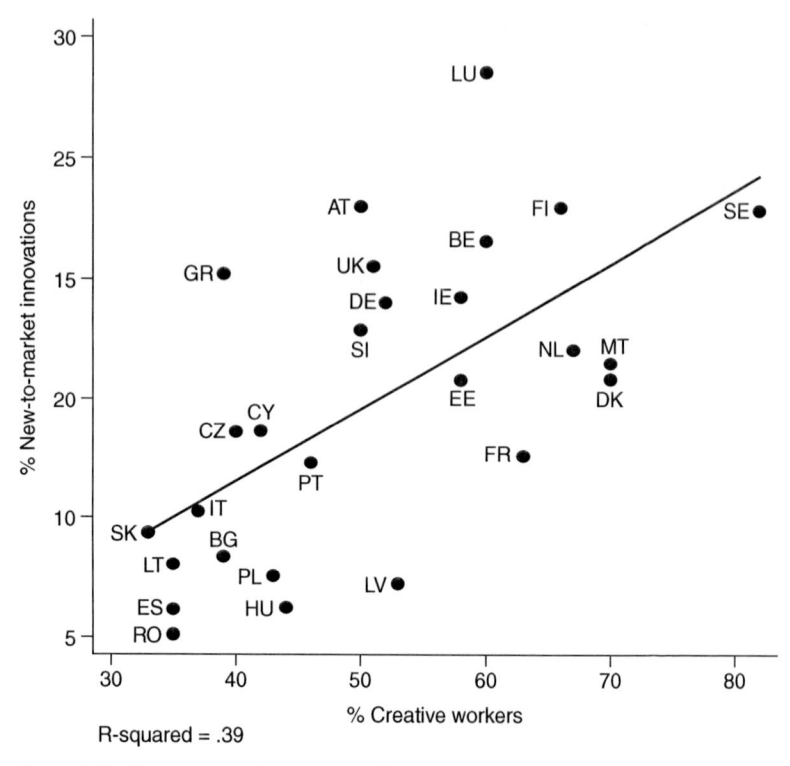

Figure 2.3 Percentage of new-to-market innovators by percentage of creative workers

also new to the market. This measure of innovation excludes cases of diffusion of innovations through imitation, and the in-house creative effort of firms classified as innovative by this measure can be expected to be relatively high. The distinction between new-to-the-firm and new-to-the-market innovations is not identical to the difference between radical and incremental innovations, since not all new-to-the-market innovations will have major transformative impacts on markets or industries. However, there is a large difference between these two categories of innovation in terms of the underlying capacity to explore new knowledge, which is conceptually similar (although on a different scale) to the difference between radical and incremental innovations. Figure 2.3 shows a positive and relatively strong correlation ($R^2 = .39$) between our measure of creativity at work and the percentage of firms in a nation introducing new-to-the-market innovations.[6] The results provide support for the view that the capacity of a nation to develop the more radical forms of innovation is closely related to the level of creativity at work.

Figures 2.4 and 2.5 extend the analysis by examining the relation between creativity at work and measures of labor market mobility and flexible security. The first Figure indicates a weak positive relation ($R^2 = .09$) between creativity and the level of labor market mobility using the same measure of mobility presented in Figure 2.1 above. The relation is not significant at the 10% level.

A simple measure of the extent to which EU nations are characterized by flexible security systems is developed by multiplying the measure of labor market mobility by total expenditures on active and passive labor market policies as a percentage of GDP.[7] Figure 2.5 shows a relatively strong positive relation ($R^2 = .29$) between this measure and the importance of creativity at work.[8] This provides support for the view that the forms of learning and knowledge exploration that underlie more radical

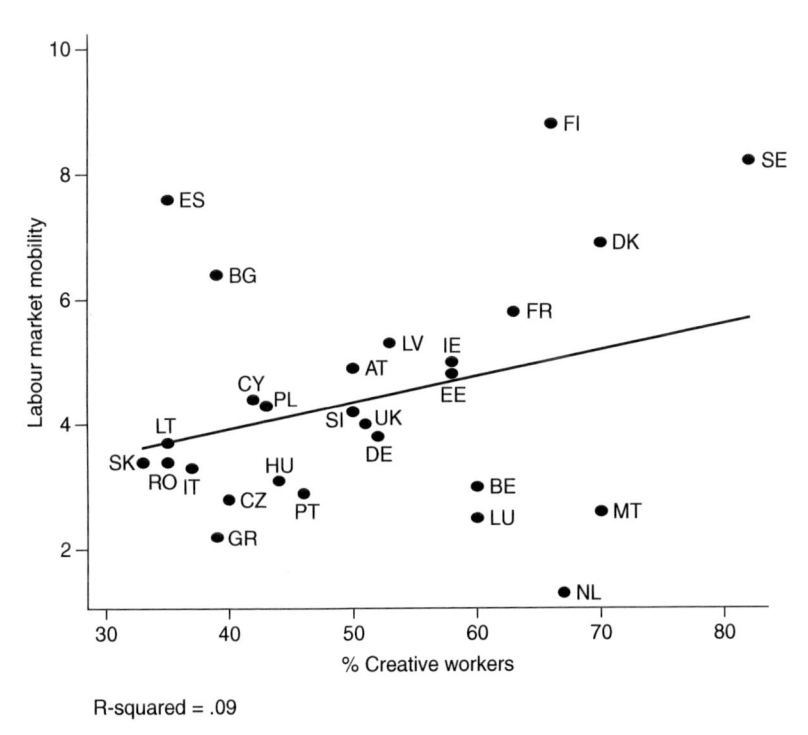

Figure 2.4 Labour market mobility by percentage of creative workers

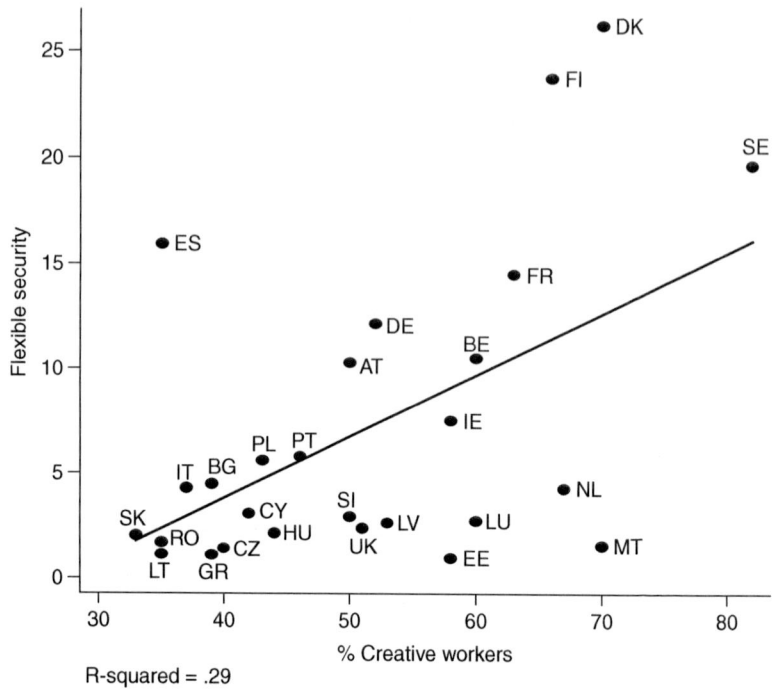

Figure 2.5 Flexible security by percentage of creative workers

innovations are more likely in settings where fluid labor markets are complemented by well developed systems of unemployment protection combined with active labor market policies.[9]

2.4 Conclusions

While the VoC approach has the merit of proposing a parsimonious theory of the relation between national institutions and innovation style, it finds little empirical support in comparisons of innovation performance across large national populations. Some authors have attempted to account for anomalous cases by arguing that firms are able to distance themselves from the constraints of domestic institutions and that they in fact enjoy much more freedom in the choice of corporate strategy than the VoC approach would allow. In this paper I support the VoC view that domestic institutions best explain differences in innovation style but take exception with the VoC account of the relational requirements for radical innovation and the institutions that best support these requirements. The idea that powerful senior management in radically innovative firms regularly imposes massive layoffs of personnel with general-purpose skills in order to develop new products or technologies is a notion that finds little support in the innovation management literature. I have argued to the contrary that radically innovative firms rely critically on the tacit knowledge of experts with industry-specific skills and this helps to explain why such firms are often grouped in localized clusters. Further, with respect to the EU-27, I present evidence which is consistent with the view that the relational requirements for radical innovation are more likely to develop in nations with well developed systems of flexible security, characterized by high levels of labor market mobility combined with generous unemployment benefit and active labor market polices.

Notes

1. The index is the one used by Hall and Soskice in their comparison of German and US patenting: a country's fraction of its total patents in a particular field is subtracted from the world's fraction of total global patents in the same field.
2. The industries include plastics, drugs, nonferrous metals, metalworking machinery, miscellaneous machinery, ships, and aircraft.
3. The measure of initial vocational education is the technical/vocational enrolment at upper-secondary level as a percentage of the total enrolment at upper-secondary level (see http://www.uis.unesco.org). The measure of labor market mobility is based on data from the Labour Force Survey on the share by country of people whose job started within the last three months. The measure is defined as the average of this share over three quarters: the second quarter of 2005 and the first and second quarters of 2006 (see *Statistics in Focus*, 'Population and Social Conditions', 6/2006, Eurostat). The reported figure of 1.7 percent for the Netherlands, the lowest for the EU-27, should be interpreted with caution. It appears to be unrealistically low when compared with figures for annual job-to-job mobility based on the European Union Statistics on Income and Living Conditions (EU-SILC) survey which covered 21 EU nations in 2005. EU-SILC results showed annual job-to-job mobility in the Netherland in 2005 as being only slightly below the EU-21 average of 8.8 percent. For an overview of the EU-SILC based results, see *Job Mobility in the European Union: optimizing its social and economic benefits*, Danish Technical Institute, April 2008.
4. The sample excludes agriculture and fishing; public administration and social security; education, health and social work; and private domestic employees.
5. The correlation is significant at the 5% level. Figures for France and the UK in Figures 2.2 and 2.3 are based on the results of CIS4 and concern innovative activities for the period 2002–2004.
6. The correlation is significant at the 1% level or better.

7. The labor market expenditure figures are taken from Eurostat's Labour Market Policy database. Total expenditures are defined as the sum of active and passive expenditures targeted at one of the following: the unemployed, the employed at risk of becoming unemployed, and inactive people who would like to enter the labor market but are disadvantaged in some way. Active measures include expenditures on training, job rotation, and job sharing, employment incentives, direct job creation, and start-up incentives. Passive measures include expenditures on out-of-work income maintenance and early retirement.
8. The correlation is significant at the 0.01 level.
9. For a more rigorous statistical demonstration of the links between work organization and systems of flexible security using multi-level econometrics, see Holm et al. (2010).

References

Akkermanns, D., Castaldi, C. and Los, B. (2009), 'Do "liberal market economies" really innovate more radically than "coordinated market economies"? Hall and Soskice reconsidered', 2009, *Research Policy*, 38, 181–191.

Arundel, A., Lorenz, E., Lundvall, B.-Å. and Valeyre, A. (2007), 'How Europe's economies learn: a comparison of work organization and innovation mode for the EU-15', *Industrial and Corporate Change*, 16 (6), 1175–1210.

Busemeyer, M. (2009), 'Asset specificity, institutional complementarities and the variety of skill regimes in coordinated market economies', *Socio-Economic Review*, 7(3), 375–430.

Florida, R. (2002), *The Rise of the Creative Class*, New York, Basic Books.

Hall, P. and Soskice, D. (2001), *Varieties of Capitalism*, Oxford, Oxford University Press.

Herrmann, A.M. (2008), 'Rethinking the link between labour market flexibility and corporate competitiveness: a critique of the institutionalist literature', *Socio-Economic Review*, 6, 637–669.

Holm, J.E., Lorenz, B-A., Lundvall, B.-Å. and Valeyre, A. (2010), 'Organisational learning and systems of labour market regulation in Europe", *Industrial and Corporate Change*, 9 (4), 1141–1173.

Lam, A. and Lundvall, B.-Å. (2006), 'The Learning Organisation and National Systems of Competence Building and Innovation', in E. Lorenz and B.-Å. Lundvall (eds) *How Europe's Economies Learn: Coordinating Competing Models*, Oxford, Oxford University Press.

Lange, K. (2009), 'Institutional embeddedness and the strategic leeway of actors: the case of the German therapeutical biotech industry', *Socio-Economic Review*, 7(2), 181–208.

Lorenz, E. and Lundvall, B.-Å. (eds) (2006), *How Europe's Economies Learn: Coordinating Competing Models*, Oxford, Oxford University Press.

Lorenz, E. and Lundvall, B.-Å. (2009), 'Measuring Creativity in the European Union', in E. Villalba (ed.) *Can Creativity be Measured*, EUR Report, DG Education and Culture.

Lundvall, B.-Å. (1992), *National Systems of Innovation: Towards a Theory of Innovation and Interactive Learning*, London, Printer.

Mintzberg, H. (1979), *The Structuring of Organizations*, Englewood Cliffs, NJ, Prentice Hall.

Nelson, R. (1993), *National Innovation Systems: A Comparative Analysis*, Oxford, Oxford University Press.

Saxenian, A. (1996), *Beyond Boundaries: Open Labor Markets and Learning in Silicon Valley*, Oxford, Oxford University Press.

Streeck, W. (1991), 'On the institutional conditions of diversified quality production', in E. Matzner and W. Streeck (eds), *Beyond Keynesianism*, Aldershot, Edward Elgar.

Streeck, W. (1992), *Social Institutions and Economic Performance: Studies of Industrial Relations in Advanced Capitalist Economies*, London, Sage Publications.

Taylor, M. (2004), 'Empirical evidence against Varieties of Capitalism's theory of technological innovation', *International Organization*, 58, 601–631.

Trajtenberg, M. (1990), 'A penny for your quotes: patent citations and the value of innovations', *The Rand Journal of Economics*, 21(1), 172–187.

Tushman, M. and Anderson, P. (1986), 'Technological discontinuities and organizational environments', *Administrative Science Quarterly*, 13(3), 439–465.

3
Organization and Innovation: The Topic of Creative Cities

Björn Johnson

3.1 Bodies of knowledge and modes of learning

In Jensen et al. (2007) we documented the existence of two different modes of learning and innovation in Danish firms. One, the DUI (doing, using, and interacting) mode, is based on informal processes of learning and experience-based know-how. The other, the STI (science, technology, and innovation) mode, is based on the production and use of codified scientific or technical knowledge. We also showed that firms which were able to combine these two modes (usually DUI firms that introduced elements of STI or STI firms that introduced elements of DUI) were more innovative than firms which relied on only one of the two modes.

There may be several explanations for this. One explanation hinges on the expansion of ICT and the acceleration of change in the globalizing learning economy. On the one hand, codified knowledge processed by information technology and sometimes taking the form of scientific information becomes increasingly important for all kinds of business – including 'low-tech' business; this requires STI competency and learning. On the other hand, this development, together with globalization, speeds up the rate of change and increases the need to learn and the speed at which new ideas must be implemented; this requires strong DUI competency and learning. Therefore firms that combine the two will be better able to both capture and develop new ideas and to implement them.

A more general explanation, not relying specifically on ICT or the acceleration of change, derives from the innovation effects of combining different bodies of knowledge in new ways. Every body of knowledge is based on certain fundamental concepts and has a particular internal structure. Every mode of learning develops rules, standard procedures, and notions of 'best practice'. This is inevitable and normally also productive. If a body of knowledge did not have an internal structure, it would be very difficult to add to it by purposeful learning, and if learning is just unintended and accidental and not, to some extent, organized and methodic, it is not very effective.

But the myopia following from the habits of thought that characterize every body of knowledge opens up new perspectives when different bodies of knowledge, like DUI and STI competencies, are made to interact and feed upon each other. This can happen without clear intentions, as when a DUI firm has to relate to codified knowledge of which it has little previous experience. But it can certainly also be encouraged by organizational change supporting mixed strategies including different bodies of knowledge.

It is important to note that mixing different types of knowledge is not always easy or even possible. They may be in contradiction with each other, and knowledge management is not like blending ingredients when baking a cake or mixing a drink. However, if the contradictions and tensions are tackled, this may in some cases open up new perspectives and options for innovation.

3.2 Organization and innovation

The creative effects of combining different bodies of knowledge can be observed in many different connections. Within the realm of STI learning it is important to notice that knowledge is not always equivalent to scientific knowledge and innovation is not only a result of R&D. It is important to recognize that technologies can be "understood as involving both a *body of practice*, manifest in the artifacts and techniques that are produced and used, and a *body of understanding*, which supports, surrounds and rationalizes the former" (Nelson, 2004). For powerful technologies like chemical and electrical engineering, biotechnology, pharmaceuticals and computer science, the supporting knowledge draws on but is not identical with science. The contribution of science to technologies is rather indirect; it provides guidelines and frameworks of understanding for what is going on in production. In large industrial firms the source of this understanding of the products and processes is the R&D laboratory – an organizational/institutional innovation from the beginning of the twentieth century, which made a combination of practice and understanding possible and led to the growth of both. Another institutionalization of the combination of the body of practice with the body of understanding was the much increased importance of university programs in old as well as new disciplines of engineering as a source of company personnel – and not only of R&D departments.

Knowledge can be 'taxonomized' in different ways and in the globalizing learning economy, as the present phase in capitalist development may be termed, such taxonomies deserve attention since they deeply influence the way we think about economic change. This, however, is not the topic of this chapter. The aim is rather to point out that almost regardless of the chosen taxonomy the combination and recombination of different types of knowledge and the tensions and contradictions these often lead to are at the heart of economic growth and development and intrinsically connected to institutional and organizational change.

A body of practice in relation to production should be thought of as including not only technical knowledge but also organizational knowledge. The body of understanding should now include 'understanding organization', that is, all kinds of organizational theory. The distinction between the bodies of practice and of understanding is somewhat less clear in the realm of organizational knowledge than in relation to process and product technology and there is no clear parallel to the R&D lab. This means that the mutual reinforcement between practice and understanding is less institutionalized. Nevertheless, 'organization' has for many years been an established discipline taught at more or less every business school in the world.

In neoclassical economics the notion of a production function, with labor, capital, and land as the main production factors, reduces firms to an input–output relation without organization. In contrast, Boulding (1981), in an early contribution to evolutionary economics, describes production in a way that brings organization and institutions to the forefront. Production, he argues, can be described as the result of three basic factors – materials, energy, and knowledge, which together transform materials into products, a transformation that requires energy, is controlled and directed by knowledge, and is organized in time and space.

Since the industrial revolution the use of energy, knowledge and materials has grown explosively and the relative importance of knowledge has been increasing in the globalizing learning economy (Lundvall, 2002). In particular, it is important to note that most of the environmental problems that accompany economic growth are connected to the use of energy and materials but the solutions hinge on the utilization and development of knowledge. It is also important to note that the organization in time and space of production gives importance to different kinds of geographical concentration of economic activities, particularly to cities. Cities have always been the locations of the main producers of knowledge and vehicles for economic growth and development. The performance of cities hinges on the organization and institutionalization of knowledge creation and utilization.

3.3 Innovative cities and the organization of knowledge

In the following I will discuss the organization of knowledge and interactive learning at the level of regional development and more specifically in the case of innovative cities.

More than 50% of the world's population lives in cities, and cities play a vital role in the social and economic development of countries. They produce almost all patents and new products and processes and in the OECD area major cities generate a third of total output (Marceau, 2008). It is clear that strong urban economies are essential for generating the resources needed for public and private investment in infrastructure, education, and health, and for improved living conditions and poverty alleviation.

Cities have long been thought of as innovative centers. Giovanni Botero (1544–1617) probably first expressed this clearly. In *The Magnificence and Greatness of Cities* (originally published in Italian in 1588, then in English in 1606), he described the importance of great cities for countries and their rulers. He suggested that neither the pleasures of living in a great city nor the necessity of the protection provided to its people explained its magnificence. What matter most, he said, are the city's diversity of industry, trades, and crafts, its interaction with surrounding agricultural districts, and the presence of a community that accepts and includes immigrants, has efficient and effective justice and education systems, and a physical location with access to good ports, which makes trade with other cities and countries possible. Only cities can provide the necessary environment for increasing incomes and power, he said.

Discussing the origins of the evolutionary alternative to mainstream thinking about economic development, Reinert (2007: 73) observed that "it was very clear to people early on that most wealth was to be found in the cities, and particularly in certain cities" and argued that Antonio Serra's 1613 observation that the larger the number of different professions present, the richer the city is still valid (Reinert, 2007: 281).

Jane Jacobs (1969) used similar arguments about the importance of diversity in trades and crafts in stimulating the innovation and economic growth of cities. Even agriculture was developed in cities, she said, since only in an area where people from different places, with different competencies and trades, met to interact were there possibilities for the new combinations that led to the transition from hunting and gathering to settled agriculture.

Peter Hall (1998) took the argument further, describing great cities in their golden ages as "innovative milieus" and "cradles of creativity" of many kinds, where artistic/cultural, technological, and organizational shifts take place and provide the intersections that can lead to new combinations. The factors that shape cultural and artistic creativity are to a large extent the same as the ones that shape technological innovation, Hall argued, and these are largely found in cities.

The reasons given for the location of innovation in cities by Botero, Serra, Jacobs, Hall, and others mostly rely on supply-side arguments. The conditions for production and growth, they say, are better in cities than in less urbanized areas because the factors of production (capital and labor) are relatively abundant, efficient, and complementary and because cities offer good infrastructure. In addition, the production structure is more diversified, which supports the development of synergies and hence the innovation activities, which make the economy robust and dynamic.

Some demand-side arguments have been added to this. These centre on the presence of a diverse population of people with not only different occupations, competencies, and social background but also with the higher wages and more sophisticated tastes that create a high and differentiated level of consumer demand. Fast consumer learning also supports the growth of demand.

In addition, when cities grow they have to constantly redesign and regenerate an urban order and especially the infrastructure of streets, water supply, sewage systems, solid waste disposal, energy, transport, and so on. The constant recreation of urban order adds a high and increasing level of public demand to the private one. In this sense, the demand side of the economy of cities harmonizes with the supply side and gives cities a higher growth potential than other places (Johnson and Meuller, 1973).

Cities in general are innovative spaces but not every city is innovative and most cities have never been noted for their innovativeness – there has to be a combination of specific factors at specific times for urban innovation to be strong. The failure of certain cities to develop and maintain growth and innovation may result from difficulties in matching technology with institutional arrangements and supply-side factors with demand-side factors.

3.3.1 Variety

The importance of variety is one of the oldest topics in the literature about creative cities. Since innovation is highly interactive and builds on the recombination of various elements of knowledge and competency, the existence of variety within a city's population and activities is a critical element of urban innovation. Variety may be seen in the population's age structure, culture, occupation, skills, competencies, and tastes, in the organization of production in terms of firm size and mode of organization, in the city's institutional variety, and in the diversity of the production and supply of public as well as private goods and services.

Variety creates the potential for innovation. Whether this potential is utilized or not depends basically on two further factors. First, it requires some kind of *proximity* between the people and organizations that have the potential to interact and recombine different kinds of knowledge, as the costs of interaction must not be too high. The relatively short physical distances and dense communication networks of well functioning cities support face-to-face as well as other types of communication, which support interactive learning and innovation.

Second, the realization of the potential provided by variety requires investment in the development of knowledge. Knowledge may be intangible but it does not recombine without costs; innovation requires expenditure on materials, equipment, testing, training, education, and associated factors. The need for investment is obvious for technical (process and product) innovation but the necessary associated organizational innovation also requires the investment of resources, not least in terms of human capital. Economically vibrant city economies provide both demand for these kinds of investment and the resources to invest. Development has been described as the mobilization of "hidden, scattered and badly utilized resources" (Hirschman, 1958); cities have often been relatively good at such mobilization and utilization, both on the supply and on the demand side.

Processes of communication, transaction, and interaction are key phenomena in city dynamics. These processes are, however, not necessarily harmonious and balanced. On the contrary, in describing the dynamics of cities, Hall (1998) uses expressions such as "structural instability," "mismatch," "lack of equilibrium," and "asynchrony." Turbulence rather than comfort is the cradle of creativity.

3.3.2 The urban order

Big congregations of people are intrinsically complex and cities are messy and disordered places. They generate problems. Large groups of people living and working in proximity put strains on natural resources and energy. Congestion puts transport systems under stress and the high costs of land mean intensive land use. While individual consumption of land and the natural environment may be relatively low, total consumption in cities is very high. Air pollution, insufficient waste treatment, and high contamination levels may engender health problems, for example. Furthermore, in cities, the redistribution of income and power between people and organizations in connection with fast growth and structural change leads to conflicts and undermines social capital. This is a general phenomenon in the globalizing learning economy, but it is accentuated in cities. Creative periods of city development are often characterized by the recognition of such long-term problems (Hall, 1998), the development of solutions for them, and an enhanced acceptance of change.

People in cities have had to be creative in developing an urban order, which is the framework for city life. Urban order is a central concept in understanding the operation of cities. A well-functioning urban order can be thought of as an arena in which problems emerge and become visible in ways, which also includes possibilities for their solution. The urban order includes the physical infrastructure but also a moral and social order backed by an institutional order composed of routines, norms, rules, and regulations. The institutional order must serve as a platform for solving, or at least alleviating, the major environmental and social problems generated by city growth if further development is to take place.

It is clear that the development and maintenance of an appropriate urban order require private and collective action, administrative and institutional innovativeness, and technological development. Innovative private and public firms, organizations, and agencies need to take regular and effective steps to solve deficiencies and problems in the existing urban order. By forming problem-solving environments, cities have been crucial engines of economic and social change.

Historically we can see that when environmental and health problems have grown to critical dimensions, radical innovations in both technology and administration have sometimes emerged in cities and contributed to urban growth and further innovation in a virtuous circle (Johnson and Hansen, 2007). Treating city waste, for example, now allows city administrators to both destroy pathogens and organic toxics and gain additional economic and other benefits. The city's problem of sludge removal has thus generated technological innovation and administrative innovation as well as new industries and resource sources. Integrating waste management with high rates of energy and materials recovery, nutrient recycling, and low negative environmental impact is also an innovative achievement led by city officials and politicians under pressure to keep towns clean and maintain the health of both citizens and environments.

3.3.3 City governance

The urban order can be regarded as an arena for problem-based interactive learning. This raises the question to what extent the governance of city innovativeness is possible. Can different modes of innovation and different bodies of competency be brought to bear productively upon each other? An increasing number of initiatives in cities around the world in the form of cooperation between urban authorities and planners, public and private companies, and universities and research organizations indicate that many urban stakeholders believe that at least some cities can develop this kind of organizing capacity (van Winden, 2008).

A rather widespread example of this is the organization of "triple helix" cooperation between knowledge institutions, firms, and public authorities (Couchman et al., 2008). This may be an important development in the governance of cities in the globalizing learning economy. It shows that policy makers and planners increasingly recognize the innovative potential of cities. At the same time it indicates the existence of the myopia that in most countries characterizes innovation policy at national level. There is a strong bias in favor of the STI mode of innovation. Triple helix cooperation is primarily seen as a way for city authorities to connect universities and other knowledge organizations to firms and strengthen science-based production. It can be argued that a broader view, which regards the city as a system of innovation and gives attention to the DUI mode and the demand side of the innovation process, would harmonize better with the view of innovation as a broadly based interactive process with many sources – a view that seems to lie behind many discussions of the creative and innovative city.

The governance of cities raises enormous challenges, not the least if their innovative potential is to be realized. Because of the complexity and density of the policy space in cities, city governance requires packages of policies and not only single-focus interventions if innovation is to be facilitated (Marceau, 2008). Another key aspect of governance is policy integration. Cities are 'served' by a host of different policy makers in different areas and on different levels. To produce coordinated packages of polices may require unattainable degrees of rationality and harmony in the policy making process. In spite of this, the question of policy integration has to be faced in order to prevent different policy makers from contradicting each other in their attempts to develop 'innovative places' and 'platforms' of policies to strengthen elements of local and regional innovation systems.

3.4 Concluding remarks

Sustainable urban development requires the intrinsic problems of urban order to be solved. It requires the efficient transport of people and goods, reliable water supply, effective land use and management, green spaces and soil protection, well functioning sewerage systems, high-quality waste management, effective energy management, and many other things. It also requires an efficient polity with effective policy makers, judiciary, arbitration, administration, and so on. There needs to be adequate social capital including, for example, forums for the participation, acceptance of responsibility, and empowerment of citizens, networks for communication and capacity building, and room for subcultures and cultural diversity.

All this calls for persistent technical, organizational, political, and institutional innovation. In particular, it should be kept in mind that solutions to the problems of urban order very often have strong institutional attributes. They may require new or reformed property rights to land, new regulations, new types of public and political attention, improved social inclusion, and new ways of thinking about sustainable development as opposed to merely the application of new technical blueprints. Conflicts and disagreements about the distribution of costs, benefits, and power in connection with public works often block the solutions and make administrative and political reform essential. It is largely a question of political will and the development of appropriate institutional capacity if the innovation potential of cities is to be realized or not.

Note

This chapter draws on Johnson, B. (2008), 'Cities, systems of innovation and economic development', *Innovation: Management, Policy & Practice*, 10(2–3), Special issue edited by Jane Marceau.

References

Botero, G. (1979), *The Magnificence and Greatness of Cities*, Amsterdam, Theatrum Orbis Terrarum.

Boulding, K. (1981), *Evolutionary Economics*, Beverly Hills, Sage Publications.
Couchman, P.K., McLoughlin, I. and Charles, R.D. (2008), 'Lost in translation? Building science and innovation city strategies in Australia and the UK', *Innovation: Management, Policy & Practice*, 10(2–3). 211–23.
Hall, P. (1998), *Cities in Civilization, Culture, Innovation, and Urban Order*, London, Phoenix Giant.
Hirschman, A. (1958), *Strategy of Economic Development*, New Haven, CT: Yale University Press.
Jacobs, J. (1969), *The economy of Cities*, New York: Vintage Books.
Jensen, M.B., Johnson, B., Lorenz, E. and Lundvall, B.-Å. (2007), 'Forms of knowledge and modes of innovation', *Research Policy*, 36. 680–93.
Johnson, B. and Hansen, J. (2007), *Systems of Innovation, the Urban Order and Sustainable Development*, Paper for the Fifth Globelics Conference, Saratov, Volga Region, Russia, September 19–23.
Johnson, B. and Meuller, A. (1973), 'Interactions of consumption and metropolitan growth', *The Swedish Journal of Economics*, 75(3), 278–288.
Lundvall, B.-Å. (2002), 'Innovation, growth and social cohesion: the Danish model', London: Edward Elgar.
Marceau, J. (2008), Introduction – 'Innovation in the city and innovative cities', *Innovation: Management, Policy & Practice*, 10(2–3).
Nelson, R.R. (2004), 'The market economy and the scientific commons', *Research Policy*, 33. 455–471.
Reinert, E. (2007), *How Rich Countries got Rich...and why Poor Countries Stay Poor*, New York: Carrol and Graf.
van Winden, W. (2008), 'Urban governance in the knowledge-based economy: challenges for different city types', *Innovation: Management, Policy & Practice*, 10(2–3). 197–210.

4
Knowledge Economy Spillovers, Proximity, and Specialization
Philip Cooke

4.1 Introduction

The complexities of where and why economic growth occurs nowadays are difficult to pin down, especially by the use of growth models that are not adequate for dealing with the exigencies of the knowledge economy. Hence the first task is to seek to show how 'knowledge economy' conventions create different and distinctive demands of people and places from the prominent – century-long and more – effects of industrialization and what came to be called the 'Industrial Age.' It is one of the surprises to many observers of the rise of globalized, web-based communication technologies that work and communities have not spread out as a result of the growth of the information society and its attendant 'footloose' locational potential for people and jobs. Rather, as globalization has proceeded, regions have become more prominent economic governance actors than they were, because many have evolved science- and technology-based (and creative) clusters requiring elements of localized policy support.

Thus in a knowledge economy, greater economic force exists than hitherto in innovation deriving from creative, scientific, and technological knowledge, often generated in university rather than corporate laboratories. It is thus important to understand, for economic purposes, the varieties of knowledge-based clustering – most notably in ICT, biotechnology, and newer fields even more focused on addressing climate change, like 'cleantech' – to pin down the rationale behind it (Burtis et al., 2004). There are very strong indications for biotechnology worldwide that clusters in geographical proximity to university labs, rather than large firms' intra-mural R&D, are the source of knowledge-based growth. In ICT there are cases of comparable lab-focused location for

R&D but also of location near customers and suppliers, or even airports (so-called Marshallian 'localization' externalities), for more routine interactions. Of central importance in the analysis of this kind of clustering compared with say, the remarkably successful clustering that generates so many employment opportunities in traditional Italian luxury design industries or those that pioneered textile manufacturing in the Great Britain of Alfred Marshall (1916) is the role of innovation and the science and research base.

Reinforcing proximity are opportunities to gain from 'knowledge spillovers' from the talent available, the novelty and quality of the 'research industry' in specific knowledge 'hotspots,' and the opportunities for 'open science' and even 'open innovation' (Chesbrough, 2003). These are often found in proximity in the form of clusters, many warranting a post-cluster 'megacenter' or 'platform' designation since they contain 'related variety' sub-clusters that may have high *lateral* absorptive capacity, major public or non-profit facilities like universities, hospitals, research laboratories, and government research institutes as anchors as well as firms, the more common element in business clusters according to Porter (1998). Within them are numerous intermediaries that are masters of many kinds of knowledge, from exploration to exploitation (March, 1991); analytic, synthetic and symbolic knowledge categories distinguish science, engineering and creative production; and at the cognitive level, tacit, codified and – as proposed elsewhere – something that frequently *mediates* between them, which we term 'complicit' knowledge (Cooke, 2005). In what follows we examine national and regional R&D and S&T specialization. This is followed by a section on the theoretical implications for contemporary regional specialization and 'related variety.'

4.2 Evidence of EU S&T specialization at national level

A region's or country's level of specialization in a given field of science or technology is measured by comparing the world share of the region/country in the particular field to the world share of the region/country for all fields combined (we refer to the 'share of scientific publications' for scientific specialization patterns, and to the 'share of patents' for technological specialization). The EU's scientific and technological output appears to be more diversified than that of the United States. Although this is a potentially rich resource in the medium and long term, additional efforts are required to ensure that activities are not too fragmented.

102 *Philip Cooke*

	BE	CZ	DK	DE	EE	EL	ES	FR	IE	IT	CY	LV	LT	LU	HU	MT	NL	AT	PL	PT	SI	SK	FI	SE	UK
Agriculture and food science																									
Basic life sciences																									
Biological sciences																									
Biomedical sciences and pharmacology																									
Clinical medicine and health sciences																									
Earth and environmental sciences																									
Chemistry																									
Engineering sciences																									
Mathematics and statistics																									
Physics and astronomy																									
Computer sciences																									

■ under specialised   ■ specialised   □ no specialistion

Figure 4.1 EU S&T specialization, 2005

The EU countries show diversity with regard to their scientific capabilities. Among the most active publishing EU countries, Germany is strong in physics and astronomy but is less involved in agriculture and food science; the UK is not highly specialized in any field according to the statistics presented in Figure 4.1 and is relatively under-specialized in chemistry, engineering sciences, and mathematics and statistics; France is specialized in mathematics and statistics as well as in physics and astronomy but is weak in agriculture and food science; finally, Italy shows under-specialization in agriculture and food science and in the biological sciences. With regard to the smaller (in terms of publications) EU countries such as Portugal and Slovakia, concerns may arise about the scope of their scientific efforts given the constraints imposed by their limited financial and human resources.

4.3 Regional specialization in the EU

In Figure 4.2 we see the EU structured according to its S&T 'meta-regions', normalized in relation to regional GDP. Methodologically the map is derived from factor and cluster analyses of numerous S&T indicators drawn from Eurostat databases. Examples of the indicators selected are shown in Figure 4.2 but others include Tertiary Education, Business R&D, and Share of Innovation Strategies. Of especial interest are, first, the presence of islands of relatively high-performing regions in the accession countries. While these generally form an S&T meta-region of high tertiary education but low GDP, the Prague, Budapest, and Gyor regions score relatively high on both. Second, the Nordic countries (Finland data not available) are the highest performing meta-region,

Regional innovation hierarchy

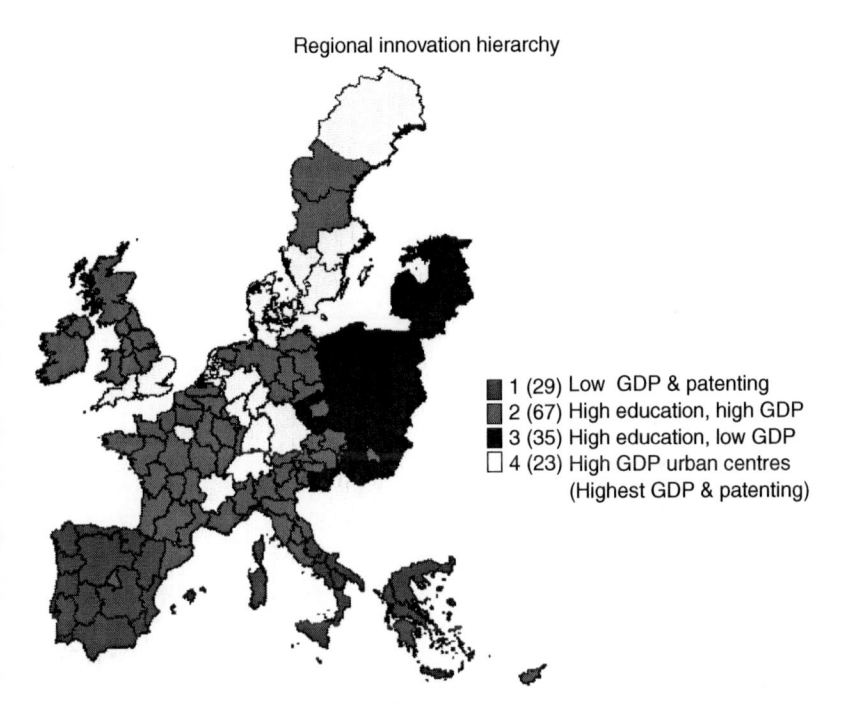

- 1 (29) Low GDP & patenting
- 2 (67) High education, high GDP
- 3 (35) High education, low GDP
- 4 (23) High GDP urban centres (Highest GDP & patenting)

Figure 4.2 EU regional S&T over GDP variations
Source: From Versapgen, 2007.

especially the peripheral regions of Sweden, where a 'knowledgeable cities' factor is the most likely explanation. Finally, Southern Europe performs weakly on these S&T indicators.

Verspagen (2007) presents a macro-sectoral manufacturing breakdown of S&T indicators using categories such as High-technology Specialized, Specialized Biochemistry, Higher and Lower Order Functions, and Absence of Patenting Activity. This analysis produces some counter-intuitive results. First Greece (and Cyprus) are not normally considered high-technology specialized countries. This can be explained partly methodologically where, amongst the S&T industry sectors analyzed in Verspagen (2007), the high-tech ones are more pronounced than any others. However, this does not mean Greece is a high-tech economy, rather the reverse. Regions specialized in biochemical S&T are less counter-intuitive (e.g. Northern England, western Norway, and the Rhine valley). Also 'no patents' occur, predictably, in a few rural, Eastern European regions.

4.4 Lineaments of proximity in the knowledge economy

In recent years, a focus on sub-national (regional) analysis has emerged as there has been a spotlight upon science-based clusters, interactive innovation, and creative, tolerant, and talented concentrations of politically desirable economic growth. This is associated with a corresponding eclipse of the notions of *ubiquity* (Maskell et al., 1998) as a condition of digital connectivity and the *death of distance* (Cairncross, 1997) as its main effect, in favor of the idea of *proximity* as a powerful economic force. In well rooted research on Italy's *industrial districts* – including traditional industries – one senses a revitalized recognition and analysis of social capital, trust, interactivity, and the notion of economic *community* as key contributors to continued small firm economic buoyancy (Becattini, 2001). Indeed, such is the dynamism of these globalizing agglomerations that many now host in their interstices communities within communities, as thousands of Chinese entrepreneurs and workers alongside fewer, but still numerous, Islamics migrated into cities like Carpi, near Bologna, and Prato, near Florence, in the early 2000s (Becattini and Dei Ottati, 2006). Foremost are agglomerative opportunities for tacit, complicit, codified, face-to-face, and tactile contact, knowledge exchange, and of course business. Such socio-economic 'communities of practice' are also the *ne plus ultra* of, especially, modern science-based economic development (Brown and Duguid, 2001).

Thus the death of distance and the end of geography were rumors much exaggerated upon the advent of innovative, knowledge-based clusters (Morgan, 2004). However, interestingly, *proximity* – which includes nearness, closeness, contiguity, and propinquity, all with traditionally geographical connotations – has evolved other, geographically unconfined meanings, involving nearness in context, domain, and even opinion. Thus digital chat-rooms are neighborly places in virtual space. A multinational company displays characteristics of organizational proximity in all its global operations because of its common rules, conventions, and resources, from job titles to the commonalities of its intranet. Zeller (2004), in an interesting article tracing the dependence of Swiss 'big pharma' on innovative biotechnology clusters elsewhere, lists, as well as geographical proximity, the following 'virtual' proximities: institutional (e.g. national laws); cultural (e.g. communities of practice); relational (e.g. social capital); technological (e.g. Linux software users); virtual (e.g. a multinational); internal and external (e.g. firm supply chain management). Actually few feature prominently in other empirical analyses and those that do are usually less important in explaining locational behavior these days than the core idea of *geographical* proximity. Thus pharmaceutical firms open R&D 'listening posts' or acquire incumbent firms capable of quarrying American biotechnology clusters. This is a strategy aimed at re-balancing the knowledge asymmetries that have arisen as university centers of excellence and DBFs have outperformed 'big pharma,' resulting in some re-establishing domestic R&D headquarters abroad, in the San Diego and Cambridge, Massachusetts biotechnology 'megacenters' (Cooke, 2005). Nevertheless, the contemporary elaboration of the notion of proximity is no longer restricted to expressly spatial 'nearness in place'. Zeller (2004) performed a useful service in this sense.[1]

Nevertheless, it is hard to escape the conclusion that much contemporary knowledge economy development is increasingly city-focused. There is little yet that engages rurality with innovative clustering, though the rise of 'cleantech' such as biofuels is beginning to change that (Cooke, 2008). The city and, even more so, metropolitan context has traditionally been the most powerful spatial determinant of growth, by and large. Now, in the knowledge economy, its force is geared up, reinforcing geographical proximity as a vehicle for achieving economic success worldwide. While the prediction of the 'death of distance' was wrong, especially in its presumption of global 'flattening,' 'knowledge economies' do exist and evolve as nodes in global knowledge connected by globally networked information flows. This rests on the observation that globalization proceeds through varieties of networks linking nodes of economic power – mainly cities, their knowledge institutions, governance mechanisms, and firms. What believers in the economist's 'spaceless playground' misunderstood until Krugman (1995) was that such nodes would be the result of increasing returns to urban agglomeration (Sternberg and Litzenberger, 2004).

By and large this has meant increasing returns derived from varieties of *spillover*, especially knowledge spillovers, which tend to concentrate in cities and in other 'knowledgeable cities' such as university or research towns. This is true for North American, Asian, and European cities, for which the required analysis has been performed. Clearly, such an array of city settings means that the growth process is by no means identical in all cases. Moreover, increased competitiveness of cities often accompanies social polarization. However, this is also a by-product of growth in the sense that immigrants are attracted because of perceived economic opportunities absent in their location of origin.

4.5 Spillovers, innovation and growth

An emergent pattern in the contemporary variety of proximities is that proximity to knowledge spillovers is nowadays crucial to city growth from the exploitation through innovation of research knowledge. This harks back to the initial contention of Glaeser et al. (1992) that human capital and scarce skills are significant factors in a city's capability to maintain or augment its economic growth. This is thus something of a progenitor of Florida's (2002) talent-led analysis of US city growth in the contemporary era. However, much of the finer detail of variations within growth trajectories is lost in these analyses, not least because of definitional, and even unit of data analysis complexities. One interesting differentiation – first hypothesized from a *static* analysis of major concentrations of knowledge economy sectoral activities derived from EU and other city- and regional-level data on high-technology manufacturing and knowledge-intensive business services (KIBS) – was that major cities, sometimes also capital cities, acquired much of the KIBS employment. Contrariwise, more specialized, satellite cities concentrated high-technology manufacturing employment to a greater extent. Current instances of this modern urbanization process include, in the US, Cambridge and numerous high-tech satellites of Boston, such as Waltham, Worcester, Woburn, and Andover; San Francisco *vis-à-vis* many such places in Silicon Valley, London in relation to Cambridge, Oxford and the Thames Valley; Stockholm and Uppsala; Helsinki and Espoo; and Copenhagen in cross-border relationship to Lund, the so-called Medicon Valley, traversed by the Øresund bridge. These 'cumulative causation' and 'spatial backwash' effects were predicted long ago by Myrdal (1957) and Hirschman (1958).

This suggests that in countries where the main financial centre is not the capital city the former will exert the stronger proximity effect but that where, as in the UK and Austria, the capital is also the leading financial services centre, a strong spatial monopoly (or more accurately quasi-monopoly) proximity effect is exerted (Cooke et al., 2007). This is the classic result modeled by Krugman (1995) in applying increasing returns to scale theory, under conditions of imperfect knowledge, to two hypothetically competing candidate cities with the consequence that one always ended up monopolizing space. Contemporary city growth theory places knowledge spillovers from (geographical) proximity at the forefront of the explanation for these observed tendencies.

To repeat, this is not to say that geographical proximity determines economic activity to an overwhelming degree. If anything, the implication of what has been concluded here is that the defining feature of knowledge spillovers from geographical proximity is qualitative and quantitative in equal measure. That is to say that a firm located in proximity to multiple and varied sources of high-grade intelligence, creativity, and connectivity is in principle at an advantage over a competitor that is not. However, connectivity to other appropriate knowledge nodes elsewhere in the relevant global knowledge networks is likely to be quantitatively less intensive, albeit qualitatively equivalent or even superior. In their discussion of precisely this relationship between geographical and virtual proximity, Owen-Smith and Powell (2004) argued for the superiority of geographical proximity along the following lines. Key processes by which dynamic proximity capabilities are expressed interactively in research or *exploration knowledge* transfer and commercialization or *exploitation knowledge* transfer include the following:

- There is a difference between 'channels' (open) and 'pipelines' (closed). The former offer more opportunity for knowledge capability enhancement since they are more 'leaky' and 'irrigate' more geographically proximately. Pipelines offer more confidential, contractual means of proprietary knowledge transfer, which may occur locally or over great geographical distances. These are less 'leaky' because they are closed rather than open.
- In high-tech fields, research centers may be a magnet for firms because they operate an 'open science' policy, promising spillover innovation opportunities. These are possible sources of productivity improvement, greater firm competitiveness, and, accordingly, localized economic growth.
- Such open science conventions influence inter-firm innovation network interactions. Although researchers may not remain the main intermediaries for long as successful firms grow through patenting and commercialization, they experience greater gains through the combination of proximity and conventions than through either proximity alone or conventions alone.

These propositions each receive strong support from statistical analyses of research and patenting practices in the Boston regional biotechnology cluster. Thus:

> Transparent modes of information transfer will trump more opaque or sealed mechanisms when a significant proportion of participants exhibit limited concern with policing the accessibility of network

pipelines [...] closed conduits offer reliable and excludable information transfer at the cost of fixity, and thus are more appropriate to a stable environment. In contrast, permeable channels rich in spillovers are responsive and may be more suitable for variable environments. In a stable world, or one where change is largely incremental, such channels represent excess capacity. (Owen-Smith and Powell, 2004)

Finally, though, leaky channels rather than closed pipelines also represent an opportunity for unscrupulous convention-breakers to sow misinformation among competitors. However, the strength of the 'open science' convention means that so long as research institutes remain a presence, as in science-driven contexts they often do, such 'negative social capital' practices are punishable by exclusion from interaction, reputational degrading, or even, at the extreme, convention shift, in rare occurrences, toward more confidentiality agreements and spillover-limiting 'pipeline' legal contracts. We noted in the introduction how open science conventions attract, in further evolutionary rounds, 'open innovation' when it might otherwise be assumed that openness should mean knowledge advantage erosion. But likely gains are perceived to outweigh losses by customers taking the plunge. This is a major factor in proximity-based economic growth since knowledge supplier firms garner a substantial share of their income from, especially, R&D outsourcing by larger customer firms.

4.6 Conclusions

With respect to other sectors, perhaps less work has been conducted than in the economics of biosciences, although 'open innovation' and varieties of 'outsourcing' research seldom focus on biotechnology as such. ICT, aerospace, even 'consumer products', as studied by Chesbrough (2003), point to the knowledge quest having brought major reductions in corporate intra-mural R&D. There is, of course, a large question over the validity, reliability, and even meaning of such an antediluvian notion as 'sector.' Here is unfortunately not the place to delve into the lethal critique of the notion due to space limitations. However, three criticisms can briefly be offered. First, the sector notion is a statistician's artifact and an increasingly misleading representation of reality. Second, sector classifications are little changed since their nineteenth-century origins to enable identification of such activities as biotechnology, nanotechnology, or 'cleantech.'

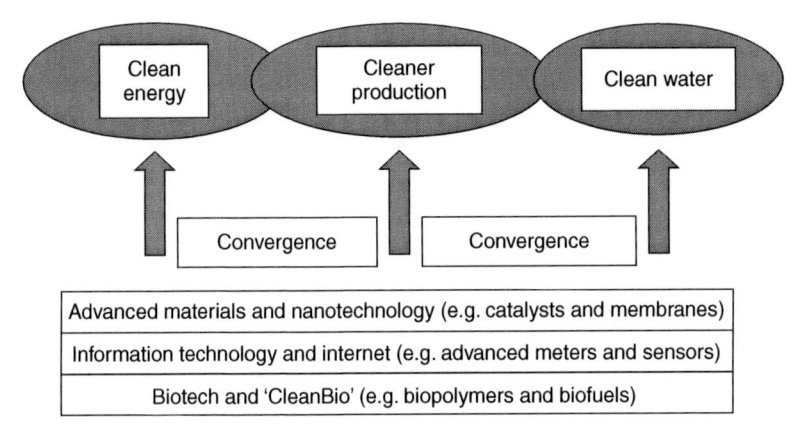

```
┌─────────────┐   ┌─────────────┐   ┌─────────────┐
│    Clean    │   │   Cleaner   │   │ Clean water │
│   energy    │   │  production │   │             │
└─────────────┘   └─────────────┘   └─────────────┘
       ▲                ▲                 ▲
       │   Convergence  │   Convergence   │
       └────────────────┴─────────────────┘
```

| Advanced materials and nanotechnology (e.g. catalysts and membranes) |
| Information technology and internet (e.g. advanced meters and sensors) |
| Biotech and 'CleanBio' (e.g. biopolymers and biofuels) |

Figure 4.3 Technology convergence in cleantech
Source: Own elaboration.

Third, as we have seen, technological innovation increasingly progresses by means of the evolution of 'platforms' that take spillover advantages, combine many technologies that are, in increasing numbers of cases, adaptable across first, related variety, later even more diverse industrial and technological applications, as a moment's reflection upon the technology platform built around 'cleantech' (Figure 4.3), let alone software or genetics, makes clear.

Note

1. A further theoretical analysis of the relations between innovation capability and varieties of proximity is presented in Boschma, R. (2005) 'Proximity and innovation: a critical assessment', *Regional Studies*, 39, 61–74.

References

Akerlof, G. (1970), 'The market for "lemons": quality uncertainty and the market mechanism, *Quarterly Journal of Economics*, 84, 488–500.
Becattini, G. (2001), *The Caterpillar & the Butterfly*, Florence, Felice de Monnier.
Becattini, G. and Dei Ottati, G. (2006), 'The performance of Italian industrial districts and large enterprise areas in the 1990s', *European Planning Studies*, 14, 1139–1162.
Boschma, R. (2005), 'Proximity and innovation: a critical assessment', *Regional Studies*, 39, 61–74.
Boschma, R. and Frenken, K. (2003), 'Evolutionary economics and industry location', *Review of Regional Research*, 23, 183–200.

Brown, J. and Duguid, P. (2001), *The Social Life of Information*, Boston, Harvard Business School Books.

Burtis, P., Epstein, R. and Hwang, R. (2004), *Creating the California Cleantech Cluster*, San Francisco, Natural Resources Defense Association.

Cairncross, F. (1997), *The Death of Distance: How the Communications Revolution Will Change Our Lives*, Boston, Harvard Business School Press.

Chesbrough, H. (2003), *Open Innovation*, Boston, Harvard Business School Books.

Cooke, P. (2005), 'Regionally asymmetric knowledge capabilities and open innovation: exploring "Globalisation 2" – a new model of industry organisation', *Research Policy*, 34, 1128–1149.

Cooke, P. (2007), *Growth Cultures*, London, Routledge.

Cooke, P. (2008), 'An analysis of the platform nature of life sciences: further reflections upon platform policies and "Cleantech"', *European Planning Studies*, 16, 375–393.

Cooke, P., De Laurentis, C., Tödtling, F. and Trippl, M. (2007), *Regional Knowledge Economies*, Cheltenham, Edward Elgar.

Florida, R. (2002), *The Rise of the Creative Class*, New York, Basic Books.

Glaeser, E., Kallall, H., Scheinkman, J. and Shleifer, A. (1992), 'Growth in cities', *Journal of Political Economy*, 100, 1126–1152.

Harrison, B. (1994), *Lean & Mean: the Changing Face of Corporate Power in the Age of Flexibility*, New York, Basic Books.

Helpman, E. (ed.) (1998), *General Purpose Technologies and Economic Growth*, Cambridge, MIT Press.

Hinoul, M. (2005), *A Mutual Learning Platform for the Regions*, Brussels, Committee of the Regions.

Hirschman, A. (1958), *The Strategy of Economic Development*, New Haven, Yale University Press.

Hodgson, G. (1993), *Economics & Evolution; Bringing Life Back Into Economics*, Cambridge, Polity.

Jacobs, J. (1969), *The Economy of Cities*, New York, Random House.

Krugman, P. (1995), *Development, Geography & Economic Theory*, Cambridge, MIT Press.

March, J. (1991), 'Exploration and exploitation in organisational learning', *Organization Science*, 2, 71–87.

Marshall, A. (1916), *Industry & Trade*, London, Macmillan.

Maskell, P., Eskelinen, H., Hannibalsson, I., Malmberg, A. and Vatne, E. (1998), *Competitiveness, Localised Learning & Regional Development: Specialisation & Prosperity in Small, open Economies*, London, Routledge.

Morgan, K. (2004), 'The exaggerated death of geography', *Journal of Economic Geography*, 4, 3–21.

Myrdal, G. (1957), *Economic Theory & Underdeveloped Regions*, London, Duckworth.

Owen-Smith, J. and Powell, W. (2004), 'Knowledge networks as channels and conduits: the effects of spillovers in the Boston biotechnology community', *Organization Science*, 15, 5–21.

Porter, M. (1998), *On Competition*, Boston, Harvard Business School Press.

Sternberg, R. and Litzenberger, T. (2004), 'Regional clusters in Germany – their geography and relevance for entrepreneurial activities', *European Planning Studies*, 12, 767–791.

Uglow, J. (2003), *The Lunar Men: The Friends Who Made the Future*, London, Faber & Faber.

Verspagen, B. (2007), Regional Innovation Clusters in the EU, Presentation to DIME Workshop 'Next Generation Regional Innovation Systems', Staur, Norway, September 30–1 October.

Zeller, C. (2004), 'North Atlantic innovative relations of Swiss pharmaceuticals and the proximities with regional biotech areas', *Economic Geography*, 80, 83–111.

Zucker, L., Darby, M. and Armstrong, J. (1998), 'Geographically localised knowledge: spillovers or markets?', *Economic Inquiry*, 36, 65–86.

Part II
Clusters, Firms and Innovation Systems

5
Combined and Complex Mode of Innovation in Regional Cluster Development: Analysis of the Light-Weight Material Cluster in Raufoss, Norway

Arne Isaksen and James Karlsen

5.1 Introduction

This chapter introduces the concept of combined and complex innovation (CCI). The concept intends to describe complex innovation processes in regional clusters, where different kinds of knowledge are combined in innovation activities. The combination occurs inside firms and in collaboration between firms and knowledge organizations found in and beyond the regional cluster. The conceptualization of the CCI mode builds on main arguments in the regional innovation system (RIS) literature, which underline that complex innovation processes most often include collaboration among many different actors (such as different kinds of firm and research organization) in order to solve technological, organizational, and other challenges. Different kinds of knowledge are used and combined in innovation processes, and collaboration and knowledge flow are stimulated by geographical and other types of proximity (Boschma, 2005). The combination of the different types of knowledge is, thus, a complex process as it includes actors in different firms and organizations, who need to develop cognitive proximity.

The CCI concept also builds on the theoretical framework of knowledge bases (Asheim and Gertler, 2005; Asheim et al., 2007; Gertler, 2008). The knowledge base approach distinguishes between analytical, synthetic and symbolic knowledge and this chapter focuses on the first two of these. Analytical knowledge includes scientific knowledge and models in the form of 'know-why' (Lundvall and Johnson, 1994). The knowledge creation process results in codified knowledge, for example as articles in scientific journals and as patents. Synthetic knowledge is experience- and context-based knowledge resulting in tacit knowing (Polanyi, 1966) and shared 'know-how' among workers in the same firm and region.

The innovation literature distinguishes between the STI (science, technology, innovation) and DUI (doing, using, interacting) modes of innovation (Coenen and Asheim, 2006; Lorenz and Lundvall, 2006; Jensen et al., 2007). The STI mode uses mainly analytical knowledge and scientific learning processes based on the formulation of abstract models, testing and documentation, which typifies some knowledge-creating activities in, for example, the biotechnology industry (Moodysson, 2007). The model is particularly useful for analyzing science and technology push or supply-driven innovation processes, which may result in radical innovations. The STI mode describes a narrower mode of innovation than the DUI mode of innovation with regard to the range of potential knowledge sources. The STI mode is thus linked to the narrow definition of innovation systems (cf. Lundvall, 2007). The DUI mode of innovation is mainly based on a synthetic knowledge base and on learning by interacting between companies in the value chain, for example between a company and its specialized subcontractors and/or a company and its customers. It is a more demand-driven innovation model than STI, and is particularly useful in analyzing incremental innovations in industries such as mechanical engineering.

Jensen et al. (2007) argue, based on data from two surveys containing answers from about 2 000 and 1 650 Danish firms, that firms combining the STI and the DUI modes of innovation are more innovative than firms that rely on either one of them alone.[1] STI and DUI represent two ideal type modes of learning and innovation "that appear in a much more mixed form in real life" (Jensen et al., 2007: 682). We refer to CCI as a third ideal type mode of learning and innovation that combines elements from the STI and DUI modes. The CCI mode also emphasizes how firms may use knowledge found in the regional innovation system and, thus, add a new element to the innovation mode concept.

The CCI mode of innovation is developed and tested through a case study in the Raufoss regional cluster of 50–60 firms in eastern Norway. It is one of the areas in Norway with the highest share of manufacturing jobs, with about 4000 employees. The core of the manufacturing industry in Raufoss is five large firms producing mainly components in aluminium and other light-weight materials for the global automotive and military industry (Johnstad, 2004; Onsager et al., 2007).

The chapter has two theoretical, one empirical and one more general research question:

1. What are the main characteristics of the CCI mode of innovation? What differentiates the CCI mode of innovation from the STI and the DUI modes?
2. How are innovation processes and knowledge-creating activities taking place in the light-weight material cluster in Raufoss?
3. What are the main theoretical lessons from the study of innovation modes in the Raufoss case?

The remainder of the chapter includes four main sections. The next section describes the main elements of the CCI, STI and DUI modes of innovation and compares these. Section 5.3 presents the context and methods used in the empirical study. Then follow analyses of innovation and knowledge-creating processes in the Raufoss light-weight material cluster. The last section sums up the analyses and discusses the more general lessons of the chapter.

5.2 The theoretical framework of the CCI mode of innovation

The concepts of knowledge bases and innovation modes contribute to new perspectives of ways to achieve competitiveness for companies, regions, and nations. Companies in high-cost locations, in particular, have to base their competitiveness on innovation. The OECD has pointed to R&D-intensive industries that are dominated by analytical knowledge and the STI mode as the most innovative ones. The favoring of R&D-intensive industries is seen, for example, in the indicators in OECD's Science, Technology and Industry Scoreboard (OECD, 2007a). The results of such indicators have also led the OECD to formulate the 'Norwegian puzzle' (2007b: 50). The puzzle seen from the perspective of the OECD is that Norwegian industry is profitable and competitive and has high productivity, even if Norway reveals a low score on most of the OECD's indicators of innovation, such as R&D intensity, number of patents, share of high-tech jobs, and innovation rate.

The 'Norwegian puzzle,' however, can be interpreted in the light of a broader and more comprehensive view of innovation (see

Asheim, 2007; Lundvall, 2007). This view emphasizes that knowledge creation and innovation can be based not only on analytical (science) knowledge-based activities but also on synthetic (engineering) and symbolic (artistic) knowledge bases. This implies that the DUI and the CCI modes of innovation promote competitiveness, and not only the 'pure' STI mode.

The conceptualization of the CCI mode of innovation is based on the typologies of analytical and synthetic knowledge. As theoretical constructs, the individual knowledge bases and innovation modes will not necessarily be found in pure forms in particular industries. Specific industries can be dominated by one of the knowledge bases and modes of innovation or they can both be of critical importance for innovation processes in particular industries.

Knowledge bases and modes of innovation are distinguished by the fact that the latter are knowing in practice (Ibert, 2007). Knowledge is then seen to be embedded in practice, which stresses the collective nature of knowing. Knowledge on the other hand is an object that exists on its own, and the concept of knowledge "gears the attention towards the socially constructed character and contextually embedded status of our knowledge" (Ibert, 2007: 106). Knowing in practice and modes of innovation denote processes, such as knowledge-creating and learning processes, where the outcomes can be innovations, such as new products, but also new routines and new knowledge. The knowledge base refers to vital knowledge that is a necessary input in an innovation process; that is, the knowledge that a firm cannot do without in order to carry out innovative activities. Thus, the knowledge base concept does not refer to all the knowledge that firms and industries need and employ in their production and innovation activities, but to the crucial knowledge input in innovation activities.

Seen as an ideal type, analytical knowledge is theoretical, codified knowledge about natural systems (Asheim and Gertler, 2005; Asheim et al., 2007; Gertler, 2008). Examples are scientific knowledge in physics and chemistry, which is vital in, for example, the production of drugs by the biotechnology industry. Analytical knowledge is abstract and universal, and rather independent of context. The meaning of the knowledge is then relatively constant between different places.

Synthetic knowledge is created in a different way. It is mainly generated from concrete problem solving in real-life situations in companies and/or in collaboration between companies. The knowledge is context-dependent knowledge; it is relevant in specific situations, industries, clusters, and regions. The concrete content of the knowledge can therefore vary somewhat from place to place. Much of the knowledge exists as shared knowing among persons who have the same kind of experience and have worked together for a long time in an organization or lived in the same locality. Some of the knowledge is shared through the use of words, as in story telling, and some of the knowledge is codified, as in routine descriptions. Other parts of the knowledge exist only as tacit knowing; that is, as knowledge that can only be identified in action, and that is difficult to formulate in words (Polanyi, 1966).

Table 5.1 reveals some differences between the STI and the DUI modes of innovation. The STI mode is characterized by the use of R&D-based knowledge and scientific methods. We will stress, however, that the STI mode is not limited to an analytical knowledge base, but can also include synthetic (and symbolic) knowledge bases (Asheim et al., 2010). The synthetic knowledge base includes applied research, which is seen as part of the STI mode. Applied research builds on basic research at, for example, university departments that create new analytical knowledge, but applied research operates on the basis of synthetic (engineering) knowledge (Asheim et al., 2011). The STI innovation process is defined and designed as a research and development process and often characterized by a technology push resulting in radical innovations.

Table 5.1 Characteristics of the STI and the DUI modes of innovation

	STI	DUI
Knowledge bases	R&D, basic or applied (analytical and synthetic) knowledge	Experience-based (synthetic) knowledge
Main type of knowledge base developed from	Research and development projects	Daily problem solving
Main method used in the process	Scientific and research methods	Methods generated from trial-and-error processes
Main external innovation partners	Universities and research institutes	Customers and suppliers, centers of real services, cf. Third Italia (consulting and training organizations, etc.)
Possible types of innovation	Technology push/ supply-driven innovation, i.e. radical innovation	Market/demand-driven innovation, i.e. incremental innovation

The most important external innovation partners of companies performing the STI mode are researchers from universities and/or research organizations.

The DUI mode is based on synthetic knowledge in the form of employees' experience-based knowledge. The knowledge is often generated from trial-and-error processes in companies and knowledge organizations. The main external knowledge sources of companies with the DUI innovation mode are customers and suppliers, which means that innovations often result from market pull and include incremental changes to satisfy individual customers. Direct collaboration with universities is less important, but the recruitment of skilled people and collaboration with applied research organizations, such as centers of real services that tailor their services to the needs of specific regional industries, may be important.

Jensen et al. (2007) maintain that firms combining the STI and DUI modes of innovation are more innovative than firms relying primarily on one of the modes. In one sense this seems obvious. Firms that build intensively on the STI mode, by relying on codified scientific and technical knowledge and collaboration with knowledge organizations, may benefit from paying more attention to the DUI mode, by drawing more on experience-based learning and ideas from customers, and vice versa. Jensen et al. (2007) do not show how firms can mix the two modes of innovation. Use of the STI mode of innovation requires a different kind of absorptive capacity in firms than use of the DUI mode. Companies making use of the STI mode need highly educated employees who are able to collaborate with researchers at universities, while the DUI mode requires experienced, skilled workers who can adapt solutions to the needs of important customers in user–producer relationships.

We approach the conceptualization of the CCI mode of innovation by drawing on main arguments in the RIS literature and building on the knowledge base approach. An RIS consists of the two subsystems of industry and the knowledge infrastructure. Knowledge flow between actors in the two subsystems (such as between firms and universities) is stimulated by policy tools and informal institutions. RISs also include extra-regional knowledge institutions, value chains, and so on (see Coenen, 2006). This strand of research argues that firms innovate by use of their internal competence, but that firms also draw on knowledge and resources in the external environment – that is, they combine different kinds of in-house and external knowledge. Although links to global value chains and distributed knowledge networks are important, resources in the local environment may, in particular, stimulate and hamper firms' innovation activity. Important local resources are the extent of related variety and knowledge spillovers in the regional industry (Frenken et al., 2007), and the extent of knowledge flow between firms and the regional knowledge infrastructure. How can firms employ external, primarily regional, knowledge?

One answer is that companies can strategically combine different kinds of knowledge in the RIS with knowledge inside the companies. The core of the CCI mode of innovation is in fact the complex combination and organization of different kinds of knowledge. The knowledge is based both on experiences from innovation projects including trial and error, as in the DUI mode of innovation, and on research-based knowledge. Such combination of knowledge requires high absorptive capacity (Cohen and Levinthal, 1990) and dynamic capability in the companies.

An important element in the CCI mode is that innovation processes include the development of the technological platform and the core competency of the company. This demands some R&D-based knowledge since this development typically takes place as an applied research project in collaboration with external R&D organizations. It includes developing the technologies and core competency to be used when developing specific products, services, and solutions for individual customers or markets. This type of technology development differs from the STI mode of innovation by being more occupied with developing and improving specific technological platforms and core competencies, while the STI mode is more geared towards the commercialization of basic research. It differs from the 'pure' DUI mode in its occupation with developing general knowledge and technology and collaborating with external knowledge organizations. The CCI mode demands both applied R&D competence and experience-based knowledge about specific products and production processes, and about the needs of specific customers and market niches (Table 5.2). The development of technological platforms and core competencies will often result

Table 5.2 Characteristics of different modes of innovation

		Experience-based knowledge	
		Yes	No
R&D-based knowledge	Yes	CCI	STI
	No	DUI	X (no innovation)

in organizational changes in a company, such as in the production process and the management of the process. Incremental innovation development will usually not result in organizational changes, while radical innovations will often result in new kinds of organization and organizational pattern.

The following analysis of the dominant mode of innovation in the Raufoss light-weight metal cluster identifies the main knowledge bases (R&D-based and experience-based) in the companies and the cluster, registers the type of innovation activity in the companies, and distinguishes the main actors and knowledge flow in the regional cluster and beyond. We particularly examine whether individual actors have different roles in developing and diffusing knowledge in the cluster.

5.3 Empirical context, method and data

5.3.1 The Raufoss cluster

The empirical setting for the study presented in this chapter is the light-weight material cluster at Raufoss. The cluster consists of about 50 companies and 4000 employees. Several of the core companies are suppliers to the global automotive industry. The cluster is world-leading in automated manufacturing technology and materials technology, especially regarding aluminum and composites (Johnstad, 2007). The cluster was appointed as one of six Norwegian Centres of Expertise (NCE) in 2006 (Isaksen, 2009). The knowledge base of the cluster has developed over the years through a combination of experience from production and applied industrial research.

Raufoss was mainly a one-company town until the mid-1990s. The dominating company was the state-owned Raufoss Ammunition Factory (RA). Until the mid-1950s RA was totally dependent on military production, but from then on it developed civil production (Onsager et al., 2007). Aluminum profiles and automotive components became particularly important: first, bumpers for Volvo in 1967, and then, step by step, other products and deliveries to most of the global car factories. In 1994 the company exported 80% of its production, with the automotive industry as its main market. A substantial restructuring was initiated at the end of the 1990s, resulting in about 35 new firms, some of them with foreign owners (Onsager et al., 2007). The period of state ownership made possible the long-term development of specialized knowledge and products inside RA, which was backed up by political initiatives such as the procurement of customers through NATO and the Norwegian army.

In 2010, Raufoss was dominated by five large companies producing mainly components in aluminum and other light-weight materials and employing about 2000 people. The leading firm is Nammo, which produces ammunition and missile engines (650 employees at Raufoss). Nammo is seen by many firms and the local research institute as the most important technology-driving force in the cluster. The other four firms develop and produce components in aluminum, brass, or composites for the global car industry. They include Hydro Automotive Structures Raufoss (now part of the Benteler Group), which produces crash systems (700 employees); Raufoss Technology, which produces suspension systems (180 employees); Kongsberg Automotive, which produces couplings (210 employees); and Plastal, which produces exterior details in plastic (200 employees). These firms are all parts of large Norwegian or international corporations. Much of the R&D activity in the corporations takes place at Raufoss, while some production is outsourced to other countries for cost reasons and to supply customers in other parts of the world.

The other firms in the Raufoss cluster consist of a number of highly specialized, niche firms, producers of machinery and equipment, engineering firms, and a few large and several smaller suppliers to the core companies and the niche firms. As regards automotive components in aluminum, the Raufoss cluster includes a total value chain from a foundry to automotive components, including development work and tool production. The firms together add up to a rather varied local production network. The cluster also contains a knowledge node: SRM (SINTEF Raufoss Manufacturing). SRM is majority owned (50.1%) by the largest technological research institute in the Nordic countries, SINTEF in Trondheim (which is the applied research organization of the Norwegian University of Science and Technology), and the rest is owned by local companies. The link to SINTEF means that SRM can draw on a large external knowledge base. SRM delivers expertise and competence within manufacturing, materials technology, technology management, and various laboratories and workshop services. It has about 80 full-time employees and is responsible for managing the NCE programme at Raufoss.

5.3.2 Data sources and method

The study was designed as a theoretically informed case study (Sayer, 1992). A case study is a study of a real system (Arbnor and Bjerke, 1997). A theoretically informed study means that precise concepts and theory are employed in order to develop precise research questions, facilitate data collection, and interpret the empirical data (Sayer, 1992). Former studies of the Raufoss cluster (such as Johnstad, 2004, 2007; Onsager et al., 2007) are used for contextual information.

With the help of two researchers at SRM, we selected 30 companies as the most relevant for our study. These include the 13 companies that participate in the NCE program at Raufoss, which are the companies defined (by the cluster participants themselves) as the core firms in the cluster (Isaksen, 2009). In addition we selected firms that are important in terms of number of employees, turnover, innovation capability, and R&D activity. Two methods were used to collect new empirical data: interviews with the managing director or technical director of 26 companies and a short web-based survey of 24 companies addressed to the same type of people (Table 5.3). In most cases the interviews and the survey cover the same companies, and in total we obtained information from 28 companies, including the research institute SRM.

The web survey gathered some key quantitative information about the companies, such as year of establishment, number of employees, education level, recruitment of employees, important knowledge sources, and innovation performance. The questions were mainly factual – that is, designed to obtain objective information from the companies. The qualitative interviews mapped the networks of the firms with regard to market-, technological-, and research-based knowledge, and gained an overview of the firms' production and innovation activities. Both authors took part in most of the interviews. The initial questions usually initiated stories about the firm and its innovation activity by the informants, which were followed up with further questions. In this way, quite detailed written stories about each firm's innovation process were obtained. Much public information exists about the firms, which made it possible to cross-check some information. We therefore assess

Table 5.3 Sample of firms in the Raufoss cluster

Type of firms	Number of firms		
	Sample	Interviewed	Answered survey
Core firms which are members of the NCE program	13	12	12
Related firms	17	14	12
Total	30	26	24

the validity and the reliability of the information to be high (Frankfort-Nachmias and Nachmias, 1992).

5.4 Knowledge creation and innovation in the Raufoss light-weight material cluster

In analyzing innovation and knowledge-creating activities in the cluster, we distinguish in many respects between the NCE companies and the related companies. The NCE companies are seen as the *core firms* in the cluster (Table 5.3). They are generally larger than the related companies, and all except one are spin-offs from RA from between 1998 and 2004. The one exception is a spin-off from the other traditional, large company in the area, O. Mustad. The core companies had about 2450 full-time workers at the time of the survey (autumn 2008). All the core companies, except O. Mustad, are located in Raufoss Industrial Park, which previously housed RA.

The *related firms* are mostly specialized contract suppliers, component subcontractors, machine builders, and engineering and consulting firms in automated production technology. Many of these firms derive the majority of their turnover from the core companies at Raufoss. Three of the related companies in the sample are spin-offs from RA, while several others were established by people that had been employed by RA. These firms had a few more than 800 workers at the time of the survey. The firms are mainly located outside the industrial park, but only a short distance from it.

5.4.1 Innovation activity

The findings from the survey reveal that the core companies in the Raufoss cluster are in general innovative and that they perform both process and product innovations. The related companies are equally innovative, by some indicators; on average they report, for example, a somewhat larger share of their turnover from new or changed products than the core companies. However, the innovation activity differs in important respects between the two types of company. Nearly all the core companies have introduced radical product innovations, have an R&D department, and have employees occupied full time with product development, whereas few of the related companies share these characteristics. Furthermore, the core companies rely more on the sourcing of technological- and research-based information from scientific publications, and from direct contact with universities and specialized research labs, and recruit more highly qualified labor from universities and R&D

institutes than the related firms. Thus, the core companies resemble the STI mode of innovation, while the related companies have more similarities with the DUI mode of innovation (cf. Table 5.1).

Looking more carefully at the innovation activity in the core firms, we can identify three main types of innovation project in these firms. The first is *technology programs* where the aim is to develop the firms' technological base and core competence. These are often long term, applied research programs in collaboration with SRM, SINTEF, NTNU (the Norwegian University of Science and Technology in Trondheim), and FFI (the Defense Research Institute near Oslo), in particular, and in some cases also with a pilot customer. In Nammo, which produces ammunition and missile engines, development of the technological base includes adopting more or less familiar technology in new and demanding contexts, such as rapid acceleration. Another example is Kongsberg Automotive, which has taken more than ten years to develop a new coupling for brakes in trucks made of composite instead of brass. This development work is based on collaboration with the research institutes SRM and SINTEF, a specialized supplier, and a machine builder in public-supported projects, on the recruiting of personnel with knowledge of plastics, and on use of the experience-based competency of skilled workers when it comes to how the new type of couplings can function and be efficiently produced. The new material made it possible to change the design of the couplings so that they can be changed faster and more easily than brass couplings (a click system instead of threads), without changing the function of the couplings. Specialized workers in the company possess experience-based knowledge about the functioning of the couplings. Volvo has in addition been a pilot customer and sparring partner and has specified requirements and performed tests of the new couplings.

The second type of innovation activity is *development projects for customers*, which are financed by the customers and have a shorter time perspective than the technology programs. Hydro Automotive Structures Raufoss, for example, develops crash systems for new car models that have to satisfy specific requirements such as safety regulations set by insurance companies. This automotive component producer at Raufoss supplements the car producers with their expert knowledge of the forming, bending, and molding of aluminum and they cooperate closely with car producers in the development phase (see Isaksen and Kalsaas, 2009).

The third type of innovation activity is *self-financed product development* without a customer, where firms see a large potential for commercialization. This is most common in the case of Nammo, which develops new products that the firm believes the Norwegian Army will endorse, which will open up other markets. One example of such a development is the supply of separation boosters, acceleration boosters devices for the launches of the European Spacecraft Ariane 5 (Aftenposten, 2009). The boosters are small rocket engines made of aluminum loaded with advanced powder fuel.

5.4.2 Knowledge creation and knowledge bases

Knowledge-creating activities in the Raufoss cluster build on both analytical and synthetic knowledge. The dominant knowledge base and innovation mode differs, however, between the companies. The core companies have much more R&D-based learning and innovation processes than the related companies. The most research-based company at Raufoss is Nammo, in particular the missile engine department of the company, which has about 45 people working in technology development. Even in Nammo, however, the core competency is described as R&D-based knowledge in some specific technological niches plus knowledge of production processes. Thus, the technology development department in Nammo Ammunition has a mix of persons with scientific and technological competencies and skilled workers (such as gunsmiths) with long experience. In another of the core companies, Raufoss Water and Gas, the managing director maintains that about half of the activity in development projects is R&D-based while the other half builds on experience-based knowledge. The first type includes knowledge about brass and composites and about calculations and testing, while the experience-based knowledge includes the design of products and the running of the production process. A similar view is expressed by the vice-president of Kongsberg Automotive, who describes the core competency of the company as knowledge about materials and couplings (the product), and about how to develop an efficient production process. Furthermore, in this company researchers and skilled operators cooperate in development projects.

The related firms more often base their learning processes exclusively on experience-based knowledge. A small contract supplier with 16 employees, specializing in the bending and machining of aluminum profiles, maintains that their knowledge is developed through experience, and that the knowledge is not documented. Its tools are an important part of the capability of the company to satisfy their local customers, and the tools have been designed and produced by the company itself. The same opinion is expressed by several other machine-building and engineering companies. The main knowledge-creating activity is seen to occur in projects aimed at finding solutions to new problems. However, some of the related companies cooperate with some national and local research institutes in defining and developing projects and in documentation and testing. Firms also appreciate the local industrial milieu as a source of information and knowledge. Thus, the managing director of a contract supplier of aluminum painting observed that "the sense of manufacturing industry spreads through the industrial park, and all aspects of production are on the common agenda here." The company moved into a new building in the park in 2008 in order, among other purposes, to be closer to its main customer.

The importance of experienced-based knowledge in learning and innovation processes is also seen in the fact that the core companies in the Raufoss cluster, in general, involve skilled workers in continuous, incremental upgrading of the production process. Firms have adapted and implemented lean forms of work organization, and have trained teams of workers on the shop floor in methods to carry out of process innovations (cf. Isaksen and Kalsaas, 2009). The methods focus on, for example, working smarter, removing idle time and unnecessary movement, and undertaking preventive maintenance. Both in the core companies and the related companies, about 20% of the workforce have higher education, most of them as engineers. The related companies, especially the engineering firms and machine- and tool-building firms, prefer engineers with a certificate of apprenticeship in addition to an engineering education. These workers have both practical experience and theoretical knowledge. Both kinds of knowledge are important in discussions of products with customers and with the shop floor workers, who have long experience of handling specialized machines for drilling and turning different kinds of metal.

5.4.3 The regional innovation network at Raufoss

The Raufoss companies seek information for their innovation activities from a number of sources. They source market knowledge first of all from direct contact with customers. Universities, customers, and SRM are the main sources of technological and R&D-based knowledge.

Although the companies, and the core companies in particular, are involved in global value chains and knowledge networks, knowledge spillovers and the regional innovation network at Raufoss are crucial for innovation and learning processes. The companies have more or less a common core competency consisting of the forging and bending of metal profiles, and in designing and carrying out automated and lean production processes. This competency is found both in the individual firms, and in the regional R&D institute SRM.

To analyze innovation processes and the modes of innovation in more detail we employ, in Figure 5.1, a simplified overview of the regional innovation network. The figure refers to the two subsystems in the RIS approach, the industry and the knowledge organizations, as well as policy tools and informal institutions that stimulate knowledge flow and interactive learning among actors in the two subsystems (Cooke, 1998). The five largest firms act as drivers for technology development in the cluster. These firms operate in the demanding global defense, aerospace, and automotive markets, which are markets that require high quality and, in the case of the automotive industry, constantly lower prices. These large firms, and to some extent the smaller niche firms, cooperate strongly in innovation projects with SRM and partly with some extra-regional knowledge organizations. These include SINTEF, NTNU, and FFI. The large firms order challenging R&D projects from SRM, and they may bring in external knowledge organizations and specialized firms as partners in these projects. The projects

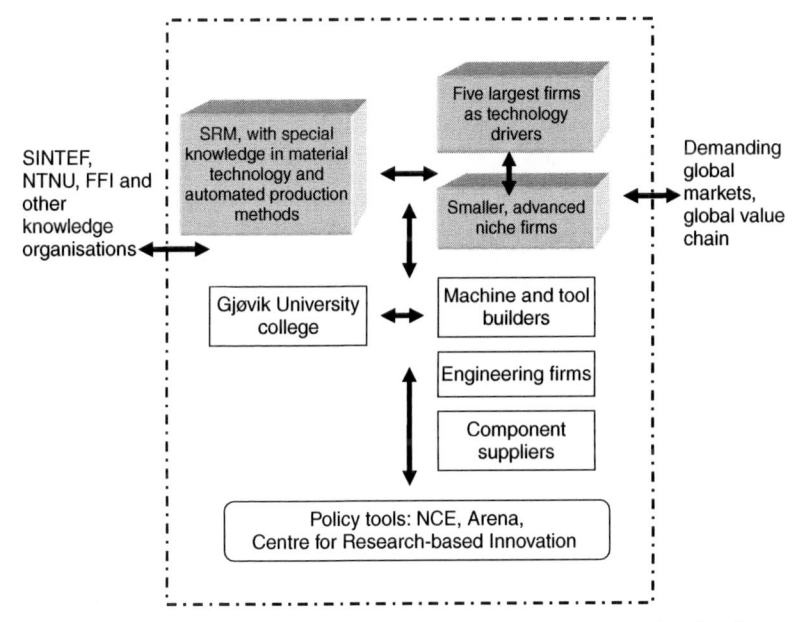

Figure 5.1 Simplified overview of the regional innovation network at Raufoss

relate to, in particular, material development, simulation technology, automation, and lean production processes. Nammo, for example, has not recruited metallurgists, but uses some dedicated personnel in SRM in projects that require such competence. Development projects in Nammo typically involve employees in the firm, in SRM, at foreign research institutes, and of local specialized suppliers. SRM performs similar types of project to several local firms, which leads to the accumulation of specialized knowledge and experience, and to the sharing of knowledge among local companies. Such activities result in technology diffusion to SRM and other actors in the Raufoss cluster, and make SRM into a local knowledge hub.[2] An important basis for the cross-company knowledge flow is the fact that the Raufoss companies are not competitors. Rather, they rely on the same or similar technological bases and have complementary core competency.

In some cases, projects that are carried out by SRM involve several local firms. Nammo has, for example, developed a new aluminum alloy for an anti-tank weapon in collaboration with SRM. The alloy is being cast at the Hydro Aluminum Foundry at Raufoss, which required the development of new casting methods. More generally, the large technology drivers and the niche firms act as demanding customers for the local related firms, for example by demanding more documentation and codification of the development process in the machine-building companies. The companies do not build internal knowledge in some areas, but rely on SRM. This raises the competence in SRM, which can be used in projects for other local and external firms. One of the niche firms (with 90 employees) performs research but sees research activity as being atypical for similar firms, however, triggered by its location at Raufoss with much specific knowledge easily available. A number of firms also maintain that they collaborate with the local university college at Gjøvik, mostly with regard to the development of specific courses for engineering education and the recruitment of students.

The Raufoss cluster includes a complete production network. Based on local demand, several machine builders specializing in automation technology have developed. Other local firms act as subcontractors for specialized work, such as small series, and make prototypes. Such firms also upgrade their competencies to meet demands from their local customers and in projects involving SRM. This also illustrates related variety (Frenken et al., 2007) within the regional cluster of firms, where related knowledge is found along the value chains, but also at specialized firms, producers of tools, and engineering firms.

The local collaboration and knowledge flow is backed up by a number of cluster-building policy tools, a Centre for Research-based Innovation in SRM, meeting places, a common culture, and so on. Thus, several initiatives have been taken in recent years by local actors, backed up by national policy instruments, to stimulate collaboration and cluster formation in regional industry. Important public initiatives are the cluster-building programs Arena and NCE administrated by Innovation Norway and the Centre for Research-based Innovation in production technology.[3]

5.4.4 The mode of innovation

The empirical analysis demonstrates that the innovation processes of the Raufoss firms share the characteristics of the CCI and the DUI mode. The 'pure' STI mode is less identifiable. The centre of the innovation activity is the collaboration between SRM, the five largest firms, and the smaller, advanced niche firms (see Figure 5.1). This collaboration resembles the CCI mode, which has knowledge spillover effects on other local companies. The spillover occurs when other firms test pilots of new products or engage in full-scale production, such as building prototypes of parts of rocket engines for Nammo. Through this process they not only produce a product but also learn to use the knowledge in new projects.

As described above, the core companies are important knowledge nodes in the cluster, they have different kinds of technological platform knowledge, and they play different roles in the cluster. The core knowledge of light-weight materials and lean management processes is mainly accumulated in the core companies and in SRM. The knowledge in SRM is partly codified and partly exists as know-how among the researchers. Know-how acquired in one project is shared and distributed in the cluster when researchers rotate among different projects. An SRM researcher with materials knowledge will always collaborate with a researcher with lean management knowledge. The knowledge that is accumulated both in the companies and, especially, in SRM is expert knowledge. An expert is a person who fully understands the context, 'reads' the situation well, and is fully involved in the situation (Dreyfus and Dreyfus, 1986).

The collaboration with SINTEF, NTNU, FFI and other national R&D organizations has been important for SRM to develop into a local knowledge node. SRM has sufficient knowledge to judge when the organization ought to acquire external knowledge to complement its own knowledge. The expert knowledge within materials and lean management also makes SRM into a national knowledge node.

5.5 Conclusion: The complex and combined innovation mode

This chapter has examined innovation processes in the Raufoss light-weight material cluster by use of the concept of a combined and complex mode of innovation (CCI). In CCI, different kinds of knowledge (highly advanced, expert knowledge, both R&D-based and experience-based) from different actors are combined in innovation processes. It is the combination of different kinds of in-house and external knowledge in complex innovation processes that differentiates the CCI mode from the more narrowly defined STI and the DUI modes, which are both based mainly on one type of knowledge (R&D- or experience-based).

We will emphasize two general theoretical lessons from the Raufoss case. First, CCI is an ideal type mode of innovation that is different from the STI and DUI modes. The case study reveals important aspects of CCI in demonstrating how core firms in the cluster create innovation by combining in-house knowledge with different kinds of external knowledge. They carry out somewhat long-term technology programs and shorter product application and process development projects. Each type of innovation project involves both analytical, R&D-based knowledge and synthetic, experience-based knowledge in the firms, although the specific combination of knowledge and innovation modes varies between the projects. The CCI mode may more generally be *one* explanation of the 'Norwegian puzzle:' R&D intensity, patent activity, and radical innovation activity may be modest in the CCI mode compared with an STI mode based on analytical knowledge, but the combination of technology platform development, the application of products and solutions to specific customers, and continuous work on improving the efficiency of operations seem to provide for competitive strength.

Second, the innovation mode approach should consider knowledge flow and interactive learning in the regional clusters and innovation networks, and not just innovation activities inside firms. This chapter thus employs the RIS approach, which focuses on innovation activities through a network of actors underpinned by an institutional framework, in order to analyze how the CCI mode can also result from collaboration, knowledge flow, and division of labor in a cluster. The regional R&D organization SRM has an especially important role in the Raufoss case as a common R&D department in materials technology and automated and lean production methods for many local firms. SRM has high research and development competency in some important areas for the regional firms, and the competency is being upgraded through demanding projects for local firms that are internationally competitive and through collaboration with external research institutes, such as SINTEF. SRM carries out much of the work in the most research based (STI-based) innovation projects , for example by documentation and testing. The Raufoss case illustrates how a regional knowledge organization that knows the local code of conduct can act as a common knowledge node, and also act as an extra-regional pipeline through its external relations to, particularly, SINTEF.

High industrial specialization may represent a (potential) weakness in the Raufoss cluster. A specific aspect of the specialization is the fact that four of the five core companies are suppliers to the global automotive industry, which has been experiencing problems in the global recession since autumn 2008. Some spin-off firms have found other market niches; however, the cluster is quite dependent on deliveries of auto parts. This points to a need to further differentiate the product and market niches among the cluster firms. Clusters and cluster firms need to undergo a constant process of renewal to enable them to change from one dominant type of product, technology, or sector to others, or move up the quality (or use-value) ladders for specific types of product. Capabilities for renewal are stimulated by the existence of a strong RIS, which is not too inward-looking (Tödtling and Trippl, 2004). Such a situation may be achieved through related variety in the regional industry and knowledge infrastructure (Boschma and Frenken, 2011), and by strategic networks to extra-regional knowledge sources. The small and specialized Raufoss cluster has by its nature low related variety, which makes extra-regional 'learning' networks particularly important. According to Boschma and Frenken (2011), extra-regional knowledge will most effectively support regional industrial growth if it is related to existing regional knowledge bases, but not too similar. This points to the need for the Raufoss rcluster firms to extent their knowledge networks beyond SRM and SINTEF found on the local and national level.

Acknowledgement

The research presented in this chapter is part of a European Collaborative Research Project on 'Constructing Regional Advantage: Towards

State-of-the-Art Regional Innovation System Policies in Europe'? 'The Norwegian part of the project is financed by the Research Council of Norway. We would like to thank Bjørn T. Asheim for his comments on drafts.

Notes

1. Gibbons et al. (1994) introduced the concepts of Mode-1 and Mode-2 knowledge production. Jensen et al. (2007) do not refer to Gibbons et al. (1994) in their discussion of modes of innovation. The STI concept is similar to the Mode-1 concept. The DUI concept and the Mode-2 concept have some similarities, such as knowledge creation in context, while other parts are quite different, such as the emphasizing of experience-based knowledge in the DUI mode. Mode-2 is a much broader and more general concept and is used by Gibbons et al. (1994) to discuss knowledge production in society, and is defined as knowledge production in a context of application.
2. Seventy percent of the earnings at SRM come from local firms and 30% from other Norwegian firms.
3. The Arena programme focuses on weak and potential clusters and aims to strengthen innovation collaboration within these. The NCE programme, on the other hand, is reserved for the most internationally competitive Norwegian clusters with the aim of strengthening the innovation and internationalization processes in these. The Centre for Research-based Innovation aims to strengthen Norwegian R&D institutes that cooperate on innovation processes with research-based companies.

References

Aftenposten (2009), *Finner opp kruttet på nytt* (Invent the powder once more). Newspaper article 4, March.
Arbnor, I. and Bjerke, B. (1997), *Methodology for Creating Business Knowledge*. Thousand Oaks, Sage Publications.
Asheim, B. (2007), 'Differentiated knowledge bases and varieties of regional innovation systems', *Innovation*, 20(3): 223–241.
Asheim, B., Coenen, L. and Moodysson, J. (2007), 'Constructing knowledge-based regional advantage: implications for regional innovation policy', *International Journal of Entrepreneurship and Innovation Management*, 7(2–5), 140–155.
Asheim, B.T. and Gertler, M. (2005), 'The geography of innovation: regional innovation systems', in J. Fagerberg, D. Mowery and R. Nelson (eds), *The Oxford Handbook of Innovation*, Oxford, Oxford University Press Oxford, pp. 291–317.
Asheim, B., Isaksen, A., Moodysson, J. and Sotarauta, M., (2011), 'Knowledge bases, modes of innovation and regional innovation policy: a theoretical re-examination with illustrations from the Nordic countries' in H. Bathelt, M.P. Feldman and D.F. Kogler (eds), *Dynamic Geographies of Knowledge Creation and Innovation*, London, Routledge.

Boschma, R.A. (2005), 'Proximity and innovation: a critical assessment', *Regional Studies*, 39(1): 61–74.
Boschma, R. and Frenken, K. (2011), 'Technological relatedness and regional branching', in H. Bathelt, M.P. Feldman and D.F. Kogler (eds), *Dynamic Geographies of Knowledge Creation and Innovation*, London, Routledge..
Coenen, L. (2006), 'Faraway, So Close', *The Changing Geographies of Regional Innovation. Meddelanden från Lunds Universitets Geografiska Institusjon*. Lund, Lunds Universitet.
Cohen, W.M. and Levinthal, D.A. (1990), 'Absorptive capacity: a new perspective on learning and innovation', *Administrative Science Quarterly*, 35: 128–152.
Cooke, P. (1998). Introduction: 'Origins of the concept' in H. Braczyk, P. Cooke and M. Heidenreich (eds), *Regional Innovation Systems*, London, UCL Press, pp. 2–25.
Dreyfus, H. and Dreyfus, S. (1986), *Mind. over Machine: The Power of Human Intuition and Expertise in the Era of the Computer.* New York: Free Press. Frankfort-Nachmias, C. and Nachmias, D. (1992), *Research Methods in the Social Sciences.* New York, St. Martin's Press.
Frenken, K., Van Oort, F. and Verburg, T. (2007), 'Related variety, unrelated variety and regional economic growth', *Regional Studies*, 41(5): 685–698.
Gertler, M.S. (2008), 'Buzz without being there? Communities of practice in context', in A. Amin and J. Roberts (eds), *Community, Economic Creativity and Organization*, Oxford, Oxford University Press.
Gibbons, M., Limoges, C., Nowotny, H., Schwartzmann, S., Scott, P. and Trow, M. (1994), *The New Production of Knowledge – the Dynamics of Science and Research in Contemporary Societies*, London, Sage.
Ibert, O. (2007), 'Towards a geography of knowledge creation: the ambivalences between "knowledge as an object" and "knowing in practice"', *Regional Studies*, 41(1): 103–114.
Isaksen, A. (2009), 'The innovation dynamics of global competitive regional clusters: the case of the Norwegian centres of expertise', *Regional Studies*, 43(9): 1155–1166.
Isaksen, A. and Kalsaas, B.T. (2009), 'Suppliers and strategies for upgrading in global production networks: the case of a supplier to the global automotive industry in a high-cost location', *European Planning Studies*, 17(4): 569–585.
Jensen, M.B., Johnson, B., Lorenz, E. and Lundvall, B.-Å. (2007), 'Forms of knowledge and modes of innovation', *Research Policy*, 36: 680–693.
Johnstad, T. (2004), 'Klynge, nettverk og verdiskaping i innlandet', *NIBR-rapport*, 2004:08, NIBR Oslo.
Johnstad, T. (2007), 'Raufoss: from a learning company to a learning region' in B. Gustavsen, B. Nyhan and R. Ennals (eds), *Learning Together for Local Innovation: Promoting Learning Regions*, Office for Official Publications of the European Communities Luxembourg.
Lorenz, E. and Lundvall, B.-Å. (eds) (2006), *How Europe's Economies Learn: Coordinating Competing Models*, Oxford, Oxford University Press.
Lundvall, B.-Å. (2007), 'National innovation systems – analytical concept and development tool', *Industry & Innovation*, 14(1): 95–119.
Lundvall, B.-Å. and Johnson, B. (1994), 'The learning economy', *Journal of Industry Studies*, 1(2): 23–42.

Moodysson, J. (2007), 'Sites and modes of knowledge creation. On the spatial organization of biotechnology innovation', *Meddelanden från Lunds Universitets Geografiska Institution. Avhandlingar CLXXIV.* Lund, Lund University, 237 s.

OECD (2007a), *Science, Technology and Industry Scoreboard 2007*, Paris, OECD.

OECD (2007b), *OECD Territorial Reviews Norway*, Paris, OECD.

Onsager, K., Isaksen, A., Fraas, M. and Johnstad, T. (2007), 'Technology cities in Norway: innovating in glocal networks', *European Planning Studies*, 15: 549–566.

Polanyi, M. (1966), *The Tacit Dimension*, New York, Doubleday.

Sayer, A. (1992), *Method in Social Science. A Realist Approach*, London, Routledge.

Tödtling, F. and Trippl, M. (2004), 'Like phoenix from the ashes? The renewal of clusters in old industrial areas', *Urban Studies*, 41(5/6): 1175–1195.

6
Facilitating Cluster Evolution in Peripheral Regions: The Role of Clusterpreneurs

Jesper Lindgaard Christensen and Dagmara Stoerring

6.1 Introduction

In the last decades cluster initiatives[1] and cluster policy have become central features of policy promoting growth at regional, national, and European level. Many regional and national government's policies aim at imitating successful clusters in the belief that their local areas may also capture the benefits of new high-technology firm formation and expected economic growth (Cooke, 2001a; Feldman et al., 2005) despite the fact that there is little empirical evidence to support a rationale for such policy, as the link between clustering and economic performance remains under-studied (Stuart and Sorenson, 2003; Maine et al., 2010). Both academic models (Brenner, 2004) and a number of consultant-made guidelines, even guidebooks (such as DTI, 2004; Rosenfeld, 2002), have been developed to assist the policy decision process.[2] This promotion of high-tech clusters is not confined to urban areas but also often takes place in peripheral regions, such as in the example studied in this chapter, the possible development of a biomedical cluster in the region of North Jutland in Denmark.

However, the effectiveness and appropriateness of transferring experiences from other regions is debatable and there are dilemmas in stimulating the development of high-tech clusters in peripheral regions. One condition for the success of cluster policy in peripheral regions has been argued to be a degree of systemic innovation in the regions, which in turn implies that institutions and actors are interlinked (Cooke,

2001a). Thus, more than twenty years ago, The European Commission pointed out that:

> It is not simply the presence of units of RTD infrastructure, but of the degree of interaction between them which is the most significant factor in local innovation. The quality of the linkage and the presence of local synergy is the key element. Therefore a systems or network approach provides the best basis for understanding and promoting regional RTD-based innovation. (CEC, 1988)

Morgan (1997) contends that less favored regions often not only are less favored in the traditional sense of having poor physical infrastructure, high unemployment rates, and low income per head, but also have poorly developed social capital. This was also pointed to at an early stage by the OECD, which stated that:

> Less favoured regions seem to have little or no social capital on which they can draw, a point which turns the spotlight on factors such as the institutional capacity of the region, the calibre of the political establishment, the disposition to seek joint solutions to common problems. These factors – the invisible factors in economic development – are just as important as physical capital. (OECD, 1993)

This emphasizes the need to focus on the carriers of the cluster policy. When policy is to a large extent about stimulating collective learning processes and building social capital, the key issues for policy become centered around human capital in both a 'supply' and a 'demand' dimension.

Despite the importance of human resources and the role of policy actors, research on cluster development and even cluster policy has generally not revealed a more precise specification of this role. This article contributes to this debate by focusing on and substantiating the concept of 'clusterpreneurs', defined as important actors in cluster formation.[3] Thus, a clusterpreneur is here regarded as a key actor in the emergence of clusters. We argue that active clusterpreneurs are relatively more important in less favored regions, and that different clusterpreneurs may act effectively in different institutional settings and in different phases of cluster evolution. The article thus contributes to the existing literature in that it combines the actors perspective and the incorporation of regional specificities in the analysis of how clusters may be promoted. Moreover, dilemmas inherent in this combination are highlighted.

We illustrate the role of clusterpreneurs by the example of a biomedical technology cluster initiative in North Jutland, Denmark, which has many of the characteristics of a peripheral region. The example could be said to be a typical case of a policy-driven cluster initiative. However, we show how the presence of clusterpreneurs comprising a diverse set of actors, spanning both the public and private spheres, can make such an initiative more effective. Moreover, we claim that this region may deviate from the usual picture of less favored regions as having poor social capital and coherence. This may provide an important condition for the further development of the cluster.

We start by presenting the concept of clusterpreneurs: its origin and main features. Then we discuss the nature of cluster policies: the principal difficulties facing cluster formation in peripheral regions; and we review theories on cluster emergence and cluster policies with an emphasis on the relation between cluster policy and the dilemmas related to implementing such policies in peripheral regions. We then describe specific characteristics of our case region, North Jutland in Denmark. Our case of a biomedical cluster initiative in the North Jutland region is used to illustrate both the concept of clusterpreneurs and their role in this specific initiative. We conclude with some suggestions for further research.

6.2 Actors in the emergence phase of cluster formation

The emergence of clusters has been studied intensively in recent years, primarily based upon historical case studies.[4] In general, the explanations given may be classified in three groups. One group of explanations emphasizes that clusters are concentrations of resources. They generate knowledge spillovers and draw upon a common pool of skilled labor and specialized intermediaries. Another group of explanations sees clusters as emerging out of random seeding, accidental or deliberately generated positive externalities at an early stage. The third group of explanations sees the internal agglomeration dynamics as decisive and explore these by network and industrial organization analysis.

Irrespective of the type of explanation for cluster evolution, cluster studies tend to fail to a large extent to specify the actors involved in the evolution and to specify the context, that is the type of region in which they operate. Some studies do, though, emphasize the role of entrepreneurship in cluster evolution. For example, Feldman (2001), Feldman et al. (2005), and Feldman and Francis (2006) see entrepreneurs as key drivers in the formation of clusters. However, these and most other studies in line with them, see the entrepreneur as an individual, private actor in cluster dynamics, whose primary contribution to cluster development is through establishing and running a business. The conceptualization of the clusterpreneur below attempts to bring in more precisely the actor perspective. Moreover, the approach is different from that of Feldman et al. (2005) and others in that it does not assume that firms have static boundaries and includes intrapreneurship as important in the dynamics of developing clusters, which is something broader than individuals starting up firms. Hence, the concept of 'clusterpreneurship' unfolded below includes also the spin-off processes, the business developers within the firms, and entrepreneurial activities in the public sector. Although some cluster studies do point to the role of actors in cluster formation it is most often not specified what these actors do and who they are.[5] We attempt to fill this gap. Although we realize that our contribution is to a large extent case-specific, we believe that it is nevertheless a positive contribution to cluster studies.

Clusterpreneurs have a crucial role to play in the cluster-emergence process and may be seen as a constellation of four types of actor: (i) key institutions in both the knowledge-generating and the knowledge-diffusing systems; in the case of high-tech cluster formation, universities and university-related institutions are the most important actors in this group; (ii) policy-makers, most often – but not necessarily – public policy bodies; (iii) private firms and industry associations; (iv) business services and venture capital organizations. The term venture capital organization as used here covers a range of relevant types of financing organization. The Triple Helix literature (e.g. Etzkovitz and Leydersdorff, 2000) includes some of these actors: university/research, private firms/industry, and policy are the foci of the analyses. However, our concept and approach are broader. These actors may in combination compromise clusterpreneurs and act with varying intensity of involvement and resources over time.

6.2.1 The collective character and changing role of different actors

Although cluster initiatives may be started by a particular set of actors, such as local government, over time a broader set of actors usually becomes involved and, more importantly, clusterpreneurs may tie the different actors together. An important function of clusterpreneurs is thus to knit regional organizations together, not only in a physical sense by creating networks, equally important by creating social capital.

Sometimes it is one type of actor (such as a private person), sometimes a group of two or more of these four types which is active in doing so. 'Quadra Helix' actors, comprising the four types of actors mentioned above, often dominate and drive the cluster development asymmetrically. Their collaboration can be loose and informal, with the result that it can be difficult to identify this kind of clusterpreneur,[6] but it can also be formalized, for instance as a group/organization devoted to the promotion of a given cluster (BioMedCommunity in our case – see Section 6.6). In the later stages of development, formalized clusterpreneurs often finance the activities of cluster initiatives by charging fees to the companies involved in the initiative.

Clusterpreneurs are particularly relevant for emerging clusters or, rather, cluster initiatives. According to Sölwell et al. (2003), cluster initiatives are often started by one person with a background in the cluster who takes the lead – a clusterpreneur. However, they also give examples of numerous other types of actor involved in starting cluster initiatives, such as policy organizations at different levels (national, regional, local), industry organizations, or even individual industry leaders.[7] It is also often underlined that the reliance on a single, key individual can turn out to be a disadvantage, especially in later stages of cluster development (Raines, 2002). Our approach thus differs from that of Sölwell et al. in that we emphasize the group character of the actors.

There may be different levels of involvement by the different types of actor during the evolution of a cluster. Also, the roles of one type of actor in one cluster may be different from that of the same type of actor in another cluster. For example, in some cases policy may have a decisive role in the early phases of the cluster life-cycle whereas policy may be only supportive in later stages. The role of active clusterpreneurs may vary over time, and will generally diminish when the cluster grows and develop its own dynamic development processes and networks. Specifically, cluster development may lead to that the roles of clusterpreneurs develop into self-organized processes rather than top-down governance. We contend that whereas the presence of the four different actors of clusterpreneurs may be a pre-condition to develop a dynamic cluster development it is in itself not enough. The specific relationships between these actors may be more decisive than is the activity and presence of a particular part of clusterpreneurs. Furthermore, we argue that whereas many studies see institutions as exogenous or lagging behind cluster formation (Feldman et al., 2005; Mason, 2007 on venture capital), we see clusterpreneurs as proactively forming cluster processes and in doing so incorporating supporting organizations.

6.2.2 Collaboration between private and public actors

Clusterpreneurs may be further grouped in different ways. One possible distinction is between, on the one hand, private individuals and organizations devoted to promoting local business through enhancing networking in clusters and, on the other hand, regional government represented by government agencies and other public bodies. These two types of actors may, at the same time, have some common and some divergent interests. Moreover, their activities are determined and controlled by different mechanisms and rationales. Private clusterpreneurs are motivated by the profit, network, image/reputation and spillover effects companies can derive from being agglomerated in a cluster, whereas public actors are primarily interested in generating new jobs in the region.

Porter (1998) emphasizes that many clusters include governmental and other public or semi-public organizations – such as universities, standards-setting agencies, think tanks, providers of vocational training, and trade associations – which provide specialized training, education, information, research, and technical support. Porter suggests a new agenda of collective action in the private sector; that it is not only government's function to invest in public goods. Cluster thinking clearly demonstrates how companies can benefit from local assets and institutions (such as trade associations establishing university-based testing facilities and training or research programs). Even if it seems obvious that private firms may in the long term benefit from such investments in public goods, it involves a classic dilemma of some firms investing while other firms free-riding as well as conflicting micro–macro objectives. Private sector investment in public goods has been claimed to be particularly problematic in the European Union in comparison to the United States (Cooke, 2001b). However, it is likely that there are substantial intra-European differences at this point.[8] Cluster building in practice is often a joint effort of public and private sector action. The shared financing of the formalized clusterpreneurs' organizations is widely seen as an example of how clusterpreneurs' activities can trigger the participation of the private sector in public goods building, thus improving collective action.

6.3 Cluster policies – the principal difficulties facing cluster formation in peripheral regions

As mentioned, cluster policy has become a central feature of economic policy in the last decade. Although cluster policy has been widely criticized by parts of the academic world (Martin and Sunley, 2003), it is extensively implemented by policy-makers (OECD, 1999, 2001). The rationale for innovation policy in general has traditionally referred to market failure, where price mechanisms fail to take externalities into account. The objective of cluster policies is then to provide access to functions that the market fails to produce, specifically networks and coordination. Following the development of innovation thinking towards seeing innovation in a system perspective, innovation policies now increasingly refer to system failures rather than market failure (Edquist, 2001). Policies to alleviate system failures may address institutions and capabilities related to the interaction between key agents in the system. As such, this perspective is more adequate for cluster policies than the market failure perspective.

Moreover, cluster promotion is not confined to urban areas, even if clusters tend to concentrate in such areas. Cluster promotion in a peripheral region may, however, involve a series of challenges additional to those present in urban areas. First, peripheral regions are generally characterized by a lack of developed physical infrastructure and social capital, as mentioned in the introduction. Second, big companies, which may play the role of driving forces in the cluster formation process, are often absent and difficult to attract. Rather, urban areas have been shown to attract high-tech/high innovative enterprises (Therrien, 2005). Third, peripheral regions lack many other factors enabling the emergence of clusters, such as a critical mass of firms, a university and other knowledge institutions, venture capital and other financing sources, and supporting business services. Fourth, it may be argued that local knowledge infrastructure and the ability to attract talented labor is less developed in peripheral regions but nevertheless is crucial (Glaeser, 2003) in such areas that often have a low-tech specialization. A low education level among the labor force is likewise often characteristic of peripheral regions. Moreover, such regions generally often lack basic Marshallian agglomeration effects rendering external economies passed on to firms as a result of savings from the large-scale operations of the agglomeration as a whole.

These factors are interconnected, and often the lack of just one of them is the reason why a cluster cannot be developed in a region which makes active policy even more necessary. Therefore, clusterpreneurs are even more crucial in these regions. It is, however, important to emphasize that the pure presence of the factors just mentioned as supporting cluster evolution is not necessarily enough. Cooke (2001b) contends that, for example, it is not the more readily available presence of venture capital and university bio-tech research that makes the US bio-tech industry outperform that of Europe, it is the system for the commercialization of the research that is more efficient in the US. This emphasizes the importance of the systemic, integrated activity of clusterpreneurs, rather than just the presence of individual factors.

6.4 Cluster policies: content, challenges, dilemmas

6.4.1 Content of cluster policy

The role of policy in cluster development has been the subject of much debate. Porter, for example, has suggested active cluster policy (1998a). However, it seems to be a general perception in the literature that in a market economy one cannot create clusters from scratch (Raines, 2002; Sternberg, 2003). Thus, Porter argues that the targets of active policies should be existing clusters that have proved sustainable, rather than the creation of new clusters (Porter, 1998a). The case in this study (Section 6.6) is to a large extent an example of active policies where cluster policies go against the general assertion and Porter's recommendation that creating clusters should not (and could not) be created by policy means.

The importance and apparent attractiveness of clusters implies new roles for government at national and regional levels. In the global economy, sound macroeconomic policies are necessary but not sufficient. Government's more decisive influences are at the microeconomic level rather than at the macroeconomic level (Porter, 2000). Cluster theory highlights the role of local actors (local/regional governments) in economic policy focused on encouraging innovation.

Cluster initiatives have developed as a new policy agenda; however, the policies following this agenda is often based on traditional policy areas such as regional policies, innovation policies, and industry policy, and is conducted heterogeneously across countries and regions. A number of common characteristics of successful cluster initiatives, such as investing in education, setting the rules of competition by establishing market institutions, creating an adequate physical infrastructure, motivating collective action by the private sector, and tolerating and even encouraging multinationals (Gambardella et al., 2002), have been listed. Cluster policies are often associated with public initiatives and actors. However, there may be both public and private actors actively pursuing cluster policies, in Fromhold-Eisebith and Eisebith (2005) these policy approaches are termed "top-down" and "bottom-up" institutionalizations.

Another approach somewhat in line with the arguments presented in this chapter is that of Keeble and Wilkinson (2000), who suggest the following measures for promoting clusters (from Spilling and Steinsli, 2003):

- diffusion of knowledge from the science and technology base, for example by reducing barriers between industry and university by supporting technology consultants helping small firms to utilise knowledge from the university
- support networking and collective learning processes by for instance supporting research collaboration between local SMEs
- business support for high-technology SMEs, for instance through education and training facilities targeted at their specific needs and development
- policies targeted to the specific needs on the regional level in order to develop policies targeting the specific challenges in each region.

Tödtling and Trippl (2005) specifically emphasize the last point. They argue that innovation policy is likely to be inefficient if a 'one-size-fits-all' approach is adopted. It is essential that the policy approach takes into account the abilities of the region and the degree of systemic innovation in the region – that is, the degree to which institutions and actors are interlinked. Peripheral regions and high-tech urban areas differ in this respect. In addition to this we highlight the role of local actors (local governments, firms, universities), the clusterpreneurs. Another important content of cluster policy is the fact that it should support networking and collective learning processes among the local actors, especially SMEs and universities, thus supporting the building of the social capital in the region, something that in later stages can be an important foundation and pre-condition of a successful cluster policy.

6.4.2 Choosing the right policy target – industry, sector, cluster

Inherently, it is difficult to plan cluster formation based on innovation. The innovation process entails uncertainty – not only technical uncertainty, but also market uncertainty. Therefore, the path of technological development is difficult to predict, as the existence of the vast literature on technology foresight illustrates. Planning clusters in this environment is extremely risky and uncertain.

Presuming that governments have a role in cluster development, policy-makers are faced with a dilemma: seeds for clusters may emerge in several areas, and resources may be restricted; how then should one choose the right area to target and at the same time secure the diversity that makes the region less vulnerable towards changes (narrow vs. broad focus)? Achieving the necessary critical mass of firms in the chosen industry may be the biggest problem.

This may be called a 'policy dilemma' that regional policy-makers face when they wish to promote such a cluster without orienting policies too much towards rewarding certain sectors at the expense of others. Therefore it is important to see the two types of actor in cluster formation – regional policy bodies and private individuals/organizations – as mutually reinforcing and dependent upon each other. In particular, the presence of private clusterpreneurs may allow local government to legitimize spending resources on specific sectors.

The specific instruments required in cluster and innovation policy are often disregarded in theoretical cluster studies, partly due to the fact that they may vary with the particular case; in other words, a general model of cluster policy is likely to be inadequate (Nauwelaers, 2001; Raines, 2002; Martin and Sunley, 2003). Cluster policies need to be adjusted to the specific conditions and strategy of the target region. At a more general level, the focus of innovation and cluster policy has moved in three phases from physical capital, such as infrastructure, R&D, and finance, to immaterial aspects related to human capital, such as knowledge, education, and training, and finally to social capital, such as networks, norms, and institutions (Nauwelaers, 2001). This poses challenges to policy-makers because the instruments of the latter types of policy are not well developed and less measurable.

Another dilemma may be related to the above-mentioned network/social capital as the target for policy. The question is how to promote social capital with policy instruments. Traditional policy instruments quickly become inadequate. Inherently, it is not easy to enforce collaboration on people. It may be possible, though, to bring the parties together and see if/how networks evolve. This, however, means that policy agents will have a positive role, conflicting with the perceived role of policy actors as being active and in control.

6.4.3 The rationale behind the promotion of low-labor-intensive high-tech industries

An additional problem may arise with the rationale behind the promotion of high-tech industries, which are usually not labor-intensive. In the case of peripheral regions it is primarily unemployment that is the biggest problem for policy-makers. This introduces a time perspective dilemma between short-term and long-term policy objectives. Although in the short term, low-tech industries provide more work places in the region, they are more vulnerable to fluctuations at regional, national, and (perhaps most importantly) global level, as when production is moved to low-labor-cost countries. On the other hand, the promotion of high-tech industries or clusters involves structural change in the region, which is a long-term process (Dalum et al., 1998). This may put pressure on policymakers to stick to stimulating the existing industrial structure.

6.5 Specific characteristics of North Jutland, Denmark

The North Jutland region has traditionally been characterized as peripheral, with the highest unemployment rate in Denmark. The industrial profile of Aalborg (the capital city of the region) has been dominated by traditional, labor-intensive manufacturing industries, while the other parts of the region have been dominated by the primary sector, especially agriculture and fishing, and in more recent decades, tourism. The regional specialization pattern for North Jutland shows that it is more specialized in primary industries and less specialized in finance and business services. Even if, during the 1990s, the region experienced a partial process of structural change toward more growth-oriented industries (some parts of the region became specialized in machinery, equipment, and electronics), it can still be characterized as relatively low-tech/peripheral in Denmark. Other indicators, such as education level, show that the share of people with tertiary education is significantly lower in North Jutland than in Denmark as a whole. Similarly, the R&D level in the region (weighted with the North Jutland's share of Danish firms) is for North Jutland approximately two-thirds of Denmark's level. Similarly, the region is lacking behind in the number of patents per 1000 inhabitants.

Thus, the region is structurally different from the rest of Denmark. Changing that is a very long process that requires considerable financial input. In sum, the region exhibits many of the characteristics of a peripheral region within Denmark, even though it is more developed than many other regions in Europe. Hence, the term 'peripheral' is used here in a relative sense.

6.6 The biomedical cluster in North Jutland

In this section we present the case of the creation of a biomedical cluster in North Jutland. We present the cluster initiative, its history, and the main actors, and we put the case in its regional and institutional context. The purpose is to reveal key characteristics of clusterpreneurs and cluster policies as discussed above.

6.6.1 Cluster competencies

The actors behind the cluster initiative had identified the following competencies in the region that were thought to be decisive for the potential emergence of a cluster.

6.6.1.1 Aalborg University (AAU)

AAU established decades ago substantial activities within health science and technology, medico-technology, biotechnology, and related areas,[9] which may overall be termed life sciences. In some areas the research has a 20-year tradition; in others, such as stem cells and nanotechnology, the research is more recent. Research at AAU in this area has now obtained international recognition. Among the established areas of activity, research within the medico-technical area at the Center for Sensory Motor Interaction (SMI)[10] developed new methods for stimulating and treating electrical signals from muscles. Advanced methods were developed for measuring and activating the human motor function system and for locating pain. Moreover, the university developed a centre for research within stem cell technology,[11] aimed at determining how stem cells may be used to develop human 'spare parts'. Another research field at AAU is biotechnology and the cluster initiative actors also see possibilities of synergy with substantial research in nanotechnology, although it seems that it is mainly within medico-technology that research is at the highest international level. In addition to a full study program in biomedical engineering, a doctoral school, which has approximately 50 Ph.D. scholarships, contributes to the high technological level of knowledge within the area as well as contributing to the pool of potential employers for local industry. A 2007 initiative was the establishment of courses in medical engineering. This was the springboard to the start of ordinary medical study from September 2010.

6.6.1.2 Aalborg Hospital, Århus University Hospital

Aalborg Hospital has a tradition of cooperation with Aalborg University and Århus University. Collaboration with AAU is primarily within biomedical research whereas research in health sciences is done in cooperation with Århus University. This cooperation is formalized in the HEALTHnTECH Research Centre (established in 2003), which offers support and evaluation of product ideas and applications developed by the industry. The close relations between doctors, scientists, and commercial partners have resulted in the set-up of a number of spin-off companies. In 2008, an 'Idea Clinique' was established with the purpose of supporting and facilitating the use – either internally or in commercial application – of good ideas from employees at the hospital.

6.6.1.3 Regional industry/companies

As already mentioned, the main high-tech companies in the region can be found within electronics and telecommunications. This sector is represented by big international companies,[12] but also many smaller companies, which play an important role in the ICT cluster. In October 2011, there were 51 companies active in biomedical technology or, more broadly, life sciences. These companies are a mixture of large firms in other industries some of whose activities related to life sciences and small development companies employing just one or two people. Some of them are spin-offs from the university research and therefore may rather be called development projects. Only a handful of the companies could be classified as pure biomedical production/manufacturing companies employing at least ten people. Another characteristic of this cluster is that its development has been turbulent, some companies disappearing and new ones having been established. We can conclude that within the biomedical area the region is characterized by a lack of big companies and a number of small companies whose specialization profile is highly differentiated. As mentioned in the description of hospital competencies, the health sector in Denmark is to a large extent a public sector, which means that the local customers of the firms within medical technology are mainly public authorities. For facilitating evolution of this kind of cluster one may expect that policy may be relatively more influential due to the large size of the health sector in Denmark, and consequently high public procurement and -demand.

6.6.2 History of the cluster initiative

The beginning of this cluster initiative can be dated back to 2000. It was the Aalborg Commercial Council[13] that, together with the Industrial Liaisons Office at Aalborg University, launched the initiative. Other actors joined them, specifically North Jutland County, Aalborg municipality, and finally industry representatives. Since the year 2000, several initiatives have been started in order to promote facilitate the evolution of biomedical technology in North Jutland. One of the origins of these initiatives is to be found in the Danish government's national strategy for the development of biomedical industries from 2000 (Regeringen,

2000). Moreover, regional policy makers were looking for industrial development potential that could supplement or eventually replace the existing mobile telecommunications (ICT) cluster, both because this cluster had experienced severe difficulties during the early 2000, and because a more diverse industry structure could reduce how sensitive the region is to business cycles.[14] In this process they had noticed local strengths in the biomedical area. The biomedical area is considered one of the most promising from the industrial development point of view in almost every European country, and it is thus naturally attracting attention.

The initiative was formalized by these actors in 2003, when BioMed Community: Science & Innovation for the Living was established.[15] BioMed Community is a collaboration aimed at developing and promoting North Jutland's cluster within life sciences. A steering committee was established representing the main actors in the region interested in this cluster initiative: Aalborg University, Aalborg Hospital, NOVI science park, biomedical companies, the County of North Jutland, Aalborg Commercial Council, and the Aalborg Region Cooperation, which means that there are agents from education, government, industry, and venture capital/supporting services. The group had administrative support from the Industrial Liaisons Office and Aalborg Commercial Council and was financed by the public actors.

The cluster is now at take off stage. It is perceived that a cluster goes through a series of stages, which may resemble the evolution of the ICT cluster in the region or follow the patterns of the cluster life-cycles described in the literature (see for example Menzel and Fornahl, 2009). According to the BioMed Community, the primary conditions for the first phases of a biomedical cluster are present in the region, namely research, education, networking, venture capital, and a well developed health sector. The region is claimed already to be above 'critical mass' in these respects. However, the small number of companies and their early development stage is regarded as a problem. Furthermore, it is only recently that the region's hospital was given the status of university hospital and its clinical research history is short. It may also be argued, as earlier in this chapter, that the pure presence of these factors will not be sufficient, that they need to be related to each other and interwoven in network constellations that may productively benefit from synergies. As also mentioned, the differences in performance between the biotech industries in the United States and Europe may be ascribed to differences in the way institutions are constituted rather than their presence or absence (Cooke, 2001a; Orsenigo, 2006). However, BioMed

Community is aware of these problems and is taking action to find solutions, as will be explained in the next section.

6.6.3 Current policies in North Jutland for the promotion of the biomedical cluster

This section is for the most part based on interviews with the actors involved in the initiative, the clusterpreneurs. Interviews were undertaken with a number of key people; Appendix 6.1 lists the interviewees and the principal issues discussed.

Publishing promotion materials, marketing, attracting new firms to the region, promotion of new and established companies have been the main activities of BioMed Community in the first years of existence. As mentioned above, an increase in the number of firms is likely to spur a virtuous circle of cluster evolution, just as in the ICT cluster, where firms were attracted to the region because of the presence of a number of key players in the industry (Stoerring and Dalum, 2008). Consequently, efforts have been made to attract firms from outside as well as stimulate spin-offs and spin-outs. However, 'soft factors' were recognized as essential to the evolution of the cluster. Therefore, it is fair to say that the cluster initiative also took a more dynamic path after this period, giving rise to a number of actions.

Shortly after the initiative was formalized, in February 2003, a so-called 'Firms Club' was established for companies from Northern Denmark (not limited to the North Jutland region: one of the biggest companies was located in Ringkøbing). The networking that takes place in the club establish synergy between companies in the region, as they learn about each other, identify and discuss common problems, agree on how to influence their cooperation with the Liaisons Office and the hospital, and how more effective support to the innovative activities within the industry is provided. BioMed Community helps members of the Firms Club to find capital and offers them administrative, organizational, and marketing support, such as providing meeting facilities and arranging common participation at national and international exhibitions. The club itself organizes visits to companies and hosts visits of outside companies. The aim is to bring companies together and support their cooperation.[16]

In their determination to develop the cluster, the cluster initiative actors have mobilized considerable financial resources, which they believe will speed up the process of cluster formation. These resources came partly from the North Jutland region and partly from the European Union funds. One of the first initiatives was the establishment of a Research House (*Forskningens hus*) at Aalborg Hospital. This initiative originated from the HEALTHnTECH Research Centre and should facilitate the cooperation and involvement of industry. In the Research Centre there is an area dedicated to students and office space to facilitate the incubation of commercial companies. The idea was to concentrate the innovation environment in one place: research and education from both medicine studies from Aarhus University/Aalborg Hospital and from the Department for Health Science and Technology at Aalborg University together with industry and emerging firms.

Three people were hired on a part-time basis to work with on initiative between 2003 and 2005: a start-ups consultant, an ambassador and a communication consultant. Their task, and especially that of the ambassador, was to attract companies from other parts of Denmark and abroad, for example by involving such companies in cooperative projects for which research would be conducted in the region. The start-up consultant should support new companies (for example, by offering the office space in the Research House), provide advice for the development of the existing ones, assist people in the Liaisons Office working with start-ups, and support the University start-up program at the medical technology department. Also at Aalborg University an intensification of activities took place. For example, at the Liaisons Office an additional person was hired to work on the biomedical cluster. From 2005, efforts focused upon attracting new companies and investors from outside the region. This required intense marketing of the life sciences expertise in the region and the cluster in particular. Supporting the development of existing firms was a priority. Finally, much effort was put into knowledge dissemination, networking, and the establishment of awareness and team spirit within the cluster. This was done through a large number of meetings, networking activities, joint participation in fairs, and so on. The most recent (2010) initiative is to establish a Business Park in association with the building of new university facilities for the medical school.

The clusterpreneurs are aware that the 'creation' of a cluster is a long process that requires building up and maintaining contacts. They refer to the way the ICT cluster in the region emerged to illustrate how the potential may be achieved only after a very long period. They believe that only one (not necessarily big) significant company wanting to establish a subsidiary in Aalborg is needed to start the process, then other firms might follow. They further believe that this initiative needs a comprehensive approach and that is why they are working with Invest in Denmark under the Ministry of Foreign Affairs. In essence, transferring competencies from the university and the hospital to industry and reaching a critical mass of companies are the main challenges, according to them.

Our case illustrates the multiple character of clusterpreneurs, as representatives university, government, and industry are involved in the initiative. The group of clusterpreneurs often consists of both public and private actors, and the presence of the latter in particular serves to legitimize cluster policy. Concerted action, where links between different actors are created through informal cooperation, is another important feature of clusterpreneurship. Such action helps to overcome a main problem of peripheral regions – the lack of social capital and ability to stimulate collective learning and action. This cluster initiative is characterized by the concerted, in many cases collective, action of the clusterpreneurs. We observe an evolution of this action, from the informal collaboration between university and hospital through the establishment of the HEALTHnTECH Research Centre to the founding of the Research House.

There is clearly a formalization process going on, spurred by the clusterpreneurs. In particular, this is seen in the establishment of BioMed Community as an organization devoted to the promotion of the cluster and, later, the creation of the "Firms Club". The formalization of a group of clusterpreneurs (such as in the form of an organization), which can be a possible outcome and continuation of the concerted action, is an important step in clusterpreneurs' development, enhancing the quality of the links between the actors and the synergy effect. Clusterpreneurs have a common vision of their cluster that is formulated in a strategy. It should be emphasized that this common vision exists in spite of any divergent interests among the actors involved in the cluster initiative, which are especially likely to be observed in peripheral regions, where unemployment is often the biggest concern of the public actors. Network policy plays an important role in clusterpreneurs' strategy. As previously mentioned, network policy is not easy to enforce collaboration and it may be the most difficult part of cluster policy.

The clusterpreneurs are united by the common vision of a prospective biomedical cluster in North Jutland in spite of the fact that they represent very different types of actor with divergent interests. This common vision is translated into a formalized strategy for the biomedical cluster development.[17] The cross-factorial character of the clusterpreneurs gives legitimacy to the initiative, which can overcome some of dilemmas connected with the promotion of high-tech clusters in peripheral regions. Local society can be more likely to accept the dedication of financial resources to a biomedical cluster if they see many different actors collaborating on its promotion.

The biomedical cluster initiative in North Jutland uses network policy as the main instrument of the clusterpreneurs' action. All the activities at Research House, including the appointment of the new consultants, and branding of the cluster by the clusterpreneurs, aim to build new contacts, particularly within the industry both in and outside the region. This is an important part of the process of building social capital in the region and, while it may be a general element in stimulating the evolution of clusters, it is arguably even more important in biotech. Maine et al. (2010) contend that knowledge in biotech is often intrinsically tacit and therefore more proximity-dependent. Despite the fact that biotech firms also source knowledge from all over the world, they benefit more than firms in many other fields from clustering. Moreover, established traditions for cooperation in North Jutland, due to the presence of an existing (ICT) cluster, have made it easier for the clusterpreneurs to realize a new cluster initiative.

6.7 Conclusions

This paper has presented and discussed the role of actors in cluster formation in different regional contexts. We use the term 'clusterpreneurs' for important actors in cluster formation and emphasize their collective/group character. Clusterpreneurs can comprise four types of actor: (i) university and other research organizations; (ii) policymakers; (iii) private firms and industry associations; (iv) business services and financing organizations. The arguments were illustrated by a single case, the promotion of a biomedical cluster in North Jutland. Our findings suggest that cluster policies in less favored regions, like North Jutland, face substantial challenges. Several reports and studies have pointed to the instruments of cluster policies and the conditions for successful cluster development initiatives. However, we find that a deficiency in the literature is the lack of emphasis on the importance of social capital (which can be symbolized by the clusterpreneurs) and discussions on how this can be stimulated. This perspective, combined with the fact that less favored regions often have weaknesses in their employment structure, specialization pattern, social and institutional structure, entrepreneurial traditions, availability of venture capital, educational level, and so on, poses substantial problems for active cluster policies.

We further believe that policies may be restricted by a need for legitimization. This problem is especially present in less favored regions. We find that the cross-factorial character of clusterpreneurs – the fact that they comprise not only government but also private agents, firms, or university representatives, as in the biomedical cluster case – helps to legitimize cluster policy.

However, we found that North Jutland may deviate from the usual picture of the less favored region. Although it has characteristics of a less favored region as far as structural indicators are concerned when compared with the rest of Denmark, it also possesses features atypical of less favored regions: the presence of social capital and a tradition of concerted action, which emerged with the successful development of a previous cluster. The challenge of promoting the biomedical cluster was taken up by clusterpreneurs in the hope of replicating that past success. This gave them both a mental and a social proximity and fostered agreement on objectives that reached further than the region's short-term unemployment problems. It was stated in the introduction that less developed regions often lack social capital. Admittedly, this one case is not a convincing reason for rejecting that assertion, but it does show that there are exceptions to this pattern.

Our analysis points to some problems in the promotion of the biomedical technology cluster in the region, the main one being the achievement of a critical mass of firms. This critical mass may be needed for the cluster to be able to compete at national and international level and to facilitate a take-off of interaction and synergy within the cluster (classic Marshallian agglomeration effects). In addition to the lack of critical mass, the biomedical cluster currently includes no large firms, which in the long run could make the cluster more sustainable through spin-offs and a more stable competence base. Finally, it is consistently a question how to ensure the transfer of competencies from university to industry or, as noted in the introduction, to ensure a well functioning system for the commercialization of research.

Our main conclusion with respect to establishing the biomedical cluster in the peripheral North Jutland region is that in spite of having the structural characteristics of a periphery, such as high unemployment, a low share of university-educated workers, a low R&D ratio, and low growth and income, North Jutland has some important beneficial institutional features that are atypical for peripheral regions. In particular there are social capital and networks to draw upon, and there is a world class research facility at the local university, which make up an important part of the competency base. Hence, together with active policy/clusterpreneurs, these institutional advantages may alleviate the traditional structural deficiencies characteristic of less developed regions.

We also found in our case study that history and context matter in another way. The Danish social welfare model, with its extensively publicly supported help for people with various disabilities, means that there is a large demand for devices and instruments produced by firms in the cluster. This may be an important condition for the way the cluster has developed so far and may be important to how it will evolve in the future. The fact that the commercialization of research is not purely technology-push, but also to a large extent demand-driven may be an important success factor for high-tech cluster development in general and for our case specifically. Further research could elaborate on how macroeconomic conditions and demand influence the viability of clusters.

Appendix

List of interviews

Charlotte Villadsen, managing clerk at Industry Liaison Office at Aalborg University

Allan Næs Gjerding, office director at North Jutland County until April 2004

Ulla Christensen, responsible for Biomedico initiative at North Jutland County, especially for the contacts with the hospital

Simon Eskildsen, graduate from the Institute of Health and Science Technology, research assistant involved in the university start-up company

Jens Haase, medical doctor in neurosurgery retired, presently professor at SMI, Aalborg University

Thomas Sinkjær, professor, head of SMI, key person for the development of medical technology at Aalborg University, Neurodan's founder

Egon Toft, medical doctor, cardiologist at Aalborg Hospital, also visiting professor at Aalborg University

Steven Rees, associate professor at the Centre for Model-based Decision Making at Aalborg University

Jeppe Vangsgaard, consultant at HealthandTEch Research Centre involved in Biomedico cluster promotion activities

Lasse Mogensen, consultant at HealthandTEch Research Centre employed until February 2005

Jens Luebeck Johansen, start-up consultant at HealthandTEch Research Centre, former administrative director at Neurodan

Jesper Nielsen, product development director at Neurodan

Morten Haugland, founder and scientific officer of Neurodan

Finn Allan Larsen, consultant at Aalborg Commercial Council responsible for Biomedico cluster initiative

Poul Ernst Rasmussen, Managing Director of NOVI A/S

Suni A Dalbø, Technology Transfer Office at Aalborg University

Notes

We would like to thank commentators on earlier drafts of the paper, especially Mike Crone, Queens University Management School; Ray Oakey, Manchester Business School; Hans Gullestrup, AAU; Pablo d'Este, SPRU; and Tessa van der Valk, Utrecht University. Errors remain our responsibility.

1. *The Cluster Initiative Greenbook* defines a cluster initiative as an organized effort to increase the growth and competitiveness of a cluster within a region, involving cluster firms, government and/or the research community (Sölvell et al., 2003).
2. See then extensive list of such reports at http://rtsinc.org/publications/index.html.
3. The concept of clusterpreneur was presented in the "The Cluster Initiative Greenbook" at the 6th Global TCI Conference held in Gothenburg, Sweden in September 2003. The purpose of this Greenbook was to give a summary of current practices in organizing and implementing cluster initiatives around the world (Sölvell et al., 2003). The Greenbook presents data from over 250 Cluster Initiatives around the world, based on Global Cluster Initiative Survey 2003 and a series of case studies.
4. One exception is Brenner (2005), who makes quantitative analyses of cluster emergence.
5. Orsenigo (2006) sees clusters as a combination of a strong academic knowledge base, entrepreneurship, venture capital, a strong IPR regime, and other infrastructure- and entrepreneurship-supporting institutions.
6. Lorenzen (1998) finds in a study of a Danish furniture cluster that key clusterpreneurs are to be found in local lodges and clubs (such as Rotary clubs), where the build-up of trust and mental coherence provides a basis for business collaboration.
7. Another example of emphasis on the role of the actors in cluster initiatives can be found in DTI (2004), *A Practical Guide to Cluster Development*. The authors of the *Guide* claim that the success of clusters is often associated with strong leadership, from either individuals or institutions. They identify the function of industry leaders in removing obstacles, assisting in cultivating collaborations between cluster stakeholders, developing a vision, and acting as 'champions' for the future strategy of the cluster (p. 50).
8. This may be reflected in the large differences between European countries in the level of private investments in vocational training, an area also characterized by free-rider problems.
9. Related areas include biostatistics, nanotechnology and model-based medical decision support.
10. http://www.smi.hst.aau.dk/
11. http://www.hst.aau.dk/lsr/
12. During the evolution of this cluster, international companies like Siemens, Motorola, Maxon, L.M. Ericsson, Texas Instruments, and Flextronics established subsidiaries in North Jutland as a part of the ICT cluster.
13. Aalborg Commercial Council provides services to more than 5000 companies, including advice on business start-up, finance, export and import, staff and management development, marketing, and obtaining subsidies.

14. In fact, it is explicitly expressed in interviews conducted by the authors that the ambition is to replicate the successful development of the ICT cluster. Policy had an important role in the later phase of the development of that cluster and policy-makers in the region are aware that active policy may likewise be decisive for the biomedical cluster.
15. www.biomedcom.dk
16. According to the creators of the club, "power is in unity".
17. Strategi for udvikling af bio/medicokompetence klynge I Nordjylland med SWOT analyse [Strategy for the development of a biomedical competence cluster in North Jutland with SWOT analyses], April 23, 2003.

References

BioMed Community, *Innovation for the Living*, Competence Catalogue, 2004.

Brenner, T. (2004), *Local Industrial Clusters: Existence, Emergence and Evolution*, London and New York, Routledge.

Brenner, T. (2005), 'Innovation and cooperation during the emergence of local industrial clusters: an empirical study of Germany', *European Planning Studies*, 13(6), 921–938.

Commission of the European Communities (1988), *Science and Technology for Regional Innovation and Development in Europe*, Brussels.

Cooke, P. (2001a), 'Regional innovation systems, clusters and the knowledge economy', *Industrial and Corporate Change*, 10(4), 945–974.

Cooke, P. (2001b), 'New economy innovation systems: biotechnology in Europe and the USA', *Industry and Innovation*, 8(3), 267–289.

Dalum, B., Laursen, K. and Villumsen, G. (1998), 'Structural change in OECD export specialisation patterns: de-specialisation and "stickiness"', *International Review of Applied Economics*, 12(3), 423–443.

DTI (2004), *A Practical Guide to Cluster Development*. Report. Department of Trade and Industry, East England.

Edquist, C. (2001), 'Innovation policy in the systems of innovation approach: some basic principles', in M.M. Fischer and J. Fröhlich (eds), *Knowledge Complexity and Innovation Systems*, Berlin, Springer.

Enright, H. (2001), Regional Clusters: What We Know and What We Should Know, Paper presented at the Kiel Institute International Workshop on Innovation Clusters and Interregional Competition, Kiel, November 12–13.

Etzkovitz, H. and Leydersdorff, L. (2000), 'The dynamics of innovation: from National Systems and "Mode 2" to a Triple Helix of university–industry–government relations', *Research Policy*, 29, 109–123.

Feldman, M.P. (2001), 'The entrepreneurial event revisited: firm formation in a regional context', *Industrial and Corporate Change*, 10(4), 861–891.

Feldman, M.P., Francis, J. and Bercovitz, J. (2005), 'Creating a cluster while building a firm: entrepreneurs and the formation of industrial clusters', *Regional Studies*, 39, 129–141.

Feldman, M.P. and Francis, J. (2006), 'Entrepreneurs as agents in the formation of industrial clusters', in B. Asheim, P. Cooke and R. Martin (eds), *Clusters and Regional Development*, London and New York, Routledge, pp. 115–136.

Fromhold-Eisebith, M. and Eisebith, G. (2005), 'How to institutionalize innovative clusters? Comparing explicit top-down and implicit bottom-up approaches', *Research Policy*, 34, 1250–1268.

Gambardella, A., Bresnahan, T. and Saxeenian, A. (2002), 'Old Economy' Inputs for 'New Economy' Outcomes: Cluster Formation in the New Silicon Valleys, Paper presented at DRUID Conference on Industrial Dynamics of the New and Old Economy – who is embracing whom?, Copenhagen, June 6–8.

Glaeser, E. (2003), 'The new economics of urban and regional growth', in G. Clark, M. Feldman and M. Gertler (eds), *The Oxford Handbook of Economic Geography*. Oxford, Oxford University Press, pp. 83–98.

Keeble, D. and Wilkinson (2000), 'High-technology SMEs, regional clustering and collective learning: an overview', in D. Keeble and F. Wilkinson (eds), *High-Technology Clusters, Networking and Collective Learning in Europe*, Aldershot, Ashgate.

Lorenzen, M. (ed.) (1998), *Specialisation and Localised Learning. Six Studies on the European Furniture Industry*, Copenhagen, Copenhagen Business School Press.

Maine, E.M., Shapiro, D.M. and Vining, A.R. (2010), 'The role of clustering in the growth of new technology-based firms', *Small Business Economics*, 34, 127–146.

Martin, R. and Sunley, P. (2003), 'Deconstructing clusters: chaotic concept or policy panacea?', *Journal of Economic Geography*, 3, 5–35.

Mason, C.M. (2007), 'The geography of venture capital investments' in H. Landström (ed.), *Handbook of Venture Capital Research*, Edward Elgar, Cheltenham.

Menzel, M.-P. and Fornahl, D. (2009), 'Cluster life cycles – dimensions and rationales of cluster evolution', *Industrial and Corporate Change*, 19(1), 205–238.

Morgan, K. (1997), 'The Learning Region: Institutions, Innovation and Regional Renewal', *Regional Studies*, 31(5), 491–503.

Nauwelaers, C. (2001), 'Path-dependency and the role of institutions in cluster policy generation', in Å. Mariussen (ed.), *Cluster Policies – Cluster Development?*, Nordregio Report, 2001, p. 2.

OECD (1993), *Territorial Development and Structural Change: A New Perspective on Adjustment and Reform*, Paris.

OECD (1999), 'Boosting Innovation: The Cluster Approach', OECD Proceedings, Paris.

OECD (2001), *Innovative Clusters. Drivers of national innovation systems*, Paris.

Orsenigo, L. (2006), 'Clusters and clustering: stylized facts, issues, and theories' in P. Braunerhjelm and M. Feldman (eds), *Cluster Genesis*, Oxford, Oxford University Press.

Porter, M. (1998a), *On Competition*, Boston, Harvard Business School Press.

Porter, M. (1998), 'Location, clusters and the "new" microeconomics of competition', *Business Economics*, 3(1), 7–17.

Porter, M. (2000), 'Location, competition and economic development: local clusters in a global economy', *Economic Development Quarterly*, 14(1):15–34.

Raines, P. (2002), *Cluster Development and Policy*, EPRC Studies in European Policy, Aldershot, Ashgate.

Regeringen (2000), *Handlingsplan – Biomedicoområdet*. Copenhagen.

Rosenfeld, S. (2002), 'Creating smart systems: a guide to cluster strategies in less favoured regions', A report to the European Union-Regional Innovation Strategies.

Spilling, O.R. and Steinsli, J. (2003), 'Evolution of high-technology clusters: Oslo and Trondheim in international comparison', BI Norwegian School of Management, Research report no.1/2003.

Sternberg, R. (2003), 'New firms, regional development and the cluster approach – what can technology policies achieve?' in J. Bröcher, Dohse, D and Soltwedel,R. (eds) *Innovation Clusters and Interregional Competition*, Berlin, Springer, pp. 347–371.

Stoerring, D. and Dalum, B. (2007), 'Cluster emergence: a comparative study of two cases in North Jutland, Denmark' in P. Cooke and D. Schwartz (eds) *Creative Regions: Technology, Culture and Knowledge Entrepreneurship*, Series: Regions and Cities, Routledge, London.

Stuart, T. and Sorenson, O. (2003), 'The geography of opportunity: spatial heterogeneity in founding rates and the performance of biotechnology firms', *Research Policy*, 32(2), 229–253.

Sölvell, O. Lindqvist, G. and Ketels, C. (2003), The Cluster Initiative Greenbook, report presented at the TCI 6th Global Conference: Innovative Clusters – A New Challenge, September 17–19, Gothenburg.

Therrien, P. (2005), 'City and innovation: different size, different strategy', *European Planning Studies*, 13(6), 873–877.

Tödtling, F. and Trippl, M. (2005), 'One size fits all? Towards a differentiated regional innovation policy approach', *Research Policy*, 34, 1203–1219.

7
Social Capital, Knowledge, and Competitiveness: The Cases of the Basque Paper and Electronics/ICT Clusters

Jesus María Valdaliso, Aitziber Elola, Maria José Aranguren, and Santiago López

7.1 Introduction

The importance of clusters and spatial networks for economic development has been largely acknowledged in economic and business literature (see, for example, Porter, 1998; Martin and Sunley, 2003; Malmberg and Maskell, 2002). Empirical evidence shows that companies in clusters experience stronger growth and faster innovation than those outside clusters, and that clusters attract more start-ups than regions without clusters (Audretsch and Feldman, 1996; Baptista and Swann, 1998; Baptista, 2000; Klepper, 2007; Swann et al., 1998). These characteristics cause clusters to be considered a prerequisite for regional prosperity (Porter, 2003; Bathelt, 2001). Many policy-makers have also recognized this phenomenon and turned to policies based on cooperative networks (Aranguren et al., 2006).

The Basque Autonomous Community (Spain) was among the earliest regions in the world to develop a cluster policy (Ketels, 2004). During the early 1990s, when the region was immersed in an economic recession, the Basque Government pioneered a competitiveness policy based on clusters (see, for example, Aranguren et al., 2005; Azua, 2003). At the moment, twelve Cluster Associations are operating in the Basque Autonomous Community, and clustered companies account for about 30% of both the industrial employment and the industrial value added of the region.

Both at the theoretical and the empirical level, much of the existing literature focuses on understanding the existence and functioning of successful contemporary clusters (Bergman, 2009). One of the most popular models for explaining cluster competitiveness is Michael E. Porter's (1990) diamond model. Porter explains cluster competitiveness in terms of four factor groups: factor (input) conditions; demand conditions; firm strategy and rivalry; and related and supporting industries. Both Porter and several other authors explicitly recognize the role of social capital and knowledge in local innovation processes and, hence, in cluster competitiveness (see, for example, Capello and Faggian, 2005; Hauser et al., 2007; Keeble et al., 1999). However, how social capital influences learning and innovation and, thus, cluster competitiveness remains a mystery (Martin and Sunley, 2003).

In this work, we aim at advancing knowledge on cluster competitiveness. For that purpose, starting from Porter's diamond model on cluster competitiveness, we introduce social capital and knowledge into the analysis. We analyze the role of these two variables in the evolution and present position of the paper cluster, and the electronics and ICT cluster of the Basque Autonomous Community. We also discuss the implications of our findings for policy-makers.

7.2 Social capital and knowledge

Knowledge is one of the most valuable intangibles in organizations (Boschma, 2005). Firms, clusters, and regions can develop sustainable competitive advantages on the basis of knowledge that other competitors cannot easily imitate or transfer (Boschma, 2004; Lawson and Lorenz, 1999; Porter and Sölvell, 1997).

Some types of knowledge are easier to transfer than others. Explicit or codified knowledge, such as scientific knowledge about nature's principles and laws, can be easily formalized, written, and reproduced. This knowledge is relatively easily transferable. On the contrary, tacit knowledge is not articulated and cannot be written, easily transferred or imitated. It needs to be acquired through experience (learning by doing) or through direct interpersonal contact (learning by interacting).

The geographical proximity of firms and other agents, such as technological centers, technological parks and business parks, is an aspect often highlighted in the study of competitiveness. This proximity results in knowledge spillovers and localization economies (Marshallian externalities), and eases firms' access to a qualified labor force, knowledge, infrastructures, and joint R&D facilities (see, for example, Malmberg and Maskell, 2002). Proximity gains special importance in the case of tacit (non-codified) knowledge, as this type of knowledge is more location-specific than explicit knowledge. But it is not only geographical proximity that plays an effective role in the generation and transfer of knowledge, in interactive and collective learning, and in innovation. Cognitive, social, and institutional proximity are also essential (Boschma, 2005; Lawson and Lorenz, 1999; Malmberg and Maskell, 2002). Learning (especially doing, using, and interacting, or DUI, learning) can be fostered by building structures and relationships, that is, through the creation of social capital.[1]

As social capital is intangible, non-tradable and difficult to imitate and/or copy (Bourdieu, 1986; Pennings et al., 1998; Westlund, 2006), the development of social capital can be a source of sustainable competitive advantage (Nahapiet and Ghoshal, 1998). Thus, differences in the performance of firms and in cluster, regional, or even national competitiveness could reflect differences in their ability to create and exploit social capital (Capello and Faggian, 2005; Hauser et al., 2007; Keeble et al., 1999; Nahapiet and Ghoshal, 1998; Porter and Sölvell, 1997; Westlund, 2006).

7.3 Social capital, knowledge and competitiveness

In the previous section we highlighted the importance of social capital. We argued that the development of social capital can be a source of sustainable competitive advantage, as it is related to positive results such as the generation and transfer of knowledge, learning, and innovation, among others. In this section we aim to explain the influence of social capital, knowledge, and learning processes on regional competitive advantage. For that purpose, starting from Michael E. Porter's diamond model, in the following sections we propose to introduce the influence of social capital, knowledge, and learning processes into the four dimensions of this framework (see Figure 7.1).

7.3.1 Dimension 1: Density of factor conditions (from fluid to sticky)

Factor (input) conditions are the conditions that must be present in a region, such as the availability of qualified labor, financing, and infrastructure (physical, computer, technological, and so on) in order to enhance its competitiveness. The existence of research and educational infrastructures that provide highly qualified human capital, collaborative social organizations such as cluster associations, social networks (of university graduates, postgraduates, and researchers), and relationships between firms and other institutional agents can create a supply of human capital specific – sticky to the region and the cluster. On the contrary, the lack of well developed educational and research

```
                    TECHNOLOGICAL REGIME, FIRM STRATEGY & INDUSTRY STRUCTURE
                              (From routinized to entrepreneurial)

- Open resources, open innovation    High turbulence                              - Proprietary information and
  system (joint R&D projects)        knowledge heterogeneity   Entrepre-            technology (patents, trade secret,
- Cooperation and competition   ⇐   and diversity              neurial   Maturity of products &   copyrights, in house R&D)
- Common base of knowledge,         Networks of specialist firms         technologies          ⇒ - In house learning
  collective learning               Strategy: innovation and             Incumbent firms         - Market power and competition
- High mobility of human capital    product differentiation              Focused knowledge
  between firms (spin-offs)                                              Strategy: scale economics
                                                                         and product specialisation

         DENSITY FACTOR CONDITIONS
            (From fluid to sticky)         Sticky                Qualified         DEMAND CONDITIONS
                 ⇓                                                              (From widespread to qualified)
                                                                                         ⇓
- Research & educational system
- Social collaborative organizations                                            - Comsumption/industrial
  (cluster association)                                                         - Standardised/experimental
- Venture and seed capital                                                        customers and niche markets
- Relational capital (social networks)                                          - Price sensitive/innovation sensitive
                                                                                - National or international
                                                  High
                                             RELATED VARIETY
                                              (From low to high)
                                                    ⇓
                                       Determined by
                                       - Diversity of related and supporting industries
                                       - Joint research projects with other clusters and industries
                                       - Related variety at regional level
                                       - Shared technological regime by suppliers
```

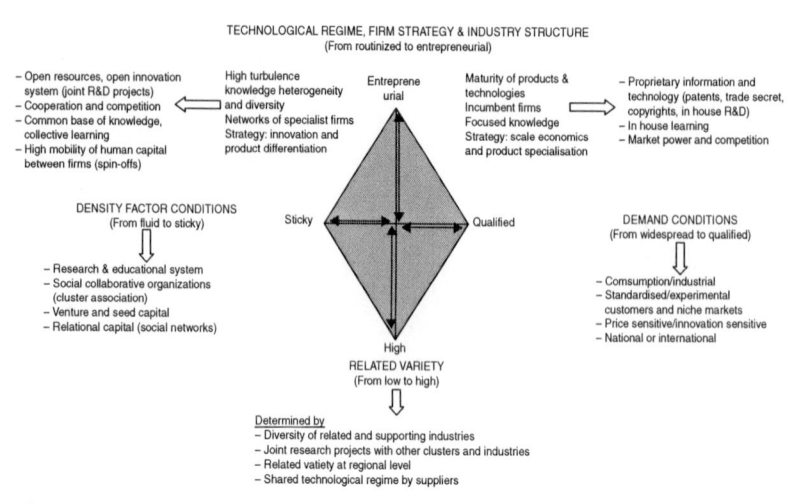

Figure 7.1 Social capital, knowledge, and competitive advantage of clusters

infrastructures, the absence of collaborative social organizations, and low levels of social capital cause factor conditions to be 'fluid', that is, easier to imitate and replicate.

7.3.2 Dimension 2: Demand conditions (from widespread to qualified)

Demand plays a crucial role in explaining firms' innovation processes and the competitiveness of the cluster as a whole. The existence of a robust and qualified demand (experimental and innovation-sensitive customers, niche markets) may speed up learning and innovation processes (Malerba, 2006; Malerba et al., 2007), while standardized and price-sensitive demand may not have such an effect. Clustered firms may benefit from the proximity of such experimental customers and niche markets. Once again, collaboration and trust between firms and customers may ease learning and the sharing of information and knowledge. It may result in joint projects that could make demand more qualified and more difficult to replicate in another location.

7.3.3 Dimension 3: Technological regime, firm strategy, and industry structure (from routinized to entrepreneurial)

Firms' strategy and rivalry co-evolves with the technological regime and life-cycle of the clustering industries, with the cluster's knowledge base, and with social (relational) capital (Bergman, 2007; Fornahl and Menzel,

2007; Malerba, 2006; Malerba and Orsenigo, 1993, 2000). We depict two opposite generic technological (and learning) regimes: entrepreneurial and routinized (Winter, 1984). An entrepreneurial regime corresponds to young industries with high turbulence (high rates of firm birth and death), low entry barriers, and high knowledge heterogeneity or diversity. These industries comprise networks of specialist firms that share resources and knowledge (which is indicative of the presence of social capital) but also compete with each other in accordance with a strategy of innovation and product differentiation. A routinized regime corresponds to mature industries with low turbulence, high entry barriers, and a more focused knowledge base. The industry is dominated by a core of incumbent firms that have a proprietary technology (therefore, the inter-firm flow of knowledge and the degree of cooperation are much more limited) and follow a strategy of product specialization, and cost and price competition based on economies of scale.

7.3.4 Dimension 4: Related variety (from low to high)

By related variety we mean inter-sectoral relatedness in terms of similar and/or complementary knowledge bases. It is argued that spillovers occur not only between firms within a sector or within a cluster but also between sectors and/or clusters with similar and/or complementary knowledge bases. Related variety is associated with Jacobs externalities, but it also shows systemic and intangible features at regional level, which make it very difficult to imitate (Asheim et al., 2009; Frenken et al., 2007). The presence of social capital and learning processes among agents in related activities generates new knowledge, which increases the probability of identifying synergies and generating related activities. At the same time, related variety makes the region as a whole less vulnerable to technological and/or market changes and can be an additional source of economic growth (Glaeser et al., 1992; Jacobs, 1969; Van Oort, 2004).

7.3.5 The role of government

Government can play an important role in the improvement of competitiveness, influencing, according to Michael E. Porter, the four vertexes of the diamond. For example, governments can provide infrastructure and education and research facilities, or promote networks and other types of collaboration (Enright, 2001), facilitating learning processes between cluster agents and government, and generating new knowledge and policies that are more closely adapted to the needs of the cluster.

7.3.6 Dynamics of the model

In principle, the bigger the diamond's size is, the more difficult to imitate is the cluster's competitive advantage and, hence, the more sustainable it becomes. Diamond's size is strongly correlated with stickier factor conditions, more qualified demand, an entrepreneurial technological regime, and a higher degree of related variety in the region. However, as time passes and technology and industry life cycles evolve, a 'downsizing tension' within the diamond seems to be in motion due to a less entrepreneurial and more routinized technological regime, an increasingly standardized demand, and fluid factor conditions. This competitive position may also generate growth, but the competitive advantage of the cluster becomes more easily imitable by other competitors and, hence, less sustainable in the long-term.

7.4 The Basque paper and electronics/ICT clusters

In this section we analyze two clusters of the Basque Autonomous Community, a paper cluster, and an electronics and ICT cluster. After a brief review of the evolution of each cluster (Table 7.1),[2] we analyze their competitiveness based on the conceptual model introduced in the previous sections.

7.4.1 Basque paper cluster

The origins of the Basque paper industry can be traced back to the late eighteenth century. The triggering factor was local demand, together with the bountiful hydro-generating resources of the region. Other factors, such as qualified labor and technology, were imported from south-western France.

During the second half of the nineteenth century, the introduction of new (Fourdrinier) technology and improvements in transportation and communications, and the subsequent increase in the available market and improvement in access to foreign raw materials, allowed the expansion of the cluster. Existing companies increased production capacity and new businesses were created. The regional concentration of firms generated economies of agglomeration, knowledge spillovers and a favorable context for cooperation among firms. The first related and supporting industries also arose during this period.

In the early twentieth century, as consumption and (national) market size grew, the average company size also increased, as a consequence of mergers among existing firms and the founding of larger new companies. During this period, new auxiliary sectors formed, considerable improvements in labor skills were made as industrial sectors fostered training colleges, and capital markets developed. Proximity and local know-how generated a climate of trust (relational capital) that yielded lower information and transaction costs, which, in turn, led to strategies of specialization.

From 1959 to 1975, the liberalization of the Spanish economy facilitated the evolution of the cluster. It opened the road to the acquisition of both raw materials and modern machinery. New institutional conditions and internal demand growth prompted companies to invest in new production machinery.

During its last three decades, the cluster faced the increasing internationalization of the paper industry, on both the supply and the demand side. As we explain in the following sections, the Basque paper cluster did not manage to adapt to this new environment and it is at present in decline.

7.4.2 Basque electronics and ICT cluster

The origins of the Basque electronics and ICT cluster date back to the late 1940s. Its development was due to local industrial demand and favorable factor conditions, including a qualified labor force and local entrepreneurs who imported foreign technology. From the 1960s, local firms improved imported technology and developed their own products and solutions. Local initiative, together with central government support, resulted in the creation of technological centers linked to firms, universities, and industry associations. Starting in the late 1950s, engineering firms were created. Later, those firms played an important role in the definition of products and solutions to be adopted by the industry.

A technological breakthrough (c. 1975) marked the beginning of the expansion of the cluster: the explosion of microelectronics and chip technology, and the transition from analogue to digital technologies. Existing firms augmented their national market share, started internationalization processes, and invested large amounts in R&D in order to develop proprietary technology. New firms were also created in the cluster, both in the existing activities and in related ones. In this period, the clustered firms benefited from favorable factor conditions, especially the availability of qualified labor. Finally, government played a notable role, creating an electronics industry association (AIEPV), and implementing technological policy programs (IMI, PET). These policy measures promoted collaboration among firms, universities, and technological centers, which materialized in training programs, joint participation in R&D programs and projects, and internationalization.

Table 7.1 Lifecycle of the Basque paper cluster and electronics/ICT clusters

Paper cluster	Emergence ca. 1800–1841	Exploratory expansion ca. 1841–1900	Exploitative expansion ca. 1900–1936	Persistence ca. 1940–1975	Decline ca. 1975–
Factor conditions	Natural resources (water) Pre-industrial technology Foreign labor and entrepreneurship	Natural resources Local and foreign entrepreneurship Technological change Improved transport and communications (imports of coal and raw materials – wood pulp)	Natural resources Local entrepreneurship Local skilled labor Existing base of resources, capabilities and knowledge	Natural resources Local entrepreneurship Local skilled labor (Paper School of Tolosa)	Foreign capital Local skilled labor Global market for raw materials, products and machinery
Demand conditions	Regional market	Growing regional and national market (protected by the state – tariffs)	Growing national market (protected by the state – tariffs)	Growing national market (protected by the state – tariffs) First exports (European market)	From national to European market (increasing imports and exports) Globalization
Firm strategy and rivalry		Market and product specialization Increasing rivalry due to new entrant firms	Concentration and mergers Scale economies in print paper Product differentiation (writing paper)	Diminishing national rivalry but increasing imports Scale economies and product specialization	Diminishing national rivalry but increasing foreign rivalry due to imports Scale economies and product specialization

	Appearance	Development (machine repairing and building industry; banks)	Development (machine repairing and building industry)	Development (machine repairing and building industry)	Development and internationalization (machine repairing and building industry)
Related and supporting industries	Few				
Number of firms	Few	Increasing	Increasing	Persisting	Diminishing
Employment	Few	Increasing	Increasing	Increasing	Diminishing
Knowledge heterogeneity (diversity)	Scarce	Increasing	Persisting	Persisting	Declining
Relational capital	Few	Agglomeration economies and knowledge spillovers Cooperation	Agglomeration economies and knowledge spillovers Cooperation (labor formation, lobbying)	Trade and research association but less cooperation and more hierarchy	Cluster association but less cooperation and more hierarchy

Continued

Table 7.1 Continued

Electronics and ICT cluster	Emergence ca. 1950–1975	Exploratory expansion ca. 1975–1996	Exploitative expansion ca. 1996–	Persistence	Decline
Factor conditions	Local skilled labor and entrepreneurship and imported technology Technical schools and universities (engineers) Central government support and local initiatives: technological centers linked to firms and universities	Technological revolution (digital divide) – entrepreneurial technological regime and low entry barriers Local skilled labor, seed and venture capital and entrepreneurship Technical schools, universities (first graduates in electronics, computer sciences and telecommunications), technological centers and parks Central and regional government support (knowledge diffusion, R&D activities and cooperation –cluster policy)	Local skilled labor, capital and entrepreneurship Technical schools, universities, technological centers and parks and R&D units Government support (cluster policy, R&D activities...)		
Demand conditions	Regional (industry) and national (electric utilities) market protected by tariffs	Liberalized national market Increasing exports and internationalization New and developing markets, products and solutions	Global and increasing market Market development and product/applications standardization Uncertainty about new markets		
Firm strategy and rivalry	High R&D expenses Development of proprietary technology	High R&D expenses Proprietary technology Product innovation Increasing rivalry, but cooperation in R&D, labor formation and internationalization	High R&D expenses Proprietary technology From firms to groups From product to integral innovative solutions Internationalization Sustaining rivalry, but cooperation in R&D, labor formation and internationalization		

Related and supporting industries	Increasing (engineering firms and electric utilities firms)	Development (automotive industry, machine-tool industry, electric utilities, engineering, financial sector)	Development (automotive and machine-tool industries, electrical utilities, engineering, financial sector) Other clusters and cluster associations
Firm's population	Few, but increasing	Increasing, start-ups and spin-offs (creative destruction)	Increasing
Employment	Increasing	Increasing	Increasing
Knowledge heterogeneity (Diversity)	Scarce, focused on electronics (professional and components)	Increasing (microelectronics, software, automation), but technological convergence among different sectors	Increasing (telecommunications, Internet, media), but technological convergence among different sectors
Relational capital	Research associations	Trade association (1983) Networks of university graduates in science and engineering colleges and master's programs: common base of learning Spin-offs Joint research projects and efforts at internationalization	Cluster association (1996) Networks of university graduates Spin-offs Joint research projects and efforts at internationalization Mutual knowledge and previous fruitful experience of collaboration

Since 1996, two characteristics stand out in the evolution of the cluster: the inclusion of new activity sectors (computing and software, telecommunications, and the content industry), and globalization. In this period, new firm creation and spin-off dynamics continued. Existing firms responded to the challenge of globalization by adopting three strategies: (i) increasing their size; (ii) continuing the internationalization process started in the previous period (increasing exports and opening subsidiaries abroad); and (iii) integrating in business groups. The former industry association (AIEPV) transformed into a cluster association (GAIA), and firms continued to count on the Basque Government's support and an already consolidated research infrastructure (universities and technological centers and parks).

7.5 Social capital, knowledge and competitiveness: the paper and electronics/ICT clusters

7.5.1 Density of factor conditions

In the case of the Basque Autonomous Community, the advantages that the paper cluster had in the early stages of its life-cycle were based on easily imitable or replicable factor conditions. Currently, local skilled labor is available (Paper School in Tolosa). However, the research and educational infrastructure related to the paper cluster is not strong, as technological centers specialized in the paper industry are absent, and there is little tradition of collaboration with universities and technological centers. In addition, although there exists a collaborative organization (Clusterpapel, the cluster association), its members are frequently reluctant to collaborate.

Firms in the electronics and ICT cluster benefit from good factor conditions, in particular from the availability of qualified human capital. The Basque Autonomous Community has a well developed system of secondary technical schools and a good science and technology infrastructure, which provide factor conditions highly specific to the needs of this cluster. In the electronics and ICT cluster, there are informal networks of university graduates, researchers, and post-graduates (IMI fellows); formal associations of graduate and postgraduate students; a high mobility of people between technological and R&D centers and firms (spin-offs); and a fluid relationship (formal and informal links) between government officials, firms, and education and R&D institutions. The progressive localization of firms and R&D centers in the four technology parks promoted by the regional government have made those relations easier and interactions more frequent (Valdaliso and López, 2008; Valdaliso et al., 2011). Since its origins, the industry association AIEPV (later, the cluster association GAIA) has also developed a proactive strategy of trust-building and inter-firm cooperation in three fields: human capital formation (postgraduate programs), R&D (support, coordination, and leadership of joint research projects and platforms), and internationalization (promoting commercial missions abroad and joint agreements and alliances with local firms in order to enter foreign markets) (Valdaliso et al., 2011).

7.5.2 Demand conditions

In the case of the paper cluster, its demand is quite standardized, and very price sensitive (paper has become a commodity). Then, companies seek scale economies and compete on prices. After the opening of the Spanish economy to the international market, this demand (as well as supply) is increasingly internationalizing.

In contrast, the electronics and ICT cluster benefited, at least since the 1970s, from a sophisticated and robust local industrial demand for innovative solutions (from electrical, machine-tool, and aeronautics companies, automotive components makers, and the banking sector, among others). Thus, the demand for Basque electronics and ICT is more 'qualified' (and growing). The cluster benefits from the proximity of experimental consumers and niche markets, and in some cases the collaboration and trust (social capital) between firms and customers results in joint projects, sharing information and knowledge.

7.5.3 Technological regime, firm strategy and industry structure

The paper sector is a mature industry, both with mature products and technologies, and with oversupply problems in Europe. Today, the paper industry is immersed in a process of concentration, growth in firm size in order to attain economies of scale, product specialization and multilocalization, and the Basque paper cluster is not unaffected by those trends (Valdaliso et al., 2008). The paper cluster is composed of a decreasing number of incumbent firms as a consequence of the concentration process, several firms being absorbed by others and some closing down. In comparison with other European counterparts, the Basque firms are small, they are not highly specialized, and their machinery is in many cases obsolete. Moreover, as a consequence of the lack of social capital in the cluster (e.g., lack of trust among cluster members), clustered firms hardly participate in joint R&D projects.

However, Basque firms in paper-machine building and repairing present quite a different picture. The existence of formal networks (an export consortium) and informal networks allows them to form a more open and collaborative system, which makes collective learning processes (joint R&D projects, for example) possible. The competitive strategy of firms in this sector is based on innovation and product differentiation. At present, some of these firms are recognized at global level and they supply firms worldwide.

The electronics and ICT industry is a young, science- and knowledge-intensive industry with low entry barriers and high turbulence (Malerba and Orsenigo, 1993; Malerba, 2006; Bergman, 2007). The cluster is composed of networks of specialist firms that cooperate (share resources and common knowledge) but also compete, following a strategy of innovation and product differentiation. As a consequence of the existing social capital in the cluster, clustered firms participate in joint R&D projects. The existence of a common base of knowledge also facilitated a process of collective learning (Keeble and Wilkinson, 1999; Keeble et al., 1999; Lawson and Lorenz, 1999) and cognitive proximity and coordination between firms (Boschma, 2005; Lorenzen and Foss, 2003). The common base of knowledge in microelectronics was created in the Basque Autonomous Community in the 1970s around the Faculty of Physics of the University of the Basque Country and several business R&D units (in particular, Ikerlan and Ikaslan). The human capital of these centers spread this knowledge in the 1980s to other university centers, technological centers, and the industry and society as a whole. One of those technicians was responsible for the technology policy of the new regional government, which in 1983 put into practice, in collaboration with the Stanford Research Institute, the IMI program (Introduction of Microelectronics in the Industry), a huge effort of collective learning and knowledge catch-up. Another, a former professor of physics at the University of the Basque Country, put into effect as the director of technology policy for the Basque Government in 1990, in collaboration with the Stanford Research Institute, the Technological Strategy Plan (PET, in Spanish), which linked the efforts of firms, universities, R&D centers, and regional government (Valdaliso and López, 2008; Valdaliso et al., 2011).

7.5.4 Related variety

In the case of the Basque paper cluster, although some related industries exist, such as printing works, the presence of these sub-clusters is not significant and there is no evidence for the existence of collaborative projects between the paper cluster and other clusters and industries.

In the case of the electronics and ICT cluster, there is far more variety within the cluster itself (electronics, computing, telecommunications) and at the regional level, due to the development of sectors such as automotive, machine-tool, and aeronautic industries, electrical companies, engineering firms and banks. The cluster association has undertaken joint research projects with other clusters. At present, collaborative projects between GAIA and four other clusters are running: the automotive cluster (ACICAE), the aeronautics cluster (Hegan), the maritime cluster (Foro Marítimo), and the energy cluster (Cluster Energía).

7.5.5 Role of government

Although government policies were, in principle, rather similar in both cases, their influence on the development of both clusters varied significantly. Since the 1980s, the regional government put in practice a technology policy that created a supportive environment for entrepreneurship, innovation, and productivity, and fostered knowledge diffusion, collaboration, and network building (Aranguren et al., 2007). In those years, technicians, scientists, and entrepreneurs linked to the electronics industry occupied almost all strategic positions in the science and technology government departments and started several programs of human capital formation and technology infrastructure building, particularly focused on new technologies related to ICT. The regional government itself promoted the creation of the Basque electronic industry association in 1983 and fostered its transformation into a cluster association when a new cluster-based competitiveness policy was adopted in the following decade (López et al., 2008). From, the early 1990s, both clusters were included in the Basque government programs to support clusters and improve regional competitiveness. The electronics and ICT cluster, which had greatly benefited from the aforementioned government programs in the 1980s, and which had a long tradition of inter-firm collaboration became one of the most proactive clusters of the Basque country in the 1990s and hereafter. However, in spite of the government effort, the cluster association in the paper industry could not be created until 1998, and then with a few affiliated firms and a lower degree of inter-firm collaboration.

7.6 Conclusions

In this chapter we have analyzed and compared the competitive advantages of two clusters in the Basque Autonomous Community, the paper cluster, and the electronics and ICT cluster. To that purpose, we based our analysis on Michael E. Porter's diamond model (Porter, 1990) but took a step further by introducing two widely acknowledged but largely neglected factors to the model, social capital and knowledge. Social capital is a socially complex phenomenon and, thus, difficult to transfer from one context to another. Therefore, the existence of high levels of social capital in a region or in a cluster may constitute a source of competitive advantage. As we see it, social capital has an effect on knowledge creation and collective learning processes and, in turn, on the four vertexes of the competitiveness diamond. According to our model, social capital contributes to competitiveness in several ways. First, social capital may help to create 'sticky' factor conditions. Second, the existence of firm–consumer networks (social capital) characterizes sectors with qualified demand. Third, social capital is critical for an entrepreneurial technological regime. And finally, higher levels of related variety are a consequence of social capital, as trust may be a prerequisite for firms in different clusters or industries to participate in joint (research) projects. On the other hand, fluid factor conditions, widespread demand, a routinized technological regime, and low related variety may reveal a lack of social capital in a cluster.

We used this framework to explain two current clusters in the Basque Autonomous Community. Our analysis presents two completely different competitive positions for each cluster. On the one hand, the present Basque electronics and ICT cluster can be classified as a cluster with sticky factor conditions, qualified demand, an entrepreneurial technological regime, and quite high related variety. As we illustrate, social capital may be the determining factor behind these characteristics, and the result of this is a growing and a highly competitive cluster. On the other hand, at present, fluid factor conditions, widespread demand conditions, a routinized technological regime, and low related variety characterize the Basque paper cluster. In contrast to the electronics and ICT cluster, social capital in this cluster is not strong (witness the lack of trust among clustered companies). A result of this may be the present situation of the cluster, which is in a decline phase, with a decreasing number of firms and employment in the cluster. The machinery sub-cluster is an exception to the general trends of this cluster. This sub-cluster presents higher levels of social capital, its demand is more qualified, and its technological regime is more of the entrepreneurial type; moreover, paper-machinery manufacturing firms compete internationally and some of them are recognized worldwide.

Our contention in this paper that social capital may impact on cluster competitiveness has some implications for policy-makers. If social capital plays such a positive role in cluster competitiveness, probably one of the most important challenges for government agencies and other organizations, such as cluster associations, is to design policies that foster the creation of social capital, which in turn facilitates collaboration among firms, and collective learning. However, this type of policy is difficult not only to design and implement, but also to evaluate. At present, the indicators that government uses in the evaluation of cluster programs does not include measurements of social capital, but measures aspects of the cluster performance that are much easier to quantify. It would be important for governments to incorporate this type of indicator and to assess how these indicators evolve over time.

Notes

Financial support from MICINN (HAR2009-09264) is acknowledged. Jesús María Valdaliso and Santiago López also acknowledge financial support from the Basque Government (IT–337–10).

1. According to Putnam (1993), social capital is the collection of intangibles such as values, norms, attitudes, and networks that are present in a community and that facilitate coordination and cooperation to obtain mutual benefits.
2. For more details, see Elola et al., 2009; López et al., 2008; Valdaliso et al., 2008.

References

Aranguren, M.J., Iturrioz, C., Aragón, C. and Larrea, M. (2005), 'La política industrial de clúster/redes mejora realmente la competitividad empresarial? Resultados de la evaluación de dos experiencias en la Comunidad de Euskadi' (Does cluster/network policy really enhance business competitiveness? An assessment of the evaluation of two programs in the Basque Community), *Ekonomiaz*, 60, 10–61.

Aranguren, M.J., Larrea, M. and Navarro, I. (2006), 'The policy process: clusters versus spatial networks in the Basque Country', in C. Pitelis, R. Sudgen and J. Wilson (eds) *Clusters and Globalisation. Development of Urban and Regional Economies*, Cheltenham, Edward Elgar, pp. 258–280.

Aranguren, M.J., Aragón, C., Larrea, M., and Iturrioz, C. (2007), 'Does cluster policy really enhance networking and increase competitiveness?', in M.J. Aranguren, C. Iturrioz and J. Wilson (eds), *Networks, Governance and Economic Development: Bridging Disciplinary Frontiers*, Cheltenham, Edward Elgar, pp. 101–128.

Audretsch, D.B. and Feldman M.P. (1996), 'Innovative clusters and the industry life cycle', *Review of Industrial Organization*, 11, 253–273.

Azua, J. (2003), 'La clusterización de la actividad económica: concepto, diseño e innovación' (The clusterization of economic activity: concept, design and innovation), *Ekonomiaz*, 53, 222–238.

Baptista, R. (2000), 'Do innovations diffuse faster within geographical clusters?', *International Journal of Industrial Organization*, 18, 515–535.

Baptista, R. and Swann, P. (1998), 'Do firms in clusters innovate more?', *Research Policy*, 27, 525–540.

Bathelt, H. (2001), 'Regional competence and economic recovery: divergent growth paths in Boston's high technology economy', *Entrepreneurship & Regional Development*, 13, 287–314.

Bergman, E.M. (2009), 'Cluster life-cycles: An emerging synthesis', in C. Karlsson (ed.), *Handbook of Research on Cluster Theory*, Cheltenham, Edward Elgar.

Bourdieu, P. (1986), 'The forms of capital', in J.G. Richardson (ed.), *Handbook of Theory and Research for the Sociology of Education*, New York, Greenwood, pp. 241–258.

Boschma, R.A. (2004), 'Competitiveness of regions from an evolutionary perspective', *Regional Studies*, 38(9), 1001–1014.

Boschma, R.A. (2005), 'Proximity and innovation: a critical assessment', *Regional Studies*, 39(1), 61–74.

Capello, R. and Faggian, A. (2005), 'Collective learning and relational capital in local innovation processes', *Regional Studies*, 39(1), 75–87.

Elola, A., Valdaliso, J.M., Aranguren, M.J. and López, S. (2009), 'Paper-making machines and microchips: a comparison of the Basque paper and ICT clusters' life cycles', working paper.

Enright, M.E. (2001), 'An overview of regional clusters and clustering', Paper presented at the TCI Annual Conference, 28–31 October, Tucson, Arizona.

Frenken, K., Van Oort, F. and Verburg, T. (2007), 'Related variety, unrelated variety and regional economic growth', *Regional Studies*, 41(5), 685–697.

Glaeser, E.L., Kallal, H., Scheinkman, J. and Shleifer, A. (1992), 'Growth in cities', *Journal of Political Economy*, 100, 1126–1152.

Hauser, C., Gottfried, T. and Walde, J. (2007), 'The learning region: the impact of social capital and weak ties on innovation', *Regional Studies*, 41(1), 75–88.

Jacobs, J. (1969), *The Economy of Cities*, New York, Vintage.

Keeble, D., Lawson, C., Moore, B. and Wilkinson, F. (1999), 'Collective learning processes, networking and "institutional thickness" in the Cambridge region', *Regional Studies*, 33(4), 319–332.

Keeble, D. and Wilkinson, F. (1999), 'Collective learning and knowledge development in the evolution of regional clusters of high technology SMEs in Europe', *Regional Studies*, 33(4), 295–303.

Ketels, C.H.M. (2004), 'European clusters', in *Structural Change in Europe 3 – Innovative City and Business Regions*, Boston, Harvard Business School.

Klepper S. (2007), 'The evolution of geographic structures in new industries', in K. Frenken (ed.), *Applied Evolutionary Economics and Economic Geography*, Cheltenham, Edward Elgar.

Lawson, C. and Lorenz, E. (1999), 'Collective learning, tacit knowledge and regional innovative capacity', *Regional Studies*, 33(4), 305–317.

López, S., Elola, A., Valdaliso, J.M. and Aranguren, M.J. (2008), *Los Orígenes Históricos del Clúster de la Electrónica, la Informática y las Telecomunicaciones en el País Vasco y su Legado para el Presente (Historical origins of the electronics, computing and telecommunications cluster in the Basque Country and its legacy to the present)*, San Sebastián, Orkestra-Instituto Vasco de Competitividad and Eusko Ikaskuntza.

Lorenzen, M. and Foss, N.J. (2003), 'Cognitive coordination, institutions and clusters: an exploratory discussion', in D. Fornahl and T. Brenner (eds), *Cooperation, Networks and Institutions in Regional Innovation Systems*, Cheltenham, Edward Elgar, pp. 82–104.

Malerba, F. (2006), 'Innovation and the evolution of industries', *Journal of Evolutionary Economics*, 16, 3–23.

Malerba, F. and Orsenigo, L. (1993), 'Technological regimes and firm behaviour', *Industrial and Corporate Change*, 2(1), 45–71.

Malerba, F.R., Nelson, L., Orsenigo, L. and Winter, S. (2007), 'Demand, innovation, and the dynamics of market structure: the role of experimental users and diverse preferences', *Journal of Evolutionary Economics*, 17, 371–399.

Malmberg, A. and Maskell, P. (2002), 'The elusive concept of localization economies: towards a knowledge-based theory of spatial clustering', *Environment and Planning A*, 34, 429–449.

Martin, R. and Sunley, P. (2003), 'Deconstructing clusters: chaotic concept or policy panacea?', *Journal of Economic Geography*, 3, 5–35.

Menzel, M.P. and Fornahl, D. (2007), 'Cluster life cycles – Dimensions and rationales of cluster development', *Jena Economic Research Papers*, #2007-076, Friedrich-Schiller-University and the Max Planck Institute of Economics.

Nahapiet, J. and Ghoshal, S. (1998), 'Social capital, intellectual capital, and the organizational advantage', *Academy of Management Journal*, 23(2), 242–266.

Pennings, J.M., Lee, K. and Van Witteloostuijn, A. (1998), 'Human capital, social capital and firm dissolution', *Academy of Management Journal*, 41(4), 425–440.

Porter, M.E. (1990), *The Competitive Advantage of Nations*, London, Macmillan.

Porter, M.E. (1998), 'Clusters and the new economics of competition', *Harvard Business Review*, November–December, 77–90.

Porter, M.E. (2003), 'The economic performance of regions', *Regional Studies*, 37, 549–578.

Porter, M.E. and Sölvell, O. (1997), 'The role of geography in the process of innovation and the sustainable competitive advantage of firms', in A.D. Chandler, Jr., P. Hagstrom and O. Solvell (eds), *The Dynamic Firm. The Role of Technology, Strategy, Organization, and Regions*, New York, Oxford University Press, pp. 440–457.

Putnam, R.D. (1993), *Making Democracy Work: Civic Traditions in Modern Italy*, Princeton, NJ, Princeton University Press.

Swann, G.M., Prevezer, M. and Stout, D. (1998), *The Dynamics of Industrial Clustering – International Comparisons in Computing and Biotechnology*, New York, Oxford University Press.

Valdaliso, J.M. and López, S. (2008), *Personas Innovando. La Industria de las Tecnologías Electrónicas y de la Información en el País Vasco, GAIA (1983–2008) (People doing Innovations. The industry of electronics and information technologies in the Basque Country, GAIA (1983–2008)*, San Sebastián, GAIA-SPRI.

Valdaliso, J.M., Elola, A., Aranguren, M.J. and López, S. (2008), *Los Orígenes Históricos del Clúster del Papel en el País Vasco y su Legado para el Presente (Historical Origins of the Paper Cluster in the Basque Country and its Legacy to the Present)*, San Sebastián, Orkestra-Instituto Vasco de Competitividad and Eusko Ikaskuntza.

Valdaliso, J. M., Elola, A., Aranguren, M.J. and López, S. (2011), 'Social capital, internationalization and absorptive capacity: the electronics and ICT cluster of the Basque Country', *Entrepreneurship and Regional Development*, 23, iFirst, 1–27.

Van Oort, F.G. (2004), *Urban Growth and Innovation. Spatially Bounded Externalities in the Netherlands*, Aldershot, Ashgate.

Westlund, H. (2006), *Social Capital in the Knowledge Economy. Theory and Empirics*, New York, Springer.

Winter, S.G. (1984), 'Schumpeterian competition in alternative technological regimes', *Journal of Economic Behaviour and Organization*, 5, 287–320.

8
Firm Heterogeneity and Trajectories of Learning: Applications and Relevant Policy Implications

Miren Larrea, Maria José Aranguren, and Mario Davide Parrilli

8.1 Introduction

In this chapter we would like to build on recent seminal, extensive work by Jensen et al. (2007), Arundel et al. (2007), and Lorenz and Valeyre (2007) on different modes of innovation and learning across firms and their production systems. On these bases we specify a particular taxonomy of firms based on the learning processes that operate within and across firms in specific local production systems. It is an important research objective as a detailed analysis of local production systems shows the extreme heterogeneity of firms within them, which needs to be taken into account to fully understand their innovation dynamics and to effectively promote their development processes (Boschma and Ter Wal, 2007). Complementarily, we also target the analysis of (non-linear) sequences of development in the learning pattern of firms; this transcends the critical analysis of typologies, which may create too narrow and rigid boundaries to learning and innovation within firms. We propose the study of actual and foreseeable sequences as a means to giving dynamism to such taxonomy, and as a basis for the discussion of relevant implications for policy-making. With these objectives in mind, we ran a survey on a network of 25 firms associated to a local development forum, called Ezagutza Gunea, which aims to create a basis for joint learning processes based on a common understanding and identification of key issues and solutions to entrepreneurial, organizational, and territorial development problems. The outcome is interesting insofar as it enables us to propose the contextual application of a relevant taxonomy of learning approaches that may help to identify relevant sequences and policy tools for innovation promotion at local level.

In the next section we discuss key aspects in the literature of knowledge flows and learning processes, including the importance of seeing the complementariness of science and technology innovation (STI) and innovation by doing, using, and interacting (DUI). In Section 8.3 we present the results of the survey based on the 25 firms associated to Ezagutza Gunea, while in Section 8.4 we discuss relevant implications for innovation policy and development within localized networks of firms.

8.2 Learning processes across firms and their systems

8.2.1 Innovation systems, knowledge flows and learning processes

The literature on innovation systems has developed considerably since the early contributions of Freeman (1987) and Lundvall (1992). The interpretation of innovation systems as collections of organizations devoted to knowledge generation and application has been overtaken by the recognition that these systems can and should also be regionally (Cooke, 2004) and/or sectorally specialized (Malerba, 2005). The existence of different primary forces within these systems is also identified, some of these being private sector-driven and others public sector-driven (Cooke, 2004). At the same time, the importance of promoting interactive learning has been understood as a means of closing the innovation gap between the (many) innovation organizations/infrastructures and the many firms that may be quite distant (in terms of geography and mindset) from those organizations, which may result in significant inefficiencies and ineffectiveness for the innovation system as a whole (Johnson and Lundvall, 1994; Archibugi and Lundvall, 2001; Jensen et al., 2007; Parrilli et al., 2010). This argument is also related to the key discussion on the transformation of 'potential absorptive capacities' into 'realized absorptive capacities' (Zahra and George, 2002; Lazaric et al., 2008), which implies the importance of targeting specific policy actions (such as using public agencies or social forums to catalyze interactions) in respect of firms and systems as a means of closing the gap and of making the system efficient and effective (Parrilli et al., 2010).

The importance of learning currently monopolizes the debate on innovation systems; it has become a key concept as it represents a catalyst of effective innovation processes. Several schools, including Aalborg,

Sophia-Antipolis, Utrecht, Copenhagen, Cardiff, Lund, Berkeley, Manchester, and Nice have targeted this aspect as a key within the analysis of the 'black box' of innovation (the set of explicit and implicit drivers and indicators of the innovation process). Asheim (2008) classifies the knowledge bases in 'analytical (typical of basic research on principles and methods, and applied in sectors such as biotech and chemistry), 'synthetic' (typical of combinatory applied research and engineering sectors), and 'symbolic' (typical of creative arts and sectors such as the movie and music industries). These knowledge bases create different economic prospects within distinct regional innovation systems, clusters and sectors. In his view the identification of these knowledge bases is more useful than the traditional distinction between tacit and codified knowledge flows to an understanding of the learning and innovation potential of firms, networks, and clusters. This view is contested by Jensen et al. (2007), who believe that tacit knowledge flows (transformed into the acronym DUI) and codified knowledge flows (transformed into the acronym STI) are keys within any sector, cluster, or innovation system and that a combination of the two (the STI+DUI mode of innovation described in their paper) allows for higher returns on knowledge flows.

Boschma (2005) extends the concept of 'proximity' in respect of innovation and learning that is implicit in the interactive (DUI) mode of innovation and learning beyond the all-inclusive 'geographical proximity' stressed by traditional cluster contributions, and stresses the role played by "cognitive, social, institutional and cultural proximities", which represent more specific, meaningful drivers to catalyze joint actions, knowledge spillovers, and learning processes. Complementarily, the role of 'related varieties' is stressed as a meaningful concept that explains the regional and sectoral knowledge relatedness that may help to connect different knowledge bases with the regional pool of capabilities, thus increasing the latter (Cooke, 2006; Asheim et al., 2008). This means that pure specialization or pure diversification are not what helps to build up dynamic (advanced) regional economies, since innovation "basically starts from...interactive learning (that) is most likely to occur between actors that are not too distant in cognitive terms, but also not too proximate" (Boschma, 2009). In Lundvall's view (2009), this consideration emphasizes the need not only to identify complementary and similar activities but also to separate them as a means to understanding what knowledge bases are combined and/or needed in a production system to make it effective. Challenging work lies ahead to identify the segments of knowledge needed in each specific innovation system to absorb new relevant (DUI and STI) knowledge and to proceed to more advanced stages of innovation. In Cooke's analysis (2009), this conceptualization may influence the "path dependence and innovative branching of new sectors and industries."

This discussion leads us to emphasize the need to analyze the "black box of innovation" (the unexplained part of innovation due to firm specificities and local idiosyncrasies) and to identify its drivers. For Cooke (2009), factors such as active knowledge spillovers and degrees of horizontal learning, social network presence and commitment to action, multi-level resources for innovation support and expenditure on innovation, and spin-out activity, are relevant for explaining and measuring the performance of innovation systems; others academics are following (NESTA, 2006; Arundel et al., 2007; Edquist et al., 2007; Storper, 2007, 2009), moving away from the literature on knowledge production function (Anselin et al., 1997) and incorporating the above aspects that stress their DUI nature (Lundvall and Nielsen, 2007; Jensen et al., 2007).

8.2.2 Taxonomy of learners

Within this debate, we consider it crucial to understand the role 'learners' (that is, firms) have within local production systems. In some sense we position our research on a complementary level with respect to Arundel et al. (2007), Lorenz and Valeyre (2007), Jensen et al. (2007), and Boschma and Ter Wal (2007); in fact, the first two contributions focus more on the organizational approach to learning (from higher levels within 'learning' and 'lean' organization, to lower levels within 'simple' and 'taylorist' organization), which in the end characterizes the profile of a country production system. Jensen et al. focus on different modes of innovation within the firm (from non-codified and non-interactive profiles to STI+DUI modes) and how these influence the overall learning process within and across firms. The fourth contribution focuses on firms' absorptive capacity and network connectivity as key determinants of economic performance. In our case, we pursue a complementary analysis as we specify a new focus, the local network of firms, and identify its internal heterogeneity and behaviors, which lead some firms to act through a low-learning approach, others through an STI approach, others through a DUI approach, and others through a mix of the last two; this analysis also helps to identify gaps across typologies that may be targeted for development purposes (e.g. advanced firms may be taking an interactive approach internally but not externally).

Our hypothesis focuses on the need to recognize this heterogeneity as a means to identifying bottlenecks and opportunities for each individual firm and by this means to set up a policy tool for the local system as a whole. For this reason, we identify a typology that may be helpful to describe the universe of firms within a network or a cluster. Such identification permits the structuring of innovation promotion actions for sub-groups of homogeneous firms as a necessary and complementary basis to organize a systemic response to the development needs of the locality/region.

In this sense, we would like to propose a hypothetical taxonomy of learners (firms) based on the firm approach to innovation (1. more focused on science and technology, here called 'structures', or 2) on 'interactive' and tacit relationships) that depicts the 'mental models' with which entrepreneurs and managers and their firms interpret the world (Senge, 1990; Dweck et al., 1996). Our 'craft learners' approximate the categories of "low learners" (Jensen et al., 2007) and "simple organizations" (Lorenz and Valeyre, 2007) that present low learning potentials with monotony of work organization. In our view, this category is also similar to a 'low DUI' mode, where traditional knowledge is conveyed through learning by doing, using, and interacting in a system that tends to reproduce the traditional mode of production with little or no creation of knowledge or innovation (for this reason it is not 0 with respect to the 'interactive variable' in Figure 8.1). It represents a different interaction with respect to advanced forms of DUI as it is a traditional interaction among local dwellers, craftsmen, and workers who exchange ideas, information, impressions, and forecasts on the basis of previous consolidated/accumulated knowledge bases. These 'craft learners' do not receive new codified knowledge inputs but utilize tacit knowledge flows through observation and conversation, the use of techniques and materials, and exchanging goods and services with clients as the only means to add value to their traditional production and commercial operations. In general, micro and small firms fit within this category, especially those operating within low-technology-intensive sectors. They may work as subcontractors for larger companies and thus not have their own design capacity but receive designs, capital goods, and production schedules from their contractors; for these reasons, they put little effort into upgrading their modes of production. In terms of social cognitive processes, this group seems to represent craft communities and organizations that are locked in, in knowledge and cultural terms, thus being limited in their capacity for dynamic insertion in the global economy. The cognitive learning processes of

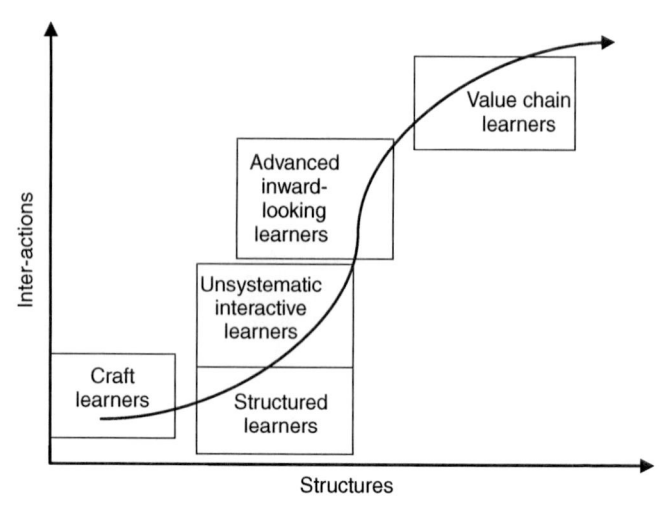

Figure 8.1 Taxonomy of learners (firms)
Source: Own elaboration.

this group of firms and their production systems are constrained by the traditional social organization of labor.

A second group is 'structured learners', which approximates to Lorenz and Valeyre's (2007) 'taylorist organizations.' We see this group as a segment of low learning organizations/firms as they tend to introduce codified knowledge mainly through structured channels, such as R&D and/or design departments, hiring highly qualified specialists, managers, and technicians, and purchasing advanced machinery or technologies in the hope that these will automatically increase productivity and innovation output (the neoclassic 'accumulation approach' to knowledge and learning; Lall and Teubal, 1998). This may be true in part, but such action does not tend to generate the highest outcome, as much potential remains latent instead of catalyzing stronger changes and improvements. This is due to the compartmentalization of work (innovation, for example, is generated only in R&D departments and by highly qualified personnel), which prevents the organization from reaping the benefits of more fruitful interactions and contributions from all workers (which, however, take place at a minimum level, which is higher than 0; see Figure 8.1). This typology points to a particular social cognitive profile, which seems to be part of a strictly hierarchical organization and/or production system in which key knowledge is possessed by only a few privileged, qualified managers and experts, who transfer their ideas and decisions to the rest of the organization/system in a direct, top-down way. Structures and procedures embody knowledge and are thus conceived as the means to transmit this knowledge and to increase the productivity and competitiveness of the organization and/or the system.

A third typology is identified as 'unsystematic interactive learners'. We observe here the first 'unsystematic' DUI practices fertilizing the pre-existent 'structured' practices, without having the thorough application of the DUI principles and methods. In fact, these firms and organizations tend to identify the importance of specific DUI practices, such as favoring the flow of information and communication across the labor force, upgrading the skills and capabilities of the staff through the organization of training courses, and introducing more autonomy for workers in innovation generation, despite expecting little effective involvement from the personnel and few effects from such an embryonic participatory approach (which may include setting up mechanisms for voicing problems and solutions without complementary incentives to implement them or parallel procedures to verify whether voiced problems are tackled and suggested solutions implemented). This also represents a top-down approach that reflects a certain social cognitive mode: the profile of an enlightened hierarchical society and organization where many are informed but only a few have the capacity to contribute to the innovation process of their firms. Increases in productivity and performance depend on the introduction of new techniques, information, and knowledge, which tend to be controlled by these key agents within the organization, whereas little material feedback is expected from the staff in spite of the communication channels that are increasingly set up.

The fourth typology represents 'advanced organizational learners' and can be split into two new categories. In the first (called 'advanced inward-looking learners'), we have a further upgrade in the learning process; the organization is geared to the possibility of contributions from workers; it is not a hierarchical organization, but one that receives bottom-up feedback, which increases the productivity and the innovation output of the firm. Contributions are systematically promoted and expected from all the staff. Interdisciplinary groups, quality circles, and autonomous work groups are DUI modes that help to exploit the STI components (such as R&D, design departments). As in Jensen et al. (2007), this typology shows the capacity of firms to reap the advantages of both DUI and STI modes of innovation and learning. The second group, 'value chain learners,' represents a top-spot kind of organization that incorporates a further step in the learning process. This type of organization not only incorporates its entire personnel through bottom-up mechanisms that favor internal innovation processes, but also applies a broader logic that extends the perimeter of the firm to include suppliers, service providers, clients, and all agents and actors who participate in the value chain and who, in interaction with the firm's own personnel, may develop insights, radical innovations, and generic improvements and consequently higher productivity. In some ways, these 'value chain learners' represent both Lorenz and Valeyre's (2007) 'learning organizations' and Jensen et al.'s (2007) 'STI/DUI' innovation mode. However, we prefer separating it from 'advanced inward-looking learners' (which is also STI/DUI based) as a means to explaining the substantial gaps that may exist within and across organizations. Indeed, real situations (Section 8.3) seem to show a gap between the logic adopted by the 'advanced inward-looking learners' and the 'value chain learners' that needs to be identified, understood, and targeted through specific business and policy actions. In some ways, the former typology still represents the case of the individual company fighting in the market vis-à-vis many competitors, whereas the latter typology portrays the case of a firm that recognizes it is part of a local system and the higher opportunities this offers to work with the system to upgrade its innovation and production capacities and increase its competitiveness. The tradition of dynamic small firms agglomerated in successful industrial districts incorporates this value and experience, as most innovations have been generated through the interaction between users and producers (Lazerson, 1990; Johnson and Lundvall, 1994).

These types of learning model single out the different types of learner psychologies. In fact, human knowledge develops and changes through social interaction on the basis of experience and consensus on attitudes, beliefs, and values (Tajfel and Forgas, 1981). This means that if a firm's collective values and beliefs are bounded (within the firm) no intense cooperation is possible with other actors in the extended local network of firms. In this connection, Carroll (1998: 707) stresses the importance of "sub-cultures [that] have somewhat distinctive logics, [whose] distinctions may help illuminate some of the conflicts and communication problems that organizations experience across occupational and hierarchical boundaries". Supporting change and improvement within organizations and systems requires not only the modification of institutional mechanisms and procedures, but also the modification of these sub-cultures and psycho-socio-cognitive profiles. For example, when complex, interdependent problems are understood in linear, cause–effect terms that result in a search for 'fixes,' it is common to find a "fixes that fail" scenario (Senge, 1990). For example, when a firm has an high number of equipment breakdowns, these tend to be attributed to poor maintenance; the solution of writing more detailed procedures and monitoring more closely is thought to ensure the quality of work; however, the reduction in errors on a particular job are then offset by the increased burden of procedures and supervision, which can be perceived by maintenance employees as mistrust and regimentation. This may result in loss of motivation, blind compliance with procedures (that may still be incomplete), malicious compliance when workers know that only rote compliance is safe from disciplinary action, the departure of skilled workers, and, ultimately, more problems (Senge, 1990: 26). As Senge notes: "Antidotes to this myopia depend upon broader participation and discussion among specialized groups, and can be facilitated by new conceptual lenses (theories), modeling tools to organize dynamic interdependencies, and feedback about effectiveness." And, in our view, also by conceptual lenses that include the collaboration of many other actors along value chains in production systems and innovation systems.

8.2.3 Sequence of learning

A second key element in our analysis is the 'sequence' of the aforementioned types of learning approaches. The five types of learner do not necessarily represent separate 'worlds;' they can represent different stages along a potential sequence of development. This does not mean that all firms actually evolve from one stage to another in a linear way; there might be firms that remain at the same stage, others that jump phases; however, some patterns might be identified and analyzed. The traditional organization (the 'craft learner') in the traditional small system/town tends to ignore new codified knowledge inputs and to reproduce former accumulated knowledge pools; however, under increasing market pressure it has to modify its approach in order not to disappear, and has to absorb external codified knowledge. As a result, this kind of organization may transform itself into a more structured organization where the entrepreneur is the one that introduces and manages new knowledge inputs (such as new machinery, techniques, or plant layout).

The 'structured learner' is often a larger organization that defines roles, responsibilities, and institutional procedures, but does not yet realize the potential of the whole organization. This organization experiences failures in internal and in market coordination with consequent high inventory costs, low quality products, high idle times, high labor conflicts, and low innovativeness. Therefore, senior management may plan to involve more workers in the process of organizational upgrading, opening the way for the transition from this stage to a more interactive phase. However, this process may be very uneven (procedures may be established yet lack incentives to promote the involvement of workers). In this context, the majority of workers would still not commit to improving their firm's performance. This development sequence may involve further steps when senior management recognizes that a further transition to a systematic approach is needed to secure the intensive participation of all workers in increasing the innovativeness, productivity, and competitiveness of their firm. This upgrading process takes place with the recognition that a set of new practices (such as TQM or JIT production) can be effectively applied only when the personnel are involved in a cooperative process that identifies internal roles and responsibilities, procedures and incentives, which motivate everyone to participate in the process of innovation generation and diffusion, and in the upgrading of the company's performance.

Yet there may be another step/transition to be made: one in which the company executives as well as the whole personnel realize that the organization and its competitiveness can be strengthened . It is when all actors in the chain are involved in such a participatory process through effective interactions and exchanges of information, ideas, and knowledge. This occurs when the learner (either the individual or the firm) becomes a 'value chain learner', able to absorb all kinds of opportunities in the process of generating value across the chain.

This sequence is neither linear nor automatic, as companies can remain stuck in a specific phase for ever; they may also jump phases; for instance, a new small high-tech company may begin directly at the structured and unsystematic interaction stage without needing first to pass through other stages; it may also target direct upgrading to the 'value chain learner' stage. Large 'structured learners' may also directly target a systematic approach to interaction as they become aware of the importance of this new logic within global markets. However, it is in general relevant to analyze trajectories that include upgrading from stages with lower to higher innovation potentials.

This is important not only in analytical terms as a means of identifying short-term potential and bottlenecks to innovation in organizations and local production systems, but also as a policy tool. In fact, this analysis allows the firm to recognize its capacities and the opportunities that can be targeted effectively in the short term by policy-makers

(Section 8.4). The use of public resources becomes more efficient and avoids frustration among producers and their production systems, as they do not waste energy in attempting to reach a step too far in the short term. This reflects on the social cognitive perspective of individuals and their firms and helps to stabilize the development path of any firm and local system.

Although this classification makes sense for both academic purposes and business/policy purposes, we need to analyze its existence and usefulness as a means of innovation promotion in a real case study, which is discussed in Section 8.3.

8.3 Case study: the learning group Ezagutza Gunea in the Basque Country

8.3.1 The case study

Using this case study we describe the process that has been developed over the past seven years in the Basque county of Urola Erdia. We illustrate how the typology and sequences proposed in section 8.2 apply to this case and how they can be used to define appropriate policies for each group of learners. The long-term research undertaken by the authors in this case study (since its creation in 2002), and the recent research focused on understanding how local firms innovate are the basis for the proposed typology. Ezagutza Gunea (EG) is a forum for the management of knowledge and training that has been promoted by the local development agency, Iraurgi Lantzen. This network is composed of the two municipal councils in the county, the local development agency, all training centers in the area, fifteen 'large firms' (with between 50 and 350 employees), representing around 90% of the large manufacturing firms in the area, and twelve 'small firms' (with between 10 and 50 employees), representing 11% of small manufacturing firms in the area; all of them are equally represented on the administration board.

Firms, training centers, municipalities, and the local development agency have targeted four key areas of organizational improvement/upgrading: 1) the organization of joint reflection and learning processes on different key aspects of the business activity; 2) the structuring of schemes for effective training and upgrading in job skillsand; 3) the adaptation of training/education to the needs of the local system; and 4) the implementation of strategies to generate an innovative atmosphere. As a means to achieving these goals, they have created various working groups and defined a process for collective decision making. Effective learning processes are promoted by forming working groups that work in coordination while retaining an important level of autonomy/auto-organization. CEOs, human resource managers, production managers, team leaders, representatives of training centers and of municipal councils, and the local development agency participate in such groups. A team of two full-time and one part-time promoters/coordinators support these learning processes and lead projects defined by the aforementioned working groups to generate new knowledge and transfer it to their companies. The current research project on innovation patterns within firms was commissioned by the working group of general managers to understand how firms innovate in order to make collective learning processes more effective. A steering committee for this highly valued research has been created and is composed of EG promoters/coordinators, one of the policy-makers in the management board, and us as applied researchers); the firms deliver crucial information and commit resources and effort to the aforementioned working groups. The research project is thus a knowledge co-generation process in which the preliminary results are already being used to orient the network's learning processes.

8.3.2 The case-study methodology

We decided to use a case-study methodology to illustrate our main proposition that company economic and socio-cognitive features characterize different learning approaches, which in addition to representing the heterogeneity of production systems also help to understand/identify the potential development trajectory of these firms and systems. Following Yin (2003), this case was selected because it epitomizes a representative network of firms in a traditional regional manufacturing economy that includes small and medium-sized enterprises in low (e.g. furniture) and medium-to-high technology (e.g. machine-tool production) sectors. It represents several local economies in southern and northern European countries such as Italy, Spain, Belgium, and Denmark, and several other SME-based economies worldwide (including several regional economies in Latin America and in Asia; see the European Observatory for SMEs, 2003; CEPAL, 2002). The selected case represents a local firm network of SMEs that develops joint learning initiatives; as such it is atypical, since it is not common to find such a positive approach among local firms in traditional sectors under increasing competition. Nevertheless, the intention of this case study is not to illustrate the success of this group and to extract indications on the way a group can succeed, but rather to show the heterogeneity of firms within a local network with respect to their learning approaches and their strengths and weaknesses, which need to be addressed when formulating innovation policy and actions.

The small size of the group made it easier to define the research project as a knowledge co-generation process between researchers and EG members; knowledge is simultaneously applied and diffused through the network. The questionnaire used for the survey was developed in cooperation with I3B, an applied research institute with long experience of analyzing innovation processes and promoting innovation strategy at firm level. We adapted their tool (designed for individual firms) to the purpose of analyzing networks of firms. The I3B questionnaire focuses on: (i) clients and markets (including questions on markets, new products and services, new markets, trends, and the socioeconomic environment); (ii) suppliers and technology sources (in cooperation with suppliers in R&D+I and knowledge management); (iii) people and change (in internal/external communication, training, professional development); and (iv) firm structure (business strategy, organizational forms). The firms were measured on a Likert scale comprising five stages, from the lowest ('this factor is neither being applied nor assessed') to the highest ('the firm applies this factor thoroughly and assesses its impact'). Criteria of coherence and consistence helped to identify what levels were achieved by respondents/firms in each question/issue. To avoid interviewer or respondent bias (such as overestimation by respondents) the interview results were discussed and processed by a group comprising the two interviewers and the researchers. The questionnaire was answered by the firms' CEOs, occasionally accompanied by production or human resources managers, between November 2008 and February 2009. Quantitative (based on the statistical mode) and qualitative (based on business and historic profiling) research was combined to assign the firms to the different groups in the taxonomy. Qualitative analysis is especially used to obtain a good understanding of the nature of innovation and learning dynamics developed by these firms on the bases of their economic, social, and institutional characteristics (Eisenhardt, 1989). To classify and describe firms in the proposed typology, a three-steps process was defined. First, a set of items of the questionnaire were selected as indicators of the level of development firms had regarding: (a) formal (science and technology) structures and institutional procedures; and (b) internal and external interaction. Depending on scores on the Likert scale for each of these items, the firms were classified in the taxonomy presented in Figure 8.1. Second, the interviews carried out alongside the questionnaire were used to make a qualitative description of each firm (Section 8.3.3.). The first classification of firms in the typology was reconsidered using these descriptions and a few firms were re-classified (see Table 8.1). Third, a set of other variables (were used to further specify the features of the learning and innovation behavior of each type of firm.

8.3.3 Empirical evidence on the taxonomy of learners

On these methodological bases, the 25 firms that responded to the questionnaire (of the total of 27 that participate in the network) were classified according to the proposed typology (Section 8.2.2). They belong to a variety of sectors, although the large majority (70%) represent machine-tools, metal products, and furniture.

The first outcome is that the size of a firm seems to be related to the way people learn within it. The small firms have all been classified in the first two groups; five of them are 'craft learners' and six are 'structured learners.' However, the inference that a minimum size is needed to create structures and procedures, and to make them work, does not fully hold, as six small firms fit within the 'structured learners.' Somehow it seems that in small firms the step towards a more structured approach is not combined with the understanding of the importance of interactive learning to catalyze significant innovation outcomes. In contrast, the large firms are mainly distributed between 'structured learners' and 'unsystematic interactive learners.' This means that most firms have defined structures and institutional procedures, but they are not yet able to actively involve a significant proportion of the workers. Innovation is still managed by a limited group of people. With regard to the 'advanced inward-looking learners' and the 'value chain learners' there is little to say. Only two of the firms in the area have been classified in the first group and none in the second. Only two firms foster advanced interactions throughout the organization and involve as many workers as possible in learning for innovation. This seems to imply that one of the big challenges for these firms, for EG, and for local policy-makers is to change mental schemes and to interpret innovation as a process that requires everybody's involvement. No firms have been classified as 'value chain learners;' this shows that there is a long way to go to make learning processes effective in the firm and across networks of firms. If two cases are found as local benchmarks for upgrading to 'advanced inward-looking learning,' for 'value chain learning' key references must be sought elsewhere.

One of the ideas regarding innovation policy presented in this chapter is the importance of identifying the groups of firms that display

Table 8.1 Types of learners in Ezagutza Gunea

'Craft learners'	'Structured learners'	'Unsystematic interactive learners'	'Advanced inward-looking learners'	'Value chain learners'
Large firms: 0	Large firms: 6	Large firms: 6	Large firms: 2	Large firms: 0
Small firms: 5	Small firms: 6	Small firms: 0	Small firms: 0	Small firms: 0
Poor structures and institutional procedures	Formal structures and procedures	Formal innovation structures and procedures	Formal structures and procedures	
Central role of General Manager	Low level of involvement of workers	Effort to involve more workers in procedures	Articulated internal systematic interactions	
Informal conversations as a source of information	Innovation mostly based on R&D (i.e. technical departments)	R&D projects: specific initiatives	R&D projects: follow the company strategic plan	
Low participation of workers in knowledge sharing and decision-making	Learning is mainly limited to a few professionals	Formal schemes for knowledge management, yet used unsystematically	Some cooperative R&D projects	
	Top-down corporate communication	Incipient interaction with clients and suppliers	More frequent, yet unsystematic, interaction with suppliers and clients	
		Mainly top-down and inter-departmental communication	Systematic interactive learning takes place inside the firm	
			Long-term strategy open	

Note: Large firms = 50–350 workers; small firms = 10–50 workers
Source: own synthesis

homogeneous economic and social cognitive behaviors as a step towards understanding their bottlenecks and potentials and to focus policies/actions on their specific needs. The following presents a deeper analysis of each of the groups identified in our case study.

8.3.3.1 'Craft learners': 5 firms

These are small firms that have poor structures and institutional procedures. They do not have a written strategic plan or formal R&D departments/activities. The general manager/owner plays a central role in all interactions inside and outside the firm, of which there tend to be few. Although he/she knows the people with critical knowledge for the firm, he/she does not set up mechanisms to encourage knowledge sharing within the company. This is evident, for example, in training processes that are organized solely to cover short-term operative needs. Informal conversations are the main source of information in the firm, whereas few exchanges are structured with clients, suppliers, and service providers as a means to improving the firm's capacity to foresee market changes and to adapt technologies to them. And most of these exchanges are conducted by the owner/manager. Overall, this situation leads to low participation of workers in decision-making and to a low learning profile.

8.3.3.2 'Structured learners': 12 firms

Twelve firms fit in this category: six small and six medium to large. These firms have formal structures and institutional procedures but involve only a small number of employees in effective learning processes. This limitation is reflected in the commercial networks that supply information about clients and markets; only a small group of managers have access to such information. Innovation activities are usually concentrated in technical (e.g. design) departments. These firms have good knowledge of their core business technology, but it is managed by a few professionals. These experts are identified, and some procedures are planned for knowledge diffusion (such as meetings, newsletters, and technical training); this notwithstanding, the dependence on such experts is high. Access to external information, benchmarks, and training is sporadic and limited to a small group of people. There is little interaction with suppliers and clients to foresee future trends and to plan the joint development of products and technologies. In general, most company divisions/departments establish formal communication channels, but they do not use them for the whole organization. Top-down communication is used, while horizontal communication is restricted to the CEOs.

8.3.3.3 'Unsystematic interactive learners': six firms

Six medium-to-large firms are in this category. They have formal innovation structures and procedures but, unlike the previous group, realize the importance of participation and try to involve more workers in those procedures. Innovation projects are not based on an overall course of action but represent specific initiatives responding to particular needs. In this respect, interaction with clients and suppliers is incipient. With reference to knowledge management and communication, these firms have defined formal schemes and procedures, whereas interaction within the organization is limited. Internal experts are identified and procedures for knowledge sharing articulated, though not systematically. Some firms plan to reduce dependence on these experts, usually by training employees. Learning from benchmarking (such as by participating in business association activities, courses, and seminars) is extended beyond CEO level to foster the assimilation of good practices. In general, the communication channels are well known and frequently used, though most often for short-term, specific issues (for example, by work teams focused on projects). These include top-down and inter-departmental communication; bottom-up communication is encouraged but is less common.

8.3.3.4 'Advanced inward-looking learners': 2 firms

Two medium-to-large firms belong to this class. These are characterized by organized formal structures and procedures and by internal systematic interactions. Innovation activities are carried out in accordance with company strategic planning; simultaneously the innovation performance is evaluated continually in each department. These companies have some R&D agreements with other firms, but they do not measure the success of such cooperation. Internal experts are identified and involved in company planning, but steps are taken to reduce dependence on these people by promoting learning among the employees who work with them. A few internal communication channels have been set up, are well known, and are used frequently for short-term targets as well as for top-down and bottom-up communication to define long-term company strategies. Innovation is a key issue that needs to be reflected in the strategic plan, which is defined in participatory terms. Interactions with suppliers and clients are more frequent than in the other types of firm, although still unsystematic. In some cases teams composed of members of different organizations work on joint projects, although their relationship is usually based on quality control standards rather than on joint problem-solving. Overall, systematic interactive learning takes place inside the firm, and not yet across the value chain.

8.3.4 Learning sequence

In this section we show the processes of change occurred within firms (in EG) help understanding the future potentials and constraints faced by these firms. Within EG, different working groups (such as general managers, production managers) regularly set a twelve-month agenda for the learning processes they want to develop together. The working group on small firms (within EG) started their group activity in April 2008; since then, they have acquired learning in three main management areas: balanced scoreboards (BSC), 5S, and objectives implementation. These represent joint learning processes oriented toward defining roles, responsibilities, and procedures; they could be classified as processes that help small firms to evolve from 'craft learners' to 'structured learners.' In 2009, these firms agreed to work on the following areas: cost, quality, and strategic management; these reflect learning processes oriented toward creating and reinforcing structures and institutional procedures that they may lack to different extents (the 'craft learners' lack it more than 'structured learners' do).

The medium/large firms are distributed across 'structured learners,' 'unsystematic interactive learners,' and 'advanced inward-looking learners.' They all have clear structures, responsibilities, and procedures, and present different levels of development in interaction and participation in accordance with their learning approach. The working group of human resources managers was created in 2003; they first worked on learning about competence-based management and then on promoting participation within their organizations; currently, they are working on how to promote participatory models of innovation. They have organized meetings to share their experience as well as learning visits to other successful Basque firms. The groups of general managers and production managers have also worked on the aforementioned areas, although the latter put a stronger emphasis on evolving from functional structures to process-based management by creating self-organized teams, stressing the importance of participation. Following the incorporation of greater numbers of personnel into these learning processes, the general managers expressed the view that EG should have learning groups where all workers participate and learn about the organizational transformations currently needed by their firms.

Overall, the learning processes developed up to now by medium/large firms (mostly 'structured learners' and 'unsystematic interactive learners') seem to emphasize their need to redefine their internal procedures, mechanisms, and incentives to foster higher levels of participation and learning for innovation. These learning processes may thus be useful to help medium-sized firms to evolve from 'structured learners' to 'unsystematic interactive learners,' or directly from these to 'advanced inward-looking learners.' In contrast, smaller firms seem to be more focused on defining structures and procedures for the first time, though some of them already are 'structured learners.'

In the next section, a thorough discussion of innovation policy is undertaken as a means of identifying possible strategies for public support based upon the identification of the local taxonomy of firms and their potentials for learning and innovation.

8.4 Policy implications

8.4.1 Relevant policy principles

Among the many distinctive theoretical approaches to innovation policy (Laranja et al., 2009), two relevant lines can be identified; they have been adopted to different extents in various periods to justify distinct types of intervention: the neoclassical approach, in which innovation policy responds to market failure, and the evolutionary approach, which emphasizes the role of policy in system failures. The former is based on the assumption that only imperfect market competition justifies public action to re-establish the former equilibrium. Within this approach, innovation is seen as a knowledge output that is influenced by three factors: the uncertainty of the innovation process, the lack of appropriability of knowledge (when this good is 'public'), and indivisibilities, which cause market failures when firms do not want to invest in non-excludable goods. These justify government intervention. In the evolutionary approach, government intervention is justified by wider system failures. In this case, the market is only one element of the system, which also includes institutions and networks. The following system failures can be identified (Smith, 2000; Laranja et. al., 2009): (i) network failure: innovation is an asset based on knowledge, which has tacit (inherent to human/personal relationships) and explicit knowledge components. Networks play an important role in innovation systems as they help to transfer and absorb both types of knowledge. Network failure appears when effective knowledge flows fail because firms are not well connected or because the members' absorptive capacity is not adequate; (ii) institutional failure, which occurs when the relevant legal, social, and normative organizations (e.g. state and sector agencies) do not promote the innovation process; and (iii) lock-in failure, which occurs in systems that remain isolated, thus adjusting too slowly to adopt new innovation paradigms. In the evolutionary approach, these three types of failure justify government intervention to build up the systemic capabilities necessary for firms and local economies to move to higher innovation levels.

The principle of 'additionality' indicates one of the key responses to these different kinds of failure. This principle refers to the subsidiary role of the state, which may intervene only if its action triggers a complementary effect that would not have taken place without any public sector involvement (Georghiou, 2002; Bach and Matt, 2002). Interestingly, Georghiou (2002) recognized three types of additionality: (i) 'input additionality,' in which the government adds resources to those invested by the beneficiaries in order to increase the scope and impact of their innovation process, which would not develop in the absence of its input; (ii) 'output additionality,' which captures the effects of policy support in the output of the innovation process; and (iii) 'behavioral additionality,' which refers to the effects on company routines and processes of public support (such as changes in business attitudes). Bach and Matt (2002) also recognize 'cognitive additionality,' which refers to the impact of such policy on the capacity of the agents to absorb and generate new knowledge. The identification of these different types of additionality seems relevant to the design and implementation of effective innovation policies; it may indeed be hypothesized that policies generating input and output additionality may respond effectively to market failures, whereas policies focusing on behavioral and cognitive additionalities offer solutions to system failures.

Until the 1980s the innovation process was interpreted as a linear process in which more inputs (such as expenditure in R&D) would produce more outputs (patents, new products); this implied that input and output additionalities were relevant. However, from the 1990s, the existence of system failures was more widely recognized and the innovation models had to change to become interactive and systemic. Innovation is now interpreted not only as a technical process but also as a social/interactive learning process developed across firms and between them and their environment. A key aspect of this systemic approach to innovation is the capacity of firms to innovate as parts of systems of thick interactions with many other firms and agents (Lundvall, 1992). As Lundvall highlights, in this model 'knowledge' is the most important resource, 'learning' is the key process, and 'cooperation' is a relevant innovation strategy. Innovation policies should consequently be designed and implemented in contexts of public–private cooperation and exchange and oriented to develop mechanisms that create, expand, and use all types of knowledge and that generate collective learning and new capabilities. In this sense, these processes may be more easily related to behavioral and cognitive additionality, as what needs to be changed is not the volume of inputs but the way these inputs are used, transformed, and exploited. Overall, the evolution from a linear approach to a systemic approach to innovation depends on a change in the rationales of policy support; thus, the type of instrument (for example, the kind of additionality) used to respond to these failures may differ from case to case.

A critical aspect of innovation policies is, therefore, to be 'context specific' in order to respond to innovation processes that are also specific to the context (region, locality, country, sector; Nauwelaers and Wintjes, 2008). The systemic approach does not recommend a 'one-size-fits-all' policy since local/regional differences in innovation capabilities call for tailored policy instruments based on effective 'policy intelligence.' This need requires the identification of the kind of firms and institutions that operate in the geographical area, as well as the main features of the local context. In this sense, our attempt to define a typology of firms could help to define actions that respond to the demand of each specific group and policies for the system as a whole. This information will help to identify the failures that are limiting the system and the kind of additionality that is needed to improve the innovation processes in the system.

In a context in which most developed economies are transiting to the innovation stage and the innovation system approach is recognized as crucial to the growth process, innovation policies should be oriented not only toward improving the elements of the system (firms, universities, technology centers) but also toward upgrading the interactions among these elements (network failures) and the interactions with other systems (lock-in failures) (Parrilli et al., 2010). According to Nauwelaers and Wintjes (2008), this new approach would change innovation policies that are focused on the institutions that foster innovation (institutional failures) but do not respond to network and lock-in failures. For this reason, the systemic approach to innovation needs to be complemented by the central idea of this chapter that may also help to structure effective innovation policies. This refers to the heterogeneity of the different types of firms, who present diverse capabilities, potentials, and constraints. This implies that agents with different absorptive capacities coexist in every system. The direct consequence is also the key message of this chapter: policies that want to be efficient and effective have to target/include these agents in a differentiated way in order to respond to their needs, bottlenecks, and potentials and to boost innovation and growth in the system as a whole. An interactive mode of policy formulation and implementation would involve design and delivery in cooperation with the beneficiaries, whereas policy implementers are also partners in action, so that learning happens in both policy implementers and firms (Nauwelaers and Wintjes, 2002; Parrilli et al., 2010).

8.4.2 Prospecting Applications

This chapter builds on the typology of Jensen et al. (2007), Arundel et al. (2007), Lorenz and Valeyre (2007), and Boschma and Ter Wal (2007), who focus on a range of innovation modes and learning behaviors across firms. Working on these typologies, we add two main contributions: the first suggests the importance of distinguishing between two types of 'learning organization:' those that learn on the basis of internal resources (people, infrastructure, organization) but do not yet learn from the value chain; and those that integrate the two kinds of learning. This limitation points to the risk of lock-in failure in the network, that is, if the firm and the local network/system do not interact with other systems, few benchmarks become available to local firms. Under such circumstances, the learning process across firms and their local systems would be severely restrained. The second specification proposes the identification of a trajectory (or several trajectories) that would help firms to transit from one type to another by a set of feasible steps in order to develop higher learning capabilities. The efforts of firms in this regard were shown to move along dynamic learning sequences (Section 8.3.4).

A complementary goal of this chapter is to discuss whether the identified typology of firms can help to make policies respond better to the needs and potential of these firms and their systems. In Section 8.4 it was argued that innovation policy needs to be contextual, which means that policies have to be adapted to the needs of each of these groups of firms. Regarding 'craft learners,' policies could focus on defining structures and institutional procedures that will enrich them with thicker codified knowledge flows. This would help them to evolve into 'structured learners.' However, this may be too restrictive, as we know the limitations of a pure 'structured approach' (top-down and exclusionary) and the difficulty of a linear approach. The combination of a structured approach with the former 'craft' (interactive) approach would help to catalyze major changes in shorter periods and enable the firms to reach the stages of 'unsystematic interactive learners' and/or 'advanced inward-looking learners.' This is coherent with the experience of EG, where the learning processes that small firm managers have decided to develop together have been those that incorporate strategic planning, TQM, and tools such as 5S. The main challenge for policies oriented toward the local firm network may be to train people in the use of such tools and to design actions that maintain an open internal atmosphere for the exchange of explicit and tacit knowledge. In fact, few interactive learning processes are generated through these procedures, which tend to be centrally executed. The main policy challenge for this group would be to promote a change in mental schemes (e.g. towards a participatory approach) through 'behavioral' and 'cognitive additionality.' Defining and executing participatory processes related to roles, responsibilities, and institutional procedures would help these firms to evolve toward the 'unsystematic interactive learners' group. This group has realized the importance of participation for innovation; however, they have not yet systematically organized participation from strategic planning to goals implementation. Actions oriented toward this group should focus on promoting the formation of more open mental frameworks and competencies for process management, auto-organized work teams, joint problem-solving, and so on. This is why the relevance of policies aimed at generating 'behavioral' and 'cognitive additionality' has been stressed, while it has been indicated that this approach should go beyond the restricted area of senior managers and reach all the workers in the organization (which, tellingly, is what is currently advocated by general managers in EG).

An interesting aspect for discussion and further research is the value of networks like EG as policy tools. A debate is currently open in the Basque Country and more widely about the role of local networks such as EG in helping firms to develop their absorptive capacity. In this regard, hypotheses should be tested regarding the best combination between top-down policies that support the local taxonomy of firms and bottom-up feedback actions promoted by local businesses that clarify their needs in terms of both structures and interactive processes.

References

Anselin, L., Varga, A. and Acs, Z. (1997), 'Local geographic spillovers between university research and high-technology innovations', *Journal of Urban Economics*, 42, 422–448.

Archibugi, D. and Lundvall, B.-Å. (2001), *The Globalizing Learning Economy*, Oxford, Oxford University Press.

Arundel, A., Lorenz, E., Lundvall, B.-Å. and Valeyre A. (2007), 'Europe's economies learn: a comparison of work organization and innovation modes for the EU-15', *Industrial and Corporate Change*, 16(6), 1175–1210.

Asheim, B., Boschma, R. and Cooke P. (2007), 'Constructing regional advantage: platform policies based on related variety and differentiated knowledge bases', *Papers in Evolutionary Economic Geography*, Utrecht University.

Asheim, B. and Coenen, L. (2006), 'Contextualizing regional innovation systems in a globalizing learning economy', *Journal of Technology Transfer*, 31, 163–173.

Audretsch, D. (2008), 'The entrepreneurial society', *Journal of Technology Transfer*, 34, 245–254.

Bach, L. and Matt, M. (2002), 'Rationale for Science and Technology Policy', in L. Georghiou and J. Rigby (eds), *Assessing the Socio-Economic Impacts of the Framework Programme*, Report to DG Research, Brussels.

Boschma, R. (2005), 'Proximity and innovation: a critical assessment', *Regional Studies*, 39(1), 61–74.

Boschma, R. and Ter Wal, A. (2007), 'Knowledge networks and innovative performance in an industrial district', *Industry and Innovation*, 14(2), 177–199.

Boschma, R. (2009), Informal communication, Workshop on 'Innovation and learning', Orkestra, San Sebastian, May 13–14.

Carroll, J.S. (1998), 'Organizational learning activities in high-hazard industries: the logics underlying self-analysis', *Journal of Management Studies*, 35, 699–717.

CEPAL (2002), 'Las pequeñas empresas industriales en America Latina', (Small industry in Latin America) Mexico City, Editorial Siglo XXI.

Cooke, P. (2004), 'Regional innovation systems: an evolutionary approach', in N. Cooke, M. Heidenreich and H-J. Braczyck (eds), *Regional Innovation Systems: Governance in the Globalized World*, London, Routledge.

Cooke, P. (2006), 'Reflections on the research and conclusions for policy', in P. Cooke, C. De Laurentis, F. Tödtling and M. Trippl (eds), *Regional Knowledge Economies*, Cheltenham, Edward Elgar.

Cooke, P. (2009), Informal communication, Workshop on 'Innovation and learning', Orkestra, San Sebastian, May 13–14.

Eisenhardt, K. (1989), 'Building theories from case study research', *Academy of Management Review*, 14(4), 532–550.

European Observatory for Small Firms (2003), 'Highlights from the 2003 Observatory of European SMEs', 8, Brussels.

Freeman, C. (1987), *Technology Policy and Economic Performance. Lessons from Japan*, London, Pinter.

Geourghiou, L. (2002), 'Impact and additionality of innovation policy', in P. Boekholt (ed.), *Innovation Policy and Sustainable Development: Can Public Innovation Incentives Make a Difference?*, Brussels, IWT Observatory, pp. 57–66.

Jensen, M., Johnson, B., Lorenz, E. and Lundvall, B.-Å. (2007), 'Forms of knowledge and modes of innovation', *Research Policy*, 36, 680–693.

Johnson, B. and Lundvall, B.-Å. (1994), 'The learning economy', *Journal of Industry Studies*, 1(2), 23–42.

Lall, S. and Teubal, M. (1998), 'Market-stimulating technology policies in developing countries', *World Development*, 26, 1369–1385.

Laranja, M., Uyarra, E. and Flanagan, K. (2009), 'Policies for science, policy and innovation: translating rationales into regional policies in a multi-level setting', *Research Policy*, 37, 823–835.

Lazaric, N., Longhi, C. and Thomas, C. (2008), 'Gatekeepers of knowledge versus platforms of knowledge', *Regional Studies*, 42(6), 837–852.

Lazerson, M. (1990), 'Knitwear industry in Modena', in F. Pyke and W. Sengenberger (eds), *Industrial Districts and Inter-Firm Cooperation*, Geneva, ILO.

Lorenz, E. and Valeyre, A. (2007), 'Organizational forms and innovative performance: a comparison of the EU-15', in E. Lorenz and B.-Å. Lundvall (eds), *How Europe's Economies Learn*, Oxford, Oxford University Press.

Lundvall, B.-Å. (1992), *National Systems of Innovation. Towards a Theory of Innovation and Interactive Learning*, London, Pinter.

Lundvall, B.-Å. (2009), Informal communication, Workshop on 'Innovation and learning', Orkestra, San Sebastian, May 13–14.

Lundvall, B.-Å. and Nielsen P. (2007), 'Knowledge management and information performance', *International Journal of Manpower*, 28(3/4), 207–223.

Malerba, F. (2005), 'Sectoral systems of innovation', *Journal of Economics of Innovation and New Technology*, 14, 63–82.

Nauwelaers, C. and Wintjes, R. (2008), 'Innovation in policy: policy learning within and across systems and clusters', in C. Nauwelaers and R. Wintjes, *Innovation Policy in Europe: Measurement and Strategy*, Cheltenham, Edward Elgar.

NESTA (2006), *Hidden Innovation*, University of Manchester, Manchester.

Parrilli, M.D., Aranguren, M.J. and Larrea, M. (2010), 'Closing the "innovation gap" in SME-based local economies', *European Planning* Studies, Vol. 18 (3), 351–370.

Senge, P. (1990), *The Fifth Discipline*, New York.

Smith, K. (2000), 'Innovation as a systemic phenomenon: rethinking the role of policy', *Enterprise and Innovation Management Studies* 1(1), 73–102.

Storper, M. (2008), Informal communication, Workshop on 'Innovation and learning', Orkestra, San Sebastian, May 13–14.

Storper, M. (2007), 'On the geographical determinants of innovation in Europe and the United States', with R. Crescenzi and A. Rodriguez-Pose, *Journal of Economic Geography*, 7, 673–709.

Tajfel, H. and Forgas, J.P. (1981), 'Social categorization: cognitions, values and groups', in J.P. Forgas (ed.), *Social Cognition*, London, London Academic Press, pp. 113–140.

Yin, R. (2003), *Case Study Research: Designs and Methods*, Sage Publications.

Zahra, S. and George, G. (2002), 'Absorptive capacity: a review, reconceptualization and extension', *Academy of Management Review*, 27, 195–203.

9
Innovation Capabilities and Learning: Virtuous and Vicious Circles

Joost Heijs

9.1 Introduction

There is no doubt about the fact that innovation is a key to economic growth (Freeman, 1994; Fagerberg, 1994, 2009) and that the development of advanced technologies is an important factor in the competitive advantage of a country, a region, or enterprise (Freeman, 1987; Porter, 1990). So it can be stated that the competitive strength of a state or firm depends, partially, on its innovation capabilities. In this chapter we analyze the improvement of such innovation capabilities in firms that have carried out publicly supported R&D projects. Therefore we study, first of all, the intensity of such learning effects based on internal projects and on the technology transfer flows between partners of the cooperative R&D projects. A second aspect of our analysis is the elaboration of the profile of the firms with higher or lower learning effects. This chapter points out that the firms with a low innovative level have a distinctly lower learning capability than the more innovative firms. Moreover, in some circumstances the firms with a free-rider behavior seem to show, at the same time, a less intensive learning effect. So the main conclusions of this chapter are that the less innovative firms are trapped in a vicious circle and can reduce the technological gap with respect to other firms only by extraordinary efforts. For this reason the improvement of the learning capabilities of a firm should be an important goal of public intervention in the field of technological change and R&D; to initiate a 'catching-up' process in the less innovative firms, financial support instruments should be combined with technical support and intensive consultancy services.

This section presents a brief discussion on the theoretical concepts of innovation and learning R&D policies. The next section analyzes the methodological problems in measuring these concepts and presents the dataset used in this study. In Sections 9.3 and 9.4 we present the outcome of our empirical work, based on a study of the learning effects of innovation projects financed by the Spanish government.

The technological or innovative capability of a firm can be described as its potential to understand, manage, assimilate, and adapt purchased technologies or innovations, and its capacity to develop or generate technological innovations, and it is the result of an accumulative learning process and experience (Bell, 1984). There has been wide attention in the literature to the importance of learning and to its diverse aspects, especially in the last decade.[1] Here we do not repeat the theoretical discussion but only highlight briefly the most important conclusions, taking into account the theoretical models of technological change. As can be deduced from the modern theories of technological change and innovation, the *corporate* technological capability of a firm is a fundamental factor in the development of R&D projects. The traditional or *linear model* views technology simply as publicly available information and R&D as an isolated activity performed in the research centers of the firms. In this model innovation is considered a sequential process, occurring in discrete stages, beginning with basic research followed by the design and industrial development of a product, and ending with its introduction onto the market. The learning process is considered less important because technology transfer is supposed to take place automatically, without significant costs or delay, through the mechanism of the 'invisible hand.' So innovation capabilities are equal for all firms because technology is seen as information that is easy to transfer and copy.

In the last three decades, an alternative model – the chain-linked or interactive model – has gained ground and fueled radical changes in the concept of innovation management and in design technology policies. The *interactive model* is based on the notion of continuous learning and interaction between different actors and elements in the innovation process – from basic research to industrial development, commercialization, and introduction onto the market. While the linear model highlights only the activities of a firm's R&D department, the interactive model stresses the firm's technological capabilities and entrepreneurial attitude, and sees innovation management as an integrated, strategic corporate activity in which the entire firm should be involved. Technology transfer is in the evolutionary theory viewed as expensive and difficult, while understanding new technologies is seen as time-consuming. A firm's technological capability consists of its know-how with a tacit, accumulative dimension determined by a range of factors, such as the human resources, the entrepreneurial attitude of the managing director, the culture, the potential to learn, the organizational structure and management of the innovation process, and the extent to which the firm is embedded in the national and regional system of innovation. So in this model, aptitude for learning is an essential part of innovative capability, which is therefore not equal for all firms, and learning or absorptive capabilities have to be built up in an active way. Technology is considered as knowledge, which is not always easy to understand and, therefore, difficult to copy or transfer. Moreover, even in cases where new technology can be considered as information, the firms or people with a good technical background have a better understanding of the potential and technical opportunities for its use and for future (incremental) improvements. In other words, even in this case, well schooled human resources are important to take advantage of new technology.

These two models reflect opposite concepts about technology and innovation. The linear model sees technology as information and the chain-linked model – based on an evolutionary perspective – describes technology as knowledge generated by a process of accumulation and learning. However, in most cases, technology is a combination of the two: some technologies are more information-orientated and others are more knowledge-based. This means that the importance of learning depends on the particularities of the technological field or sector. The literature, especially the evolutionary theory of technical change, has made it clear that the capacity for learning of a firm is fundamental to the improvement of its technological capabilities (Lundvall, 1992).

Because knowledge and resource accumulation are cumulative and path-dependent processes, firms hold asymmetric assets of resources and competencies and this diversity of knowledge, together with the growing multi-disciplinarity of R&D, means a greater potential for learning based on new combinations of complementary knowledge. In fact, the use of knowledge created by others speeds up the innovative activities of most agents in an innovation system or in the productive system of a country. In relation to this learning capability we can underline the importance of the absorptive capability, defined as the ability of firms to understand and interpret external knowledge and to use technological opportunities for their own interests. One of the basic obstacles of the absorptive capability – besides the lack of talent and training of the scientists and technicians – is the distance between the technological level of the available internal knowledge in relation to the external technological opportunities. If the technological distance is too great, the firm cannot absorb the new external technologies due to the lack of understanding; if it is too small, the technology-receiving firm will generate only marginal or incremental improvements. A way to increase learning effects would be to improve the interaction and linkages between the agents in the innovation system. Learning often requires a high level of interaction, especially in the case of the transfer of tacit knowledge. Therefore, cooperation could be a good mechanism through which to disseminate new knowledge and build up technological capability.

From the work of Lane and Lubatkin (1998), Van den Bosch (1999, 2003), Zahra and George (2002), or Narula (2004)[2] we can deduce that absorptive capacity depends on: (i) the R&D activities of the firm, including prior knowledge (accumulation of experience; pool of knowledge, innovative culture; regularity of R&D activities, and so on); (ii) the stability or dynamics of the environment of the firms (knowledge and competitive environment); (iii) the organizational setting of the firms (organizational structure; interaction between departments; networking and interaction with external agents, for example); and (iv) the quality of the human resources (e.g., their educational level, training).

The empirical part of this chapter is based on a dataset of firms that have received support for (cooperative) R&D projects. Therefore it is important to take into account the theories of cooperation in R&D, including the motives and problems involved in cooperation. The data show an increasing level of cooperation in R&D and innovation (Hagedoorn, 2002; Narula, 2004). Some general trends have led to this: new scientific challenges are increasingly capital-intensive; the life-cycles of products and technologies – and therefore the payback period of new products – are increasingly short; and the complexity and the interdisciplinary nature of the technologies needed for the development of a new product have increased in parallel with the need for capacity in different technological areas. If we look at the outcomes of the empirical studies (see, for example, Table 9.1), we observe that cost-saving (which can be considered as a way of risk-sharing) seem to be less important motives to cooperate in R&D. In fact, most studies show that access to new knowledge, or infrastructure and equipment, not available within a firm and the creation of synergies in R&D activities are the most important reasons to cooperate, while financial motives seem to be less important (Heijs/Buesa, 2007; Schmidt, 2007; Arvantis,

Table 9.1 Motives for cooperation with research centers (percentage of firms that attach each level of importance)

Motives	Importance			
	Low	Intermediate	High	Total
Cost-saving	39	33	28	100
Obligation to obtain public support	30	35	35	100
Access to expertise and qualifications not available in own firm	22	32	44	100
Access to infrastructure and equipment not available in own firm	22	29	44	100
Following-up of technical advances	23	37	40	100
Acquisition of experience and knowledge	18	38	44	100

Note: The survey asked about the importance of the impact on a scale from 0 (irrelevant) to 5 (very important) in the tables with three values we reclassified the range. The value 0 or 1 expressed a low level of impact. The scores 2 and 3 an intermediate level and 4 and 5 a high level of impact.

Source: Heijs and Buesa, 2007.

2009). To conclude, incoming R&D spillovers and learning – based on synergies in R&D – seem to be the most important reason to cooperate in R&D.

9.2 Measuring learning effects, methodological remarks, and the empirical dataset

In this chapter we will make use of two databases (see Table 9.2), which are the result of two different questionnaires designed by the Spanish Institute of Industrial and Financial Analyses (IAIF), and analyzes the impact of publicly supported R&D and innovation projects. The first survey – the IAIF/CDTI survey – evaluated the impact of all kinds of projects supported by the Center for Technological and Industrial Development (CDTI), and the second – the IAIF/FECYT survey – analyzed the impact of cooperative projects financed by the CDTI. Both surveys comprised a large number of questions about firms' general characteristics and innovative behavior and included a section about

Table 9.2 Short description of the surveys and the main variables (dependent variables)

The IAIF/CDTI survey: of 1995 was answered by 545 firms of the total of 1354 that carried out innovation projects supported by the Center for Industrial Technological Development (CDTI). Both individual and cooperative projects analyzed.

The IAIF/FECYT survey: Carried out at the end of 2003. Analyzes the impact of public support for cooperative R&D projects. Answered by 505 firms of the total of 1562 that received financial aid from the CDTI for R&D projects that required cooperation between firms and public or private research institutes.

LEARNING EFFECT	IAIF/CDTI survey	IAIF/FECYT survey
Improvement of the training of the R&D employees	1 variable	
Improvement of the knowledge base of the firm	1 variable	
Improvement of the R&D management	1 variable	
Improvement of the conversion of innovations into products	1 variable	
Transfer of knowledge from the cooperation partner to the firm		1 variable
Transfer of knowledge from the firms to the cooperation partner		1 variable

the evaluation of the possible impacts of public support for R&D and innovation.

The IAIF/CDTI questionnaire offers three indicators that measure the learning effects derived from the supported projects. Two indicators analyze the improvement of the technical capabilities of the firm by analyzing improvement in the quality of the human resources and increases in the knowledge base of the firm. The third indicator analyzes improvement in the innovation management system. More precisely, this indicator studies improvement in the integration of the R&D department with other units of the firm. This is an important factor, because we should not forget that the modern theories of technological change (like the system approach) show that the success of innovation depends on the ideas and experiences of all actors (or factors) in the innovation process. Therefore, innovation management should be an integrated part of a firm's corporate strategy and the improved integration of departments in the R&D process is considered very important.

The IAIF/FECYT survey analyzed the learning effects deriving from cooperative projects measured by the importance of the inward and outward flows of knowledge (technology transfer) between the partners in these projects. Moreover, as mentioned above, the most important motives for cooperation relate to learning processes (such as the acquisition of experience and knowledge and access to external knowledge – see Table 9.1).

To analyze which kind of firms have improved their innovation capabilities most significantly, we use in the following sections two kinds of statistical instrument. First, an exploratory study analyzing the correlation between each of the variables reflecting the learning process (dependent variables) and the independent or explanatory variables (such as size, sector etc...). However, such analyses cannot take into account all the possible interactions between the dependent and explanatory variables. Therefore, we introduce a second statistical method based on a logistic regression model. This method takes into account the simultaneous effects of the independent variables on the explanatory variables, revealing possible relationships not detected in the Pearson's Chi-square test of associations. In section 3 of this chapter we will present the main statistical results of these two forms of analysis.[3]

An important methodological problem of the surveys is the use of qualitative indicators based on the opinions of the managers or researchers. In other words, one should take into account that the results of most of the studies are based on the subjective perception of only one person involved in the R&D activities of a firm. Another well known problem of the questionnaires in general is that some of the respondents are prone to overestimate the importance of the learning process, especially in the case of publicly supported projects. To resolve this problem this study characterizes firms in terms of their learning capabilities, in relation to the average level of learning.[4] So the main objective of this article is not to find out the exact level of improvement in the technological capability of each firm, but to find out what kind of firms differ from the average level. Two further limitations of the surveys have to be pointed out. First, the questionnaires analyze the impact of CDTI projects – or their learning effects – at firm level and not at project level. To solve this problem we included, as a control variable, the number of publicly supported projects carried out by the firms. A second limitation or methodological problem is that the impact of a project on innovation capabilities can be related to – among other things – the complexity and size of the project. Therefore, we included in the analysis several characteristics of the projects such as the novelty of the innovative activity for the firm and the size (budget) of the project (we included a variable that reflects the size of the projects measured by their budget or the financial resources allocated to them). Moreover, in Section 9.3 we distinguish between two types of project. The first type is the cooperative projects that are considered more complex projects that had to be carried out in collaboration with public research centers and be focused on basic R&D. The second type is technology development projects, which were focused on more simple incremental or applied research related closely with their introduction market.

9.3 Internal learning as a consequence of R&D projects

The IAIF/CDTI survey offers information (see Table 9.3) showing the percentage of firms that consider the learning effects deriving from the innovation projects financed by public funds as very, fairly, and not very important. Around 80% showed an improvement in the training of their personnel, 83% indicated an increase in the knowledge base of their firm and 64% of the firms considered that the R&D department improved its integration with other areas of the company. Studying the

Table 9.3 Impact of R&D project in relation to several modes of learning

The importance from	Improvement in human resources (%)	Improvement of knowledge base (%)	Improvement in integration of R&D with other departments (%)
0 Not relevant	17	15	28
1 Very low importance	4	2	8
2 Certain importance	10	8	12
3 Important	29	27	23
4 More than important	29	36	22
5 Very important	11	13	7
Total	100	100	100

Source: own elaboration based on the IAIF/CDTI questionnaire and Heijs, 2000a. See also the note of Table 9.1.

three modalities of learning simultaneously, it can be seen that fewer than 10% of the firms indicated that the projects did not have an impact on their technological capabilities.[5]

In this section we present the profile of the firms that show a lower or higher learning capability. To identify this profile we use simultaneously the results of the exploratory analysis (association tests) and the confirmative analysis or logistic regression models). In relation to the explanatory analysis we have not included an exhaustive summary of the contingency tables and the corresponding association tests but the main results are reflected in Table 9.4 (a, b), while the results of the logistic regression models are presented in Table 9.5. It should be pointed out that all the relations and empirical results mentioned in this article are statistically significant unless otherwise stated.

The data from the CDTI/IAIF survey (see Table 9.2) indicate that the relationship between size of the firm and each of the three modalities of learning is weak, although statistically significant, and not always linear. The exploratory analysis, based on a test of association, indicates that the large firms showed a below-average learning effect, reflected by a relatively low improvement in the training of the R&D personnel and in innovation management. Similar results were also found in other evaluation studies (Becher et al., 1989; Meyer-Krahmer, 1989; Kulicke et al., 1997) and could be explained by the fact that large firms have a higher number of well educated employees devoted to R&D (critical mass) than small firms. In other words if you have a small critical mass the possibility that you can or need to learn something new (the learning potential) is bigger.

According to logistic regression model analysis, however, the role of size as an explanatory variable should be revised. In two of the three modalities of learning we did not find any relationship between size and learning. The discriminatory role of the variable size disappeared in the logistic regression models estimated in the case of the improvement in the training of R&D personnel and innovation management. It seems that the associations detected can be explained by interaction with or the bias of other explanatory variables of the model. Probably it is not the size which really determines a larger impact on the R&D management, however probably the effect is explained or caused by the innovative level and orientation of the firms.

As already mentioned, one of the methodological problems to measure the relationship with the firm's behavior as the determinants of the learning effects is the relation of the impact of a project to – among other things – the characteristics of the project. Therefore, we included

Table 9.4a Principal results of the exploratory analyses of generic impact (percentage of firms that considered the impact as very important – 4 or 5 points on the scale from 0 to 5)

	Improvement in the training of the Human Resources	Improvement of the knowledge base	Improvement in innovation management
Small firms (up to 50 employees)	43	NS	29
Medium-size firms (50–500 employees)	40	NS	32
Large firms (over 500 employees)	28	NS	16
Firms with foreign participation	NS	NS	30
Public enterprises	NS	NS	19
National private firms	NS	NS	30
Producers of traditional consumer goods	29	43	32
Suppliers of traditional intermediate goods	49	56	44
Specialized suppliers of intermediate goods and equipment	29	35	29
Mass production assemblers	33	46	26
R&D-based sectors	53	58	26
Service providers	53	59	25
Firms with R&D expenditure of < 1% of sales	27	46	NS
Firms with R&D expenditure of 1–5% of sales	38	48	NS
Firms with R&D expenditure of > 5% of sales	54	58	NS
All	40	48	29

Source: Own elaboration based on the IAIF/CDTI questionnaire and Heijs (200a: 35–36). Cells marked 'NS' denote that results were statistically not significant.

in the analysis several characteristics of the projects carried out by the firms. In fact, the type of project is, together with the innovative level of the firm (see below), one of the most important explanatory variable. The association tests for the type of project showed that the firms with cooperation projects showed a higher level of learning capability for

Table 9.4b Principal results of the exploratory analyses of generic impact

	Improvement in the training of the RR.HH	Improvement of the knowledge base	Improvement in innovation management
R&D considered as not important	67	79	NS
R&D considered as important	86	64	NS
R&D considered as very important	90	87	NS
Firms with cooperative projects	94	89	NS
Firms with only technological projects	79	75	NS
All	89	83	64

Note: Cells marked 'NS' denote that results were statistically not significant See also the note of Table 9.1.

Source: Own elaboration based on the IAIF/CDTI questionnaire and Heijs (2000a: 35–36).

each of the three indicators. The logistic regression models confirmed those tendencies found in the contingency tables except for that regarding improvement in innovation management. So it can be concluded that cooperation projects generate a clearly higher learning impact than technological projects. This result is not surprising because cooperation projects are normally larger and oriented to basic R&D, while technological projects were usually innovative activities close to the market, less complex, and less ambitious. Besides the type of the project, other characteristics were taken into account in the analyses, such as the number of projects financed by the CDTI, the total budget of the projects financed by the CDTI, and the level of novelty of the innovative activity. The main results are that the firms with a larger number of projects or with a higher total budget show, in general, a higher overall impact level. This may not be surprising, but their inclusion in the logistic regression model serves as control variables, assuring the absence of any bias in relation to the validity of the other explanatory variables included in the models.

We also analyzed the innovative level and orientation of the firms. Possibly the most notable conclusion is the fact that the most innovative firms show, in general, a higher level of impact on their technological capabilities than the firms with a less consolidated innovative culture. The statistical results of the IAIF/CDTI questionnaire show that the less innovative firms, which should have more need to improve their innovative capabilities, do not take so much advantage of their projects as the more innovative firms – a conclusion confirmed by the logistic regression model analysis. Moreover, it can be seen that the group of firms that indicated that the learning effect of the CDTI projects was irrelevant is characterized by a very low innovative level. On the one hand, this result seems to be surprising because it could be expected that the less innovative firms should have more margin for learning and improving their innovative capabilities, but on the other hand, those findings coincide with the results of other studies and also with the theory on technological change (see, among others, Cohen and Levinthal, 1989; Becher et al., 1989; Kulicke et al., 1997).

On the one hand, analysis of the results of the logistic regression analysis reveals that, the less innovative firms do not take as much advantage of their projects as the more innovative firms. Although in the case of the improvement of the innovation management a different relationship between the innovative level and the learning capability was defined. The variables measuring the innovative efforts and orientation of the firms included in this model reflect opposite tendencies.[6] Some of them confirm that the less innovative firms do have a lower level of impact (like expressed by the variables such as importance of R&D or technological development carried out by the firm, and percentage of sales corresponding to innovative products), while others reflect the opposite relationship (number of employees in R&D and expenditure on R&D relative to sales), indicating that the more innovative firms have a lower learning capability level. This apparent contradiction should be interpreted in the following way. The more innovative firms do show greater improvement in their innovation management, but once they reach a certain innovative level, this impact is less pronounced. Highly innovative firms have already a clear, well defined innovation management system. So their innovative activities are well designed, with few deficiencies, and are less open to improvement.

Additional analyses showed that the higher level of learning among the more innovative firms is not due to possible differences in the characteristics of the projects they carry out, for two reasons: first because the same tendency was found in the association tests made on the sub-samples by expenditure on R&D as a percentage of sales (ERDs); second, it can be pointed out that the type and size of the projects were included in the logistic regression models as a control factor to the differences in the projects carried out. Furthermore, additional logistic

Table 9.5 Explanatory factors for learning capability: a logistic regression model

	Improvement in training of HH.RR		Improvement of the knowledge base		Improvement in innovation management	
	Individual projects	Cooperative projects	Individual projects	Cooperative projects	Individual projects	Cooperative projects
FIRM CHARACTERISTICS						
Small (up to 50 employees) versus medium-size and large firms (over 50 employees)	n.s.	n.s.	n.s.	n.s.	n.s.	n.s.
SMEs (up to 500 employees) versus large firms (over 500 employees)	n.s.	n.s.	n.s.	n.s.	n.s.	n.s.
Year of creation of the firm	n.s.	n.s.	n.s.	n.s.	n.s.	n.s.
Competitive position in its main market	n.s.	n.s.	n.s.	n.s.	n.s.	n.s.
National individual private firm	n.s.	n.s.	n.s.	n.s.	n.s.	n.s.
Firm belonging to a national group/holding	n.s.	n.s.	n.s.	n.s.	n.s.	n.s.
Firm with foreign capital	n.s.	−0.36*** (0.19)	n.s.	n.s.	n.s.	−0.25*** (0.03)
Public enterprise	n.s.	−0.79** (0.14)	n.s.	n.s.	n.s.	n.s.
Producers of traditional consumer goods	n.s.	−1.19** (0.12)	n.s.	n.s.	n.s.	n.s.
Suppliers of traditional intermediate goods	n.s.	−0.65*** (0.11)	n.s.	−1.04*** (0.25)	n.s.	n.s.
Specialized suppliers of intermediate goods and equipment	−0.27*** (0.12)	n.s.	−0.17* (0.05)	n.s.	+0.23* (0.09)	n.s.
Mass production assemblers	n.s.	n.s.	n.s.	n.s.	n.s.	n.s.

R&D-based sectors	n.s.	n.s.	n.s.	n.s.	n.s.
Service suppliers	n.s.	n.s.	n.s.	n.s.	n.s.
TECHNOLOGICAL ORIENTATION AND EFFORT LEVEL					
Expenditure on R&D as percentage of sales up to 1% versus 1% or more	n.s.	n.s.	−0.63* (0.04)	n.s.	−0.22* (0.07)
Expenditure on R&D as percentage of sales up to 5% versus 5% or more	n.s.	n.s.	n.s.	n.s.	n.s.
Staff in R&D (up to 25 versus 25 or more)	n.s.	n.s.	n.s.	−0.78*** (0.19)	−0.46*** (0.11)
Regularity of the innovative activities	n.s.	+1.11** (0.11)	n.s.	n.s.	n.s.
Importance of basic R&D carried out by the firm (TOE1)	n.s.	n.s.	n.s.	+0.17* (0.06)	n.s.
Importance of applied R&D carried out by the firm (TOE2)	n.s.	n.s.	+0.14* (0.04)	+0.56*** (0.28)	+0.23*** (0.12)	n.s.
Importance of technological development carried out by the firm (TOE3)	n.s.	n.s.	+0.22** (0.07)	n.s.	n.s.
Importance of own R&D in general (TOE4)	+0.27*** (0.11)	+0.44** (0.11)	n.s.	n.s.	n.s.
Technical autonomy	n.s.	n.s.	n.s.	+0.02** (0.14)	n.s.	n.s.
% of sales corresponding to the introduction of new products or new processes in the last five years	+0.20*** (0.06)	n.s.	n.s.	n.s.	+0.51*** (0.19)
CHARACTERISTICS OF THE PROJECTS					
Number of projects financed by the CDTI	n.s.	n.s.	n.s.	+0.26* (0.05)	n.s.

Continued

Table 9.5 Continued

	Improvement in training of HH.RR		Improvement of the knowledge base		Improvement in innovation management	
	Individual projects	Cooperative projects	Individual projects	Cooperative projects	Individual projects	Cooperative projects
Total budget of the financed projects	n.s.	n.s.	n.s.	n.s.	+0.33** (0.05)	+0.55** (0.11)
Novelty of the project	n.s.	n.s.	n.s.	n.s.	0.54* (0.05)	n.s.
Constant	−0.71**	+0.45^{NS}	+0.97^{NS}	−0.04^{NS}	−0.60***	−1.01***
Percentage of cases correctly classified by the model	67%	83%	71%	91%	67%	65%
Chi square of the model	21***	29***	12*	22***	37***	23***

Notes: To make possible the use of a logistic regression model we dichotomized the dependent variables, joining on one side the values 0–2 (irrelevant or less important) and on the other side the values 3–5 (important to very important). Level of significance (* 10%; ** 5%; *** 1%). The estimated models contained several variables not included in this table because they were rejected. For expenditure on R&D, three dummy variables were used (up to 1%; between 1% and 5%; more than 5%); for the social or control capital four dummies were used (individual national firms, firms belonging to a national group, firms with foreign capital, and public enterprises); for the personnel in R&D two dummies were used: up to 25 employees versus more than 25 employees). It is worth mentioning that all the variables with TOE (technological orientation and efforts) can substitute each other. Excluding TOE1 from the model implies that the betas of other variables will be get statistical significant such as TOE2, TOE3, or TOE4. But this substitution implies a lower level of statistical significance, a lower number of correctly classified firms, or a lower Chi-Square for the model. This could imply that the model has some problems of co-linearity due to the variables for technological effort and orientation (the same could be said for the variable personnel in R&D in relation with the variable employment) but during the construction of the model, and earlier estimations, we did not find any evidence or indications that this is a real problem.

n.s. means 'not statistically significant'

Source: Own elaboration based on the IAIF/CDTI questionnaire.

regression models were also estimated for two sub-samples by type of project (firms with cooperative projects and firms with only technology projects) and both models confirmed the results mentioned before.

The tests of association indicate (see Table 9.2) that the sector[7] to which the firm belong seems to be correlated with the level of learning capabilities, although in the association tests for the additional sub-sample of the most innovative firms (with a level of R&D expenditure of above 5% of sales) the sectoral differences fade away. In this case all sectors showed a high level of learning. The logistic regression model distinguishes those preliminary results.

The models that analyze the impact of the cooperative projects show that in each of the three learning modes the traditional sectors reached a lower level of learning impact while in the case of the other sectors no statistically significant differences where found. In the case of the models for technological (or individual) projects only the sector of specialized suppliers shows a different level of learning. In this case the firms in this sector have a lower level of learning impact in relation to improvement of their human resources and the knowledge base of the firm. However, in the case of organizational learning (improvement in innovation management) those firms have an above-average level of learning impact. All other sectoral differences faded away in the regression models and have to be related by other sectoral differences such as size and level of innovation effort.

The analyses of learning capability, taking into account also the ownership of the firms (E.g. the control capital). The survey distinguish four types of firm: those belonging to a group of enterprises, national private firms, public enterprises, and firms with foreign financial input. As in the case of the sector analysis, most of the differences detected in the association tests between the control capital and the impact fade away once we estimate the logistic regression model. Only the regression models of the cooperative projects show some statistically significant differences. In this specific case the improvement in the training of human resources is lower in the case of foreign-controlled firms and public enterprises, and improvement in innovation management is somewhat lower in the case of the foreign-controlled firms, where all the other differences detected in the association tests have to be caused by other explanatory variables of the model (like size, type of project or innovative behavior).

The level of learning capability seems not to be correlated with the competitive strength of the firms. The IAIF/CDTI database also includes a broad range of variables[8] that measure the competitive strength of the firms. These variables – not included in the tables in this chapter – were analyzed in the preliminary versions of the exploratory analysis and the logistic regression models. Of all modalities of learning only the improvement in the integration of R&D activities with other areas of the firm showed statically significant differences in the exploratory analysis. The association tests indicated that the learning effects seem to be somewhat higher in the more competitive enterprises. However, this weak relationship was not confirmed by the logistic regression model.

9.4 Flows of knowledge between partners in cooperative R&D projects

9.4.1 Impact of cooperative R&D projects on inward and outward knowledge flows

The IAIF/FECYT survey provides us with information about knowledge flows between the partners in the R&D projects. These flows can be considered as learning effects. The firms were asked about the importance of the technology transfer, in the form of incoming and outgoing flows of knowledge and information. It should be emphasized that the data in this section – including results relating to the importance the technology flows given by the research institutes – are based on the opinions of the supported firms. Table 9.6[9] indicates that 33% of the firms consider the knowledge acquired from the cooperation partner as very important, 37% consider this type of inward technology transfer important, and 30% estimated the learning effects as not important. On the other

Table 9.6 Impact of public support projects on form of learning

		Not important	Important	Very important	Total
Transfer of knowledge and information to the firms	Not important	16	8	7	31
	Important	8	20	8	36
	Very important	5	4	24	33
	Total	29	32	39	100

Transfer of knowledge and information to the research centers

Note: It is important to note that the learning effects for the research centers were measured by the opinions of the firms.

Source: Own elaboration from the IAIF/FECYT survey.

hand, the firms consider that they transferred very important knowledge and information to 39% of the research institutes, another 32% transferred important knowledge and for 29% of the research institutes the incoming knowledge flows (as an indicator of the learning effects) can be considered – in the opinion of the firms – as minimal. Analyzing simultaneously both directions of technology transfer we found that for 16% of the projects there was no knowledge transfer at all. In these projects neither the firm nor the research centre seems to be involved in an important or very important learning process. For 56% of the firms there was an intensive mutual transfer of knowledge – considered as important or very important. For the other 31% the transfer was one-way. An interpretation of these results could be that for 56% of the firms the policy meets their objectives in creating synergies by a process of mutual or collective learning between firms and other agents of the innovation system. For 31% the learning process is individual while for 16% there is no learning effect.

The directions of the technology transfer were also analyzed[10] in order to calculate 'net impacts' (Table 9.7). This showed that 12% of the firms received much more knowledge and information than they had transferred to the research centers while 14% considered that they had learned rather more than their partners. Overall, 26% of the firms considered that they had learned more from the research institutes than these institutes had learned from them, while the opposite

Table 9.7 Direction or orientation of knowledge transfer (learning) between firm and research center (by type of firm: size and R&D intensity)

Size of firm	Level of R&D intensity	The transfer of knowledge from the research centre to the firm is higher — Clearly (%)	Moderately (%)	Equal level of learning (%)	The transfer of knowledge from the firm to the research centre is higher — Moderately (%)	Clearly (%)
Small	Low	12	14	53	12	10
	Medium/high	7	1	55	14	23
Medium	Low	10	7	59	11	14
	Medium/high	9	14	48	18	11
Large	Low	13	8	59	12	8
	Medium/high	7	10	57	20	7
Total		10	9	55	14	12

Note: It is important to note that the learning effects for the research centers were measured by the opinions of the firms.

Source: Own elaboration from the IAIF/FECYT survey.

situation – that the research centers were net receivers – was reflected in almost 20% of cases. In 10% of cases the research centers clearly learned more from their cooperation partners while for 9% their learning advantages were only moderate. In particular, the smallest low-tech firms were net receivers of scientific and technological knowledge (26%), while in only 7% of the small high-tech firms were the incoming flows of knowledge and information more important than the transferred technologies. The opposite situation – research centers as net receivers – was found for 37% of the small high-tech firms and only for 20% of the small low-tech ones. For the other subsamples of firms no statistically significant differences were detected.

9.4.2 Promotion of cooperation in R&D and the profile of the firms with a lower or higher impact level: an econometric model

In this part of the chapter we analyze more broadly which type of firm is more influenced by the public support measures and which kind of firm could be characterized as free-riders. For this purpose we estimated logistic regression models. First we divided the sample between firms with a low level of impact and firms with a high level of impact (or learning) and second we estimated the model. Table 9.8 shows the profile of the firms with a low or high impact or level of learning and the profile of the firms in relation to the direction of the knowledge flows. The profiles are very succinct or concise and include only a few explanatory variables. As in the case of the other learning effects discussed in Section 9.3, the main explanatory variable is, again, the innovative behavior. The most R&D-intensive firms showed a higher level of learning during the execution of the cooperative R&D projects than the less innovative ones. This tendency is confirmed by both surveys (IAIF/CDTI and IAIF/FECYT) and by different variables of the firms innovative behaviour and orientation. In fact it is confirmed by the variables that reflect the input of the innovation process (R&D expenditure as a percentage of sales), by the technical results or outcome of the innovation process (percentage of sales related to new or improved products), and by some variables measuring the orientation of the R&D activities[11] (such as the importance of the basic R&D or the regularity of R&D activities).

However, some variables measuring the absolute level of R&D (such as number of researchers) reflect a lower level of learning. This could be explained by the fact that larger research departments – with a higher number of scientists – probably have a broader complementary set of knowledge and experiences and this high potential probably reduces the need for learning.

As mentioned in Section 9.2, access to complementary knowledge and information is an important motive for cooperation. Other important motives are access to technological infrastructure and equipment and to follow-up or to get aware or of the latest technological tendencies. This kind of motive implies that the firms cooperate to assure new knowledge which convert learning is a specific objective of the cooperation. In other words it can be supposed that this kind of motives should be directly be related with the learning effects. However, the results of the survey showed that the firms that consider the 'purchase of knowledge and experience' an important motive for cooperation have an on-average level of incoming knowledge flow (i.e. learning effect). However, the outgoing knowledge flows for this type of firm – the transfer of knowledge to their R&D partners (which are the public R&D centers) – are above average. This is surprising because in this case it could be expected that the firms that are looking for such knowledge available in the public research centers would have learn more. However, another interpretation could be that the firms in search of new knowledge oblige the public research centers to develop or assimilate new activities and to invest in new R&D fields – initially based on the knowledge transferred from the firms – to adjust this new knowledge to the firms' requirements. This interpretation could mean that both have a very high level of learning. In any case, this interpretation can not be proved with our dataset. Some conclusion could be drawn from these results.

First, the intensive level of learning of the public research organizations could confirm the theoretical idea that learning depends on technological capacity – for example, that the agents need to have a certain level of knowledge and to be specialists to absorb new technological knowledge and take advantage of the potential learning effects.

Second, these results could reflect an important aspect of the cooperation, the confidence and real interest of the collaboration partners in cooperative projects, which could conflict with their mutual interest in the technology transfer in both directions. For both partners, knowledge is part of their business and could be considered a strategic asset. For the firms, knowledge is part of their business strategy to compete in the market with new products or processes. However, for the public research centers, innovation and knowledge is the core of their business. They are selling technological capabilities and knowledge (through cooperation or contract research) and can attract customers

Table 9.8 A logistic regression model to reflect the profile of the firms or R&D centers with a lower or higher learning effect

	Learning effect in the firms		Learning effect in the public R&D centers		Orientation to the firms	
	1	2	1	2	1	2
Size	n.s.	n.s.	n.s.	n.s.	n.s.	n.s.
Export propensity	n.s.	n.s.	n.s.	n.s.	n.s.	n.s.
Age	n.s.	n.s.	n.s.	n.s.	n.s.	n.s.
Individual private enterprises (reference category)	Ref.	Ref.	Ref.	Ref.	Ref.	Ref.
Enterprise belonging to a national group	++	+	n.s.	++	n.s.	+
Foreign enterprises	n.s.	n.s.	n.s.	n.s.	n.s.	n.s.
Producers of traditional consumer goods	n.s.	n.s.	n.s.	n.s.	n.s.	n.s.
Providers of traditional intermediate goods	n.s.	n.s.	n.s.	n.s.	n.s.	n.s.
Providers of specialized machinery and equipment	n.s.	n.s.	n.s.	n.s.	n.s.	n.s.
Scale-intensive sectors and mass assemblers	n.s.	n.s.	n.s.	n.s.	n.s.	n.s.
Science-based sectors	n.s.	n.s.	n.s.	n.s.	n.s.	n.s.
Other manufacturers	n.s.	n.s.	n.s.	n.s.	n.s.	n.s.
High-tech services	n.s.	n.s.	-	n.s.	-	n.s.
Other services (reference category)	Ref.	Ref.	Ref.	Ref.	Ref.	Ref.
R&D intensity (R&D expenditure as % of sales)	n.s.	n.s.	n.s.	n.s.	n.s.	n.s.
Innovative intensity (expenditure on innovation as % of sales)	n.s.	+	n.s.	n.s.	n.s.	+
Personnel in R&D	--	--	-	-	-	--
Innovative regularity	n.s.	n.s.	n.s.	n.s.	n.s.	n.s.
Importance of basic research	n.s.	n.s.	n.s.	n.s.	n.s.	n.s.
Importance of applied research	+		++	+	n.s.	n.s.
Importance of technical development	n.s.	n.s.	n.s.	n.s.	++	n.s.
Percentage of sales related to 'innovative' products	+	+	n.s.	+	n.s.	+

Percentage of exports related to 'innovative' products	n.s.	n.s.	n.s.	n.s.	n.s.
Cost saving	Exc.	Exc.	Exc.	Exc.	Exc.
Acquisition of experience and knowledge	Exc.	Exc.	Exc.	Exc.	Exc.
Following-up of technical advances	Exc.	Exc.	Exc.	Exc.	Exc.
Access to expertise and qualifications not available in own firm	Exc.	n.s.	Exc.	n.s.	n.s.
Access to infrastructure and equipment not available in own firm	Exc.	++	Exc.	n.s.	++
Obligation to obtain public support	Exc.	n.s.	Exc.	n.s.	n.s.
Percentage of cases correctly classified by the model	57	65	60	57	60	65
Yes	68	73	65	68	65	73
Total	64	70	64	64	64	70
X^2 of Nagelkerke	0.12	0.21	0.14	0.12	0.14	0.21
−2 Log likelihood	414	389	399	414	399	389
Number of cases No	112	112	106	112	106	112
Yes	247	247	253	247	253	247
Total	359	359	359	359	359	359

Notes: The symbols indicate the level of statistical significance and the orientation of the relationships: positive relationships (+++ = 99%; ++ = 95%; + = 90%); negative relationships (−−− = 99%; −− = 95%; − = 90%). The dependent variable of the model is the importance incoming knowledge flows -measured on a scale from 0 (irrelevant) to 5 (very important)- which is interpret as the intensity of the learning effect (i.e. technology transfer). To carry out the logistic regression model these values were aggregated to two. As in table 9.4 the cases with the values 0 to 3 are considered as low impact and the cases with values 4 and 5 are classified as the high impact group.

n.s. means 'not statistically significant'; Ref. means the reference group; and Exc. means excluded from the model.

Source: Own calculations based on the IAIF/FECYT survey.

(firms) only if they continue to be at the technological cutting edge. So they also try in a certain way to assure to limit or restrict the outward flows of strategical knowledge and capabilities. Thus, they find themselves in paradoxical situation, simultaneously putting on the market R&D-related services and trying on the same time to prevent an to excessive outward flow of knowledge. To conclude, the different actors in cooperative projects try to minimize outward flows and to maximize inward flows of knowledge. This tendency is contradictory to the policy propositions in which mutual and collective learning based on a maximum level of flows in both directions- is the primordial objective.

Research centers probably have a better learning capability than firms due to their continuous interaction with different enterprises and other clients, from which they receive complementary knowledge which they can use for benchmarking. This is the trial-and-error process of learning by doing, generated by collaboration or contract research with a broad number of firms prevent them for making mistakes during their services their next clients and avoids to entrance to the wrong technological paths.

Another conclusion of this article concerns the relationship between learning and the nature of the firm. In this case, the logistic regression model shows that national firms belonging to a group have a higher learning capability than individual or foreign-influenced firms. However, in terms of the direction of the technology transfer, the model shows that in the case of foreign firms the inward transfer is more important than the outward knowledge flow.

The logistic regression model also shows that the direction of the knowledge flow is related to the innovative behavior of the firms. In the case of firms with a relatively high R&D effort (high level of R&D expenditure relative to sales), the inward flow is higher than the outward flow. However, in the case of firms with an R&D unit with more than 25 researchers, the outward flow is greater. This could be explained by the fact that groups of more than 25 researchers could have a broad knowledge base while smaller units lack the 'critical mass' and therefore have to be more specialized or oriented to some limited aspects. This tendency confirms this relationship which also was detected in the case of the internal learning process for cooperative projects, mentioned in Section 9.3.

The logistic regression model offers also an estimation that includes variables that express the motives behind cooperative projects. It should be noted that hardly any of the motives were statistically significantly related to the learning level. However, the firms that consider "access to infrastructure and equipment not available in their own firm" as an important aspect showed a higher level of learning, while for those same firms the inward knowledge flows were higher than the outward flows.

9.5 Conclusion: profile of firms with a lower/higher leaning intensity from R&D

Both surveys (the IAIF/CDTI survey and the IAIF/FECYT survey) produced similar conclusions in relation to the profile of the firms with a higher or lower level of learning capability. In general terms, we can conclude that there is almost no correlation between learning capability and most of the firms' structural characteristics. In general, we found only some small differences both in the explorative analysis and in the results of the logistic regression models. Moreover the models could be considered as rather weak because generated only a relatively low percentage of well classified firms.

The exception are, without any doubt, the innovative level and/or orientation of the firm, which can be seen as the most important explanatory variable for learning capability. The firms with a low innovative level and/or orientated to less complex R&D activities have a markedly lower learning capability than the more innovative firms. Moreover, in some additional analysis –not included in this chapter (See Heijs, 2007) – we detected a group of small and less innovative firms that scarcely improved their technological capabilities. It seems that within this group the learning process is not assured due to lack of experience in the highly specialized and complex field of innovative activities. In other words, in spite of the fact that less innovative firms carry out R&D projects, they remain in a backward position (with a low level of technological capabilities) in relation with more innovative firms.

On the one hand, this result seems to be surprising because the less innovative firms could be expected to have more margin and need for learning and improving their innovative capabilities, but on the other hand, the findings coincide with the results of other studies (see, among others, Becher et al., 1989; IMADE, 1992; Kulicke et al., 1997; Schmidt, 2005) and with the theoretical literature on absorptive capacities (Cohen and Levinthal, 1989; van den Bosch et al., 1999; Zahra and George, 2002; Narula, 2004). Moreover, the empirical work of Heijs (2000, 2001) points out that less innovative firms (in terms of R&D expenditure in proportion to sales) have a similar level of goal achievement. This means that their low learning capability does not impede the effective development of their R&D projects.

The only variable with regard to innovative behavior that has an opposite effect is the size of the research unit. The firms with more than 25 researchers show – in general – an average or below-average learning capability. This fact could be explained by the 'critical mass' phenomenon. Firms with large research units have a broad knowledge pool in which the researchers have complementary knowledge, while smaller firms often require – as in the case of the cooperative projects under consideration – new complementary knowledge from their research partners. Moreover, for certain projects their researchers probably have to complement their existing knowledge with specialized information through study or external training or advice.

With regard to the characteristics of the projects carried out by the firms, we observed that, together with the innovative level of the firm, the type of project seems an important explanatory variable. The association tests for the type of project showed that the firms with cooperative projects showed a higher level of learning capability for each of the three indicators. The logistic regression models confirmed those tendencies found in the contingency tables except for improvement in innovation management. So it can be concluded that cooperative projects generate a higher level of learning than technological projects.

These results can lead to two final conclusions. The first could be that less innovative firms embedded in their normal everyday innovative activities, while highly innovative firms carry out projects at the cutting edge of technology. However, in Section 9.4, we showed that the differences in learning capabilities are not only based on the differences in the kinds of project carried out by the firms. Therefore, the second conclusion could be that it seems very difficult for less innovative firms to close the technological gap with more innovative firms. Less innovative firms need not only financial support but also other types of support such as technical consultancy and training. The need for such support has been highlighted in a study on innovative enterprises in Madrid (IMADE, 1992). Analyzing the opinion of the innovative firms about the support they regarded as necessary, this study showed that they require not only financial help (70% of the firms asked for financial support to buy modern equipment and over 50% financial support to carry out R&D projects) but also technical advice to initiate their projects (42%), supervision and orientation during the development of the projects (17%), and training for their managers (36%) and their personnel (56%).

As a third important conclusion, emphasis must again be put on the importance of the technological capabilities of a firm and the fact that those capabilities are the result of an accumulative process. The most innovative enterprises show a higher learning capacity than the less innovative ones. So learning capability depends on innovation capabilities, which depend on the accumulation of experiences and acquired knowledge. This means that less innovative firms are enclosed in vicious circle and can only escape – that is, reduce the technological gap between themselves and the high-innovation firms – with extraordinary effort. To initiate such a 'catching-up' process, innovation policies should develop special instruments for less innovative firms, based not just on financial support but on a combination of financial and technical support and intensive consulting.

Notes

1. See, among others, Freeman, 1994; Bell, 1984; Cohen/Levinthal, 1989; Lundvall/Borras, 1998; Lane and Lubatkin, 1998; Zahra and George, 2002; Lundvall et al., 2002; Van den Bosch et al., 2003; Schmidt, 2005; Autio et al., 2008; Vega-Jurado et al., 2008.
2. Dagfhous (2004) offers a good overview of this subject.
3. Details of these analyses can be found in Heijs, 2001 and Buesa and Heijs, 2007.
4. Calculated as the simple average for the whole sample
5. The IAIF/CDTI survey measured the learning effects from the CDTI projects by the following question: "Evaluate each of the following aspects of the impact arising from the CDTI project, according to their level of importance (from 0 not relevant, 1 unimportant to 5 very important)." Only 54 firms valued all the three aspects of learning with 0 or 1 points.
6. The inclusion of a large number of indicators to measure the innovative level of firms could generate a problem of co-linearity. To avoid this problem I used a stepwise method to estimate the models. Moreover, the preliminary estimations of the models showed that the inclusion or exclusion of different variables for innovative level makes little change within that group of variables. Those experiments did not influence the inclusion and the sign of the effect (positive or negative beta coefficient) of other variables of the model. This confirms that the models presented in this paper are stable and consistent and can be considered as valid.
7. The aggregated sectors used in this article are: Producers of traditional consumer goods (CNAE 15–22, 26, 36, 37), Suppliers of traditional intermediate goods (CNAE 27, 28), Specialized suppliers of intermediate goods and equipment (CNAE 25, 29, 33), Mass production assemblers (CNAE 30–32, 34, 35 except 35.3), R&D-based sectors (CNAE 24, 35.3), as proposed by Archibugi et al. (1991) and Pavitt (1984), and Service suppliers (CNAE 51–92).
8. This aspect is measured by ten variables. The first two are the position of the firm in its main market. In this case the survey asked for its competitive position (inferior, equal or superior) in relation to other firms related to national of foreign competitors. Moreover it include indicators about the firms level (inferior, equal or superior to its competitors) in relation with their national and international competitors in reference to their: product quality; price level; level of customer services; the commercial position; and the technological level of the firm.

9. In this case the five options to answer were aggregated to three levels (Very important; important; not important).
10. Therefore we compared for each firm the value of the importance of the received and the transferred knowledge and information.
11. The survey asked about the importance of three types of R&D. The firms evaluate (on a likert scale from 1 -low importance- to 5 -very important-) the importance of basic R&D, Applied R&D and the technological development.

References

Archibugi, D., Cesaratto, S. and Sirili, G. (1991) 'Sources of innovative activities and industrial organisation', *Research Policy*, 20, 357–368.

Arvanitis, S. (2009), 'How do different motives for R&D cooperation affect firm performance? An analysis based on Swiss micro data', KOF Working Papers No. 233, July.

Autio, E., Kanninen, S., Gustafsson, R. (2008), 'First- and second-order additionality and learning outcomes in collaborative R&D programs', *Research Policy*, 37: 59–76.

Becher, G.; Kuhlmann, S.; Kuntze, U.; Walter, G.H.; Gielow, G.; Herden, R.; Hornschild, K.; Edler, D. (1989) *FuE-Personalkostenzuschüsse: Strukturentwicklung, Beschäftigungswirkungen und Konsequenzen für die Innovationspolitik*, ISI-Fraunhofer/DIW., Fraunhofer Institutit für System und Innovationforschung, Karklsruhe, Germany.

Bell, M. (1984), 'Learning and the accumulation of industrial technological capacity in developing countries', in K. Kim and M. Fransman (eds), *Technological Capacity in the Third World*, London, Macmillan.

Brown, J.S. and Duguid, P. (1991), 'Organizational learning and communities-of-practice: toward a unified view of working, learning, and innovation', *Organization Science*, 2(1), 40–57.

Cohen, W. and Y Levinthal, D. (1989), 'Innovation and learning: the two faces of R&D implications for the analysis of R&D investment', *Economic Journal*, 99. 569–596.

Daghfous, A. (2004), 'Absorptive capacity and the implementation of knowledge-intensive best practices', *SAM Advanced Management Journal (1984)*, 69(2), 21–27.

Fagerberg, J. (1994), 'Technology and international differences in growth rates', *Journal of Economic Literature*, 32. 1147–1175.

Fagerberg, J., Srholec, M. and Verspagen, B. (2010), 'Innovation and economic development.',. In B. Hall and N. Rosenberg (eds), *Handbook of the Economics of Innovation, Volume 2 Elsevier,* North Holland.

Freeman, C. (1994), 'The economics of technological change', *Cambridge Journal of Economics*, 18, 463–515.

Hagedoorn, J. (2002), 'Inter-firm R&D partnerships: an overview of major trends and patterns since 1960', *Research Policy*, 31, 477–492.

Heijs, J. (2001), 'Política tecnológicas e Innovación: Evaluación de la financiación pública de I+D en España', Published by the *"Consejo Económico y Social de España"*, Madrid, Spain..

Heijs, J. and Buesa, M. (2007), 'Cooperación en innovación en España y el papel de las ayudas públicas', Editorial: Instituto de Estudios Fiscales. Madrid, Spain.

Heijs, J. (2003), 'Freerider behaviour and the public finance of R&D activities in enterprises: the case of the Spanish low interest credits for R&D', *Research Policy*, 32(3), 445–461.
IMADE (1992), *La Industria y los Empresarios Madrileños ante la Innovación Tecnológica*, Madrid, Imade.
Kulicke, M., Bross, U. and Gundrum, U. (1997), *Innovationsdarlehen als Instrument zur Förderung Kleiner und Mittlerer Unternehmen*, ISI-Fraunhofer. Fraunhofer Institutit für Innovation und System Forschung, Karklsruhe, Germany.
Lane, P.J. and Lubatkin, M. *(1998)*, 'Relative absorptive capacity and inter-organizational learning', Strategic Management Journal, 19, 461–477.
Lundvall, B.-Å. and Borras, S. (1998), 'The globalising learning economy: implications for innovation policy', The European Commission, DG XII-TSER, Brussels.
Lundvall, B.-Å., Johnson, B., Sloth Andersen, E. and Dalum, B. (2002), 'National systems of production, innovation and competence building', *Research Policy*, 31, 213–231.
Meyer-Krahmer, F. (1989), *Der Einfluss Staatlicher Tecnologiepolitiek auf Industrielle Innovationen*, Nomos-Verlag, Berlin..
Narula, R. (2004), 'R&D collaboration by SMEs: new opportunities and limitations in the face of globalisation', *Technovation*, 24, 153–161.
Pavitt, K. (1984), 'Sectoral patterns of technical change: towards a taxonomy and a theory', *Research Policy*.
Porter, M. (1990), *The Comparative Advantage of Nations*, Free Press and Macmillan, Harvard University.
Schmidt, T. (2005), 'Absorptive capacity – one size fits all?', Center for European Economic Research, Discussion paper 05–72.
Schmidt, T. (2007), 'Motives for innovation co-operation – evidence from the Canadian survey of innovation', ZEW, Discussion paper 07–018.
Van Den Bosch, F.A.J., Van Wijk, R. and Volberda, H.W. (2003), 'Absorptive capacity: antecedents, models, and outcomes', in Mark Easterby-Smith and Marjorie A. Lyles, *Blackwell Handbook of Organizational Learning & Knowledge Management*, pp. 278–301.
Van den Bosch, F.A.J., Volberda, H.W. and de Boer, M. (1999), 'Co-evolution of firm absorptive capacity and knowledge environment: organizational forms and combinative capabilities', *Organization Science*, 10, 551–568.
Vega-Jurado, J., Gutiérrez-Gracia, A. and Fernández-de-Lucio, I. (2008), 'Analyzing the determinants of firms' absorptive capacity: beyond R&D', *R&D Management*, 38(4), 392–405.
Zahra, S.A. and George, G. (2002), 'Absorptive capacity: a review, reconceptualization, and extension', *Academy of Management Review*, 27, 185–203.

10
Typologies of Innovation Based on Statistical Analysis for European and Spanish Regions

Mikel Navarro and Juan José Gibaja

10.1 Introduction

Innovation is increasingly regarded as one of the key engines of economic growth and prosperity (Lundvall, 1992; Nelson, 1992; Nelson and Rosenberg, 1993; Verspagen, 1995). One of the most relevant levels for the analysis and policy-making on innovation is the regional level (Lundvall and Borras, 1997) and the most influential strand of literature that deals with them is the regional innovation system (RIS) (Asheim and Coenen, 2005).

Typologies of RIS have been elaborated aiming at capturing the diversity and variety of regional patterns of innovation. These help us to understand causality and other relations in a systematic context (Lundvall, 2007) and to design policies better suited to the characteristics and needs of each region (Cooke, 1998). Among the two types of RIS typology – conceptual typologies based on case studies and typologies based on statistical analysis –we have opted for the latter in this chapter. There have been few attempts at a typology covering all the regions of the EU-25; and even fewer covering Spain (Navarro and Gibaja, 2009). This chapter will present the main findings of our recent research to identify a typology of innovation for the EU-25 regions (Navarro et al., 2009), and will offer a new typology for the Spanish regions.

Probably the main obstacle to the development of RIS typologies based on statistical analyses is the lack of statistical data about core aspects of an RIS (Bruijn and Lagendijk, 2005). The shortage of data is more pronounced in some countries than in others, depending by and large on the level of decentralization existing in the country. In Spain, for instance, the availability of data is quite high and it allows us to take into consideration some issues (interactions, government policies, openness of the region, and so on) that in typologies for many other countries – and, as a result, in typologies for all the EU regions – are unknown.

The second objective of this chapter is, precisely by exploiting the aforementioned data availability for Spanish regions, to explore the consequences of considering or not considering such issues when elaborating typologies for all the European regions. In order to do this, we conduct a multiple factorial analysis. This statistical technique allows us to compare the two typologies of innovation obtained for the Spanish regions (the one obtained with available data from Eurostat and the one obtained by adding to them data collected from other Spanish sources) and assess whether the data structure of both is stable and those typologies can be regarded as similar.

10.2 Regional typologies of innovation in the RIS literature

The RIS framework is a useful tool for studying regional economic and innovative performance and for policy-making (Asheim and Coenen, 2005; Mullers et al., 2008). Following Tödtling and Trippl (2005), we distinguish the following components in the RIS:

- The knowledge generation and diffusion subsystem. Crucial actors are R&D organizations, educational bodies and technology-mediating and other innovation-supporting organizations.
- The knowledge application and exploitation subsystem. This subsystem refers to the region's business sector.
- The regional policy subsystem, composed of government organizations and regional development agencies.
- The socio-institutional factors specific to a region, which largely influence its innovation capacity.
- The linkages with other RIS or national innovation systems.

The RIS components have particular characteristics in each territory. The relevance and nature of these components will depend on the innovation and learning mode prevailing in the region. According to Jensen et al. (2007), two main modes can be distinguished: the STI and the DUI modes. The former is based on searching and exploring, related to a great extent to R&D activities; the latter is based on doing, using, and interacting. As regions differ, so must their innovation systems and the policy stances adopted in pursuit of them (Cooke, 1996).

As a result, several types of RIS can exist and the created typologies can shed important light on both analytical terms and policy design (Asheim and Isaksen, 2002). Following Lundvall (2007), clustering procedures that result in dividing the population into different 'subspecies' or 'families' with common characteristics are more useful when it comes to study systems of innovation and search for causality than statistical procedures that look for causality patterns general for the whole population. In this regard, typologies constitute an analytical tool for characterizing regions according to their similarity in a certain combination of criteria. By allowing for a systematic comparison of economic and innovation activities across various regions, typologies serve as a general comparative classification that helps us to gain insight into development patterns.

There have been two main approaches to obtaining RIS typologies. The first uses case studies – sometimes as an iterative dialogue, very often in order to test previous conceptual work. A second group of authors have considered large groups of regions and have performed statistical data analyses – mainly factor and cluster analyses – on regional economic and innovation data in order to cluster regions with similar RIS characteristics.

A compilation of the main conceptual typologies can be found in Table 10.1.[1] Despite the specific differences in the factors describing the different typologies, all these case study-based classifications present the advantage of providing detailed insights into the innovation processes accruing in different territories. They manage to clearly identify governance structures, types of knowledge, and nuanced descriptions on the linkages between the different innovative agents and innovation broker institutions. However, they fail to provide comprehensive and quantitative measurement of the economic and innovation performance of the European regions.

In order to deal with this caveat and generate an RIS typology applicable to a larger number of regions, statistical analyses could be used. Until recently, the RIS literature hardly ever worked with aggregated data coming from secondary sources and pertaining to a broad group of regions (Malmberg and Maskell, 1997). Certainly, the limitations in regional data availability restrict the extent to which it is possible to take into account interactions among agents and other important aspects related to the systemic nature of innovation processes. Still, the analysis of traditional indicators available in secondary sources might help

Table 10.1 Review of RIS conceptual typologies

Author	Factors considered	Typology obtained	Regions analyzed
Cooke (1992, 1998, 2004)	1. The type of governance infrastructure: where the process is initiated (local, regional, federal, supranational), who provides the funding (banks, government agencies ...), which research competence prevails (basic, applied, or near to the market), and the levels of coordination and technical specialization (high or low)	Three categories according to the first dimension: grassroots, network, and dirigiste	Cooke (1992), Braczyk et al. (1998) and Crooke et al. (2004): Tuscany (IT), Southwest Brabant (NL), Catalonia (ES), Midi-Pyrénées (FR), Quebec and Ontario (CA), California (Silicon Valley/Hollywood) (US), Tampere (FI), the village economy of Denmark (DK), Baden-Württemberg (DE), Wales (UK), North Rhine-Westphalia (DE), Tohoku (JP), Singapore (SG), Gyeonggi (KR) and Slovenia (SI).
	2. The type of business innovation: who is the prevailing firm (large or small, indigenous, or multinational), the research reach of firms (internal or external), the innovation supporting infrastructure (public or private) and the degree of associationism (among firms or between firms and policy-makers)	Three categories according to the second dimension: localist, interactive, and globalized	
Asheim and Isaksen (1997, 2002).	Extent to which they are internally and externally integrated: the location of knowledge organizations (locally or outside the region), the knowledge flow (interactive or linear), and the stimulus for cooperation (geographical, social and cultural proximity); planned and systematic network functioning; sharing the same education and experiences	Three categories: territorially embedded regional innovation networks, regional networked innovation systems and regionalized national innovation systems	Asheim and Isaksen (1997 and 2002): Norwegian regions (especially Jaeren Horten and Sunmore)
SMEPOL research group: Kauffman and Tödtling (2000), Isaksen (2001), Nauwlaers and Wintjes (2002), Tödtling and Tripp (2005)	Main barriers to innovation: organizational thinness, fragmentation, and lock-in	Linked to organizational thinness: peripheral areas Linked to fragmentation: fragmented regional clusters and metropolitan regions Linked to lock-in: old industrial regions, and transition- and raw material-based peripheral areas	Regions investigated in the SMEPOL project: Upper Austria (AT), Wallonia (BE), Jutland (DK) Lombardy and Apulia (IT), Limburg (NL), northern and south-eastern Norway (NO), Valencia (ES), Lee Valley and Hertfordshire (UK) Regions investigated in the REGIS project non high performers: Styria (AT), Tampere (FI), Wales (UK), Basque Country (ES), Wallonia (BE), Aveiro and Friuli (IT), Féjer (HU), and Lower Silesia (PL)

to shed some light on the relations between knowledge inputs, socio-economic characteristics of the territory, and innovation and economic outputs (Bruijn and Lagendijk, 2005). As a result, both for academic reasons and to help policy-makers to design regional and innovation policies, some researchers have recently started following a promising path of defining RIS on the basis of statistical sources.

Table 10.2 presents synoptically a review of the works on statistical typologies of innovation for the EU regions: the type of publication (academic journal or report), the region under consideration, the sources of data, the reference year for data, the statistical technique used, the variables employed, and the typology obtained. A more detailed presentation of these typologies can be found in Navarro et al. (2008, 2009). There are reasons we decided to develop our own typology of innovation for the European regions. The first was that many of the typologies did not span the whole EU-25, contained few variables, or were based on old data. The second reason was that, even though many of the existing typologies claimed to be based on an RIS framework, the model on which they relied was not explicit (this is the case with many of the report-type typologies) or their connection with the model was not direct (except in the case of the Martínez-Pellitero typology).

Similarly, Table 10.3 presents a review of the typologies of innovation for the Spanish regions. In fact, only the typologies of the IAIF group (Martínez-Pellitero, Buesa, Heijs and Baumert) and of the Orkestra-Institute (Navarro and Gibaja) was elaborated with statistical techniques. Although there are many differences between the methods these two teams applied to produce their typologies, probably the most important is that a relatively high number of variables were applied in absolute terms by the former, and practically all the variables were applied in relative terms by the latter. The strange and, in our view, unsatisfactory typology resulting from the IAIF team's work is probably due to their use of a large number of variables in absolute terms. Unlike the typology offered by Navarro and Gibaja (2009), the typology elaborated in this chapter does not work with 133 variables grouped into 29 factors (employed as variables in the subsequent factorial analysis), but directly with variables: firstly, with 21 variables taken from Eurostat, so as to make a typology more comparable with the ones elaborated by the RIS literature for European regions; secondly, with 31 variables, 10 of them taken from Spanish sources, related to key issues of the RIS literature that cannot be studied with data coming from Eurostat (see Table 10.4).

10.3 Data, sources and methodology for our typology of EU-25 and Spanish regions

The variables that should nurture our statistical analysis were determined according to the components a conceptual RIS should have. Figure 10.1 shows the types of indicator used in our typology, grouped according to their connection with the main components of an RIS and the effect of the RIS on innovation and economic output. Let us look at them briefly.

The most simple and basic indicators of competitiveness or economic output are GDP per capita and productivity (Porter et al., 2008). Although, as mentioned before, innovation is increasingly regarded as one of the key engines of economic growth or competitiveness (Lundvall, 1992; Nelson, 1992; Nelson and Rosenberg, 1993; Verspagen, 1995), reaching a threshold of economic development might be a necessity before a region can increase its technological base (Clarysse and Muldur, 2001; Bilbao-Osorio and Rodríguez-Pose, 2004; Dory, 2008). The RIS affects economic output, but in turn the economic output conditions the RIS' innovation performance.

Despite some weaknesses, patents are the most appropriate indicator for measuring technological output based on R&D (Jaffe, 1989; Feldman, 2000). But not all innovations come from R&D, and variables such as the percentage of sales due to new products can be used as indicators for overall innovative activity (OECD, 2005; UNU-MERIT, 2009). Unfortunately, for this last indicator there is no available data for all European regions, because the Community Innovation Survey (CIS) is not collected on a regional basis in most of European countries. But the Spanish official statistical institute (INE) provided us with data on this variable for the Spanish regions.

As previously shown, several components could be differentiated within the RIS. First, the knowledge generation and diffusion subsystem, which in the figure has been abbreviated to 'supporting system.' In this subsystem, according to the aforementioned distinction between the STI and DUI modes, it is convenient to differentiate between indicators for the R&D infrastructure and for the innovation infrastructure (the public R&D infrastructure excluded). Additionally, unlike some other typologies, in the R&D infrastructure we make a distinction between the two kinds of public R&D: government and university. The reason for doing so is that the weight and role assigned to public administration and to universities is different in each country; and, whereas tertiary education is quite widespread over the territory,

Table 10.2 Synoptic review of works on statistical typologies of innovation for the EU regions

Authors	Type of publication	Regions considered*	Data source	Year of data
Clarysse and Muldur (2001)	Academic journal	102 regions in EU-15: NUTS 1 (BE, DE, UK) and NUTS 2 (rest)	Eurostat	1995 (for variables of level); 1989–1995 (for variation variables)
Hollanders (2003)	Report	171 regions in EU-15: NUTS 1 (UK, BE) and NUTS 2 (the rest)	Eurostat and CIS II innovation survey	1995–2000, depending on the variable
Hollanders (2006)	Report	206 regions in EU-25: NUTS 1 (BE, UK, POL) and NUTS 2 (the rest)	Eurostat	2002–2004 (or last available year), depending on the variable
Brujin and Lagendijk (2005)	Academic journal	206 regions in EU-15: NUTS 2	Eurostat	2000–2002 (variables of level); 1995–2000, 1999–2001 and 1999–2002 (for variation variables)

Statistical technique	Variables employed	Typology obtained
Factorial and cluster	Five variables of level and three of variation: GDP per capita, employment in agriculture, total R&D, patents per capita, unemployment rate, GDP variation, patents variation, unemployment variation	Six groups: industry leaders, clampers-on, slow growers, technological catchers-up, economic catchers-up, laggards
Cluster	14 variables of level: tertiary education, life-long learning, medium- and high-tech manufacturing employment, employment in knowledge-intensive services, public R&D expenditure, business R&D expenditure, patents, high-tech patents, innovative companies in manufacturing, innovative companies in services, innovation cots in manufacturing, innovation costs in services, sales of products new to the firm in manufacturing and GDP per capita	Six groups: two high-tech groups with three regions each; and four others with a much higher number of regions, especially those located close to the EU average or below this
Cluster (hierarchical)	Six variables of level: HRST, life-long learning, public R&D expenditure, business R&D expenditure, employment in medium- and high-tech manufacturing, employment in high-tech services, patents	12 groups, ranked according their innovation performance
Factorial and cluster	Seven variables of level and seven of variation (for the same variables): per capita GDP, GDP per employee, workforce with tertiary education, tertiary students, R&D expenditure, employment in high-tech manufacturing, employment in technology-intensive services, employment in life-long learning, patents	Six groups: with very strong diversified position, with strong position in knowledge-intensive services, with strong growth in knowledge-intensive services, with strong position in high-tech sectors, with strong growth in high-tech sectors, laggards

Continued

Table 10.2 Continued

Authors	Type of publication	Regions considered*	Data source	Year of data
Ecotec (2005)	Report	About 150 regions (varying with cluster) in EU-15: NUTS 1 (BE, UK) and NUTS 2 (the rest). Not included: DK and IRL	Eurostat and ESPON.	1999–2002, depending on the variable
Technopolis et al. (2006)	Report	215 regions in EU-25	MERIT, based on Eurostat data	Mostly referring to 2002–2003

Statistical technique	Variables employed	Typology obtained
Z-score analysis and three-cluster analysis: re-scaled data for four individuals, two compound indicators and average of the six indicators	Six variables of level for the z-score analysis and the third cluster analysis: three of R&D capacity: R&D expenditure, R&D staff, HRST core; and three of innovation: employment in medium- and high-tech manufacturing, employment in knowledge-intensive services, population with tertiary education Four variables of level for the cluster analysis: business R&D intensity, HRSTC, patents per capita, high-tech employment	Z-score analysis: five types of area: lack of capacity, average capacity, rich innovation, rich R&D, knowledge centers. Cluster analysis: First analysis: five clusters: worst R&D performance and lowest share in high-tech employment; mediocre R&D performance and strong HRSTC base; mediocre R&D performance and average share of high-tech employment; second best R&D performance and average share of high-tech employment; top R&D performance, strong HRSTC base and highest share of high-tech employment. Second analysis: five clusters: low R&D capacity and low innovative capacity; medium R&D capacity and low innovative capacity; medium R&D capacity and medium innovative capacity; high R&D capacity and medium innovative capacity; high R&D capacity and high innovative capacity Third analysis: five clusters: very high capacity for R&D and innovation; high capacity for R&D and innovation; above average capacity for R&D and innovation; average capacity for R&D and innovation; below average capacity for R&D and innovation
Factorial and cluster	16 variables: GDP per capita and 15 additional variables in four groups: public knowledge (higher education, HRSTC core, high-tech services employment, public R&D expenditure), urban services (value-added share services, value-added share industry, employment in government administration, population density), private technology (high- and medium-tech manufacturing employment, value-added share agriculture, business R&D expenditure, HRSTO occupation), learning families (population share under ten, life-long learning, activity rate females)	11 types of region, in four strategic groups: global consolidation regions (science and service center, Nordic high-tech learning), sustaining competitive advantage regions (learning, centrral techno and high techno), boosting entrepreneurial knowledge regions (local science and services, aging academia), entering knowledge economy regions (southern cohesion, rural industries, eastern cohesion, low-tech government)

Continued

Table 10.2 Continued

Authors	Type of publication	Regions considered*	Data source	Year of data
Martínez-Pellitero (2007)	Academic journal	146 regions in EU-15: NUTS 1 (BE, D, UK) and NUTS 2 (the rest)	IAIF-RIS (EU) database elaborated with Eurostat data (with estimates of missing values), supplemented by Infostate and Economic Freedom	Average of 1998–2000
Dory (2008)	Report	189 regions in EU-25: NUTS 1 (BE, D, UK) and NUTS 2 (the rest)	Eurostat	2002

Statistical technique	Variables employed	Typology obtained
Factorial and cluster	29 variables of level, grouped into six factors: national environment (employment, population, GDP, gross added value, compensation of employees, gross fixed capital formation, HRST in services, HRST in knowledge-intensive services, HRST in high-tech), regional environment (venture capital, economic freedom index, seed and start-up capital, ITC penetration), innovative companies (business R&D, business R&D headcount personnel, business R&D FTE personnel, patents high-tech per GDP, patents high-tech per capita, patents per GDP, patents per capita), universities (university R&D headcount personnel, university R&D FTE personnel, university R&D expenditure, postgraduate students), public administration (government R&D headcount personnel, government R&D FTE personnel, government R&D expenditure), demand (GDP per worker, GDP per capita)	Ten groups, divided by the author into three categories: atypical, intermediate, and least developed
Factorial and cluster	13 variables of level: some relating to knowledge creation and absorption capacity (business R&D intensity, volume of R&D, business R&D personnel, educational qualifications, HRST) and some to the economic structure and industrial specialization (level of regional income, sectoral specialization, labor market characteristics, degree of agglomeration)	Seven region types, three of which have two subtypes each: types 1A and 1B predominantly agricultural and diversified agro-industrial; type 2 tourism-based; type 3 re-industrializing or industrial catchers-up; types 4A and 4B newly industrialized and diversified; type 5 restructuring industrial; type 6 high-income industrial leaders; types 7A and 7B diversified industry-based high-income economies and diversified service-based high-income economies

Continued

Table 10.2 Continued

Authors	Type of publication	Regions considered*	Data source	Year of data
Muller et al. (2008)	Academic journal	55 regions in EU-12 (enlargement): NUTS 2	Eurostat; PATDPA, SCI, eEurope + database, Fraunhofer ISI/CWTS; and Merit	From 2001 to 2004 (most variables of level) 1996–2001 (two additional variables of level) and 1995–2001 (for variation variables)
Navarro et al. (2009)	Academic journal	188 regions in EU-25: NUTS 1 (BE, D, UK) and NUTS 2 (the rest)	Eurostat and Schurmann Talaat index	2005

(*) In Denmark, Ireland, Luxemburg, Estonia, Cyprus, Latvia, Lithuania, Malta and Sloven data correspond to the whole country in all the works.

Statistical technique	Variables employed	Typology obtained
Double factorial: (1) with five variables included in knowledge creation; (2) with the factor of knowledge creation and the 20 remaining variables	23 variables of level and two variables of variation, arranged in five groups: knowledge creation (R&D expenditure, R&D employees, patents, publications in life sciences, publications in nanosciences), knowledge absorption (business R&D, university R&D, tertiary education, secondary education, secondary and tertiary education, lifelong learning, IS population), diffusion of knowledge (technology diffusion infrastructure, employment in high-tech services, employment in manufacturing industries, employment in agriculture, IS enterprises), demand (GDP per capita, cumulated growth of GDP, unemployment rate, population density, change in population density), governance capacity (participation in EU initiatives, e-government and web presence of regions)	Five groups: capitals, with tertiary growth potential, qualified manufacturing platforms, with industrial challenges, agricultural laggards
Factorial and cluster	21 variables of level: GDP per capita, employment, GDP per worker, population density, peripherality index, employment in agriculture, employment in industry, employment in business and financial services, employment in medium- and high-technology manufacturing, employment in high-tech services, youth educational level, tertiary education, life-long learning, HRSTC, total R&D expenditure, government R&D expenditure, university R&D expenditure, business R&D expenditure, R&D expenditure per person engaged in R&D, patents, high-tech patents	Eight groups: peripheral agricultural regions with strong economic and technological lag, restructuring industrial regions with considerable weaknesses, peripheral regions with an economic and technological lag, central regions with a certain technological lag, industrially restructured regions with an increasing technological capacity, service-oriented regions with average economic and technological capacity, technologically advanced regions with an industrial specialization, innovative capital regions, specialized in high added value

Table 10.3 Review of typologies of innovation for the Spanish regions

Authors	Data source	Year of data	Statistical technique
Coronado and Acosta (1999)	INE and OEPM	1989–1995 (average)	No
Martínez-Pellitero (2002), Buesa et al. (2002a, 2002b)	IAIF database (created from data from INE, EPO, CINDOC, CDTI, FEDIT, Departamento de aduanas e impuestos especiales, webcapitalriesgo.com)	1996–1998 (average)	Factorial and cluster analysis

Variables employed	Typology obtained
Seven variables: Spanish patents, total R&D expenditure, total R&D personnel, total researchers, business R&D expenditure, business R&D personnel, business R&D researchers	Three groups: technologically outstanding region (Madrid), technologically over average regions (Catalonia, Basque Country, Navarre and C. of Valencia), technologically peripheral regions (others)
33 variables grouped into four factors: variables related to regional environment (VA* and employment* in high and medium technology manufacturing, VA* and employment* in low technology manufacturing, exports* in high- and medium-high-tech manufacturing, exports* in medium low- tech manufacturing, exports* in low-tech manufacturing, CDTI's R&D projects*, GDP*, number* and percentage of patents in Spain, number and percentage of patents* in Europe), variables related to administration (government R&D expenditure, personnel and researchers, stock of scientific capital*, stock of scientific capital per inhabitant, stock of technological capital*, investment in venture capital*, venture capital as % of total), variables related to universities (university R&D expenditure, personnel and researchers, students enrolled in tertiary education, students finishing tertiary education, students enrolled in doctoral programs, students that became PhD, university's quality index), variables related to firms (business R&D expenditure, personnel and researchers, stock of business technological capital*, HRCT, number and turnover of technological centers*)	five groups, of which four have only one region: Madrid, Catalonia, Basque Country, Navarre, rest

Continued

Table 10.3 Continued

Authors	Data source	Year of data	Statistical technique
Buesa et al. (2007), Buesa and Heijs (2007)	IAIF database (created from data from INE, EPO, CINDOC, CDTI, FEDIT, Departamento de aduanas e impuestos especiales, webcapitalriesgo.com)	1994–2004 (every year)	Factorial and cluster analysis
Navarro and Gibaja (2009)	REGES database (created from data from INE, Eurostat, OECD, OPE, D.G. Aduanas, Ministry of Industry, SABI-Informa, Fedit, APTE, ASCRI, Madri+d, Schurmann and Talaat	2006	Factorial and cluster analysis

* Variable applied in absolute terms

Variables employed	Typology obtained
23 variables, grouped into five factors: variables related to regional environment (employment* in low-tech industry, employment* in high- and medium-high-tech industry and exports*, CDTI's R&D projects*, venture capital*, GDP*), variables related to innovative firms (R&D expenditure, personnel and researchers, innovation expenditure, stock of business R&D); variables related to government (R&D expenditure, personnel and researchers, and stock of scientific capital), variables related to university (R&D expenditure, personnel and researchers, students enrolled in tertiary education, students enrolled in doctoral programs, university's research quality), variables related to supporting institutions (number* of technological centers, turnover* of technological centers)	Five groups, of which four have only one region: Madrid, Catalonia, Basque Country, Navarre, rest
133 variables, grouped into 29 factors, relating to eight areas: two factors of economic output (economic output, profitability), two factors of S&T&i output (S&T output, innovation output), six factors of the business subsystem (business R&D, innovation expenditure, structure of services and agriculture, manufacturing structure, industry's technological level, size and firms' group, five factors of the supporting subsystem (university R&D, government R&D, technological centers and parks, venture capital and business services, and ICT), eight factors of the socio-economic setting (demography, educational attainment, labor market, road and railroad infrastructure, air transport infrastructure, seaport infrastructure, accessibility, region size), three factors of government (regional and local administration support, central and European administration support, public funding of R&D), one factor of firm cooperation, two factors of internationalization (trade internationalization, productive internationalization)	Five groups: agricultural laggards (Extremadura, Castile-La Mancha). peripheral tourist without manufacturing and a technological lag (Canary Islands, Balearic Islands and Andalusia), intermediate regions with certain economic and technological lag (Murcia, Valencia, Galicia, Asturias, Cantabria, Castile-Leon, La Rioja, Aragon), economically and technologically developed industrial regions (Basque Country and Navarre), developed regions with high urbanization (Madrid and Catalonia)

Table 10.4 Variables used to obtain the innovation typologies of EU-25 and Spanish regions

Component of the model	Code	Indicator	Available for EU-25 regions
Economic output	GDP pc	GDP per capita (€)	Yes
	GDP pw	GDP per worker (€)	Yes
Innovation output	Patents	Patents (per million habitants)	Yes
	Pat High Tech	High-tech patents (per million inhabitants)	Yes
	New Sales	Sales of new-to-firm and new-to-market products (% of turnover)	No
Business subsystem	GERD	Total R&D (% GDP)	Yes
	BERD	Business R&D (% GDP)	Yes
	NoR&Dinnov	Expenditure of innovative firms in acquisition of machinery, equipment, software, and other external knowledge (% GDP)	No
	Agric	Agriculture (% employment)	Yes
	Ind	Industry (% employment)	Yes
	HTManuf	High- and medium-tech manufacture (% employment)	Yes
	KIServ	Knowledge intensive services (% employment)	Yes
	Special	Export specialization index (*)	No
	RelVar	Export-related variety index (**)	No
	Firms>500	Firms with 500 or more employees (%)	No
Infrastructure subsystem	HERO	Higher education R&D (% GDP)	Yes
	GOVRD	Government R&D (% GDP)	Yes
	GERDpr	R&D per researcher (€million)	Yes
	FBServ	Financial and business services (% employment)	Yes

R&D activities linked to public administration tend to be concentrated in certain regions (Oughton et al., 2002; Mowery and Sampat, 2005). Besides, unlike other RIS typologies, our work also takes into account R&D expenditure per person employed in R&D activities. As the European Commission (2007) shows, R&D workers' wages are much lower in less developed regions. If we look only at R&D expenditure without making allowances for disparities in researchers' wages, differences between developed and less developed regions could be inflated. As for the innovation infrastructure, the percentage of employment in financial and business services will be used like an indicator, because its value is positively correlated with the summary index of European innovation and with the regional economic and technological performance (Miles, 2005; Arundel et al., 2007).

The analysis of the application and exploitation subsystem ('business subsystem' in Figure 10.1) should be split according to three factors that condition a firm's innovative output. First, as the literature on knowledge production function has shown since Griliches (1979), a firm's innovation inputs influence the innovation output. Once again, following the distinction between the STI and DUI modes of innovation, we consider it convenient to collect separate indicators for firms' R&D activities and for firms' innovative activities not based on R&D. For the former, as almost all the existing typologies do, we will turn to business R&D expenditure as a percentage of GDP. For the latter, we will take innovation expenditure (the one in R&D excluded) as a percentage of GDP. As has been explained, the CIS is not conducted on a regional basis in most European countries and therefore such indicators can not be used to obtain a typology of EU-25 regions. But innovation expenditure (R&D excluded) can be obtained for the Spanish regions from the innovation survey.

Second, the size of the firm is a factor conditioning its innovation output (Cohen, 2010), taken into account explicitly by Cooke's and Asheim's typologies. Although the average size of manufacturing firms can be obtained from Eurostat for the EU-25 regions, our examination of the available data raised serious doubts about its comparability and therefore we decided to exclude them from our EU-25 typology. On the contrary, firm size data for the Spanish regions are elaborated with a uniform methodology that makes them truly comparable and these were thus used to obtain the typology of Spanish regions.

Third, the region's production structure affects its innovation performance, as acknowledged by all the RIS typologies. Usually, this factor is taken into consideration by entering some indicators about the

```
                    ┌──────────────────────────┐
                    │  Other innovation systems │
                    └──────────────────────────┘
                              ↕
                      Internationalisation
                              ↕
┌─────────────────────────────────────────────────────────────┐
│                   Regional innovation system                 │
│              ┌────────────────────────────────┐              │
│              │      Socio-economic setting     │              │
│              │  Demography, human resources,   │              │
│              │ labour market, accesability and size │          │
│              └────────────────────────────────┘              │
│                           │                                  │
│              ┌────────────────────────────────┐              │
│              │       Government subsystem      │              │
│              └────────────────────────────────┘              │
│                    ╱                      ╲                  │
│   ┌──────────────────────┐  Interaction  ┌──────────────────────┐ │
│   │ Supporting subsystem │  ⇆⇆⇆⇆        │ Business subsystem   │ │
│   │  S&T infrastructure  │               │ Business R&D         │ │
│   │Innovation infrastructure│            │Other innovative activities│ │
│   └──────────────────────┘               │Production structure  │ │
│                                          │Firms structure       │ │
│                                          └──────────────────────┘ │
│                              │                                  │
│                   ┌──────────────────────┐                      │
│                   │  S&T and Innovation  │                      │
│                   │        output        │                      │
│                   └──────────────────────┘                      │
│                              │                                  │
│                     ┌──────────────┐                            │
│                     │   Economic   │                            │
│                     │    output    │                            │
│                     └──────────────┘                            │
└─────────────────────────────────────────────────────────────┘
```

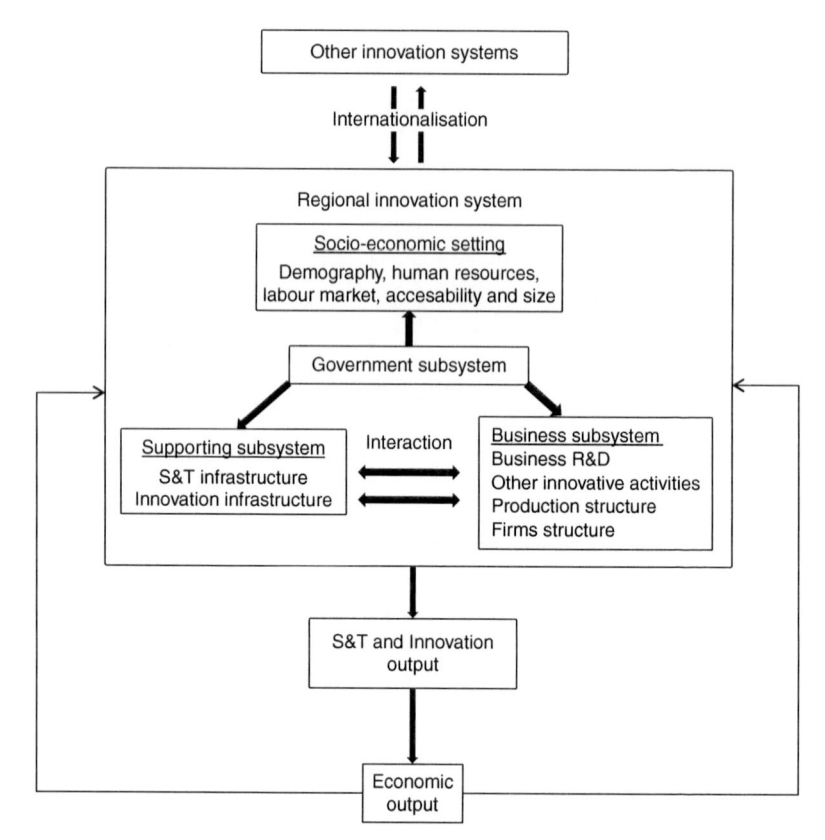

Figure 10.1 Aspects considered to build a RIS typology

share of the main economic sectors (agricultural, industry, or services) or the share of the industries intensives in technology or knowledge into the statistical analysis. Nevertheless, the existing RIS typologies have not considered indexes of specialization or related variety, even though since the paper of Glaeser et al. (1992) on dynamic knowledge spillovers, the literature on geography of innovation has highlighted the relevance of these factors for innovation. The main reason is that Eurostat does not offer enough breakdown in the data by industry for all the European regions. Once again, the availability of export data for the Spanish regions allows us to obtain these indexes and use them to obtain the typology of Spanish regions.

One of the major contributions of the innovation system framework to the understanding of innovation is its emphasis on the interactions of the agents (Edquist, 1997). In fact, this is one of the main obstacles to the existence of an RIS (Kauffman and Tödlting, 2000). But as Bruijn and Lagendijk (2005) state, limitations in regional data availability mean that interactions among agents cannot be taken into account by regional typologies. However, the existence of regional data in Spain from the innovation survey permits us to calculate the percentage of innovative firms that cooperate with other firms or with S&T infrastructures.

With regard to the government subsystem, despite the importance attributed to this element by the RIS literature and by the conceptual typologies developed by Cooke and Asheim, it has not been considered by typologies based on statistical analysis, due to the lack of data about the role played by regional governments. Here, again, the innovation survey conducted in Spain allows us to know the percentage of innovative firms funded by regional or local administrations. This variable will be used as a proxy to measure the involvement of regional government in RIS development.

According to Crescenzy et al. (2007) and Rodríguez-Pose and Crescenzy (2008) there are three types of "social filter" that, being part of the socio-economic setting, affect regional ability to transform R&D into innovation and economic growth: demography, education, and employment factors. As proxies for these we have taken: for the first, population density; for the second, HRST, percentage of students with five and six ISCED levels, percentages of those aged 25–64 with tertiary education level and with life-long learning; and for the third, the employment rate. As can be deduced from Table 10.1, all of them have been used for other EU regional typologies of innovation. Additionally, considering that proximity to markets and developed technological locations facilitates the presence of spillover and external economies (Crescenzi et al., 2007), we have also incorporated a peripherality index – understood here not as an indicator of economic development, but as an indicator of accessibility.

Finally, with regard to the methodology of data analysis, the analysis – performed using R and the FactoMineR package – consisted of a principal components analysis (PCA) and a cluster analysis, complemented by a multiple factorial analysis (MFA). Although our research uses more than twenty indicators, it does not use synthetic indicators, as do some other typologies (for instance, Muller et al., 2008). Working with the original indicators facilitates the interpretation of the econometric results, and therefore the suggestions of policy recommendations, without losing much explanation capacity.

10.4 Typology for the EU-25 regions

We developed a PCA with the 21 selected variables for the 188 regions of the EU-25. Figure 10.2 presents the positions of the variables regarding the first two principal components. The first principal component, measured along the horizontal axis, explains 43.2% of the variance and represents, to a great extent, the economic and technological development of the region. As shown by the coordinates, this factor is closely correlated with per-capita GDP, productivity, accessibility, HRST, employment in knowledge-intensive and financial/business services, inputs in R&D, results of R&D activities, and agriculture employment. The second component, measured along the vertical axis, explains 14.1% of the variance and represents the regional sectoral specialization, as shown by the coordinates of industrial employment and employment in medium-high and high-tech manufacturing.

Based on the findings of the PCA, a cluster analysis was carried out in order to put the regions into homogeneous groups. This analysis resulted in the creation of eight groups of regions named as follows (see Table 10.5):

G1 Peripheral agricultural regions with a strong economic and technological lag
G2 Restructuring industrial regions with considerable weaknesses
G3 Peripheral regions with an economic and technological lag
G4 Central regions with an intermediate economic and technological capacity

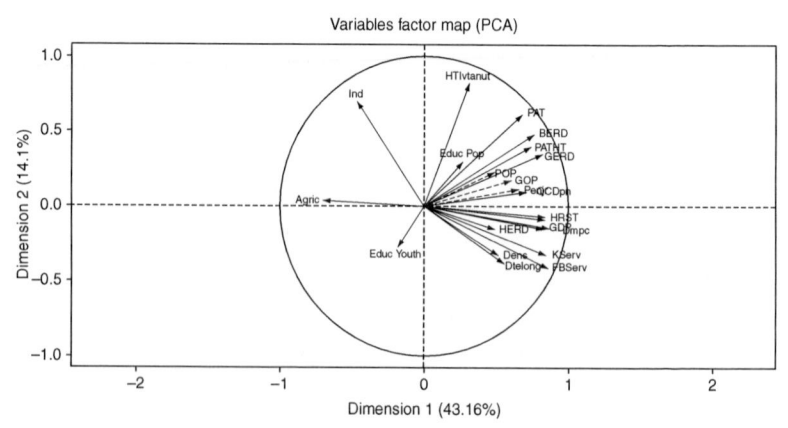

Figure 10.2 Results of the principal components analysis for the EU-25 regions

G5 Industrially restructured regions with some economic and technological capacity
G6 Service-oriented regions with a certain economic and technological capacity
G7 Technologically advanced regions with an industrial specialization
G8 Service-oriented innovative and capital regions.

The grouping of regions reveals three blocks of regions at different levels of technological and economic development: low – regions in groups 1, 2, and 3; medium – regions in groups 4, 5, and 6; and high – regions in groups 7 and 8. Moreover, regions with the lowest and highest development levels (G1 and G2, on the one hand; and G5, G6, G7 and G8, on the other) can be grouped according to their economic structure: G1 agricultural; G2 industrial; G5 and G7 industrial; G6 and G8 services). Whereas in regions with a medium-to-low level of development (G3 and G4), sectoral specialization seems less relevant to their allocation. A possible interpretation of this is that in order to achieve a significant level of economic and technological development, regions tend to opt for an industrial or service orientation.

Figure 10.3 positions the EU-25 regions regarding the two principal components. The centre of gravity of each of the eight groups of regions identified in the cluster analysis is also illustrated. The size of each centroid represents the population size of the regions pertaining to each group. The regions belonging to the EU-10 accession countries and to the EU-15 countries that formed the Union before the enlargement are identified by symbols as shown in the key. Finally, the peripheral regions (peripherality index <=100) are highlighted. In short, the figure can be interpreted as follows: regions with high levels of economic and technological development are located on the extreme right; regions with a high percentage of industrial employment and of employment in medium-high or high-tech manufacturing are at the top.

Figure 10.3 also reveals a relationship between economic and technological development and peripherality. Although there is not complete determinism, the more accessible regions tend to be concentrated on the right, i.e. among the developed regions, while less accessible regions tend to be concentrated on the left, related to low levels of development and innovation (peripheral regions). The main exceptions to this rule are the Nordic countries, showing that geographic peripherality is not always incompatible with high economic and technological development levels.

Table 10.5 Groups of EU-25 regions obtained through the cluster analysis

Group	Prevalent country	Regions			
G 1	GR, PL, PT	Castilla-la Mancha (ES) Thessalia (GR) Peloponnisos (GR) Észak-Alföld (HU) Malopolskie (PL) Podlaskie (PL) Opolskie (PL) Algarve (PT)	Extremadura (ES) Ipeiros (GR) Voreio Aigaio (GR) Dél-Alföld (HU) Slaskie (PL) Wielkopolskie (PL) Kujawsko-Pomorskie (PL) Centro (PT)	Anatoliki Makedonia, Thraki (GR) Ionia Nisia (GR) Notio Aigaio (GR) Lubelskie (PL) Zachodniopomorskie (PL) Warminsko-Mazurskie (PL) Alentejo (PT)	Kentriki Makedonia (GR) Dytiki Ellada (GR) **Kriti (GR) (G3)** Latvia (LV) Podkarpackie (PL) Lubuskie (PL) Pomorskie (PL)	Dytiki Makedonia (GR) Sterea Ellada (GR) Dél-Dunántúl (HU) Lódzloe (PL) Swietokrzyskie (PL) Dolnoslaskie (PL) Norte (PT)
G 2	CZ, HU, SI	**Strední Cechy (CZ) (G3)** Moravskoslezsko (CZ) **Stredné Slovensko (SK) (G1)**	Jihozápad (CZ) Közép-Dunántúl (HU) Východné Slovensko (SK)	Severozápad (CZ) Nyugat-Dunántúl (HU)	Strední Morava (CZ) Észak-Magyarország (HU)	Západné Slovensko (SK)
G 3	CY, EE, ES, IT, MT, SI	Burgenland (AT) Principado de Asturias (ES) Comunidad Valenciana (ES) Corse (FR) Molise (IT) Sicilia (IT)	Cyprus (CY) Cantabria (ES) Illes Balears (ES) Valle d'Aosta (IT) Campania (IT) Sardegna (IT)	Jihovýchod (CZ) (G2) La Rioja (ES) Andalucía (ES) Umbria (IT) Puglia (IT) Malta (MA)	Estonia (EE) **Aragón (ES) (G4)** R. de Murcia (ES) **Marche (IT) (G4)** Basilicata (IT) Mazowieckie (PL)	Galicia (ES) Castilla y León (ES) Canarias (ES) Abruzzo (IT) Calabria (IT) **Slovenia (SI) (G4)**
G 4	FR	Salzburg (AT) Saarland (DE) Itä-Suomi (FI) Lorraine (FR) Limousin (FR) P. A. Trento (IT) Zeeland (NL)	**Tirol (AT) (G6)** Sachsen-Anhalt (DE) **Champagne-Ardenne (FR) (G3)** Pays de la Loire (FR) **Attiki (GR) (G6)** Friuli-Venezia Giulia (IT) **Lisboa (PT) (G6)**	R. Wallonne (BE) Schleswig-Holstein (DE) Basse-Normandie (FR) Bretagne (FR) (G5) Közép-Magyarország (HU) Toscana (IT) Norra Mellansverige (SE)	Brandenburg (DE) **País Vasco (ES) (G5)** **Bourgogne (FR) (G3)** Poitou-Charentes (FR) Liguria (IT) Friesland (NL) Mellersta Norrland (SE)	Mecklenburg-Vorpommern (DE) Cataluña (ES) Nord-Pas-de-Calais (FR) Aquitaine (FR) P. A. Bolzano-Bozen (IT) Drenthe (NL) Småland med öarna (SE)

G 5	AT, FR	Niederösterreich (AT) Vlaams Gewest (BE) Thüringen (DE) Alsace (FR) Piemonte (IT) **Border Midlands and Western (IE) (G4)**	Kärnten (AT) Niedersachsen (DE) C.F. de Navarra (ES) Franche-Comté (FR) Lombardia (IT)	Steiermark (AT) Nordrhein-Westfalen (DE) Picardie (FR) (G4) Midi-Pyrénées (FR) (G7) Veneto (IT) (G4)	Oberösterreich (AT) Rheinland-Pfalz (DE) Haute-Normandie (FR) Rhône-Alpes (FR) Emilia-Romagna (IT)	Vorarlberg (AT) Sachsen (DE) Centre (FR) Auvergne (FR) Limburg (NL)
G 6	UK	**Bremen (DE) (G8)** Lazio (IT) Bratislavský kraj (SK) West Midlands (UK) Southern and Eastern (IE)	C. de Madrid (ES) Overijssel (NL) North East (UK) South West (UK)	Aland (FI) (G4) Gelderland (NL) North West (UK) Wales (UK)	Languedoc-Roussillon (FR) Flevoland (NL) Yorkshire and The Humber (UK) Scotland (UK)	P. Alpes-Côte d'Azur (FR) Övre Norrland (SE) East Midlands (UK) **Northern Ireland (UK) (G4)**
G 7	DE. FO, SE	Baden-Württemberg (DE) Pohjois-Suomi (FI)	Bayem (DE) Noord-Brabant (NL)	Hessen (DE) Sydsverige (SE)	**Etelä-Suomi (FI) (G8)** Västsverige (SE)	Länsi-Suomi (FI)
G 8	LU, NL, DK	Wien (AT) Denmark (DK) Noord-Holland (NL) London (UK)	R. de Bruxelles (BE) Île de France (FR) Zuid-Holland (NL) South East (UK)	Praha (CZ) Luxembourg (LU) Stockholm (SE)	Berlin (DE) Groningen (NL) Östra Mellansverige (SE)	Hamburg (DE) Utrecht (NL) Eastern (UK)

Note: Regions in bold are the most distant from the center of their group. After them, in brackets, is shown their next nearest group.

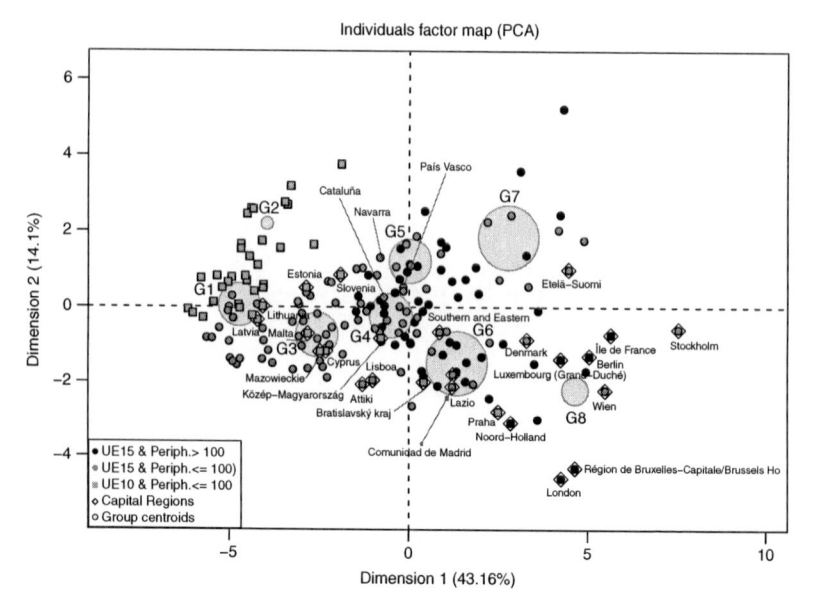

Figure 10.3 Location of the EU-25 regions in terms of the first two principal components: regional typology according to the cluster analysis

It can also be seen that regions belonging to the accession countries tend to be concentrated on the left of the figure. Finally, the EU-25 capital regions[2] are mainly located at the bottom, which makes clear the low level of employment in industrial activities in this type of region, the main exception being the Finnish region Etela-Suomi. Capital regions pertaining to the EU-15 are in the bottom right corner (except Lisbon and Athens), and those pertaining to the accession countries in the left (except Prague and Bratislava). All of them are located to the right of the rest of the regions in their countries, which makes explicit the link between being a capital region and achieving a high level of economic and technological development.

10.5 Typologies for the Spanish regions

This section aims to offer a new typology for the Spanish regions and, above all, explore how a typology might be affected by omitting variables about which there is no available data in Eurostat or other international data sources, even though they are considered as key aspects of an RIS by the literature. In order to conduct this analysis we will start by looking at the typology of Spanish regions obtained from data taken from Eurostat and then will replicate the analysis, but adding some new variables taken from other Spanish sources.

The PCA carried out for the seventeen Spanish regions (Ceuta and Melilla excluded, due to the lack of data on them for a high number of variables), based on data from Eurostat (Figure 10.4), lets us again identify two factors that explain even higher percentages of the variance of the variables: 63% and 14%. As in the EU-25 regions, the first factor, measured along the horizontal axis, represents to a great extent the economic and technological development of the region; and the second factor, measured along the vertical axis, the regional manufacturing specialization. The differences between the results of both principal components analyses (see Figures 10.2 and 10.4) could be described as minor.

Figures 10.5 and 10.6 represent, respectively, the dendrogram of the cluster analysis of the Spanish regions and the location of Spanish regions

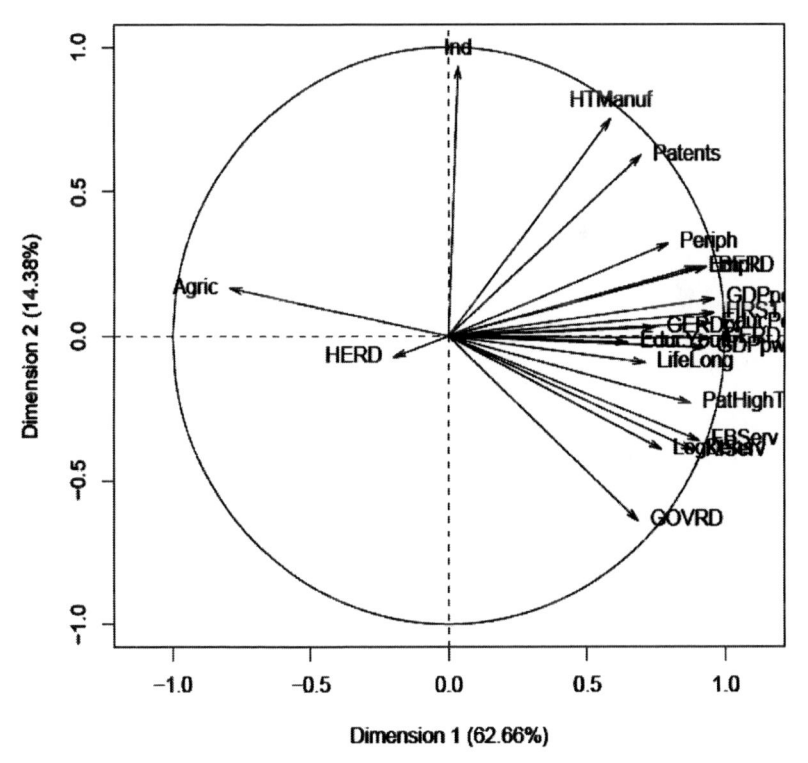

Figure 10.4 Results of the principal components analysis for the Spanish regions, using Eurostat data

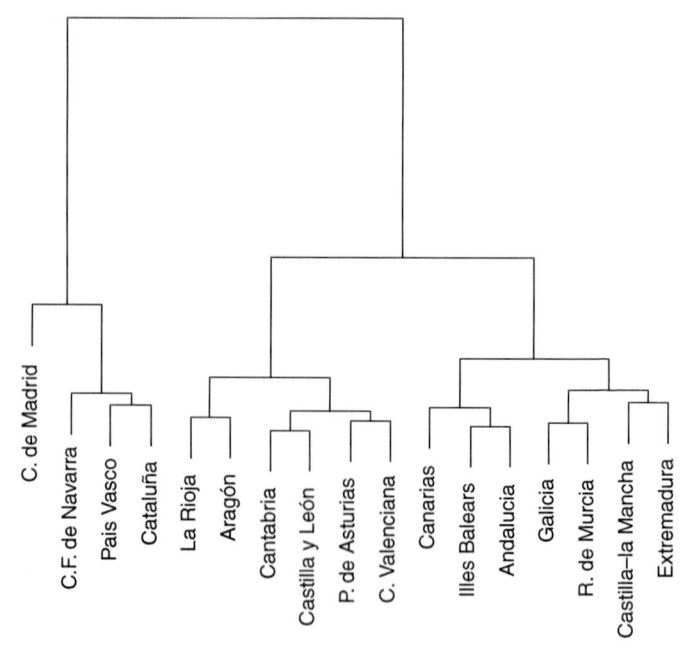

Figure 10.5 Dendrogram of Spanish regions, using Eurostat data

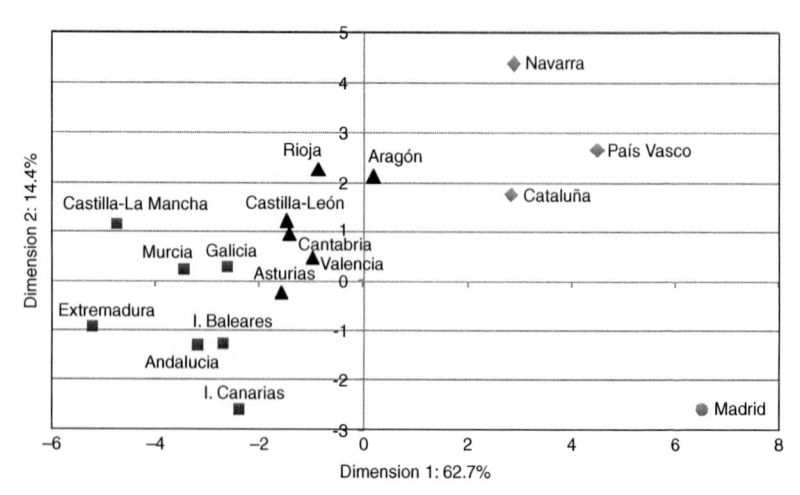

Figure 10.6 Location of Spanish regions in terms of the first two principal components, using Eurostat data

regarding the first two principal components of the factor analysis. The dendrogram shows a clear division into four groups of regions:

G1 Capital region specialized in advanced services: Madrid
G2 Medium/high-tech industrial regions: Basque Country, Catalonia, and Navarre
G3 Medium/low-tech regions: Aragon, Asturias, Cantabria, Valencia, La Rioja, Galicia, Castile-Leon
G4 Agricultural or tourist (less developed) regions: Balearic Islands, Canary Islands, Castile-la Mancha, Andalusia and Murcia

On the other hand, leaving aside the capital region, a positive relation appears between specialization in manufacturing and level of economic and technological development, perhaps because, apart from Barcelona (in Catalonia), there are no large cities or areas of high population density to foster the development of advanced services.

Figures 10.7, 10.8, and 10.9 show the same analyses, but conducted with variables taken from Spanish sources added to the ones taken from Eurostat.

In comparison with the previous factorial analysis, the percentage of the variance of variables explained by the two main components is lower (72% versus 77%), which seems logical considering the higher number of variables employed in this new analysis. On the other hand, the weight of the second component increases (from 14.4 to 17.7%), because several of the new variables (mainly goods exports, cooperation in innovation, and regional government's financial support to innovative firms) appear positively correlated with specialization in manufacturing industry. On the other hand, as could be expected, the percentages of sales of new products, direct investment, firm size, and non-R&D innovation expenditure are positively correlated with a high level of economic and technological development. Finally, indexes of specialization and related variety do not have high loadings and therefore do not seem so relevant to differences between Spanish regions; and while the related variety index tends to be linked more closely to high economic and technological development, in the specialization index the opposite applies.

As far as the cluster dendrogram is concerned, there are some changes. As in the previous cluster dendrogram, the number of region groups that seems meaningful is four. But two regions have moved from one group to another: Aragon from G3 to G2; and Galicia from G4 to G3. Also, regions are often arranged differently within each group. Overall,

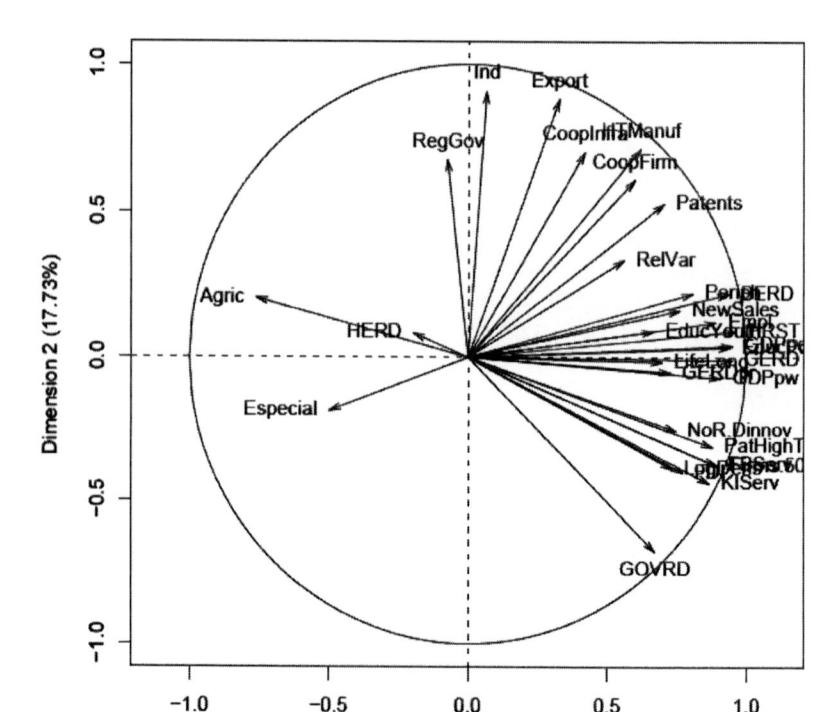

Figure 10.7 Results of the principal components analysis for the Spanish regions, using data from Eurostat and Spanish sources

the new classification fits better with our perception of the characteristics of the Spanish regions and shows a clearer geographical arrangement (see Figure 10.10). By and large, leaving aside the capital region (located in the middle of Spain), the most advanced regions are located in the north, middle and east of Spain and the less developed ones in the south and islands.

G1: Madrid
G2: Basque Country and Navarre; Catalonia and Aragon
G3: Asturias, Cantabria, and Valencia; Galicia, Castile-Leon, and Rioja
G4: Murcia, Andalusia, Castile-la Mancha, and Extremadura; Balearic and Canary Islands

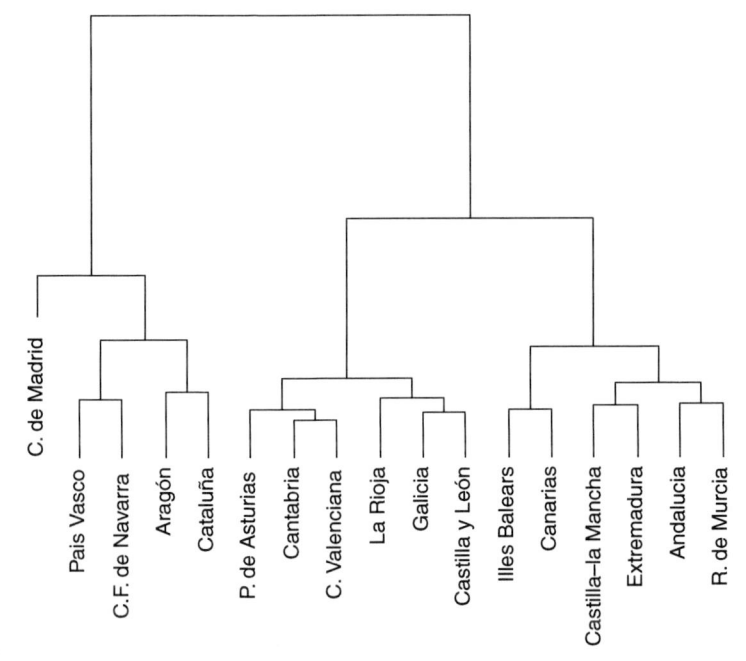

Figure 10.8 Dendrogram of Spanish regions, using data from Eurostat and Spanish sources

Regarding the location of the Spanish regions with respect to the two main components of the PCA, the differences in the results between the two analyses (only with data from Eurostat, on the one hand; and with data from Eurostat and from other Spanish sources, on the other) are less evident than in the dendrograms. Some apparently strong movements from one group to another in the cluster dendrograms (do compare Figures 10.5 and 10.8) turn out to be relatively small shifts from borderline regions in the individual factor maps (Figures 10.6 and 10.9). In fact, the individuals factor map seems more appropriate to understand the similarities between regions than the cluster dendrogram.

In order to assess the extent to which the first typology of Spanish regions, elaborated from data taken only from Eurostat, changes when new variables related to RIS issues about which Eurostat does not offer information are added, we carried out a multiple factorial analysis (MFA). MFA is used to analyze a set of observations described by several groups of variables. The analysis generates an integrated picture of the observations and of the relationships between the groups of variables (the different principal component analyses).

Figure 10.11 shows the regions' positions regarding the two main dimensions of this multiple factorial analysis. When the position is shown by a triangle, it means that only the 21 variables taken from Eurostat are considered; when shown by a square, that all the 31 variables are considered (those coming from Eurostat and from other sources).

Figure 10.11 allows us to see that, in general, regions do not move far from their initial (Eurostat) positions. In addition, regional changes occur mainly along dimension 2 and are more evident in some regions than in others. Basque Country and Navarre (regions with strong regional governments, specialized in manufacturing, and advanced technologically) move upwards along dimension 2. Galicia, La Rioja and Aragon move also upwards, but to a lesser extent. On the contrary, Balearic Islands, Canary Islands, and Castile-la Mancha move downwards. By and large, the differences between regions on dimension 2 have increased, because regions with a higher score in this factor go even upwards; and regions with lower score go downwards.

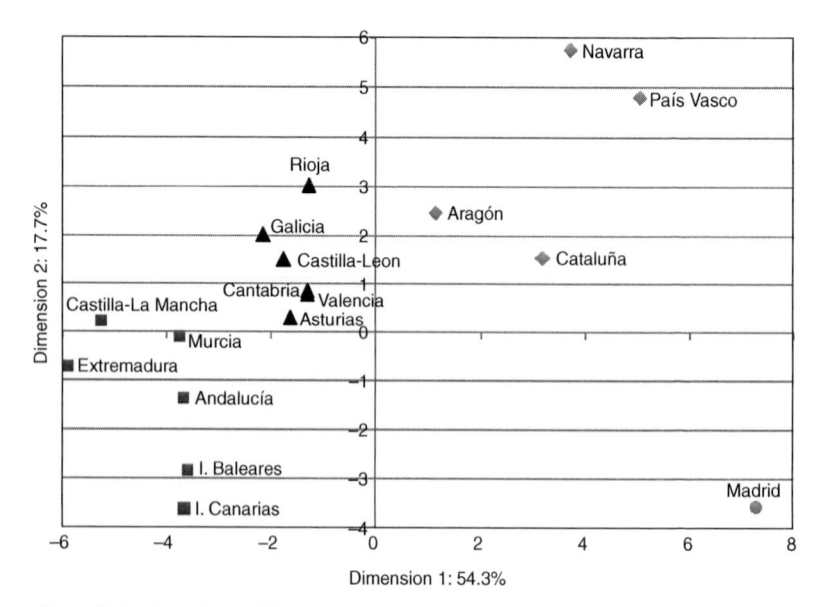

Figure 10.9 Location of Spanish regions in terms of the first two principal components of the factorial analysis, using data from Eurostat and Spanish sources

Figure 10.10 Geographical location of Spanish regions, and their cluster groups

As well as producing this visual depiction, the MFA measures the similarity between the two PCAs by looking at the stability of factors by means of RV and Lg coefficients. This is a more accurate and appropriate way of comparing the structure of the two typologies than the traditional one based on a correspondence analysis of the coordinates obtained by the regions in the two factorial analyses (the one with the 21 variables from Eurostat, and the one with all 31 variables).

Table 10.6 shows that the groups in the two typologies have a similar dimensionality (as can be seen by the coefficients of the main diagonal in the L matrix) and an internal structure practically equal (as the coefficients of RV matrix confirm). In short, the typology of Spanish regions does not undergo significant changes as a result of operating with a large number of variables connected to the system nature of an RIS, about which Eurostat does not provide information.

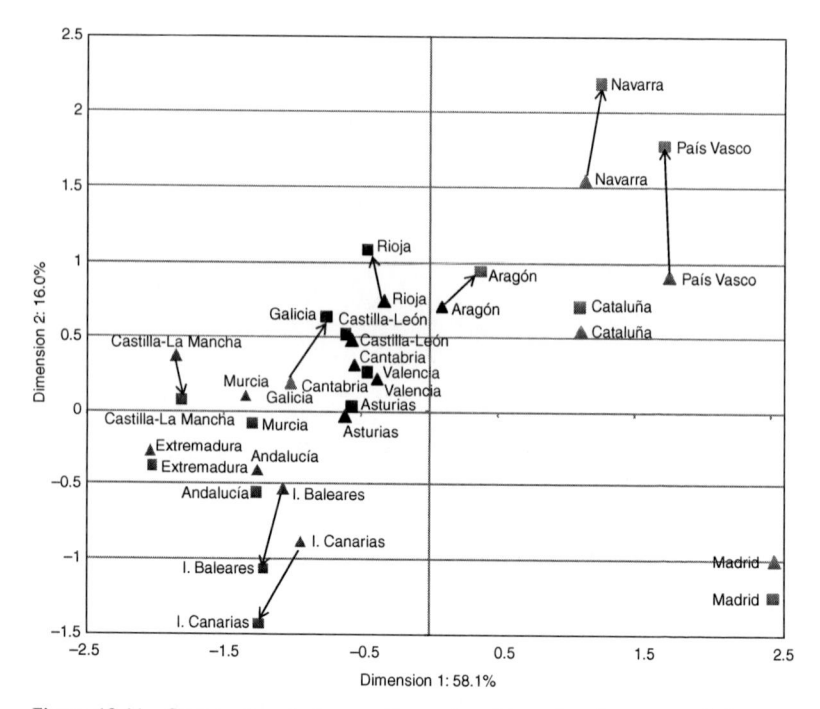

Figure 10.11 Comparison between the regions' location in terms of the two principal components in the two-factor analyses, using only Eurostat data and using data from Eurostat and Spanish sources

Note: Triangles shows region locations according to data only from Eurostat; squares, from Eurostat and other Spanish sources.

Table 10.6 Relation coefficients between groups

```
        Lg coefficients              RV coefficients

      |   1       2    AFM          |   1      2     AFM
------+----------------------    ------+----------------------
    1 | 1.079                        1 | 1.000
    2 | 1.096   1.156                2 | 0.981  1.000
  AFM | 1.089   1.127  1.110       AFM | 0.995  0.995  1.000
------+----------------------    ------+----------------------
      |   1       2    AFM          |   1      2     AFM
```

This suggests that a typology resulting from an analysis using only sources that do not allow those aspects to be taken into consideration will differ little from a typology obtained from an analysis that also considers them.

10.6 Conclusions

RIS typologies allow regional patterns of innovation to be captured and, therefore, help understanding and policy-making. To obtain RIS typologies there have been two main approaches: initially, conceptual typologies based on case studies were developed; more recently, some researchers have developed regional typologies of innovation based on statistical analysis (factorial and cluster analysis). The first approach presents the advantage of providing detailed insights into innovation processes, but fails to provide comprehensive and quantitative data on the economic and innovation performance of all EU regions. The second approach, working with data coming from secondary sources, can deal with all the EU regions and shed some light on the relation between knowledge inputs, the socio-economic characteristics of the territory, and innovation and economic outputs, but the current limitations in regional data availability do not allow important aspects of RIS to be taken into account. Table 10.2 offers a synthetic review of the existing conceptual typologies and Tables 10.3 and 10.4 of the typologies for the EU and Spanish regions based on statistical analysis.

This paper has reviewed the main results of a recent innovation typology developed for the EU-25 regions by Navarro et al. (2009) and has developed a brand new typology for the Spanish regions. Among the principal findings of the former could be mentioned the fact that, in order to classify regions, it is important to take into account not only their level of economic and technological development but also the kind of sectoral specialization in the region, except for regions with medium-low level of development. On the other hand, the EU-25 typology work highlighted the relevance of good accessibility and being the capital of the country to be positioned, within the groups of regions that have higher economic and technological development Additionally, despite decades of national policies and EU structural funds in favor of less developed regions in Greece, Portugal, Spain, and Italy or the embracement of market mechanisms by accession countries since early 90s, most of the disadvantaged regions of the EU-25 have not been able to reverse their adverse situation, which raises questions about the adequacy of these policies.

As for the Spanish regions typology, our analysis confirmed the existence of two main factors, representing to a large extent regional economic and technological development and regional manufacturing or services specialization. According to the new typology, Spanish regions can be classified in four groups: capital region (Madrid), medium–high-tech industrial regions (Basque Country, Navarre, Catalonia, and Aragon), medium-low-tech regions (Asturias, Cantabria, Valencia, La Rioja, Galicia, and Castile-Leon), and less developed, agricultural or tourist regions (Balearic Islands, Canary Islands, Castile-la Mancha, Andalusia, and Murcia). Leaving aside the capital region, the analysis also revealed a positive relation between specialization in manufacturing and level of economic and technological development; and a clear geographical pattern: the most advanced Spanish regions are located in the north, middle and east and the less developed ones in the south and islands.

The higher availability of regional data in Spain allows us to analyze the effects of adding to the currently available Eurostat data some variables that, despite being closely connected to the system nature of an RIS, are not available from the European statistics office. Based on additional Spanish regional sources, some aspects more connected with the DUI mode of innovation and learning have been considered such as:

- sales of new products and innovation expenditure other than R&D, as proxies for innovation output and input, respectively
- export specialization and related variety indexes, as proxies for agglomeration economies and the characterization of the firm subsystem
- firm size, as a proxy for the climate of competition or monopoly as well as the characterization of the firm subsystem
- firms' cooperation in innovation with other firms and with S&T&i-supporting infrastructures, as proxies for RIS internal interactions
- regional and local governments' financial support to innovative firms, as a proxy for regional government involvement in RIS development
- goods export and foreign direct investment, as proxies for the internationalization and linkages of the region with foreign innovation systems.

In the new typology, obtained by adding the aforementioned variables, the weight of the second principal component increases, because some of the new variables taken into account (goods exports, cooperation in innovation, and regional government support for innovative firms) appear positively correlated with specialization in manufacturing. Regions that move upwards along the second axis are by and large those that had a high score on that axis in the previous typology (that is, regions specialized in manufacturing); and regions that move downwards, the opposite. Somewhat unexpectedly, specialization and related variety indexes do not appear related to this second principal component (which broadly reflects orientation towards manufacturing or services) but to the first principal component (which broadly reflects level of economic and technological development). In any case, these two indexes do not appear so relevant to differences in this factor among Spanish regions, and if the latter is more closely linked with high economic and technological development, in the former case, the opposite applies, as it is positively related to low economic and technological development.

Finally, this chapter has shown the utility of multiple factorial analyses in comparing different typologies and assessing the similarities among them. When applied to Spain, the typology of regions does not undergo significant changes when operating with a large number of variables connected to the system nature of an RIS about which Eurostat does not provide information. This suggests that a typology resulting from an analysis using only sources that do not allow those aspects to be taken into consideration will differ little from a typology obtained from an analysis that also considers them.

Notes

1. In addition to them, Asheim has developed a distinction between RIS based on their knowledge base (see Asheim and Coenen, 2005, 2006; Asheim and Gertler, 2005; Asheim et al., 2007a, 2007b, 2007c; Moodysson et al., 2008). This distinction could be considered an RIS typology. Asheim proposes to distinguish three knowledge bases – the analytic, the synthetic, and the symbolic – based on the nature of the knowledge (science-, engineering-, or art-based), the key knowledge type (know-why, know-how or know-who), the way they mix tacit and explicit/codified knowledge, and some other features.
2. We use the term capital region only if the country has sub-national administrative levels. We therefore exclude from this category Luxembourg, Denmark, Cyprus, Estonia, Latvia, Lithuania, Malta, and Slovenia.

References

Abascal, E. and Landaluce, M.I. (2002), 'Ánalisis factorial multiple como técnica de studio de la estabilidad de los resultados de un análisis de componentes principales', Qüestiió, 26(1–2), 109–122.

Arundel, A., Kanerva, M., Cruysen, A. and Hollanders, H. (2007), *Innovation Statistics for the European Service Sector*, INNO Metrics 2007 report, Brussels: European Commission, DG Enterprise.

Asheim, B.T. and Isaksen, A. (1997), 'Location, agglomeration and innovation: towards regional innovation systems in Norway', *European Planning Studies*, 5(3), 299–330.

Asheim, B.T. and Isaksen, A. (2002), 'Regional innovation systems: the integration of local "sticky" and global "ubiquitous" knowledge', *Journal of Technology Transfer*, 27, 77–86.
Asheim, B.T. and Coenen, L. (2005), 'Knowledge bases and regional innovation systems: comparing Nordic clusters', *Research Policy*, 34, 1173–1190.
Asheim, B. and Gertler, M. (2005), 'The geography of innovation. Regional innovation systems', in J. Fagerberg D.C. Mowery and R.R. Nelson (eds), *The Oxford Handbook of Innovation*, Oxford, Oxford University Press, pp. 291–317.
Asheim, B., Boschma, R. and Cooke, P. (2007a), 'Constructing regional advantage: platform policies based on related variety and differentiated knowledge bases', *Papers in Evolutionary Economic Geography*, 0709.
Asheim, B.T., Coenen, L., Moodysson, J. and Vang, J. (2007b), 'Constructing knowledge-based regional advantage: implications for regional innovation policy', *International Journal of Entrepreneurship and Innovation Management*, 7(2–5), 140–155.
Asheim, B., Coenen, L. and Vang, J. (2007c), 'Face-to-face, buzz, and knowledge bases, sociospatial implications for learning, innovation, and innovation policy', *Environment and Planning C, Government and Policy*, 25 (5), 655–670.
Asheim, B., Coenen, L. and Moodysson, J. (2008), 'Explaining spatial patterns of innovation, analytical and synthetic modes of knowledge creation in the Medicon Valley Life Science Cluster', *Environment and Planning A*, 5(40), 1040–1056.
Bilbao-Osorio, B. and Rodríguez-Pose, A. (2004), 'From R&D to innovation and economic growth in the EU', *Growth and Change*, 35(4), 434–455.
Bruijn, P. and Lagendijk, A. (2005), 'Regional innovation systems in the Lisbon Strategy', *European Planning Studies*, 13(8), 1153–1172.
Clarysse, B. and Muldur, U. (2001), 'Regional cohesion in Europe? An analysis of how EU public RTD support influences the techno-economic regional landscape', *Research Policy*, 30, 275–296.
Cohen, W. (2010). 'Fifty years of empirical studies of innovative activity and performance', in B.H. Hall and N. Rosenberg (eds). *Handbook of the Economics of Innovation*. Amsterdam. North Holland, pp. 129–213.
Cooke, P. (1998), Introduction: 'Origins of the concept', in H.J. Braczyk P. N. Cooke and M. Heidenreich (eds), *Regional Innovation Systems. The Role of Governances in a Globalized World*, London, UCL Press, pp. 2–25.
Cooke, P., Heidenreich, M. and Braczyk, H. (2004), *Regional Innovation Systems*, London, Routledge.
Crescenzi, R., Rodríguez-Pose, A. and Storper, M. (2007), 'The territorial dynamics of innovation, a Europe–United States comparative analysis', *Journal of Economic Geography*, 7, 673–709.
Dory, T. (2008), *RTD Policy Approaches in Different Types of European Regions*, Luxembourg, Office for Official Publications of the European Communities.
Ecotec (2005), *The Territorial Impact of EU Research and Development Policies*, ESPON 2.1.2.
ESPON (2006), *Scientific Report II. Applied Territorial Research. Building a Scientific Platform for Competitiveness and Cohesion*, Autumn.
European Commission (2007), *Key figures 2007 on Science, Technology and Innovation*, Luxembourg, Office for Official Publications of the European Communities.

Feldman, M.P. (2000), 'Location and innovation: the new economic geography of innovation, spillovers, and agglomeration', in G.L. Clark M. P. Feldman and M. S. Gertler (eds), *The Oxford Handbook of Economic Geography*, Oxford, Net Library Incorporated.

Hollanders, H. (2003), *European Innovation Scoreboard 2003 – Technical Paper No. 3, Regional Innovation Performances*, European Trend Chart on Innovation.

Hollanders, H. (2006), *2006 European Regional Innovation Scoreboard (2006 RIS)*, European Trend Chart on Innovation.

Husson, F., Josse, J., Le, S. and Mazet, J. (2008), FactoMineR, Factor Analysis and Data Mining with R. R package version 1.10., http://factominer.free.fr, http://www.agrocampus–rennes.fr/math.

Jaffe, A. (1989), 'Real effects of academic research', *The American Economic Review*, 79, 957–970.

Kaufmann, A. and Tödtling, F. (2000), 'Systems of innovation in traditional industrial regions: the case of Styria in a comparative perspective', *Regional Studies*, 34(1), 29–40.

Lundvall, B.-Å. (ed.) (1992), *National Systems of Innovation. Towards a Theory of Innovation and Interactive Learning*, London and New York, Pinter.

Lundvall, B.-Å. and Borrás, S. (1997), *The Globalising Learning Economy, Implications for Innovation Policy*, UE, Commission of the European Union.

Lundvall, B.-Å. (2007), 'Innovation system research. Where it came from and where it might go', *Globelics Working Paper Series*, 2007–01.

Malmberg, A. and Maskell, P. (1997), 'Towards an explanation of regional specialization and industrial agglomeration', *European Planning Studies*, 5(1), 25–41.

Martínez-Pellitero, M. (2002), 'Recursos y resultados de los sistemas de innovación, elaboración de una tipología de sistemas regionales de innovación en España', IAIF Working Paper, 34.

Martínez-Pellitero, M. (2007), 'Los sistemas regionales de innovación en Europa, tipología y eficiencia', in M. Buesa and J. Heijs (eds), *Sistemas regionales de innovación, nuevas formas de análisis y medición*, Madrid, Fundación de las Cajas de Ahorros, pp. 215–256.

Martínez-Pellitero, M. (2008), *Tipología y eficiencia de los sistemas regionales de innovación. Un estudio aplicado al caso europeo*, Doctoral thesis, Complutense University of Madrid.

Maskell, P. and Malmberg, A. (1999), 'Localised learning and industrial competitiveness', *Cambridge Journal of Economics*, 23, 167–185.

Miles, I. (2005), 'Innovation in services', in J. Fagerberg D.C. Mowery and R.R. Nelson (eds), *The Oxford Handbook of Innovation*, Oxford, Oxford University Press, pp. 433–458.

Muller, E. and Nauwelaers, C. (eds), (2005), *Enlarging the ERA: Identifying Priorities for Regional Policy Focusing on Research and Technological Development in the New Member States and Candidate Countries*, Report to the European Commission DG Research, Karlsruhe, Fraunhofer Institute for Systems and Innovation Research and MERIT.

Muller, E., Jappe, A., Héraud, J.A. and Zenker, A. (2006), 'A regional typology of innovation capacities in New Member States & Candidate Countries', *Working Papers Firms and Regions R1/2006*, Fraunhofer Institute for Systems and Innovation Research (also published as *Document de travail 2006–18*, Bureau d'économie théorique et appliquée (BETA)).

Muller, E., Doloreux, D., Heraud, J.A., Jappe, A. and Zenker, A. (2008), 'Regional innovation capacities in new member states: a typology', *Journal of European Integration*, 30(5), 653–669.
Nauwelaers, C. and Wintjes, R. (2002), 'Innovating SMEs and regions: the need for policy intelligence and interactive policies', *Technology Analysis & Strategic Management*, 14(2), 201–215.
Navarro, M., Gibaja, J.J., Bilbao-Osorio, B. and Aguado, R. (2008), 'Regional innovation systems in EU-25: a typology and policy recommendations', Paper presented to the DRUID Conference. San Sebastian, Spain, September 2008.
Navarro, M. and Gibaja, J.J. (2009), 'Las tipologías en los sistemas regionales de innovación. El caso de España', *Ekonomiaz* 70: 240–281.
Navarro, M., Gibaja, J.J., Bilbao-Osorio, B. and Aguado, R. (2009), 'Patterns of innovation in the EU-25 regions: a typology and policy recommendations', *Environment and Planning C, Government & Policy*27: 815–840.
Nelson, R.R. (1992), 'National innovation systems: a retrospective on a study', *Industrial and Corporate Change*, 1(2), 347–374.
Nelson, R. R. and Rosenberg, N. (1993), 'Technical innovation and national systems', in R.R. Nelson (ed.), *National Systems of Innovation: A Comparative Study*, Oxford, Oxford University Press, pp. 3–21.
OECD (2005), *Oslo Manual. Guidelines for Collecting and Interpreting Innovation Data*, Paris, OECD.
OECD (2007), *Regions at a Glance*, Paris, OECD.
Porter, M.E., Delgado, M., Ketels, C. and Stern, S. (2008), 'Moving to a new global competitiveness index', *The Global Competitiveness Report 2008-2009*, Geneva.
R Development Core Team (2008), *R: A Language and Environment for Statistical Computing*, R Foundation for Statistical Computing, Vienna, Austria. ISBN 3-900051-07-0, http,//www.R-project.org.
Rodríguez-Pose, A. and Crescenzi, R. (2008), 'Research and development, spillovers, innovation systems, and the genesis of regional growth in Europe', *Regional Studies*, 42(1), 51–67.
Schurmann, C. and Talaat, A. (2000), *Towards a European Peripherality Index. Final Report*. Mimeo.
Tödtling, F. and Kaufmann, A. (1999), 'Innovation systems in regions of Europe – a comparative perspective', *European Planning Studies*, 7(6), 699–717.
Tödtling, F. and Trippl, M. (2005), 'One size fits all? Towards a differentiated regional innovation policy approach', *Research Policy*, 34, 1203–1219.
UNU–MERIT (2009), *European Innovation Scoreboard 2008. Comparative Analysis of Innovation Performance*, Pro Inno Europe INNO METRICS.
Verspagen, B. (1995), 'Convergence in the global economy. A broad historical viewpoint', *Structural Change and Economic Dynamics*, 6(2), 143–165.

11
Academia and Public Policy: Towards the Co-generation of Knowledge and Learning Processes

Mari José Aranguren, Miren Larrea, and James R. Wilson

11.1 Introduction

The role of universities in society has become a key area of debate in recent years, coinciding with movement towards a more globally integrated economy in which processes of learning and knowledge-generation are widely recognized as central to competitive advantage. Alongside the traditional functions of educating and conducting research, the importance of a broader interface between university and society has been emphasized in concepts such as 'systems of innovation,' the 'triple helix of industry, government, and university' and the 'entrepreneurial university.'

This chapter contributes to analysis of the role of universities in society in two important respects. First, we consider an under-researched subset of the university–society interface of relevance largely for the social sciences: that between academia and public policy. Second, we explore the issue of balance in the role of the academic with regard to public policy. We build our analysis around an ongoing experience from the Basque Country region of Spain in which the authors are involved: the emergence and development of the Basque Institute of Competitiveness. We focus specifically on the integration of action research principles into research projects, where our analysis highlights processes of co-generation of knowledge and learning between academics and policy-makers as a key axis of the interface.

11.2 Towards a 'third mission' of universities

In general, universities have traditionally been acknowledged as playing two primary and strategic roles in society: first, with regard to teaching, facilitating the development of knowledge and skills among people (human capital development); second, with regard to research, generating and diffusing potentially useful research ideas that may lead directly or indirectly to innovations in socio-economic outputs and processes. Both roles are strategic in the sense that they are important contributors to processes of socio-economic development. Indeed, elements of both human capital and research have featured strongly in the development of theoretical and empirical literature seeking to explain economic growth (Lucas, 1988; Romer, 1989; Mankiw et al., 1992; Temple, 1999). Moreover, following the pioneering work of Becker (1964), the economic and social returns from higher education are frequently calculated and analyzed. The OECD, for example, has integrated such analysis into its influential annual *Education at a Glance* set of indicators (OECD, 2007).

In recent years, however, interest in the role of universities in socio-economic development processes has intensified. In particular, there has been strong growth in research analyzing the significance of universities for *local* and *regional* economic development processes, accompanied by increasing demands of universities from regional actors (Karlsen, 2007). The emphasis is typically on combining both of the traditional human capital and research roles of the university to create a more active contribution to regional development. This intensification of concern around an active *regional* role of the university corresponds broadly with the advance of processes of *globalization*. While globalization itself can be variously defined (Sugden and Wilson, 2005), it is generally associated with the increasing geographical integration of socio-economic relationships, facilitated at a great pace in recent years by new transport and communication technologies. Thus for Scholte (2000: 46), for example, "the proliferation and spread of supraterritorial – or what we can alternatively term 'transworld' or 'transborder' – connections brings an end to what could be called 'territorialism', that is, a situation where social geography is entirely territorial." This 'de-territorialization' of socio-economic relationships at global level, however, has simultaneously emphasized the importance of proximity-based relationships rooted in regional and local systems (Morgan, 2004). Authors such as Ohmae (1995), Storper (1997), Cooke and Morgan (1998), and Scott (1998), for example, have been influential in emphasizing regions as important economic and policy units in an increasingly globalized world.

Part of the reason for growing interest in the role of universities in this context is the widespread acknowledgement of the critical importance of processes of knowledge and learning as sources of competitive advantage. Dunning (2000: 8), for example, expresses a widely accepted view when he argues that "over the last three centuries, the main source of wealth in market economies has switched from natural assets (notably land and relatively unskilled labor), through tangible assets (notably buildings, machinery and equipment, and finance) to intangible created assets (notably knowledge and information of all kinds)." Moreover, the theory of 'stages' of economic development proposed by Porter (1990) and adopted by the World Economic Forum in its annual *Global Competitiveness Report* makes a related distinction between 'factor-driven,' 'efficiency-driven,' and 'innovation-driven' economies, suggesting that knowledge and learning processes are even more critical in the most advanced economies (World Economic Forum, 2008).

Thus it is no coincidence that the role of universities in society, particularly in advanced economies, has become a key area of analysis as globalization has intensified, and no accident that this has taken place with an increasingly regional frame of reference. Indeed, universities are today seen as key actors in moving territories towards what Morgan (1997) terms "learning regions" (Feldman, 2001; Lazzeretti and Tavoletti, 2005). Thus a 'third mission' of universities has been identified and progressively explored (Laredo, 2007). Building on universities' long-acknowledged functions of educating and conducting research, the importance of the interface between university and local economies has been emphasized in specific concepts such as "systems of innovation" (Freeman, 1987; Lundvall, 1992; Nelson, 1993; Cooke et al., 1998), the "triple helix of industry, government and university" (Etzkowitz and Leydesdorff, 1997) and the "entrepreneurial university" (Etzkowitz, 1997, 2004). Together, these present a powerful imperative for universities to seek to move *closer* to the societies in which they are situated, thereby stimulating the hypothesized benefits from knowledge flows in interaction with other (public and private) socio-economic agents.

11.3 Academia and public policy

Our focus in this chapter is on examining the implications of this 'third mission' for a specific subset of the university–society interface, that between academia and public policy. Our focus is thus not on the role of the university within the triple helix or the innovation system as a whole, which incorporates its relationship with a range of public and private agents, involving both market and non-market relationships. Rather we are interested specifically in the interface between academic research and the government agents responsible for designing, implementing, and evaluating public policies. This implies that our focus is primarily on the social sciences (economics, business, sociology, political science, etc.), which marks a further change from much of the traditional analysis of the third mission in terms of innovation systems and the entrepreneurial university, where the natural focus is on transfer of science- and engineering-based knowledge between academia and industry.

With regard to analysis of the academia–public policy interface, it is important to consider that a key feature of policy environments is that they are characterized by concentrations of power, similar to imperfect market environments. Democratic mechanisms are imperfect in representing the whole range of interests in society and providing a constraint to the power of certain groups. Moreover, it is clear that political power and economic power are frequently interrelated. This would imply that there are dangers that academic processes may be captured by certain interests as academics engage more closely with public policy agents – a similar argument to that which has been widely expressed regarding the closer engagement of academia in market environments (Aronowitz, 2000; Bailey, 2008; Bok, 2003; Grönblom and Willner, 2009; Levin and Greenwood, 2008; Lundvall, 2002; Sparkes, 2007; Sugden, 2004; Wilson, 2009).

For example, there is evident concern among some academics as to the boundaries between policy-related academic research and policy consultancy. Consultants clearly provide a 'product' that must in some sense be tailored to the expectations of the purchaser (the policymaker): outputs are well defined from the beginning; and future contracts are likely to depend on providing solutions that both are sensitive to the interests of the particular client and encourage a certain 'dependence' of the client. Academic research, however, cannot be framed as a 'product' in the same way: it is a flexible process whose outcomes and even methodologies are often uncertain at the time of formulating the research question; and it must be truly independent if it is to attract respect among peers and be considered genuinely 'academic.' Despite these clear differences, however, as academic research moves closer to policy environments, the distinction can become blurred. This is particularly so in a context where there are often strong pressures on both sides to interact: on academics to bring in external research funding and to be seen to be fulfilling their 'third mission;' and on policy-makers to validate (or at least be seen to validate) their policies with 'independent' academic expertise.

The heterogeneity of policy environments suggests that there is likely to be a strong contextual element to analysis of these tensions. First, there are different levels of public policy with which academics interact; from the most local (municipality) through regional and national to international or global institutions. Second, there are different areas of policy (macroeconomic, microeconomic, social, cultural, etc.), although Layard (2006) argues convincingly that these cannot in fact be analyzed in isolation and require collaboration between different branches of social sciences. Finally, in each particular policy environment the culture of academic engagement with policy-makers will have a distinct history and tradition, determined in part by the institutional characteristics of the university system and the government agencies, and also potentially by the characteristics of key relationships between individual researchers and policy agents. This suggests the importance of case analysis in exploring issues of balance in the academia–public policy relationship. In the remainder of this chapter we introduce a self-reflective case that describes and analyzes a specific set of experiences with which the authors have been involved in the Basque Country region of Spain.

11.3.1 Introducing our case: the Basque Institute of Competitiveness

The Basque Institute of Competitiveness was founded in March 2006 as an initiative of the Deusto Foundation, an institution devoted to making scientific knowledge available to society. It is a research centre based at the University of Deusto (a private, Jesuit-run university) and funded for the first four years by a group of stakeholders that included the Society for the Promotion of Industry of the Basque Country Autonomous Government (SPRI), the Provincial Council of Gipuzkoa, and several firms. It was established with the aim of supporting activity by public administrations, socioeconomic agents, and all of the universities in the Basque Country aimed at improving the competitiveness of the region. Within this broad field, research within the centre has been focused on three sub-areas: (i) clusters, regional development, and innovation; (ii) entrepreneurship; and (iii) strategy.[1]

Researchers forming the Institute were drawn initially from various research groups at the University of Deusto, and these maintain around 30% of their annual hours complement for teaching in the University. Researchers have also been recruited directly by the Institute, with agreements that these academics can also become faculty members and engage in certain teaching activities within the University. The Institute had 29 staff (including doctoral students) at the time of writing the case, 23 of whom were directly engaged in research and research-support activities. While the research of the centre has a strong territorial focus, this is complemented by involvement in international research networks, the aim being to ensure that research on the Basque Country reaches an international audience and that cutting-edge research from around the world permeates analysis of Basque competitiveness. There has hence been an effort to recruit researchers from outside of the Basque Country and of Spain, and research activities have been developed with various international partners and networks.[2]

The stated mission of the Institute to support the activity of a range of socio-economic agents in enhancing the competitiveness of the region has been operationalized explicitly through three inter-related activities: research, interaction, and teaching.[3] The combination of these is seen as crucial for engaging both with the frontier of international knowledge on competitiveness and competitiveness policy, and with the actual situation of the Basque Country. Thus research, interaction, and teaching combine in impacting on the competitiveness of the Basque Country Autonomous Community (through 'actions') and contributing to the international pool of knowledge (through 'outputs'). Our own interpretation of this general model of operation is illustrated in Figure 11.1.

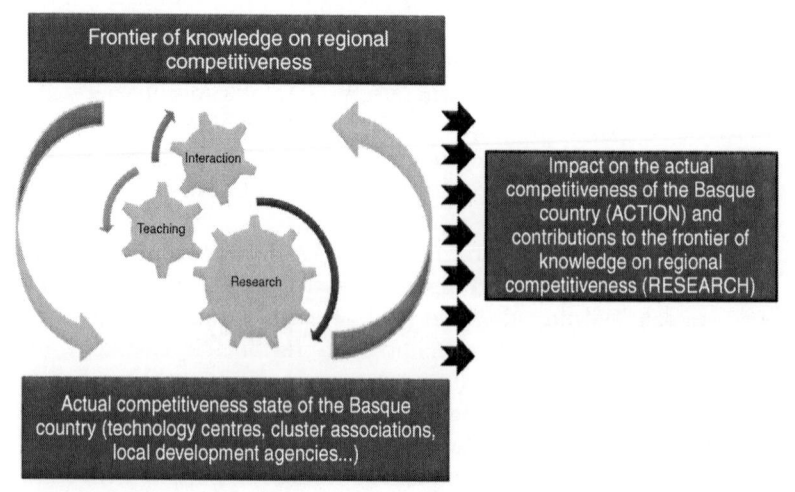

Figure 11.1 The Basque Institute of Competitiveness model of operation

11.4 Different approaches to combining interaction and research

Within this overall structure, various methodologies are employed by different academics and groups of academics within the Institute in undertaking their activities; there is freedom for individual academics to select how they work. Nevertheless, there has emerged discussion among researchers in particular surrounding questions of balance between 'research' and 'interaction,' and the ideal forms that these activities should take individually and/or in combination. 'Teaching' is seen as less controversial, probably because academics are very used to combining research and teaching, while explicit recognition of interaction as an academic activity alongside research is more novel.

Simplifying somewhat, across the various research projects currently under way within the Institute we can identify two broad approaches to the research–interaction balance:

1. In what we might label a *traditional university approach* there remains a fairly clear distinction between 'research' and 'interaction.' A combination of established disciplinary research techniques are employed in the definition and undertaking of research (literature analysis, theoretical development, qualitative and quantitative analysis, etc.). Interaction with the users of research occurs in processes of peer review, conference presentation, publication of articles and reports, press releases, dissemination workshops, and so on. While there may be some interaction with users of research in the design phases (response to calls for research proposals, research proposal feedback, and so on), most interaction takes place in the later stages of the research, in the dissemination and discussion of results. Thus there is not only a distinction between research and interaction but also a clear separation of the two processes in different phases of the projects.
2. In what we might label an *action research approach* the distinction between 'research' and 'interaction' is considerably more blurred. Mixes of the same established disciplinary research techniques are employed in the definition and undertaking of research (such as literature analysis, theoretical development, and qualitative and quantitative analysis), but throughout the process a consistent interaction with the agents at whom the research is targeted is maintained. Thus systematic interaction in the form of meetings, participatory workshops, and focus groups with agents, for example, is present alongside

more traditional forms of interaction in the proposal and dissemination stages. A result is that the targets of the research become an integral part of the research process itself, meaning that the distinction between research and interaction is far less clear.

Individual researchers within the Institute do not generally adopt one or another of these approaches exclusively. However, while all researchers come from a tradition of research in mode 1 and continue much of their activity along these lines, there is a small group of researchers (which include the authors of this chapter) who have recently begun to explicitly develop research projects in mode 2. In practice, the two approaches demonstrate complementary responses to the requirements placed on academic researchers in an institute with an explicit mission to conduct research that supports the activities of government and other socio-economic agents in enhancing a territory's competitiveness. Moreover, in their different forms of interaction, both approaches carry risks of crossing the line that separates academic research from consultancy. In the case of mode 1, the danger is the more traditional one of safeguarding independent analysis during interaction with (politically and/or financially) powerful interests in the proposal and dissemination phases. In the case of mode 2 the danger is often argued to be greater given the systematic nature of the interaction, but on the other hand it can be argued that such interaction enhances the sophistication with which academic research can truly engage with and impact on society. For both of these reasons, in the following sections we reflect on our experiences as researchers in developing projects in mode 2.

11.5 Learning from action research

The group of researchers who have explicitly sought to develop projects according to the mode 2 approach to research and interaction have sought to learn from the principles of action research, and to frame certain projects explicitly as action research projects. Following Greenwood and Levin (2007) we understand action research as socio-economic research carried out by a team that encompasses a professional action researcher and the members of an organization, community, or network (stakeholders) who are seeking to improve the participants' situation. In line with Reason and Bradbury (2008: 1), it is "not so much a methodology as an orientation to inquiry that seeks to create participative communities of inquiry in which qualities of engagement, curiosity and question posing are brought to bear on significant practical issues." The practical issues addressed have been mainly related to local economic development policies and the Basque Government's cluster policy, including policy evaluation issues.[4] Hence, participative communities of enquiry have included policy agents from the Basque government's Department of Industry, Commerce and Tourism, local development agencies, and the umbrella organization for local development agencies (GARAPEN). In one particular research project designed to evaluate the 'cluster policy' of the Basque Government, the specific institutions and firms targeted by this policy are also included in the community of enquiry (Aragón et al., 2008).

Another project was initially suggested by the administrative board of the Institute, which comprises its financing stakeholders. The proposal was to use data on numbers of establishments in different industrial sectors in each of the 250 municipalities of the Basque Country to produce a study that mapped agglomerations of specialized activity and enabled an identification of potential local 'clusters.' A team of researchers from the Institute adapted a methodology employed for a similar study in Catalonia aimed at mapping local production systems (Hernández Gascón et al., 2005), and initially set out to produce a similar report for the Basque Country. During the research process, however, it became clear that there were significant methodological difficulties in determining which sectors were related; in short there was a lack of detailed local and industry knowledge in the research team. Other studies have solved this problem from a distance by interviewing a sample of industry experts and then making a series of judgments about the relationships between industry categories. However, in this case the project coincided with awareness within the research group of: (i) a pool of local knowledge present within local development agencies; and (ii) the desire of Basque Government policy-makers to introduce a sub-regional element to their cluster policy. A decision was therefore made to re-orient the project from the straightforward production of a research report based on our analysis of data, to a process-oriented project involving policy agents from the local development agencies and the Basque Government.

A flexible online tool was developed by the research team to make the data available in an easy-to-use format and to provide the capability to draw geographical maps of the results. A series of five workshops was then held over a five-month period with around twenty local development agency representatives. At these workshops the research team taught the policy agents the basics of the methodology, alongside some of the theoretical and practical principles of clusters and cluster policy, and worked with them as each undertook a mapping of their own group of municipalities. In a sixth workshop, the local development agencies presented their analysis to cluster policy-makers from the Basque Government as an input to ongoing considerations regarding adding a local dimension to the regionally administered cluster policy.

As a consequence of this systematic interaction with policy agents, the results of this research process have been quite different from those initially envisaged. A disadvantage has been the lack of complete coverage of the Basque Country territory in the mapping exercise,[5] although the gaps can potentially be filled by the research team in the future. However, at least four significant advantages can be identified from the interactions inherent in the adopted approach:

1. The approach has enabled a potent combination of the theoretical and methodological knowledge of the research team with the on-the-ground knowledge of the policy agents. Thus when it came to making the ultimately subjective judgments about where to draw lines around agglomerations in terms of activities and location, the decisions could be made on the basis of far greater knowledge of the local industrial texture.
2. The approach has facilitated significant learning processes on both sides as these different knowledge bases have been able to systematically interact. This has led to, for example, an empowerment of both sides in terms of knowledge that can be used in future projects.
3. The approach has ensured that advantages can be made of synergies and work already in progress in the local development agencies in identifying potential clusters for further strategic analysis.
4. The involvement of policy-makers from the Basque Government in a process with local development agencies has opened the way for future dialogue and closer coordination between policy initiatives at regional and local levels that are based often on very similar principles and processes.

Reflections on our experience with the above-cited projects suggest that adopting the research principles associated with enquiry and with action research can be of great help in preserving the line between research and consultancy, at least with regard to academia–public policy relations. In a research environment that is subject to new public management principles (Levin and Greenwood, 2008; Grönblom and Willner, 2009) and/or where pressures to design and publish research are required to interact with powerful external interests, there are serious dangers in crossing that line and producing research as a 'product' in the mold of a consultancy relationship. Crossing the line can both play to powerful interests, potentially skewing research, and create dependence of the policy agent on the consultant/researcher. At first glance it might appear that the deeper and systematic interaction required by action research implies greater dangers. However, the interaction inherent in this approach also brings the potential for the development of qualitatively different relationships that, with appropriate safeguards, can in fact reinforce the line, generating respect for academic independence and empowering rather than creating dependence among policy agents. In particular, we refer to the mutual understanding and respect for different viewpoints on sensitive questions that can emerge through participative democratic *processes* that facilitate the *co-generation of knowledge*. Indeed, Greenwood and Levin (2007: 10–11) "equate democracy with the creation of arenas for lively debate and for decision making that respects and enhances the diversity of groups."

11.6 Concluding remarks

In this chapter we have built on an analysis of some of the general concerns that surround the changing roles of universities in society to reflect on the specific interface between academia and public policy. As in other areas of the university, academics in the social sciences are today required to play a far more active role – in their local and regional policy contexts – than in the past, responding in their own disciplinary niches to the so-called 'third mission' of universities. However there are two different, and often conflicting, problems that emerge as universities and their academics seek to engage more effectively with the societies in which they are situated. First, there is the issue of making an effective bridge between academic research and policy, ensuring that the process is attractive to the people involved on both sides. Second, there is the issue of ensuring that in making that bridge, the independence of both the academic and policy processes are maintained to a sufficient degree. From the academics' perspective this can be framed in terms of treading an often difficult line between policy-related academic research and policy consultancy, the latter being more output determined and (explicitly or implicitly) sensitive to the interests of those 'purchasing' the research.

Our case analysis points to a series of conclusions with relevance both for academics engaged in policy-related research and for the design of research institutes and funding mechanisms. In particular we would emphasize the benefits of processes that facilitate the open co-generation of knowledge between academics and policy agents. Moreover, successful knowledge co-generation processes require development over the medium to long term, so as to avoid interaction being reduced to the design of closed, outcome-oriented research projects that are then 'sold' to policy-makers. Long-term processes also critically provide the necessary space for aims to be clearly articulated and assimilated by the different agents involved, and mutual respect over roles to be built. All of this has implications for financing, which typically takes a shorter time-horizon, suggesting the need for institutional bridging of research finance between externally funded projects and/or for the development of long-term relationships between research centers and research funders.

In addressing resource issues we suggest that it is particularly important to bear in mind the need for researchers to be given the space to detach themselves from processes of intense interaction and engage in academic reflection (reading and writing). This time is crucial both for ensuring an independent, critical academic perspective on the ongoing research and for enabling the development of research outputs in terms of publications that are able to generate the respect of peers. Finally, our reflections on the Spanish context point to the need for improved training in research methods that are explicitly designed for a world in which engagement with other socio-economic agents is expected of academics. Doctoral programs in the social sciences should expose students to the alternative methodologies offered by action research, to the advantages of multi-disciplinary research, and to debates around the dangers present in all research processes with regard to the capture of the research process by powerful interests.

Notes

1. A fourth area, welfare, has been defined but not yet developed.
2. For example, the European Network on Industrial Policy (EUNIP), the Global Entrepreneurship Monitor (GEM), the Max Planck Institute for Economics, the China Europe International Business School (CEIBS) and the Institute for Strategy and Competitiveness at Harvard University.
3. In Spanish, these translate as the three 'i's of 'investigación', 'interacción' and 'instrucción'.
4. See Aranguren et al. (2006) for detailed accounts of the genesis and evolution of the Basque cluster policy and the establishment and role of local development agencies in the Basque Country.
5. An open call for participation was made to all local development agencies. While the take-up was extremely good, it was not 100% and the system of local development agencies also does not have 100% coverage of the Basque territory.

References

Aragón, C., Aranguren, M.-J., Diez, M.-A., Iturrioz, C., Larrea, M. and Wilson, J.R. (2008), 'Una metodologia partecipativa per la valutazione della politica dei cluster nel Paese Basco' [A Participatory methodology for evaluating the cluster policy of the Basque Country], *Sviluppo Locale*, 12, (9–30), 155–180.

Aranguren, M-J., Larrea, M. and Navarro, I. (2006), 'The policy process: clusters versus spatial networks in the Basque Country', in C. Pitelis, R. Sugden and J.R. Wilson (eds), *Clusters and Globalisation: The Development of Urban and Regional Economies*, Cheltenham, Edward Elgar.

Aronowitz, S. (2000), *The Knowledge Factory: Dismantling the Corporate University and Creating True Higher Learning*, Boston, MA, Beacon Press.

Bailey, R.W. (2008), 'Is the university in ruins?', *Institute for Economic Development Policy Discussion Paper 2008–02*, Birmingham, UK, University of Birmingham.

Becker, G.S. (1964), *Human Capital: A Theoretical and Empirical Analysis, with Special Reference to Education*, New York, National Bureau of Economic Research.

Bok, D. (2003), *Universities in the Marketplace: The Commercialisation of Higher Education*, Princeton, NJ, Princeton University Press.

Cooke, P., Gomez Uranga, M. and Etxebarria, G. (1998), 'Regional systems of innovation: institutions and organisational dimensions', *Research Policy*, 26(4–5), 475–491.

Cooke, P. and Morgan, K. (1998), *The Associational Economy: Firms, Regions and Innovation*, Oxford, Oxford University Press.

Dunning, J.H. (2000), 'Regions, globalization, and the knowledge economy: the issues stated', in J.H. Dunning (ed.) *Regions, Globalization and the Knowledge-Based Economy*, Oxford, Oxford University Press.

Etzkowitz, H. (1997), 'The entrepreneurial university and the emergence of democratic corporatism', in H. Etzkowitz and L. Leydesdorff (eds), *Universities and the Global Knowledge Economy: A Triple Helix of University–Industry–Government Relations*, London, Cassell.

Etzkowitz, H. (2004), 'The Evolution of the Entrepreneurial University', *International Journal of Technology and Globalisation*, 1(1), 64–77.

Etzkowitz, H. and Leydesdorff, L. (eds) (1997), *Universities and the Global Knowledge Economy: A Triple Helix of University–Industry–Government Relations*, London, Cassell.

Feldman, J.M. (2001), 'Towards the post-university: centres of higher learning and creative spaces as economic development and social change agents', *Economic and Industrial Democracy*, 22(1), 99–142.

Freeman, C. (1987), *Technology Policy and Economic Performance. Lessons from Japan*, London, Pinter.

Greenwood, D.J and Levin, M. (2007), *Introduction to Action Research*, Second edition, London, Sage Publications.

Grönblom, S. and Willner, J. (2009), 'Destroying creativity? Universities and the new public management', in S. Sacchetti and R. Sugden (eds), *Knowledge in the Development of Economies: Institutional Choices Under Globalisation*, Cheltenham, Edward Elgar.

Hernández Gascón, J.M., Fontrodona Francoli, J. and Pezzi, A. (2005), *Mapa de los Sistemas Productivos Locales Industriales en Cataluña*, Barcelona, Generalitat de Catalunya.

Karlsen, J. (2007), *The Regional Role of the University: A Study of Knowledge Creation in the Agora between Agder University College and Regional Actors in Agder, Norway*, PhD thesis, Trondheim, Norwegian University of Science and Technology.

Laredo, P. (2007), 'Revisiting the third mission of universities: toward a renewed categorization of university activities', *Higher Education Policy*, 20, 441–456.

Layard, R. (2006), 'Happiness and public policy: a challenge to the profession', *The Economic Journal*, 116, March, C24–C33.

Lazzeretti, L. and Tavoletti, E. (2005), 'Higher education excellence and local economic development: the case of the entrepreneurial university of Twente', *European Planning Studies*, 13(3), 475–493.

Levin, M. and Greenwood, D.J. (2008), 'The Future of universities: action research and the transformation of higher education', in P. Reason and H. Bradbury (eds), *The SAGE Handbook of Action Research: Participative Enquiry and Practice*, Second edition, London, Sage Publications.

Lucas, R.E. Jr. (1988), 'On the Mechanics of Economic Development', *Journal of Monetary Economics*, 22, 3–42.

Lundvall, B-Å. (2002), *The University in the Learning Economy*, Danish Research Unit for Industrial Dynamics (DRUID), Working paper 02–06.

Lundvall, B-Å. (1992), *National Systems of Innovation. Towards a Theory of Innovation and Interactive Learning*, London, Pinter.

Mankiw, G.N., Romer, D. and Weil, D.N. (1992), 'A contribution to the empirics of economic growth', *The Quarterly Journal of Economics*, 107(2), 407–437.

Morgan, K. (1997), 'The learning region: institutions, innovation and regional renewal', *Regional Studies*, 35(5), 491–503.

Morgan, K. (2004), 'The exaggerated death of geography: learning, proximity and territorial innovation systems', *Journal of Economic Geography*, 4, 3–21.

Nelson, R.R. (ed.) (1993), *National Systems of Innovation*, Oxford, Oxford University Press.

OECD (2007), *Education at a Glance 2007: OECD Indicators*, Paris, OECD.

Ohmae, K. (1995), *The End of the Nation State: The Rise of Regional Economies*, London, HarperCollins.

Porter, M.E. (1990), *The Competitive Advantage of Nations*. London, The MacMillan Press.

Reason, P. and Bradbury, H. (2008), Introduction, in P. Reason and H. Bradbury (eds) *The SAGE Handbook of Action Research: Participative Enquiry and Practice*, Second edition, London, Sage Publications.

Romer, P.M. (1989), 'Human capital and growth: theory and evidence', *National Bureau of Economic Research Working Paper Number 3173*, Cambridge, MA.

Scholte, J.A. (2000), *Globalization: A Critical Introduction*, Basingstoke, Palgrave.

Scott, A.J. (1998), *Regions and the World Economy: The Coming Shape of Global Production, Competition and Political Order*, Oxford, Oxford University Press.

Sparkes, A.C. (2007), 'Embodiment, academics and the audit culture: a story seeking consideration', *Qualitative Research*, 7(4), 521–550.

Storper, M. (1997), *The Regional World: Territorial Development in a Global Economy*, London, Guildford Press.

Sugden, R. (2004), 'A small firm approach to the internationalisation of universities: a multinational perspective', *Higher Education Quarterly*, 58(2–3), 114–135.

Sugden, R. and Wilson, J.R. (2005), 'Economic globalisation: dialectics, conceptualisation and choice', *Contributions to Political Economy*, 24, 13–32.
Temple, Jonathan (1999), 'The new growth evidence', *Journal of Economic Literature*, 37(1), 112–156.
Wilson, J.R. (2009), 'Higher education and economic development: do we face an intertemporal trade-off', in S. Sacchetti and R. Sugden (eds), *Knowledge in the Development of Economies: Institutional Choices Under Globalisation*, Cheltenham, Edward Elgar.
World Economic Forum (2008), *The Global Competitiveness Report 2008–2009*, Geneva, World Economic Forum.

Index

Aalborg University (AAU), 148, 149
Abramowitz, Moses, 41
absorptive capacity, 10–11, 182, 184, 208–9
academia
  see also universities
  public policy and, 275–86
action research, 275, 281–5
adaptive learning, 6
additionality principle, 200
adhocracies, 78
advanced inward-looking learners, 186, 187–8, 194, 195, 197–8, 203
agglomeration economies, 22
analytical knowledge, 6, 115–16, 118, 183
application development, 7–8
Arrow, Kenneth, 33, 36
Australia, 4
autonomy, 6, 18, 51, 52, 81

Barcelona Declaration, 1
Basque Autonomous Community, 21, 161–77
  electronics and ICT cluster, 167–77
  Ezagutza Gunea case study, 191–9
  paper cluster, 166–7, 168–71, 172–6
Basque Institute of Competitiveness, 275, 279–80
behavioral additionality, 200
best practices, 91
biomedical clusters, 20–1, 147–56
biotechnology, 8–9, 73–4, 100, 118
Botero, Giovanni, 93
Bush, Vannevar, 33

Canada, 4, 60, 74
capital
  human, 2, 4, 5, 276
  mental, 33
  social, 17, 18, 21, 25, 57–64, 65, 140, 146, 162–3
capital cities, 106

capitalism, varieties of, 1, 15, 18, 23, 72–88
Center for Technological and Industrial Development (CTID), 210
Centers of Expertise (CoE), 8–9
change, 43
  acceleration of, 90
  organizational, 50–1
  technological, 207
channels, 107–8
China, 4, 10, 43
cities, 105
  capital, 106
  creative, 19, 90–8
  satellite, 106
city governance, 97–8
civil society, 59–61
cleantech, 100, 109
clusterpreneurs, 20, 137–56
clusters, 20, 183
  in Basque, 161–77
  biomedical, 147–56
  competitiveness and, 161–77
  demand conditions, 164, 173
  drivers of, 21
  emergence of, 139–42
  factor conditions, 172–3
  formation of, 137–56
  government and, 145–6, 165, 176
  high-tech, 20–1, 47, 146–7
  input conditions, 164
  knowledge-based, 100–1, 104–5
  in North Jutland, 147–56
  in peripheral regions, 142–7
  policies, 19–20, 137–8, 142–7
  Raufoss regional cluster, 116–17, 122–33
  regional, 116–17, 122–33
codified knowledge, 18, 40–1, 49, 116, 162
collective entrepreneurship, 16
collective learning, 24, 163

291

common knowledge, 39
Community Innovation
  Survey (CIS), 16
comparative advantage, 3
competitive advantage, 3, 6, 24,
  162–6, 206, 275, 277
competitiveness, 21, 117
  clusters and, 161–77
  innovation as driver of, 1–2
  social capital, knowledge and,
    163–6, 172–5
complex and combined innovation
  (CCI), 20, 115–34
complicit knowledge, 101
constrained problem-solvers, 81–2
cooperation, in R&D, 209–10,
  222–5, 228–9
coordinated market economies
  (CMEs), 4, 18–19, 23, 73–7
core competency, 121–2
craft learners, 185–6, 195, 196
creative cities, 19, 90–8
creative knowledge environment, 23
creative workers, 4, 81–3
creativity, 19, 80–6

David, Paul, 41
demand conditions, 164, 173
demography, 255
Denmark, 5, 52, 192
  North Jutland, 147–56
developmental learning, 6
development projects, 126
DG Research, 2–3
discretionary learning, 51–4, 62,
  64, 66–7
distributed knowledge base, 5–6
doing, using, interacting (DUI), 2,
  6–7, 10, 16–18, 23, 44–9, 90, 116,
  119–22, 163, 185

economic development
  clusters and, 161
  education and, 41–2
  innovation and, 9–15, 106–8,
    206, 234
  knowledge and, 9–15, 33–42
  stages of, 277
  universities and, 55–7, 276–86
  welfare states and, 58–9

economic equality, 60–4
education, 40, 255
  see also universities
  approach to, 16–17
  economic growth and, 41–2
  in learning economy, 49–57
  learning organizations and, 52–5
  policy, 57
  public funding of, 36
  role of, 34
  science and engineering,
    54–7, 65, 92
egalitarianism, 60–1, 64
employees
  interaction between
    management and, 58
  skill requirements for, 50–1
  training, 53–4, 75–6
  work organization and, 51–2
employment, 255
engineering education, 54–5, 92
entrepreneurial regime, 165
entrepreneurial university, 277
environmental innovation, 68
EU-25 regions, 256–60
European Innovation Surveys, 10
European Union (EU)
  competitive environment, 1–4
  national specialization in, 101–2
  regional specialization in, 102–3
European Working Condition
  Survey, 80
evolutionary theory, 199, 207–8
experience-based learning, 58
experts, 78–9
exploration knowledge, 120
external knowledge, 120–1
Ezagutza Gunea, 181–2, 191–9, 203

factor conditions, 163–4, 172–3
Finland, 8–9, 58, 64, 74, 77
firm heterogeneity, 184–91, 201–2
firm size, 253
firm strategy, 164–5, 173–4
flexible security, 15–16, 18–19, 24,
  72–3, 79–87

geographical proximity, 19–20, 95,
  100–1, 104–7, 162–3, 183
Germany, 4, 52, 73–4, 76–7

global financial crisis, 24
 country responses to, 4–5
 European competitive environment, 1–4
globalization, 1, 3, 24, 59, 90, 100, 277
governance
 city, 97–8
 corporate, 73
 inclusive, 19
 multi-level, 3
 top-down, 141
government
 cluster development and, 145–6, 165, 176
 role of, in knowledge production, 36
 universities and, 277–86
Greece, 52, 103, 269
Greenspan, Alan, 34

Hall, Peter, 94
heterogeneity of firms, 184–91, 201–2
higher education, 53
 see also universities
 innovation and, 42, 55–7, 65
high-tech clusters, 20–1, 47, 146–7
human capital, 2, 4, 5, 276

IAIF/CDTI survey, 210–16, 221
IAIF/FECYT survey, 210–12, 222–4
incremental innovation, 73, 78
India, 43
industrial districts, 36, 68n2, 104–5
industrial dynamics, 3
industry structure, 164–5, 173–4
inequality, 61–4
information, 35, 39
information and communication technology (ICT), 8, 21, 77, 90, 100–1
information signals, 79
innovation
 activities, 125–7
 approaches to, 21–2
 black box of, 13–15, 183, 184
 capabilities, 206–32
 combined and complex, 20, 115–34

 competitiveness and, 1–3, 117
 defined, 2
 drivers of, 15–17
 DUI, 6–7, 10, 16–18, 23, 44–9, 90, 116, 119–22, 163
 economic growth and, 9–15, 106–8, 206, 234
 environmental, 68
 expenditures, 253
 higher education and, 42, 55–7, 65
 incremental, 15, 73, 78
 inputs and outputs, 253
 learning and, 10–13, 22
 modes of, 44–9, 117–22, 131
 new-to-market, 83–5
 open, 101, 108
 organization and, 91–3
 radical, 15–17, 23, 73–5, 77–80, 116, 119
 regional, 234–71
 science-driven, 3–4
 STI, 6–8, 10, 17–18, 23, 44–9, 90, 116, 119–22
 systems of, 275
 technology and, 207–9
 traditional approach to, 4–9
 typologies of, 234–71
 universities and, 55–7
 variety and, 95
innovation policy, 24–5, 48–9, 64, 143, 194, 196, 199–203
innovation style
 flexible security and, 79–87
 VoC perspective on, 73–80
innovation systems, 182–4
innovative cities, 93–8
input additionality, 200
input conditions, 163–4
Institute of Industrial and Financial Analyses (IAIF), 210
institutional dynamics, 3
interactive knowledge, 15
interactive learners, 187, 197, 203
interactive learning, 2, 16, 163, 182, 183
internal learning, 213–22, 226–7
Ireland, 4, 5, 52
Italy, 10, 52, 192, 269

Jacobs, Jane, 93

know-how, 37–8, 116, 208
knowledge
  analytical, 115–16, 118, 183
  as asset, 35, 68n1
  bodies of, 90–2
  codified, 18, 40–1, 49, 116, 162
  co-generation of, 275–86
  common, 39
  competitiveness and, 163–6, 277
  complicit, 101
  economic role of, 33–42
  external, 120–1
  flows, 21, 182–4, 222–5, 228–9
  interactive, 15
  localized, 36
  organizational, 92
  organization of, 93–8
  public and private nature of, 39
  as public good, 35–6
  scientific, 33, 40, 56, 65, 91, 116, 118
  social capital and, 162–3, 172–5
  symbolic, 118, 183
  synthetic, 116, 118–20, 183
  tacit, 10, 15, 18, 40–1, 49, 58, 65, 79, 119, 162, 185, 209
  terminology, 37
knowledge-based industries, 5
knowledge bases, 115–18, 127–8, 183
knowledge creation, 4–9, 36, 118, 125–31
knowledge economy, 1, 18, 33–4, 41, 100–9
knowledge inputs, innovation, economic results and, 9–15
knowledge-intensive business services (KIBS), 106
knowledge production function, 22, 253
knowledge spillovers, 19–20, 105–8, 121, 162–3
knowledge transfer, 36, 107, 162–3, 209
know-what, 37–8
know-who, 37–9
know-why, 37–8, 116

labour market mobility, 15–16, 18–19, 72–3, 76
  creativity and, 80–6
  radical innovation and, 77–80

labour markets, 72–80
lean production, 51–2, 53
learners
  advanced inward-looking, 187–8, 194, 197–8, 203
  craft, 185–6, 195, 196
  interactive, 187, 197, 203
  low, 185
  organizational, 187–8
  structured, 186–7, 189–90, 195, 196, 202–3
  taxonomy of, 184–9, 194–8
  value chain, 190, 195
learning
  from action research, 282–5
  aptitude for, 208
  capabilities, 208–9, 213–22, 226–7, 229–31
  change and, 43
  collective, 163
  competitiveness and, 277
  continuous, 207–8
  cooperative R&D and, 222–5, 228–9
  discretionary, 51–4, 62, 64, 66–7
  firm profile and, 229–31
  interactive, 2, 16, 163, 182, 183
  internal, 213–22, 226–7
  life-long, 57
  measuring effects, 210–13
  modes of, 44–9, 90–1
  organizational, 44, 48–9
  sequence of, 189–91, 198–9
learning economy, 18, 34, 41–4, 92
  education in, 49–57
  European, 51–2
learning organizations, 17, 23, 52–5, 202
learning processes, 25, 118, 127–8
  across firms, 181–91
  at Ezagutza Gunea, 191–9
  innovation and, 10–13
  innovation systems and, 182–4
  R&D and, 22
learning regions, 25, 277
learning society, 34
learning work organization, 5–7, 14–15
liberal market economies (LMEs), 15, 19, 23, 73–7

life-long learning, 57
Lisbon Strategy, 1
List, Friedrich, 33
local environment, 120–1
localization, 100–1, 162–3
localized knowledge, 36
local production systems, 23, 24
lock-in failure, 200, 202
low learners, 185

market economy
  coordinated, 4, 18–19, 23, 73–7
  liberal, 15, 19, 23, 73–7
market failures, 199
Marshall, A.P., 36
Marx, Karl, 33
mental capital, 33
Mintzberg, H., 78
monopolistic competition, 3
multi-level governance, 3
multiple factorial analysis
  (MFA), 255, 271

nanotechnology, 8
national systems of innovation
  (NSI), 72
Nelson, Richard, 33, 36, 41–2
neoclassical economic theory, 59,
  92, 199
Netherlands, 4, 5, 6, 52
network connectivity, 184
networks, 199
new economy, 34, 41
new growth theory, 58
new-to-market innovations, 83–5
niche markets, 1
Nordic countries, 4, 52
  see also specific countries
  inequality in access to
    learning in, 61–4
  social capital and trust in, 57–64, 65
North Jutland, Denmark, 147–56
Norway, 5, 9
  absorptive capacity, 10–11
  oil and gas industry, 14
  Raufoss regional cluster, 116–17,
    122–33
Norwegian puzzle, 117–18

OECD, 33–4, 41, 59, 117, 138

open innovation, 101, 108
organization, 91–3
  of knowledge, 93–8
  of production, 92–3
organizational change, 50–1
organizational knowledge, 92
organizational learners, 187–8
organizational learning, 44, 48–9
  inequality in access to, 61–4
output additionality, 200

paper industry, 166–76
patents, 36, 74–5
peripheral regions, clusters in, 142–7
Phelps, E. S., 41–2
pipelines, 107–8
Porter, Michael, 162, 165
Portugal, 52, 64, 102, 269
principal component analysis
  (PCA), 255
product development, 126–7
production
  organization of, 92–3
  system of, 184
production function, 92
productivity, 42
professional networks, 79
proximity, 19–20, 95, 100–1, 104–7,
  162–3, 183
public expenditures, 59
public good, knowledge as, 35–6
public policy
  academia and, 275–86
  on education, 57
  innovation and, 24–5
  knowledge and, 40–1
  learning economy and, 43–4
  universities and, 22–3

radical innovation, 15–17, 23, 73–5,
  77–80, 116, 119
Raufoss regional cluster, 116–17,
  122–33
regional advantage, 2–3, 6
regional clusters, 116–17, 122–33
regional development, 276–7
Regional Innovation Strategies, 25
regional innovation systems (RIS), 7,
  20, 115, 120–1, 128–31, 234–71
regionalization, 100

regional specialization, 102–3
Reinert, E., 93
related variety, 165, 174–5, 183, 270–1
research and development (R&D), 2–9, 41, 44–5, 92, 119–20
  cooperative, 209–10, 222–5, 228–9
  expenditures on, 22
  innovation capabilities and, 206–32
  internal learning and, 213–22, 226–7
  investment in, 33
  learning process and, 206–32
research institutes, 101
resource accumulation, 208
routinized regime, 165

satellite cities, 106
Scandinavian countries
  see also specific countries
  welfare model in, 58–61
schools, *see* education; universities
Schultz, T.W., 42
science, technology, innovation (STI), 2–3, 6–10, 17–18, 23, 44–9, 90, 101–3, 116, 119–22
science-driven innovation, 3–4
science education, 54–7, 65
science policy, 33
scientific knowledge, 33, 40, 56, 65, 91, 116, 118
Silicon Valley, 36
simple organizations, 53, 185
skill-biased technical progress, 43
skilled labor, 41–3
skill requirements, 50–1
small and medium-sized enterprises (SMEs), 21–2, 24, 42
Smith, Adam, 33, 44
social capital, 17, 18, 21, 25, 57–65, 79, 140, 146
  competitiveness and, 163–6, 172–5
  knowledge and, 162–3, 172–5
social distance, 61
social filters, 22, 255

social networks, 79
Spain, 10, 52, 192, 269
  see also Basque Autonomous Community
Spanish regions, 234–71
spatial networks, 161
  see also clusters
specialization, 270–1
  at national level, 101–2
  pure, 183
  regional, 102–3
spillovers, 105–8, 121, 162–3
structured learners, 186–7, 189–90, 195, 196, 202–3
sub-cultures, 188–9
Sweden, 5, 9, 74, 75, 77, 103
Swedish paradox, 9
symbolic knowledge, 6, 118, 183
synthetic knowledge, 6, 7, 116, 118–20, 183
system failures, 199–200

tacit knowledge, 10, 15, 18, 40–1, 49, 58, 65, 79, 119, 162, 185, 209
Taylorist work organization, 5, 52, 53, 81–2, 187
technological capability, 208, 230–1
technological change, 207
technological platform, 121–2
technological regime, 164–5, 173–4
technological specialization, 74
technologies, 91–2, 206, 207–9
technology convergence, 109
technology development, 7–8
technology policy, 22
technology programs, 126
technology transfer, 207–8, 222–5, 228–9
tertiary education, 53
training
  learning organizations and, 52–5
  vocational, 53–4, 72, 75–6
trust, 59–61, 65

unemployment insurance, 73, 77, 79
United Kingdom, 4, 52

United States, 4, 74, 101
universities, 8, 22–3, 92, 100, 101
  action research approach and, 281–5
  collaboration between industry and, 120
  public funding of, 36
  regional development and, 276–7
  role of, 34, 55–7, 65, 275–86
unsystematic interactive learners, 186, 187, 190, 203
urban order, 95–7

value chain learner, 190, 195

varieties of capitalism (VoC), 15, 18, 23, 72–88
  innovation style and, 73–80
  labor markets and, 73–80
variety, 95, 165, 174–5
vocational training, 53–4, 72, 75–6

welfare states
  economic performance and, 58–9
  innovation style and, 76–7
  trust and, 59–61
Winter, Sidney, 35
work organization, 5–7, 14–15, 51–3, 63, 66–7, 185–8
World Bank, 59
World Economic Forum, 277